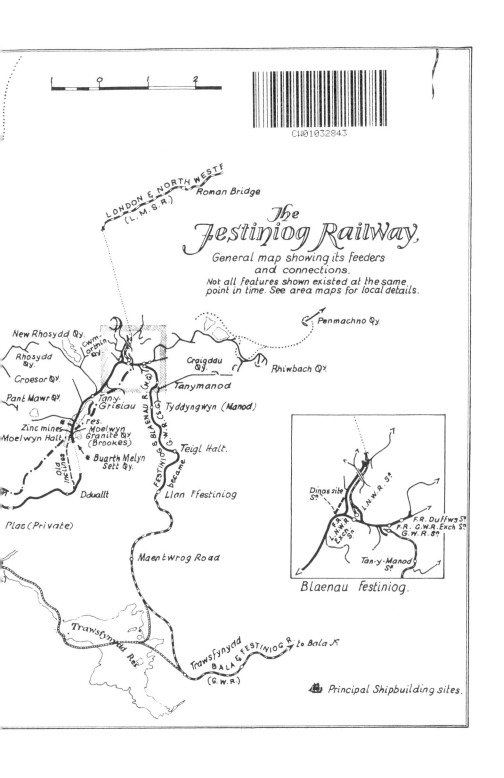

The
Festiniog Railway,

General map showing its feeders
and connections.

Not all features shown existed at the same
point in time. See area maps for local details.

LONDON & NORTH WEST (L.M.S.R.) · Roman Bridge

New Rhosydd Qy.
Cwm-orthin Qy.
Penmachno Qy.
Rhosydd Qy.
Croesor Qy.
Craigddu Qy.
Rhiwbach Qy.
Pant Mawr Qy.
Tanymanod
Tan-y-Grisiau
Tyddyngwyn (Manod)
Zinc mines
res.
Moelwyn Granite Qy. (Brookes)
Moelwyn Halt
Teigl Halt
Buarth Melyn Sett Qy.
Old inclines
FESTINIOG & BLAENAU R. (N.G.) G.W.R. (S.G.) became
Ddualt
Llan Ffestiniog
Plas (Private)
Maentwrog Road

Dinas site S?.
L.N.W.R. S?.
F.R. L.N.W.R. Exch S?.
F.R. Duffws S?.
F.R. G.W.R. Exch S?.
G.W.R. S?.
Tan-y-Manod S?.

Blaenau Festiniog.

Trawsfynydd Res.
Trawsfynydd
BALA & FESTINIOG R. (G.W.R.) → to Bala J?.

🚢 Principal Shipbuilding sites.

Books from the Oakwood Press by the Same Author

In Print

Festiniog Railway
  Volume One: History and Route, 1800-1953
*
The Isle of Man Railway,
  Volume Two: 1905 - 1994
*
The Isle of Man Railway,
  Volume Three: The routes and rolling stock
*
Narrow Gauge in North Caernarvonshire
  Volume Two: The Penrhyn Quarry Railways
*
Narrow Gauge in North Caernarvonshire
  Volume Three: The Dinorwic Railways
*
Narrow Gauge in South Caernarvonshire
  Volume One
*
Schull & Skibbereen Railway
*
Wrexham, Mold & Connah's Quay Railway

Out of Print

The Isle of Man Railway,
  Volume One: Pre-1873 - 1904
*
Narrow Gauge Railways in Mid-Wales
*
Narrow Gauge in North Caernarvonshire
  Volume One: The West
*
Narrow Gauge in South Caernarvonshire
  Volume Two: The Welsh Highland Railway

THE
FESTINIOG RAILWAY

A History of the Narrow Gauge Railway linking the Slate Quarries of Blaenau Ffestiniog with Portmadoc, North Wales: together with outline histories of quarry undertakings connected to the Railway.

1800 – 1974

by

JAMES I. C. BOYD

with drawings by J. M. Lloyd

Vol. 2 – Locomotives, Rolling Stock and Quarry Feeders

THE OAKWOOD PRESS

© Oakwood Press & J. I. C. Boyd 1975

British Library Cataloguing in Publication Data
A Record for this book is available from the British Library
ISBN 0 85361 168 8

First Edition 1975
Reprinted 2002

Printed by Ebenezer Baylis & Son Ltd, Worcester.

CONTENTS

VOLUME 2

INDEX TO PLATES

To the Memory of Geoffrey Hoyland

A Headmaster who brought me to the Mountains and Narrow Gauge Railways of North Wales many years before this became a fashionable scholastic exercise.

His Algebraic administrations are among the subjects I have largely forgotten, but his love of the railway, his description of locomotive cylinders and valve events, remain as vivid today as they were to me in my thirteenth year.

All drawings, diagrams etc., are to scale where circumstances permit; to admit detail in layout plans some latitude has been allowed. A compromise between official documents and the evidence of fieldwork and photographs is occasionally practised where these conflict.

Welsh spelling is currently going through an appraisement which seems to satisfy neither Welshmen nor English visitor. 'Railway Spelling' (such as was used by the Festiniog Railway Company or Bradshaw's Timetables) is therefore used; so for instance, there has been no temptation to alter 'Portmadoc' into the current 'Porthmadog'. However, 'Blaenau Ffestiniog' has been adopted to agree more naturally with Llan Ffestiniog, and from a considerable choice, each quarry has been given a title which will serve to identify even though it may fail to please!

'Blessed are the dead which die in the Lord from henceforth. Yea, saith the Spirit, that they may rest from their labours, and their works do follow them'.

Rev. XIV 13.

(from the inscription on the gravestone of Charles Easton Spooner)

CHAPTER FOURTEEN

MOTIVE POWER—NINETY YEARS 1863–1953

A considerable portion of the history of steam and other mechanical power has been given as it occurred in the historical section which precedes this chapter, and reference to individual engines therein should be made through the Index. This chapter is therefore confined to (a) a summary of events leading to the introduction of steam engines; (b) the four-wheeled engines; (c) the Fairlie engines; (d) rail tractors; (e) Welsh Highland Railway engines.

In general, events after 1953, except where overlapping of period cannot be avoided, will be found in Chapter Twenty. (In the summaries for each engine, the term 'Engine Rebuilt' and date is taken from the Work's records. Rebuilding implied dismantling, complete repair and renewal where required, a virtual 'new engine' returning to traffic; and often officially described as such.)

PROPOSALS FOR, AND BUILDING OF, LOCOMOTIVES, AND THEIR TRIALS
(Drawings of such as have appeared in
Festiniog Railway Magazine marked ⋆)

24 August 1860: At Board Meeting Secretary instructed 'to make enquiries as to practicability of using locomotives on the line'. Suggested that he visits the railway of the Neath Abbey Ironworks to see their 2 ft. 7½ in. gauge locomotives at work.

Though not referred to in the Minutes, he is also recommended to communicate with Charles Menzies Holland, nephew of Samuel Holland, Junior, who is an Engineer and acquainted with the subject.

9 April 1861: Letter from Spooner to Holland referring to earlier correspondence of 26 November 1860; a four-wheeled locomotive with tender and tank separate, coupled to it, of not more than 5 tons suggested, to have oval boiler and low centre of gravity, outside cylinders and inside valve gear. Wheels 2 ft. 6 in. diameter maximum to operate over sharp curves and 30 lb. rails at 8 m.p.h. Up and 10 m.p.h. Down, engine to run Down light without train. Requests plans in time for next annual meeting (this would take place during late summer 1861). Spooner sketches oval boiler to be recessed beneath to accommodate upper rims of wheels.

28 August 1861: Letter from Holland to Spooner regarding design sub-

mitted by Jones of Liverpool on 8 August 1861 for single cylinder engine.* (No. 5, p. 11.) Holland considers design 'unsafe' but suggests they might build engine to his design. Underlines difficulty, however, of supervising work done in Liverpool.

1 September 1861: Holland recommends to Spooner that a tank on the engine would not be too heavy for it and would improve adhesion (sketches end-on sections of saddle, etc., tanks—'which gives the term "tortoise backed" ').

7 September 1861: Holland to Spooner detailing curious provision of trunk cylinders used in first design, and recommending adoption of injector rather than pump.

November 1861: Spooner visits the Neath Abbey Railway and sees their locos at work during this month (date not given).

2 November 1861: Neath Abbey send sketch of four-coupled engine to Spooner incorporating firebox dropped between coupled axles [as in Fletcher's Patent—Author]. Wheelbase thus 7 ft. Springing under-hung. Frames to be bent outwards to accommodate large firebox. [This system was employed by De Winton when using large vertical boilers on 3 ft. gauge locomotives with *outside* frames—Author.]

December 1861–January 1862: Correspondence between Holland and Spooner regarding wheelbase, safety, etc., resulting in specification forwarded from Holland during January for four-wheeled coupled engine with 4 ft. 6 in. wheelbase, to cost £900–1,000. Jones of Liverpool recommended for building.* (No. 7, p. 13.) Letters follow concerning water and coke consumption.

28 February 1862: Spooner makes Report to Directors summarising his visit to Neath Abbey and submitting Holland's specification for a locomotive, 'more suitable' than an engine to plans already supplied. A description of the work done on the Neath Abbey Railway by their locomotives is given, together with a reference to the Neath Abbey being in a position to supply a locomotive. Based on figures obtained from engines at work at Neath Abbey, Spooner submits estimate of locomotives and wagons required to work Up goods traffic, 'Back goods traffic' including conversion of horse boxes into wagons. Suggests three engines will be required, two in use and one spare.

Calculations in respect of Festiniog Railway based on an Up train with 1 locomotive and 60 empty slate wagons, plus 10 tons Back Carriage of total weight 40 tons to be worked at 8 m.p.h. and work approximately three trips per day. At that time one horse drew 8 wagons at 3 m.p.h. Cost of horses £1,300 per annum. Estimate of loco costs £873 4s. 9d. including interest on capital.

One locomotive could do the work equivalent to 3·43 horses. In view of the sharp curves and the steepest grade of 1 in 75, suggested that 2 locomotives be employed, 'one to meet the other half-way when the whole traffic can be easily accomplished by having 5 trains instead of 3 . . .'

Alternative of 6 trains running at slower speeds suggested. On this basis one hour would be allowed for each engine to work over half the total distance.

Spooner now awaits Directors' instructions to send out tenders 'to the most approved makers'. The cost will now be nearer £1,000 rather than £750 which Mr. Holland previously estimated.

Recommended that the track be left unaltered except 'the long sharp curve near where the first stone was laid at Creua' (the relaid curve is shown in plate 6R). In an estimate of costs is included 'Lengthening the turnout at Hafod Llyn on Mrs. Oakeley's property'. 'Three water tanks for supply of engine.' 'Alteration in Six Pass Byes.'

Provision also made for inserting additional sleepers. The train was to be staffed by 'Two engine Drivers and Stokers . . .' (The Driver is both Driver and Stoker). [From this it seems that the intention was to have the engines single-manned.—Author.] Additionally there were to be 'Two men attending to Breaks on Train and acting as Guard'.

On the matter of Back Carriage, Spooner recommends that this be let out on contract, the Company to find the motive power, wagons, grease, etc., and the contractor to be responsible for loading and unloading. Note that present carrier cannot undertake this work, but in view of great increase in Back Carriage anticipated when locomotives are set to work, it should not be difficult to find contractor. This traffic should be developed.

The question as to whether two or three engines should be ordered is put before the Board.

3 April 1862: Spooner advises Holland that Company have decided to 'have Locomotive Engines on their line . . .' Suggests engine be shorter with overall length 11 ft. 6 in., boiler top 4 ft. 6 in. from rail 'width to suit gauge of 2 ft. 1 in. from Centre to Centre of Rail'. Height to top of chimney 8 ft., wheelbase 5 ft. Tender to be separate or attached in manner of rear pony truck, i.e. pivoted section carrying fuel and driver. Two engines will be required at first. Holland's professional charges for plans and superintendence during construction requested.

7 May 1862: Holland submits amended design restricting overhang due to cylinders and introducing another set of 2 ft. diameter wheels having side play. Holland considers engine 'too top heavy' for wheelbase 'and although it would not capsize with careful management yet a slight accident might upset it and endanger life, etc.'. Recommends laying an extra rail outside the running rails (giving 3 ft. 6 in. gauge), on longitudinal sleepers. Locomotives to run on broader gauge and

stock on existing gauge. Jones again recommended. Holland favours cautious approach to the problem and has new idea of placing 'boiler under the wheels'.†

23 May 1862: Holland submits new design of his own to Spooner of freak machine having central firebox with mid-feather and boiler at one end of it.‡ Driving unit fixed under one end with four-coupled wheels; other end carried the boiler on an ordinary pivoted bogie. Single chimney near centre of boiler but offset away from driving end.

Holland now engaged on six-coupled design with one pair wheels having side play.* (No. 20, p. 20.)

21 August 1862: (This letter follows others of detailed matter.) Holland to Spooner advising that only one engine be built at first in order to rectify defects, etc., before second is added. Recommends *The Engineer* for the advertisement and that a builder be found in the London area to allow Holland to supervise. His terms to be 5% on cost of engine. He feels England & Co. are the best builders, being the only regular locomotive builders in London of whom he is aware.

2 October 1862: Holland reports he has called on England's. England said he had not intended to tender if only one was required—he had not replied to correspondence (presumably from Spooner). He would make three for £3,000, he and Holland to design it but giving him the liberty of altering the design to suit his method of construction, the first engine to be ready in 4 months. England objected to being tied by time and payment, not knowing beforehand how much the engines would cost. Holland tells England Spooner would probably call with him the next day. Advises Spooner that England would agree to make 2 engines at £1,000 each.

6 October 1862: Holland adds that England's engines would last twice as long as any from an 'inferior' maker.

8 October 1862: Holland replies to Spooner enquiry regarding suitable carriage builders in either Liverpool or Manchester. Holland prefers Manchester and mentions Butterworth of South King Street.

10 October 1862: Advertisement appears in *The Engineer*.

11 October 1862: Letter of Introduction for Spooner addressed to John Ramsbottom (this would be with reference to Spooner's visit to see the Crewe Works narrow gauge tramway engine).

16 October 1862: Galloway & Sons, Knott Mill Foundry, Manchester, and Forresters of Liverpool recommended by Holland for the supply of wagons.

October (various dates): Replies being received to advertisement. Twenty-nine makers show interest in the following date order:

† This idea was not new to standard gauge practice.
‡ A container for water and coal was carried at the extremity of the driving unit end, with footplate between the container and the firebox.

Hawthorns, Leith	11.10.62
John W. Marsden	11.10.62
Fletcher Jennings & Co.	11.10.62
Isaac W. Boulton	11.10.62
W. Butlin	11.10.62
J. Harris, Darlington	11.10.62
Brown & May, Devizes	11.10.62
Belliss and Seekings	11.10.62
Slaughter, Gruning & Co.	11.10.62
Haigh Foundry, Wigan	13.10.62
J. C. Evans, E. Greenwich	13.10.62
W. Syrett, Bury St. Edmunds	13.10.62
Adamson	13.10.62
W. G. Armstrong	13.10.62
James Swan, Worcester	13.10.62
Wm. Cafferata, Newark	16.10.62
Blaylock and Pratchitt, Carlisle	18.10.62
Thos. Dunn & Co., Manchester	18.10.62
Geo. Law, Newark	20.10.62
Geo. Skelton	20.10.62
Beyer Peacock & Co., Manchester	20.10.62
Thos. Worsdell	20.10.62
Vulcan Foundry, Ayr	21.10.62
Vulcan Foundry, Warrington	21.10.62
H. M. Lawrence, Liverpool	23.10.62
Close Burlinson & Co., Sunderland	23.10.62
Carrett Marshall & Co., Leeds	25.10.62
Bryan Johnson, Chester	28.10.62
Manning Wardle & Co., Leeds	7.11.62

November 1862 (various dates): Correspondence concerning design and photograph submitted by Manning Wardle & Co. England preferred to either Manning Wardle or Hawthorns.

6 December 1862: Holland writes Spooner on the relative merits of 4 and 6 wheeled engines, the latter advocated by Holland. England now prepared to accept 3 engines for £950 each.

10 February 1863: England agrees to make 3 engines for £900 each and advises the Directors of the F.R. accordingly. Further letter of 13 February suggests payment in thirds viz: at commencement of contract, at Trials under steam, at time of delivery.

14 February 1863: Holland advises Spooner that he will accept F.R. Company's terms of payment of 5% upon *two* engines for his attention and superintendence on building of three engines by England.* (No. 20, p. 23.)

15 February 1863: Holland advises England, on behalf of the Festiniog Directors, that they will pay in thirds for the two engines they require delivered by 1 June, immediately, the remaining payments as suggested by England. The third engine to be delivered by 1 March 1864 and to be paid for on delivery; this engine not to be brought to a forward state until the first two have been tried out.

20 February 1863: Boiler design amended by England to reduce large surface area liable to condensation in steam space.

4 March 1863: England advise Spooner they have accepted Holland as the railway's appointed Engineer for the three engines. The suggested price to be £1,000 each for the first two and £800 for the third.

The matter is duly settled and a first instalment of £666 13s. 4d. is acknowledged by England on 23 March; between this event and the foregoing correspondence letters have been exchanged between Directors and Spooner regarding charge for third engine should extensive alterations have to be made in the light of experience, and England attempts to charge more than £800 as quoted. This matter is settled.

28 March 1863: Holland advises progress on the locomotives.

(There is no surviving correspondence between 28 March and 4 August—a vital period in the completion of the engines. Nor is there any reference to date of despatch, method of delivery, etc. Two engines were delivered on 18 July.)

4 August 1863: Letter to England from Spooner '... Your man tried one of the Locomotives today (*The Princess*) for a couple of miles up the line on an Inclination of 1 in 82 with a couple of trucks behind it ... very unsatisfactory ... water flowed into the cylinder in such quantities that it was thrown out of the funnel in volumes, and the injector would not work for the whole distance—the Engine ran at a rate of about 4 miles an hour with a pressure of 60 lb.—when she came to a standstill, by which time there was left about 12 inches of water in the tanks & the fire was obliged to be put out—. No doubt you will be able to explain the cause of all this & I trust to make an early remedy.

'I fear there must be something wrong with the bearings for we had to go back over the before named Inclination of 1 in 82 without steam, and it was as much as the men could do to get the Engine back again ...

'Having made arrangements to work the traffic on the line with Locomotives next week ...'

5 August 1863: Holland acknowledges letter from Spooner written 28 July commenting favourably to Holland on appearance of 'Engine'. This may suggest that they were not delivered before the last week in

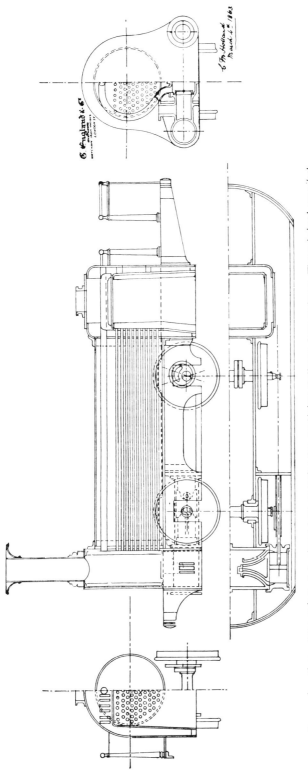

Reconstruction of the original England & Co. drawing for Festiniog Railway locomotives. The original, on oiled tracing paper, has been stored folded flat with the result that when discovered it was in a number of separate tattered pieces. This is an accurate copy but there is some evidence that it was drawn to a bastard form of projection and not as arranged here. The original is drawn to scale ¼ full size, the copy is to scale ⅓ of the original. *Note* the domeless boiler and the suggestion on the elevation (but not on the plan) of leather dumb buffers.

July. Holland hopes to hear an equally good report of 'their' capabilities. Buffers appear to have been omitted from the original drawing (this fact is confirmed by the reproduction of it). Four are to be made (two per engine) and sent to Portmadoc.

A postscript to this letter acknowledges receipt of Spooner's letter stating the trial was unsatisfactory. Holland states that workshop trials were satisfactory and attributes failure to driver's mismanagement. If further improvement does not take place, means to be adopted to 'give the Engine more steam room'.

Subsequently Holland reports to England concerning priming in the engine cylinders. England suggests that the steam pipe lies too close to the water level in the boiler and water is being drawn into it along with steam (letter from Holland to Spooner 10 August). Holland had spoken to James Cleminson over this matter during construction, but was reassured that priming would not take place. Holland recommends the driver to take the utmost care to keep the water level 'above the level of the top of the firebox and yet beneath the level of the steam pipe . . . I own it is a rather ticklish thing to manage'.

Arrangements had been made by Holland to ask England to fit 'two small domes on the boiler, etc. . . .' but in the event only a single dome was fitted. Holland considered England should pay for this work but there is no record of payment.

Engines Nos. 1-6

No. as delivered	No. as amended by 1886	Named	Re-named	Built by Geo. England & Co. Maker's No.	Date	Cost	Withdrawn from traffic
2	1*	The Princess	Princess		1863	c. £1,000	
4	2	The Prince	Prince		1863	£975 7s. 6d.	
1		Mountaineer	—		1863	c. £1,000	1879
3	4	Palmerston	—		1864	£975 7s. 6d.	
5		Welsh Pony	—	234	1867	£1,005	late 1938
6		Little Giant	—	235	1867	£1,005	1939

*Early pictures show as 'No. 1' very early in service.

No. 1 *The Princess* and No. 2 *The Prince* (ex No. 2 and ex No. 4).
No. 3 *Mountaineer* and No. 4 *Palmerston* (ex No. 1 and ex No. 3).

The requirements laid down in April 1862 were for two engines, but later counsels prevailed. By March 1863, when the order was confirmed, three engines were to be supplied, two by 1 June 1863 and a third by 1 March 1864. Eventually six four-coupled engines were supplied (the final pair being larger than the originals), the second pair arriving in

1864. A letter from Spooner relates that *The Princess* was the first engine in steam and other evidence points to *The Princess* (then numbered 2) and *Mountaineer* (then numbered 1) being the first to arrive.*

They were four-coupled tank engines with auxiliary tenders for carrying coal; they had inside frames and outside cylinders whilst water was carried in side tanks whose tops were level with the top of the boiler lagging. The chimney was bell-mouthed, there was a front weather-board curved towards the top, brass dome with whistle thereon, safety valve in a brass cover on the firebox whilst the footplating was curved at front and rear presumably to give adequate clearance between vehicles on curves and to push open the many gates then across the line. At the front of each tank was a rectangular box for carrying sand; this tapered at the bottom into a feed pipe on to the rails. Although all engines carried sandboxes and feed pipes in these early years, the pipes were removed later as, due to leaking, the sand was trailed along the rails and frequently brought the gravity trains to a standstill. For this reason, unfortunate firemen had to ride on the fronts of their engines and, dipping their hands into the sandboxes, drop it on to the running rail before the engine. The vacuum brake fitting, with which the engines were equipped atterly, formed a useful 'marker' for this purpose as it fell into line with the rail and was an essential to dropping sand accurately in Moelwyn Tunnel!

The side tanks are thought to have been joined over the top of the boiler by sheeting. The footplate was side sheeted to waist height and there was an opening in the centre rear sheet for passing on to the tender. There were no proper weatherboards initially, only a minute 'stand' on which the pressure gauge was mounted. *Princess* later received a weatherboard with turned-over top. *Prince* may have been delivered with larger board but the turn-over was smaller than *Princess* and more like those put on Nos. 5 and 6 originally.

The tenders were intended to carry coal, tools and extra sand, but were unusual in not having a water tank. In practice they might carry almost anything; coal, bicycles, laundry baskets, boxes of cakes, etc., are among items which have been seen therein. At the back was a wooden tool box. The early tenders had plain unsprung bearings and were virtually slate wagon chassis with sheet-iron bodies.

Closer inspection of the first engines revealed spoked driving wheels, Allan's straight link motion inside the frames, marine pattern connecting and coupling rods, ash-pan doors which could be operated from the footplate and cleaned out easily from the trackside, two Giffard injectors, centre buffer-couplers (the tender having secondary securing chains in case of breakage of the screw link between engine and tender) whilst the tender rear coupling hook was supported by a chain carried over the

* Confirmed by a note of William Williams.

the tender backsheet to the footplate.* This enabled the crew to cast off the slate wagons by fly-shunting and pulling up the hook at the crucial moment when the couplings were slack. The handbrake screw on the footplate was mounted horizontally after later rebuilding (as on some Caledonian Railway goods brake vans) and worked on to wooden shoes (as first fitted) on the driving axle only. Driving was from the left-hand side.

It is the plan of the engine which shows its most striking points; in order to obtain an adequate firebox the main frames are carried only between valve chests and firebox frontplate. At the rear end these frames are bracketed to the box, whilst a lighter pair of frames are bracketed to the firebox back and carry the drag beam. At the front end the cylinders and valve chest assembly form a complete unit across the width of the engine and the frames are carried through it, projecting forward as shallow plates to carry the smokebox and front beam. To help to take the strain of haulage, the frames as just described are secured to heavy valances which run the full length of the engine, immediately below the running plate. This forms, in effect, a secondary outside frame (note that on the earlier four-wheelers it was straight whilst on the later it was raised over the motion) without which the engine might quickly pull itself into a number of dismembered sections! By dividing up the inner frames in this manner the firebox, free of any limit of width, is as wide as the distance across the face of wheels and is carried down to the lowest possible depth.

The first two engines cost £1,000 each, the next two £975 7s. 6d. each and were designed to haul 50 tons at 10 to 15 m.p.h. They could haul 60 empty wagons on the ascent. Until turntables were installed they worked Up chimney first and ran Down light (at this time all Down trains ran by gravity).

The original water tanks were too small; ultimately larger ones were fitted. To improve adhesion round-topped cast-iron weights ('Dummy Tanks') in sections, were added to the flat-top tanks, giving the appearance of extra water tanks. Known dates for this addition are; *Palmerston* 1880, *The Prince* 1881, *The Princess* 1882. At the same time two whistles were placed on the dome and the semi-circular hand-grips on the chimney front, opened out to make two vertical grips and allow the lamp to fall between. In addition, cast-iron weights were hung under the running plates and dropped into the bottoms of the water tanks.

Possibly the two larger engines, Nos. 5 and 6, worked on the main line, and certainly No. 4 was the Harbour shunting engine for much of this period. The boilers of Nos. 4, 5 and 6 required replacing in the late 1880s, and new frames and 2 ft. 3 in. wheels were fitted. New frames

* For further notes on valve gear fitted to all these early engines see *Festiniog Railway Magazine* No. 1 (Summer 1958, p. 10) and No. 2 (Autumn 1958, p. 9).

were fitted to Nos. 1 and 2 in 1891; these two engines were never exactly alike.

No. 1 received an unusual alteration before new frames were fitted in the shape of an open-back cab.

When new water tanks were made, the names of 1 and 2 (later series) were shortened by dropping the *The*, new plates being made.

Mountaineer had a short life and was never rebuilt. An 1879 Report states it was worn out and beyond repair, and recommended to be 'dismounted, being unroadworthy'. Its spare parts were used later for repairing similar engines—during its lifetime it was always No. 1.

No. 4 as new has not survived in pictorial form, but new frames, 2 ft. 3 in. diameter driving wheels and a new boiler (from Daniel Adamson) were supplied in 1888.

A curious accident (but not unique) befell No. 3 on 12 September 1876 when the chimney broke off when running under a bridge at Duffws.

No. 1 *The Princess* (latterly *Princess*)

Designer, C. M. Holland. Builder, George England & Co., 1863. 0–4–0 Tank/Tender type. Cylinders, 12 in., stroke, 8 in. diam. (later $8\frac{3}{8}$ in.). Weight in Working Order, $7\frac{1}{2}$ tons; $8\frac{1}{2}$ tons; 12 tons, as rebuilt. Heating Surface, 377 sq. ft. Grate Area, $4\frac{5}{8}$ sq. ft. Pressure, 200 lb. (later reduced approx. 140 lb.). Tractive Effort at 85% B.P., 4,624 lb. Wheelbase, 4 ft. 6 in. Driving Wheel diam. 2 ft. Tank Capacity, 239; 418 gallons, as rebuilt.

1891—Steel frames fitted and cab.

1895—New boiler fitted, purchased 1892 from Vulcan Company* Engine rebuilt. 2 ft. 3 in. diam. driving wheels.

1922—New boiler from Adamson fitted, purchased 1918, delivered 1921. Engine did not re-enter traffic until 1923. Engine out of use 1919–23.

1937—Heavy boiler repairs and refit (instead of new boiler). Engine rebuilt. Engine out of service end 1935–early 1937.

This engine was one of the first two to be delivered in July 1863, and was the last to be in service, 1 August 1946.

No. 2 *The Prince* (latterly *Prince*)

Principal features, etc., and dimensions similar to but not identical with *The Princess* when new. Tractive Effort, 4,489 lb. Amended details as rebuilt as for *The Princess*.

---

* Williams had recommended it to be supplied by R. & W. Hawthorn Leslie & Co. Ltd.

1890—Open-back cab fitted (to *Princess* 1891).

1891—Steel frames fitted, and 2 ft. 3 in. diam. driving wheels.

1892—New boiler fitted. Engine rebuilt.

1915—Engine taken out of service, boiler condemned.

1919—New boiler ordered from Adamson; delivered end 1919.*

1921—Engine returns to traffic, rebuilt.

1930—Engine rebuilt: painted red.

1937—Engine taken out of service, boiler condemned. (Engine only used in emergency after 1935.)

1943—New boiler ordered from Adamson; delivered 1945.

★   ★   ★

Note—All figures are nominal only especially cylinder dimensions, pressures and wheel diameters.

Weights and Tractive Effort taken from official figures—1921.

No.3 *Mountaineer* (No. 1 of the early series of locomotive numbering.)

Built 1863. Principal features, etc., and dimensions as for *The Princess* when new. Tractive Effort, 3,177 lb. (1879 Report states *Mountaineer* 'was worn out . . . accordingly the next new engine will be numbered No. 1 in its place'.) Same Report gives age of *Mountaineer* and *The Princess* as 16 years, with *Palmerston* 15 years.

This engine was the first to be withdrawn, and was not rebuilt. Officially withdrawn 1879, but parts used later in other locomotives.

Probably carried No. 3 before being scrapped.

No. 4 *Palmerston*

Built 1864. Principal features and dimensions as for *The Princess* when new. Tractive Effort, 4,489 lb.

1886–8—Engine out of service.

1888—Steel frames fitted, new boiler from Adamson, and 2 ft. 3 in. diam. driving wheels. Engine rebuilt.

1891—New cylinders, smokebox, shortened footplate and cab cut back 8 in. to use as Top Shunter.† New tank.

1907—Engine taken out of service 14 October; boiler condemned.

1910—New boiler from Adamson fitted, purchased 1909.

1913—Engine rebuilt.

1930—Engine rebuilt but needs new boiler.

---

* But carried Plate '3/5451 Davies & Metcalfe, Manchester, 1921'.

† To give more clearance in the L.M.S. and G.W. goods sheds.

1932—Boiler barrel condemned, but that off *Little Giant* fitted.*
1940—Fitted up as stationary boiler to work steam hammer in connection with lease of part Works and machinery.

No. 5 *Welsh Pony* and No. 6 *Little Giant*

It was found that the first series of four engines was too small for the growing work and the next two engines remedied some of their shortcomings.

Larger driving wheels of disc pattern, extended footplates, weatherboards and cylindrical sandpots were fitted; the footplate was raised over the wheels and motion, large saddle tanks completely shrouded the boiler and on the maker's photograph of No. 6 the double slide bars are replaced with a single rod pattern. Unlike the earlier engines, the smokebox saddles were waisted in and the motion was of rectangular section rodding. The wheelbase was lengthened to improve the riding, and a boiler 6 inches longer than previously was used. Apparently both engines were originally alike regarding slide bars etc., but by mid-1868 it appears new crossheads, slide bars etc. had been purchased for alteration. An account from George England of April 1869 refers to coupling, connecting rods, slide bars, cylinder covers, slide blocks, piston rods, motion bars etc. Total £373 8s. 0d.

The last two engines had different links and suspension link and valve rod from the first four. (The Allan Patent 1747 is dated 2 August 1855 and provides for either curved or straight links.) No. 5 had a hand-painted name and maker's plate, now preserved.

These engines were a definite improvement and it was proposed that the Bessbrook & Newry Railway in Northern Ireland should be worked by engines of the *Little Giant* type. (This line was built in 1885 to the three-foot gauge, but from the first was electrified.)

No. 5 received new frames, boiler and 2 ft. 3 in. wheels in 1889–90, and No. 6 was reconstructed in 1887–8 and 1890.

The name *Little Giant* has a local origin; it was the name given to the smaller two-masted schooners built at Portmadoc.

For No. 6 a new steel boiler was supplied by Vulcan Company in October 1904, whilst new cab, new smokebox, new shorter chimney 'to clear bridge', extended frames under the cab, new front footplate and copper firebox were added. The Superintendent's records state that only the water tank and wheel centres of the old engine survived—which would be true in large measure. The engine was not a success, a new cylinder being 'porous'; Williams declined to reduce the blast pipe orifice as had been done on the *Pony* as 16 stays of the latter had had to be replaced due to the blast 'tearing' the copper stayheads 'by small coal

---

* Originally proposed to use section of *Taliesin* 0-4-4 boiler.

and sulphur'. *Little Giant* he called 'a stupid steamer'. Again, as originally supplied, the Works plates were painted simply on iron sheet, glazed and framed (four engines had this feature).

No. 5 *Welsh Pony*

Designer, C. M. Holland. Builder, George England & Co., 1867. Works No. 234. Cylinders, 12 in. stroke, 8¼ in. diam. (later 8⅜ in.). Weight in Working Order, 10 tons; approx. 13 tons as rebuilt. Heating Surface, 377 sq. ft. Grate Area, 4⅝ sq. ft. Pressure, 150 lb. Tractive Effort, 3,312 lb. Wheelbase, 5 ft. Driving Wheel diam. 2 ft. 2 in. Tank Capacity, 418 gallons.

1890–1—New boiler from Vulcan Ironworks fitted (cost £227), new smokebox, cab, water tank. Engine rebuilt. Work not urged as traffic poor. Steel frames fitted, and 2 ft. 3 in. driving wheels.

1910—Boiler condemned, engine taken out of service.

1912—New boiler ordered from Adamson.

1915—New boiler fitted, engine rebuilt. (*Prince* withdrawn same day).

1938—Boiler fails hydraulic test, engine taken from service.

The engine lay out of service between late 1910 and 1915, awaiting new boiler.

No. 6 *Little Giant*

Principal features and dimensions as for *Welsh Pony*. Works No. 235.

1887–8—New boiler fitted from Adamson. Engine rebuilt; new tank, smokebox, allover cab, chimney.

1890—Engine dismantled and cracked frame replaced by new steel frame (originally intended to use 2 ft. driving wheels according to drawing).

1904—Steel frames fitted and 2 ft. 3 in. driving wheels, new boiler from Vulcan Company fitted; being last England engine to receive larger wheels, new frames etc. (Williams lays blame for condition of 1887 boiler on failure to rebuild earlier: difficult to keep time in traffic whilst in pre-1904 condition.)

1929—Consideration given to using boiler for connection to steam hammer.

1932—Engine officially withdrawn, firebox condemned. Boiler barrel put on to *Palmerston*, engine dismantled and many parts left at Glan-y-Mor.

General Remarks on Engines Nos. 1–6

At the present time or at the time of their withdrawal, these early engines reached a stage where no two were alike. Each unit had begun to evolve in a form all its own, so that as years went by they were far from a uniform class by any standard. Even so, discarded boilers, tanks, cabs, wheels and cylinders might be re-used (at one time No. 4 ran with one pair of spoke and one pair of disc wheels), but it was mainly tubes and the less 'individual' items. Nos. 1–4 had one pattern of cylinder, Nos. 5–6 another. Springs were individually made for each engine.

The single line staff was carried in a pocket on the cab side sheet on the driver's side.

The valve gear was naturally somewhat inaccessible and, apart from holes in the main frames provided for lubrication, could only be reached when over a pit.

All engines had lamp brackets. These were an open rectangular frame into which a square lug on the bottom of the lamp was dropped at the top of the smokebox.

As to the usage of these small engines, in 1870 Nos. 3, 5 and 6 were sharing the brunt of the work. Later, Nos. 1 and 3 were relegated to Spare Engines and laid off. At this period there were four main-line crews; they did not have the outright use of one engine but shared two with another crew.

Tenders

Originally were built in the Works incorporating slate wagon frame chassis; the original small plain-bearing variety chassis were replaced with larger ones having unsprung axleboxes. The body frames were of wood faced with iron; it appears that only four tenders were in use, though possibly six were built in all. Larger sprung tenders were given to Nos. 5 and 6 from the start.

Hand brakes were once fitted, but after 1889 when vacuum brakes were introduced the tenders were probably unique in having vacuum but no hand brakes.

Five tenders were in service in 1889 and this number survived to 1953, two being steel-framed; one is attached to *Welsh Pony*.

Engines Nos. 7-11

No. 7 *Little Wonder*

On 25 September 1868 England wrote offering to build a double Fairlie for £1,950 to quoted dimensions; '. . . will run round curves down to 2 chains radius . . .'

This engine was the fourth narrow gauge one built to the Fairlie Patent and was the seventh and last engine to be built for the Company by what had been George England's Works, but in fact the firm had gone out of business and become the Fairlie Engine & Steam Carriage

No. as delivered	No. as amended	Named	Built by	Works No.	Date	Cost	Withdrawn from traffic
7	7	Little Wonder	Fairlie Engine & Steam Carriage Co. (ex: Geo. England & Co.)	—	1869	£1,905 (also given as £2,006 and £1,600)*	1882
8	8	James Spooner	Avonside Engine Co.	929/930	1872	£1,000	1933
9 1885	7	Taliesin	Vulcan Foundry	791	1876	£1,305	1932
10	10	Merddin Emrys	Boston Lodge	—	1879		Extant in 1953
11	3 c. 1886	Livingston Thompson (later Taliesin)	Boston Lodge	—	1885		Extant in 1953

* Half year Report.

Company Limited, though still occupying the same premises. [Earlier, three engines had been built by James Cross & Co. of St. Helens for Queensland's 3 ft. 6 in. gauge in 1866; these were, to put it mildly, unsuccessful, and were disclaimed by Fairlie. They were eventually rebuilt to standard gauge by Yorkshire Engine Co. two going to Uruguay and one becoming Burry Port & Gwendraeth Valley Railway No. 8 *Victoria*.] The bogie wheelbases were the elongated form of the later four-wheeled engines and the driving-wheel diameter was increased once again. The water tanks reverted to the form used on the first engines, having a box-like shape enveloping the boilers; the chimneys too appeared with bell-mouth tops. Salter valves were encased in the domes which contained also regulator valves with horizontal sliding faces worked from a horizontal handle on top of the firebox. There was no cab but weatherboards were fitted. To clear stones or snow off the line, small ploughs hung in front of the cylinders. The side tanks carried long plates reading 'Fairlie's Patent', and *Little Wonder*. Coal was carried in each tank top on the fireman's side. The later form of smokebox of ' ∩ ' section was used, the footplate being attached to the bogie frames and sliding beneath it when the bogie turned.

The fireboxes themselves were of novel section, resembling two letter 'Ds' joined back to back when seen in plan. Unlike previous double Fairlie engines, there was a double firebox each fired from the same side.

Gooch's motion was fitted. (Further reference will be found in *Festiniog Railway Magazine*, No. 2 (Autumn 1958), p. 9.)

The bogie pivots were central and the bearings plain. No balance weights were hung at the trailing ends of the bogies to counter-balance the weight of the cylinders and motion; later engines had ballast to equalise the weight of cylinders. Local tradition has it the engine literally shook itself to pieces on the rough track of those early times, whilst the plain bogie bearings and lack of steadying devices on the bogies contributed to the effect. (Perhaps the steadiness of its footplate was gained through punishment to the running gear?) It was the condition of the boiler which led to withdrawal, however.

The engine was fitted with a bell which was later used at Boston Lodge shed; there were india-rubber delivery pipes from the sandpots. The sandpots were later taken off the footplate and fixed to the tank ends. Whistles were moved from within to outside the cab sheets.

Vignes describes the boiler as being made of 'Sir John Brown's Iron', and the engine as 'a very steady machine'. The cost of it was £2,006 and it did its work on 75% of the fuel required for the other engines when doing the same work.

It is odd that little mention is ever made in the minutes of this engine; only when the order is given for the *Livingston Thompson* is it recorded that this new engine was to replace the *Little Wonder*, 'abandoned'. The engine can only have had a life of about twenty years, but the boiler report of June 1882 reads 'Boiler in very bad state, otherwise in fair working order; worked up to 98 lb.'. The boiler was condemned at the year end.

No. 7 *Little Wonder*

Designer, Robert F. Fairlie to Fairlie Patent. Builder, Fairlie E. & S. C. Co., 1869. 0–4–4–0 double bogie type. Cylinders, 13 in. stroke, $8\frac{1}{4}$ in. diam. (later $8\frac{1}{2}$ in.). Weight in Working Order, $19\frac{1}{2}$ tons. Heating Surface, 730 sq. ft. Area Grates, 11 sq. ft. Pressure, 160 lb. Tractive Effort, 5,357 lb. Wheelbase, 19 ft. total; 5 ft. bogie. Driving Wheel diam. 2 ft. 4 in. Tanks Capacity, 680 gallons.

1879—Engine worn out, withdrawn, but returned to traffic after 'thorough repairs'.

1882—6 December; officially condemned.

No. 8 *James Spooner*

A second double Fairlie engine was supplied by the Avonside Engine Company to the designs of Charles Spooner's son, George Percival Spooner. Delivery was delayed owing to a strike at the builders but it began work in December 1872. Avonside, in common with other constructors, built engines to the requirements of the Fairlie Engine & Rolling Stock Co. whose plate is clearly visible on at least two Fairlie double engines. Fairlie himself was now associated with the Narrow Gauge Rolling Stock Company. The builders looked upon this new engine as two locomotives, and gave it two Works Nos. 929 and 930. It was numbered 8 by the Company and named *James Spooner*. Larger than the *Little Wonder*, it was the prototype of the remaining single and double Fairlie engines which the Company built later. Compared with No. 7, the wheelbases of the bogies were reduced, the design of the fireboxes and ashpans altered, and the bogies pivoted off-centre to counter-balance the weight of the cylinders. When delivered the engine had cast-iron stove-pipe chimneys, no cab but two weatherboards, and no smokebox saddles. A nautical flavour was imparted by the provision of a bell mounted on a sandpot saddle behind each chimney; a whistle stood on each bell bracket. Each bell was engraved '*James Spooner*' and the clapper was worked by hand by a rod from the footplate. Unlike the *Little Wonder* whose footplate at each end was slightly rounded, No. 8 had full rounded ends; the frames carrying the disc pattern wheels, cylinders and motion were not attached to the footplating in any way. The domes had brass covers. Roltz safety valves were fitted. Vignes draws attention to the coil springs at the rear ends of the bogies to steady them, a feature absent on the *Little Wonder*.

Though the published drawings show the engine to have been built to them, there are a number of drawings in the Festiniog archives, dated 3 November 1871. Here the engine is shown to have capped chimneys like the succeeding double engines, and there are conical devices in the crowns of the fireboxes which may have been water-circulators.

A further drawing, dated 1888, shows that part of the original boiler was unsafe and Neilson & Co. of Glasgow supplied a new parallel type in steel for £390. The ornate sandboxes came off in 1885 and the engine was given a cab in 1887. The second boiler was used for the reconstruction of the engine in 1889 but it was troublesome having been made asymmetrical and the side tanks etc. were trimmed to fit it.

Williams always maintained that when Neilson came to build the boiler they found they had undercosted and built it of 'inferior material'; hence its short life. He also found the existing cylinders of 'bad design' and the engine was very inferior in the work it would do at 120 lb. alongside either of the later double engines. (February 1902.)

In 1907 the boiler was condemned. In the previous September Vulcan Foundry had supplied a new steel wagon-top boiler (referred to officially as 'a hump-back boiler') and in reassembly, four new cylinders, new smokeboxes and new boiler mountings were given, so that at first glance, the 'new' engine was to all intents and purposes standard with the later two double engines, except of course, it was shorter in length. The existing cab and tanks were again 'shaved' to fit the new boiler.

No. 8 *James Spooner*

Designer, G. P. Spooner. Builder, Avonside Engine Co. Works Nos. 929/930 of 1872. 0–4–4–0 double bogie type, Fairlie Patent. Cylinders, 14 in. stroke, $8\frac{1}{2}$ in. diam. Weight in Working Order, 22 tons. Heating Surface, 713 sq. ft. Area Grates, 11·2 sq. ft. Pressure, 140 lb. Tractive Effort, 5,410 lb. Wheelbase, 18 ft. 8 in. total; 4 ft. 6 in. bogie. Driving Wheel diam. 2 ft. 8 in. Tanks Capacity, 720 gallons.

1878—'Thorough repairs'.
1889—New parallel boiler fitted, built by Neilson & Co.
1891—Withdrawn for heavy repairs.
1906—New wagon-top boiler ordered from Vulcan Foundry.
1908—Wagon-top boiler fitted.
1919—New frames.
1930—'Laid off, requiring heavy repairs'.
1933—Engine condemned and later dismantled.
Lay out of use between late 1904 and 1908 awaiting fitting of new boiler. Engine condemned and partly dismantled 1926, awaiting decision on advisability and costs of fitting new boiler. Emergency repairs undertaken and engine returned to service 1928. Failed in traffic repeatedly but remained as stand-by engine in case of failure of *Merddin Emrys*, until late 1930, when *Livingston Thompson* entered traffic again. Finally condemned 1933 though had lain out of use for considerable period. Parts left at Glan-y-Mor.

No. 9 *Taliesin* (renumbered 7 about 1882).

Possibly something on the lines of the next engine had been contemplated for some time as there is an 'Outside Plan of Locomotive for Festiniog Railway 1874' in the Records, a sort of half *James Spooner* with 0–4–4T wheel arrangement and G.N.-Stirling wrap over cab having a circular spectacle in each side.

In 1876 Vulcan built one single Fairlie type engine for the Festiniog; it was similar in many respects to engines for the N.W.N.G. (of which there were two) but embodied the driving bogie dimensions of the *James Spooner*. This engine, to G. P. Spooner's designs, went into service in 1876 as No. 9, *Taliesin*; its name being that of a chief of the bards who died in A.D. 570. It took the number 7 when the *Little Wonder* was withdrawn. The drawings are dated 14 October 1875.

It is safe to draw the conclusion that whilst the double engines were eminently suitable for heavy work, and the four-coupled engines for light work, something in between was needed. The *Taliesin* proved to be the fastest and most economical engine on the line, and was the best all-purpose engine the Company owned. It was always placed on mail and fast trains. As built the engine was alike to the *James Spooner* except that the middle ring of the boiler carried the large brass dome with safety valve on it, and at the rear end was a roomy footplate with an open-backed cab on it. There was a goodly sized coal bunker in the rear and this was surmounted by a weatherboard with spectacle glasses. Behind the bunker was a wooden toolbox. The driving bogie was exactly as the *James Spooner* and as built the rear bogie had disc wheels with oval slots in them, just as did the driving wheels. The rear bogie frames were *inside* and there were brake blocks on all its wheels. The driving pair of wheels were also braked with wood blocks, but the trailing bogie shoes were of cast-iron. Later, when the rear bogie was replaced by one with outside frames at unknown date and without brakes, only the single set of brakes on the driving pair of wheels remained. These made the wheels so hot on the down journey that in 1891 new wheels were cast having the tyres integral with the centres; this prevented unequal expansion between the wheel and tyre due to heating. Cast-iron weights were bolted inside the tank top to improve adhesion.

Other points of interest included the double whistles, Stroudley type regulator and the new flexible steam jointing involving ball and socket joints.

The engine was first in service on 17 August 1876 but the angled cab roof was damaged in the tunnel; it came out again on 26 November with modified cab contours. Between 1887 and 1893 the cab was completely roofed in: ultimately a completely new cab was given in the 1898–1900 rebuilding—it was then tested in the Moelwyn Tunnel making 24 stops '. . . and the stoker managed somehow to get out on left side 15 times, right side 7, shall see to altering of windows so that stoker can get through'.

Everyone liked this engine; when new cylinders were fitted in 1900 Williams also wrote well of it '. . . proved to be a better engine than ever . . .'.

No. 9 *Taliesin* (Took number of *Little Wonder* in 1885.)

Designer, G. P. Spooner. Builder, Vulcan Foundry. Works No. 791 of 1876. 0-4-4 single bogie Fairlie type. Cylinders, 14 in. stroke, 9 in. diam. Weight in Working Order, 17 tons. Heating Surface, 342·5 sq. ft. Grate Area, 6·25 sq. ft. Pressure, 150 lb. Tractive Effort, 3,029 lb. Wheelbase, 13 ft. 11 in. total; 4 ft. 6 in. bogie. Wheel diam., 2 ft. 8 in. Tank Capacity, 430 gallons.

1891—New smokebox, chimney and steel bogie wheels.

1894—Cracked main frame; new frame and cylinders fitted.

1899—New boiler ordered from Vulcan Foundry; cab and side tanks etc. enlarged/renewed. New cylinders.

1900—New boiler fitted.

1924—Boiler condemned and engine dismantled for fitting new one. Vulcan Foundry quote for replacement, but Board refuses to sanction purchase although recommended by both Locomotive Superintendent and the Engineer. Engine not scrapped but re-erected.

1925—Officially returns to traffic early in year but boiler not passed at inspection. Used spasmodically on light work until 1927 at least.

1932—Engine dismantled but not used latterly. Parts to Glan-y-Mor. Boiler sold for scrap 1935.

(See *Festiniog Railway Magazine* (Summer 1960), No. 6 for earlier proposed design.)

No. 10 *Merddin Emrys* and No. 11* *Livingston Thompson*

Consideration was given in January 1876 to the saving in cost by building a double engine in the Works. Using *James Spooner* as a guide, it was estimated that an outside order would cost £2,150 but this could be done for £1,698 at home.

In a Minute dated 14 January 1877 it is recorded, 'that a new bogie engine be built and that an erecting shed be made to accommodate the work'. Thus was born No. 10; it was completed in 1879. Larger still than the *James Spooner*, it is believed to have been constructed entirely, excluding boilers which were supplied by Adamson, at Boston Lodge. No. 10 (and No. 8) had the designer's wheel-operated regulators in addition to the conventional handle.

When built the two last engines had wagon-top boilers. No. 10 had stove-pipe chimneys for a time. No. 11 appeared with capped chimneys. Subtle variations have taken place since then, a detail difference between the engines may be seen in the size of tanks and cab-openings; the latter have been altered in size on both engines and gutter strips added.

No. 10 had water circulators when new and was perhaps without sandboxes at first; No. 11 had plain fireboxes. Maker's drawings show square sandboxes, but in this and other minor respects they do not agree with the engine as put into traffic.

Merddin Emrys (or more correctly, Myrddin Emrys) was a legendary figure from the Dark Ages, one of the three Christian Bards of this Island, of whom Taliesin was another.

The Minute dated 15 August 1882 authorises the construction of a

* Accounts dated December 1884 refer to this engine as 'New No. 7'.

new double bogie engine to be completed in three years and to replace the *Little Wonder*. *The Railway Engineer* published plans in October 1884 and the engine entered traffic in June 1886 as *Livingston Thompson*.

Again, the boiler was supplied ready for fitting and the side frames delivered complete ready for erecting. The Works plates read 1885 but the engine was not ready until early 1886, requiring two years to build. It carried the name of a Director who was in office between 1836 and 1873, being Chairman for seven years, at intervals. The accounts suggest that when first tested, painting was incomplete.

In 1905 *Livingston Thompson* received a new boiler, the engine being in the Works between 28 April and 7 July. New smokeboxes with new chimneys, $1\frac{1}{4}$ inches shorter than the old ones, were fitted (just which bridge was giving clearance difficulties is hard to say but this was the stated reason).

No. 10 *Merddin Emrys*

Designer, G. P. Spooner. Builder, Boston Lodge Works, 1879. 0–4–4–0 double bogie type, Fairlie Patent. Cylinders, 14 in. stroke, 9 in. diam. Weight in Working Order, 24 tons. Heating Surface, 887 sq. ft. Area Grates, 12·4 sq. ft. Pressure, 160 lb. Tractive Effort, 6,059 lb. Wheelbase, 20 ft. total; 4 ft. 8 in. bogie. Driving Wheels, 2 ft. $9\frac{1}{4}$ in. diam. Tanks Capacity, 667 gallons.

1896—New boiler fitted from Vulcan Foundry.

1915—Boiler condemned; engine taken out of traffic.

1919—New boiler ordered from Vulcan Foundry.

1920—December, new boiler delivered Blaenau Ffestiniog: special train sent Up to collect.

1921—New boiler fitted and engine returned to traffic. Bogies swopped with No. 3.

1934—Heavy boiler and firebox repairs carried out at Avonside Engine Co. (instead of new boiler). Engine rebuilt.

Engine lay out of use 1915–21 owing to difficulties of obtaining new boiler during First War; also for period 1930–4.

With *Princess*, was one of the last two engines in service before the closure. It lay derelict between 1946 and restoration. In 1972 it was found that the wheels and axles are off *James Spooner*.

No. 11 *Livingston Thompson* (*Taliesin* from 1931)

According to accounts dated 1884 this engine was to have been No. 7, taking the vacant number left by *Little Wonder*. This number was given to *Taliesin* instead, in 1885; although then allotted No. 11, doubtful if this was carried even when new. Given No. 3 (ex *Mountaineer*)—unless at first carrying No. 11—within twelve months of entering traffic.

Principal features, etc., and dimensions as for *Merddin Emrys*. Built, March 1885–6. To traffic, 1886.

1905—New boiler delivered from Vulcan Foundry, April.

1908—New boiler fitted and engine returned to service.

1920—New tanks (partly from materials in stock).

1924—Boiler condemned.

1929—Boiler sent to Avonside Engine Co. for repairs, including a new firebox.

1931—Repaired boiler refitted, engine returned to service.

Engine lay out of use awaiting new boiler 1905–08 and again for a new boiler (which Company could not afford to purchase) 1921–31. Took name *Taliesin* after withdrawal of that engine.

In 1939 the engine was put in the erecting shop for repairs which could not be energetically pressed owing to shortage of men and pressure of other work. Consequently, the work was still unfinished when Boston Lodge employees were paid off in 1946. (A 1972 inspection showed the wheels were off No. 10).

Snowploughs

These possibly started as 'lifeguards' recommended by B.O.T. inspection on 27 October 1864 which proved as useful for snow as rocks. In December 1888 Nos. 1, 2, 6 and 10 were given them and others were listed from time to time. Each engine had its own plough(s): the method of use was to run an engine to and fro in places where drifting occurred . . . often resulting in failure and the engine having to be dug out.

Rail Tractors

(*No Number or Name*) 'Simplex' type four-wheeled petrol tractor by Motor Rail Ltd., Bedford, built 1917 for War Department, Indent No. 10350. Dorman engine. Weight, 6 tons. 40 horsepower. Driven by petrol though paraffin used experimentally. Purchased July 1923 from Kent Construction & Engineering Co., Ashford, Kent, for £350. Length, 11 ft. 1½ in. Width, 6 ft. 8 in. Height, 8 ft. 4 in. Wheelbase, 4 ft. Driving Wheels, 1 ft. 6 in.

Limited usage at first owing to width; platforms and wharves altered to suit. First used at Minffordd, then between Boston Lodge and Portmadoc as Bottom Shunter. Pre-1939 taken to location of work by attaching to rear of suitable trains, out of gear. Not run independently along main line unless actually shunting. Also used on Croesor Tramway for collecting traffic from Croesor Junction.

Maximum load about 4 tons on Croesor duty. In normal duty, load equivalent one third England engine.

No. 11 *Moelwyn*

Class 4–50/1. I.C. 629 four-wheeled petrol tractor by Pittsburgh Model Engine Co. Works No. 49604 of 1918. Built under sub-contract for Baldwin Locomotive Co. for War Department use of French Government, petrol engine. Weight, 7½ tons. 45 horsepower. Purchased February 1925 from E. W. Farrow & Sons, Engineers' Merchants, Spalding, Lincs., per Honeywill Bros. Ltd. (Agents) for £373. Length, 15 ft. 3 in. Width, 5 ft. 3 in. Height, 8 ft. 4 in. Wheelbase, 4 ft. Driving Wheels, 2 ft. 2 in.
1928—Vacuum brake fitted in connection with proposal to use tractor for winter passenger work on Welsh Highland Railway.

(*No Number or Name*) Four-wheeled paraffin tractor by Muirhill with Fordson engine; on trial only; property of Aluminium Corporation, Dolgarrog. (Cost of new tractor £250.) Built Muirhill (E. Boydell & Co. Ltd.) 1922. 4 cylinder, 20 horsepower engine. Wheelbase, 2 ft. 11 in. Driving Wheels, 1 ft. 8 in. Weight, 4 tons. Period of loan, April–August 1924.
Tractor loaned at instigation of Dolgarrog to test capacity with a view to withdrawing all steam locomotives and working railway with fleet of these tractors. Delivered between Dolgarrog and Blaenau Festiniog (F.R. station) by Foden steam wagon. Having only normal 'road-type' gear box, with only one reverse gear, engine had to be turned or else work at 2½ m.p.h. in reverse. Also used as stationary engine at Boston Lodge before Tangye engine installed. Found unsuitable; too light for work involved. When shunting, wagons would run away with tractor. Returned to Dolgarrog.

(*No Number or Name*) Four-wheeled petrol tractor by Austro-Daimler of about 20 horsepower. (Other dimensions not available.) Purchased by Colonel Stephens from contractors of North Devon & Cornwall Light Railway in July 1925 for use on Welsh Highland Railway. In operation by early 1926, running trials between foot of final incline on Croesor Tramway and Portmadoc Wharves, in place of a horse. Used with Hudson carriage 25 January 1928 between Portmadoc and Croesor Junction but overloaded—journey time 45 minutes.
Tractor not suitable general purposes; too light. Filled with rocks to increase weight! Relegated to Boston Lodge Works as shunter, later stored in paint shop 1929. Offered for sale or hire March 1930, and again for £10 in July 1933. Cut up for scrap 1934.

1L The Princess, carrying its second style of weather board, at Duffws in the early 1870s. The first vehicle is brake van No. 1, attached to two forms of closed and one open coach. The train stands on the mineral line; to its left is Palmerston and the building at rear reads 'Refreshment Room'. The track is still un-fished T section rail. The new slate mills above the van are in the Votty & Bowydd quarry.

(F.R. Co.)

2L   Somewhat later than the period as Plate 1L, a Festiniog & Blaenau Rly. train from Blaenau stops near the wooden viaduct approaching Tan-y-Manod. Standard gauge sleepers nearby suggest repair work using crossing timbers, perhaps to the viaduct?

(National Library of Wales)

3L   The Princess, *attached to a F. & B.R. coach, in the F. & B.R. station, Blaenau. Its tender carries 'No. 6'. Behind the driver reads 'Duffws Station'. c. 1876.*

(National Library of Wales)

4L   *Bottom Shunting Engine* The Princess *on the Sluice Bridge, Portmadoc. Open cab as carried May 1891 to 1894 (the cab was also carried by* Prince *October 1890 to May 1891) and 'Dummy Tanks'.*   *(Alan Pratt)*

5L *No. 2 with 'Dummy Tanks,' later cast-iron chimney, second type of weather board and later tender. On the Cob, 1887.* (F.R. Co.)

6L Princess *in ultimate form at Duffws. 1927.* (L.P. Co.)

7L Prince *at Tan-y-Bwlch, as restored 1955. July 1958.* (J. I. C. Boyd)

8L Mountaineer, *with second pattern of chimney as fitted 1876 and newly-acquired whistle mounting.*   (L.P. Co.)

9L Palmerston *on Boston Lodge shed; late 1920s.*   (K. A. C. R. Nunn)

10L Prince *back in harness; leaving Harbour station. 1957.*   (J. I. C. Boyd)

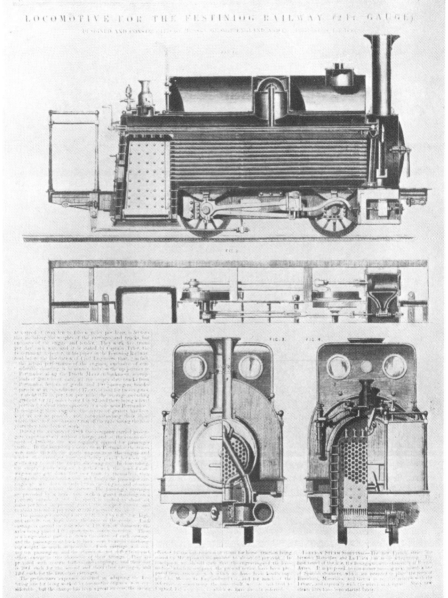

11L *Inaccurate in certain widths, engraving from 'Engineering' of 4 October 1867
purporting to show* Welsh Pony.

12L   *Maker's photograph of* Little Giant *showing several unusual features mentioned in the text.*   *(J. I. C. Boyd)*

13L   Little Giant, *modified from above state, and with sprung tender having wooden-frame faced with iron. On the Cob, 1887.*   *(F.R. Co.)*

14L   Welsh Pony *with sundry modifications and attached to 'No. 2' tender, at Duffws. c. 1876*   *(National Library of Wales)*

15L *Top Shunter, Duffws, about 1876.* Little Giant *as fitted with painted name, maker's and owner's plates.* (*National Library of Wales*)

16L Little Giant *at Portmadoc, fitted with 1888 boiler but before receiving steel frame and larger driving wheels.* (*L.P. Co.*)

17L *Last years;* Little Giant *in ultimate form, acting as Top Shunter, Duffws.* (*L.P. Co.*)

(*No Number or Name*) Six-wheeled diesel tractor by Kerr Stuart Ltd. Works No. 4415 of 1928. First diesel tractor by makers. Engine, McClaren-Benz 4 cylinder, with J.A.P. engine for starting purposes. Chain drive. 60 horsepower. Wheelbase, 5 ft. Driving Wheels, 2 ft. diam. On loan to Welsh Highland and Festiniog Railways before despatch to Sudan. Delivered to Dinas Junction July 1928 and worked principally on Bryngwyn branch. Transferred to Festiniog Railway 14 March 1929, but cab too high for Minffordd Cemetery road bridge—cut down at Boston Lodge and several Minffordd wharves cut back. Undertook duties of Bottom Shunter in place of Baldwin tractor. Returned to Stoke, 1929, used later by contractors in making East Lancashire Road at Kirkby, August 1929, then passing to the Castleder & Victoria Bridge Tramway in Ireland for which it was converted to 3 ft. gauge. Later to Mauritius per Hunslet Engine Co., rebuilt to 60 cm. gauge. Colonel Stephens not impressed by performance of this tractor, considering it to be uneconomical when compared with petrol consumption of his standard gauge Ford railcars, but made the comment when the makers announced it was going back, 'I thought you had given her to us'.

In 1920, Drewry & Co. were asked to supply a petrol engine 'to drive an Inspection Car': nothing more is known of this.

Painting—Locomotives

1863—(Probably) red with black lining. Domes: polished brass.

1878—Brick red, lined gold or yellow. Area outside lining solid black. Footplate, smokebox, cab roof: black. Valance, running gear: black or green or vermilion.

1880s—Lining-out now more ornate on double engines, having black border, then red(?), yellow, black and finally thin red lines on area perimeters.

1925—Dark green (similar to 'Swindon' green). Yellow lining. Panelling as 1878 with black surround. Later no lining at all.
England engines: yellow numerals on front beam and rear tender. Cab interiors: dark cream. In 1942 No. 3 was sea-green with orange lining edged white. Tender fitted was 7 ft. 10 in. long, 4 ft. 10 in. wide over sides and 5 ft. 2 in. wide over floor plating. Tractors: green.

★   ★   ★

Engines Nos. 11-13 (1934 numbering)

Although strictly outside the scope of the Festiniog Railway proper, the links formed through the Welsh Highland Railway meant that three other steam locomotives should be added to the Festiniog's own roster. Their individual story has appeared in NARROW GAUGE RAILWAYS IN

SOUTH CAERNARVONSHIRE, and a summary is sufficient here. The
number prefix was added to follow on from the Festiniog loco list, being
applied only from the date of leasing, 1934.

No. 11 *Moel Tryfan*

Designer, G. P. Spooner. Builder, Vulcan Foundry, 1875. Works No.
738. 0–6–4 tank, single bogie Fairlie type. Cylinders, 14 in. stroke,
8½ in. diam. Weight in Working Order, 14 tons. Heating Surface, 366
sq. ft. Grate Area, 5·9 sq. ft. Pressure, 140 lb. Tractive Effort, 3,855 lb.
(ref. official lists). Wheelbase, 14 ft. 11½ in., total; 6 ft. bogie. Driving
Wheels, 2 ft. 6 in. diam. Tank Capacity, 350 gallons.
This engine was one of two supplied to the North Wales Narrow Gauge
Railways, the other being named *Snowdon Ranger* (Works No. 739). It
was the first engine of the 0–6–4 wheel arrangement in the British Isles.
(N.W.N.G. Railways stock was fitted with Westinghouse brakes.)

1903—Engine despatched for heavy overhaul at Davies & Metcalfe,
near Stockport, and fitting of new boiler.
(*Snowdon Ranger* had been likewise repaired in 1902.)

1917—Frames of *Snowdon Ranger* placed under *Moel Tryfan* and the
latter put into best working order possible under conditions of
extreme economy and wartime restrictions. Best parts of each
engine utilised to provide a survivor, *Snowdon Ranger* thereafter
being nominally withdrawn.

1937—Taken into Boston Lodge for boiler and firebox repairs. This
work was not completed though the engine was dismantled, parts
being stacked in the Works yard, and the boiler and driving bogie
in the locomotive shed.

1954—Decision taken by new owners to scrap remaining parts. Boiler,
etc., towed across from locomotive shed to Harbour station where
cut up for scrap.

This engine and *Russell* were the only two N.W.N.G. Railways engines
to come into Festiniog stock lists in 1923. They worked through to
Portmadoc Harbour from the first time after the systems had been
connected. In 1923 *Moel Tryfan* was taken into Boston Lodge to have
cab and boiler mountings reduced in height to enable it to work over the
Festiniog. Vacuum brake was fitted and the Westinghouse removed.
The engine worked regularly between Blaenau and Dinas Junction
between 1924 and 1936, occasionally being turned so as to run bunker
first Up to Blaenau. Like the Festiniog single Fairlie, she was a good
steamer, free running and well-liked by the enginemen.

No. 12 *Russell*

Designer and Builder, Hunslet Engine Co., 1906. Works No. 901.

2-6-2 tank locomotive. Cylinders, 15 in., stroke 10¾ in. diam.* Weight in Working Order, 20 tons. Heating Surface, 381 sq. ft. Grate Area, 6¼ sq. ft. Pressure, 160 lb. Tractive Effort, 7,425 lb. Wheelbase, 15 ft. 6 in., total; 5 ft. 6 in. rigid. Driving Wheels, 2 ft. 4 in. Tank Capacity, 440 gallons.

(Records of this engine were not kept at Boston Lodge and details of repairs not available.)

This engine came into Festiniog stock lists in 1923. It had been intended for the P.B. & S.S.R., being an enlargement of the maker's design for Sierra Leone.

The engine was cut down at Boston Lodge in 1923 and the Westinghouse brake system removed. Vacuum brake was fitted. After trials it was found that the engine was still too wide to be used through the Festiniog tunnels with safety, consequently although it ran to Boston Lodge for repair, it was not used above this point. In the main, it spent its life between Beddgelert and Dinas Junction. Although numbered in the Festiniog series, its other connections with the Festiniog Railway were more figurative than real. Heavy repairs apart, it never had reason to run over Festiniog metals.

No. 13 (Not Named) (ex R.O.D. No. 590)

Builders, Baldwin Locomotive Works, Philadelphia, U.S.A. Class 10–12–D, 13. Indent D.R.T. 887 of 1 March 1917. Works No. 45172 of 1917. 4–6–0 Pannier Tank. Cylinders, 12 in. stroke, 9 in. diam. Weight in Working Order, 14½ tons. Heating Surface, 254·5 sq. ft. Grate Area, 5·6 sq. ft. Pressure, 178 lb. Wheelbase, 12 ft. 2 in., total; 5 ft. 10 in. rigid. Driving Wheels, 1 ft. 11½ in. Tank Capacity, 496 gallons.

This engine was used on the Welsh Highland main line and Bryngwyn branch throughout its life. It was not used on the Festiniog line at all but was repaired at Boston Lodge and occasionally stabled at Boston Lodge shed overnight.

Stored at Boston Lodge after end of summer season 1936 and taken 'dead' to Dinas Junction June 1937 and cut up there in 1941.

(This engine was purchased for the Welsh Highland services and could not work beyond Cemetery Bridge, Boston Lodge, on account of loading gauge.)

* F.R. records of 1921 state 14 in. × 9½ in.

CHAPTER FIFTEEN

CARRIAGES AND WAGONS 1836–1953

(The Roman Numerals are for identification in Dimension List at chapter end.)

Slate Wagons I II III

The slate wagon is the earliest form of railway vehicle in North Wales. It has the lesser distinction of being the most numerous form of narrow gauge vehicle in the British Isles. The Festiniog Railway had 1,095 of them on its books.

The earliest quarry railways in North Wales appear to have been in the Penrhyn Slate Quarry and it is likely that wagons for internal use were in operation before the end of the eighteenth century. When the Penrhyn Railway, on the two-foot gauge, was opened in 1801, the wagons, hauled by horses, differed but little from the slate wagon of the present day. The *Repertory of Arts and Manufactures*, Volume III (Second series), illustrates a train on this railway in 1803 showing the familiar slat-sided wagons carrying the finished slates to the port. This pattern has remained ever since, the frame sides being constructed of wood at first and later of angle-iron.

Clause 7 of the F.R. Specification of 22 December 1832—already quoted—required 'one hundred wagons each to contain twenty-three hundred weight of slates to be made for the use and benefit of the said Company'.

In general terms the slate wagon is a plain, unimposing and strictly utilitarian vehicle. It is small, carried on four wheels in simple bearings without springs, and apart from some method of hooking on to another wagon, it is usually without decoration in the form of buffers, etc. The early forms on the Festiniog were made in wood, the laths forming the sides being carried on iron rod uprights, threaded with cast-iron spacers. The bearings were large and were embodied in a casting having a large grease hole in it, covered by a hinged flap. At each end was a single link with hook attached, and the end of the floors had a protrusion faced with metal which took the buffing shocks. In later forms the wooden floors were replaced with sheet iron floors which rusted away so quickly in the wet climate (frequently having a pool of water in them) that wooden floors were reinstated.

The wagon wheels could be broken down into:

1. Curve spoked variety (no separate tyre) supplied by Hadfields.
2. Straight spoke variety: cast-iron with tyre of rolled iron shrunk and riveted on.
3. Disc variety: cast-iron with either integral or separate tyres.

Apart from a certain number of the earliest wagons having inside bearings, the running gear has remained unchanged; the wheels are 1 ft. 6 in. diameter, some having steel tyres; they are either spoked or disc, with spokes either straight or curved (the latter were fitted when knowledge of casting faults was more widely appreciated). Some wheels are in cast-iron throughout without separate tyres: in this form they

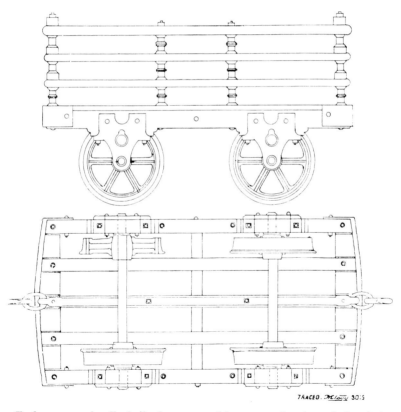

TRACED. *McLeoy* 30:5

Early pattern, locally-built slate wagon (from an undated rough drawing)

may be of disc or straight spoke pattern. With inside bearings the wheels were loose on the axles and held to them by a split pin and washer on the end of the axle. With outside bearings the wheels were a fixture—in either case, Low Moor iron was used. Due to tread wear the flanges of these wagons became so deep that they struck the cheeks of the chairs on the track and to counter this the design of chair was modified several times over the years, the most modern castings having cheeks much reduced in height. The only effective cure for this was to take the wheels from the wagons and turn down the flanges relative to the reduced tread once more. At one time it was the practice to put steel-tyred spoked wheels under ordinary wagons and cast-iron disc wheels under braked wagons. About one in six of all slate wagons had hand brakes, this being a necessity for the gravity-worked slate trains.

Wagons numbered 1–805 were practically all original wooden wagons taring 10–12 cwt., or the smaller iron wagons (first introduced in 1857) taring 13–16 cwt. There were a few of the large iron wagons in this series tare 19 cwt., followed by a complete set of large iron numbered 806–998, but after 1,001 the small iron wagons were reverted to for the rest of the series. The small wood and iron wagons held two tons of slate, the large iron wagons three tons. Some of these were built at Boston Lodge Works, but the large type (the first batch built by Brown, Marshalls & Co., 1869) was found to be too wide for comfortable loading by hand; the reach required to pack the slate was too great. The series thus ended with the small iron wagons.

Other disadvantages of the larger wagons were that they could not pass each other on inclines or, singly, they fouled equipment near the track in the quarries; their wheelbase was also too long for certain quarry turntables.

The slate is stacked into the wagons with wooden mallets, in two or three tiers as required; wagons find their way into the workings and as the clearances here or in slate mills, underground workings, etc., are often limited, they are suitably small and capable of manhandling even when loaded.

The non-F.R. wagons built at Earlestown and Swindon were very similar to the above, but had different patterns of bearings and bearing castings; these conveyed slate from the quarries to the L.N.W.R. or G.W.R. yards at Blaenau Ffestiniog. They had small cast builder's plates on them, whilst the Festiniog patterns had merely 'F.R.' on the bearing casting. It should be emphasised that the Company provided wagons for the use of fifteen quarry systems, there being no privately owned wagons running over Festiniog tracks, save for gunpowder vans.

Slate Wagon Summary up to 1928
(from Minffordd Tare Book, April 1928)

Numbered 1–1,079*

Series	Notes
1–500	Mainly original wood and small iron. A few large iron among list.
501–805	Almost all small iron wagons with a handful of original wood and less than 20 wagons large iron.
806–998	With exception 853, all large iron.
999–1,000	Original wood.
1,001–1,079	All small iron.

Miscellaneous Conversions

Large iron (no brake) temporarily converted for Macadam, 12/1910 (No. 926).
Large iron (brake) temporarily converted for setts, 12/1919 (No. 167).

Summary of Types in March 1911

Original Wood (brakes)	Original Wood (no brakes)	Small Iron (brakes)	Small Iron (no brakes)	Large Iron (brakes)	Large Iron (no brakes)
18	176	117	522	72	176

At a Board Meeting held at the Harbour Offices on 23 September 1892, and in the presence of the following quarry representatives, a resolution was passed that:

1. All slate wagons be marked.
2. Quarry owners to marshal similarly marked wagons together to obviate shunting unnecessarily.
3. A list of allotments would follow.

J. W. Greaves & Sons	J. E. Greaves
	C. W. Roberts
Votty & Bowydd Slate Co.	F. S. Percival
	C. W. Logan
Oakeley Slate Co.	C. Benson
	R. Roberts
	D. Morris

* 26 converted to solid sides for granite chipping traffic as below:

Large iron (braked) converted to end door tip wagons, 1914–20	Nos. 167, 338, 365, 443, 825, 873, 875.
Large iron (no brake) converted to side door tip wagons, 1914–20	Nos. 830, 846.
Large iron (no brake) converted to end door tip wagons, 1914–20	Nos. 40, 52, 258, 387, 808, 810, 812, 815, 821, 827, 840, 843, 851, 860, 926, 978, 988.

Maenoffleren   W. C. Andrews
Craig Ddu   R. Bowton
Wrysgan   J. Davies
New Welsh Slate Co.   Robert Owen

Though not commercially correct, the titles are quoted from a circular letter sent from the Secretary (who had his own Office Seal-marked envelopes) to all interested parties on 30 September by J. S. Hughes. Allotment was to be by labels, and numbers of wagons would be:

Oakeley—400; Greaves—190; Votty & Bowydd—120; Maenofferen—90; New Welsh—70; 'the surplus to be divided among the smaller quarries by the Festiniog Railway Company in the best way possible'.

Colour coding was introduced as below, in March 1911, when the labelling scheme was discontinued:

Quarry	*Colour Mark*
Oakeley	Blue on Middle Rail
Greaves	Red on Middle Rail
Votty & Bowydd	Green on Middle Rail
Maenofferen	White Square on Black Ground
Wrysgan	Green on Vertical Rail
Diphwys Casson	Yellow on Vertical Rail
Rhiwbach	2 White Rings flanking Red Square on Middle Rail
Bwlch-y-Slater	White on Middle Rail
Unallotted	(Unmarked)

Slab Wagons (Flat) IV

Local lore has it that the first slab wagons were used for constructing the Embankment. Be that as it may, there was little slab traffic over the Festiniog Railway, most of the rock being sent down in finished slate form. The slab wagons had the same bearings and wheels, and the same form of painting, as the slate wagons. The floors were a sheet of iron, having wooden cross members on which the rock was placed and, if necessary, to which it was chained down. Small hand cranes were used to load and unload. The records show that at one time slab wagons were numbered 1 to 41 but by 1928 a third of these had disappeared. Their average tare was 15 cwt. and each held 3 tons of stone. The first slab wagons used for constructing the Cob were not of this later style. (The Billington aquatint also shows typical contractor-type swivelling tip wagons on the Cob construction.)

Slab Wagons (Vertical)

These were known by the staff as 'donkey trucks' and were built from certain parts of old slate wagons for carrying either slate slab or sheet iron plates, glass, etc. They were really travelling trestles as the sheeting was allowed to lie against a central trestle which ran lengthwise along the wagon. Similar vehicles were used on most Welsh quarry tramways where there was an output of slabs. These wagons are now extinct.

[In late 1918 it was the intention to paint the tare on all slate and slab wagons to prevent overloading, but only goods and coal wagons were so treated. Where in doubt, a low loading was rated. A typical cause for this intention was occasioned when Moelwyn Zinc Mine sent down a 4 ton wagon loaded to $7\frac{1}{4}$ tons (October 1919).]

Open Wagons V VI VII

(the majority of these built at Boston Lodge, 1862–64)

Apart from the two bogie open wagons referred to elsewhere which were designed for coal or ballast, and a single six-wheeled wagon to which reference is made later, the rest of the four-wheeled open wagons fell into two official classifications, 'small coal' and 'large coal'. Each of these broad descriptions could be sub-divided many times, and there were many variants among them including stone and coke wagons introduced in 1871–2. The early wagons, of which many have vanished, their forms being known only from photographs, were narrow in body but high in side, they had inside bearings and no centre buffers. Most had end doors, either single or double, and a few had side doors. The later variety to carry 4 tons, introduced in 1875, had outside bearings and sprung buffer-couplings, with a hand-brake. The smaller types carried 3 tons or 1 ton.*

Besides the above, there were a smaller number of 'iron coal trucks' of 2 tons capacity, built at Boston Lodge. They had end doors and brakes. VIII

The need for large numbers of open wagons for coal, lime, manures, merchandise, etc., which formed a very heavy traffic at a time when ships brought cargoes for inland towns and the Festiniog carried all commodities for inland use, was amost extinguished (so far as the hinterland of Portmadoc was concerned) when standard gauge railways reached Festiniog and water-borne cargoes dwindled in importance.

During the years when the railway was closed (1946–54) the surviving open wagons fell victim to the weather and the majority have been scrapped. Other than slate wagons, the Company possessed another 200 or so four-wheeled wagons, a large percentage of which comprised the above. Thus there were wagons which held smaller loads and were not

---

* Large open, end-door coal wagons having outside framing and inside beamings were 7 ft. 6 in. length over beams, 7 ft. 1 in. over body, 3 ft. 6 in. wide in body, height from rail 4 ft. 8 in. with 3 ft. $7\frac{1}{2}$ in. wheelbase, were used by Oakeley Quarry and probably F.R. origin.

of the general description given above. Number plates were swopped about, and logical loadings did not always agree with the lettering on the sides. Batches of wagons were not constructed identically.

Six-wheeled Open Iron Wagon IX

This was an experimental wagon built in 1880 (ref: stock list 1887) after the N.W.N.G. Railways' experience with Cleminson's six-wheeled flexible wheelbase system on their carriages. It seems possible that the Festiniog intended to apply the system to further wagons and carriages too, but the outcome was this single vehicle, No. 8. It is a massive wagon and was intended for coal traffic. For a Welsh Show, held in Portmadoc, the wagon was roofed in corrugated iron to carry prize cattle. Later it was used for flour traffic between Blaenau Ffestiniog and the Co-operative Wholesale Society's flour store in Penrhyn station. It has end doors and still exists. It was loaned to the Shell Factory during the First War and used to run over to the harbour for unloading into ships. Such loads of shells broke its axles firstly on the harbour in July 1918 and again when overloaded causing an awkward derailment in Moelwyn Tunnel during the following September when attached to an Up train. The staff called it 'The Iron Bogie'. The brake works on a drum on the centre axle. Vignes' *Atlas* shows a hypothetical bogie version of this wagon, and a similar drawing is in the Company's possession.

Open Wagon Conversions

Some large iron slate wagons were fitted up with wooden sides for granite chippings traffic. Iron side-tipping wagons were also built for it, and any suitable wagons were used for granite setts. These wagons worked between the Moelwyn or Festiniog granite quarries, and Blaenau. Only wagons marked with a white spot could enter the Moelwyn sidings where there were severe loading gauge restrictions. (It was intended to use the existing wooden coal wagons for the chippings but in 1919 they were in short supply.)

Large slate wagons were the basis for conversion, having additional rails put on their top sides for setts and wooden planks for chippings. Nos. 926 and 167 were among the first. Brookes submitted to Boston Lodge what they thought was a cheap conversion of a L.N.W.R. slate wagon (as all their converted chippings' wagons were at the premises of the Zinc Mine) only to be told they had converted one of the F.R.'s precious large slate wagons.

Bolster Wagons X

The first seven wagons resembled abbreviated flat slab wagons, having sheet-iron floors, small bolsters and known as 'Iron Bogies'.

After 1874 the remainder had very short wheelbases and a very large bolster which overhung the wagon sides; these were the 'Wood Bogies'. Match trucks ran between the bolster when the load was long; spare screw couplings were used with chains to lash the load. A pair is shown carrying long timber in Vignes.

Ganger's Flat Wagons XI

These were light flat-topped wagons with low sides used by men working on the line. They had inside bearings and a crude brake. Unlike the modern trolley, they had coupling gear and could be used in a train.

Carriage Wagon

This was another form of flat wagon, having a long wheelbase and built to a drawing dated 10 May 1884. It was used for carrying road carriages, the road vehicles straddling the length of the wagon and the road wheels being carried on what appeared at first to be side steps slung low below the axle bearings. These were, in fact, channel-shaped runners which allowed the road vehicle to run on and off, and held it securely when travelling. In later life it was used as a match truck for the mobile crane jib.

Gunpowder Vans XII

One or two of these are still in use in the quarries though not of F.R. origin. They were made of sheet-iron and once carried the powder from the Boston Lodge magazines to their users. The sides were wrapped over the top to form a roof and the doors substantially padlocked. These vans operated on behalf of Messrs. Curtis & Harvey (latterly I.C.I.), contractors for the gunpowder. Latterly, they were the only privately owned wagons on the system.*

Hearse Van

This remarkable vehicle is still in existence and has double end doors through which the coffin was passed. It was converted from a Type 2 quarrymen's coach in 1885–6. It has inside bearings and no one can remember when it was in use. A funeral touch is added by four Grecian urns, one on each corner of the roof. It was painted black and remained in use until the 1920s although some correspondence suggests it may have been used in 1946: this is hardly feasible.

* A Return of 1890 states there were 21 wagons belonging to private owners running on the line 'and these are of similar construction to those belonging to the Company'.

Horse Dandies (and conversion to Coal Wagons)

These were first known as Iron Horseboxes, a name which they did not lose when, their purpose superseded, they were put to carrying coal. They were narrow iron-bodied trucks with a single end door, placed at the Up end. The other end was swan-necked; bodies were 6 ft. long (6 ft. 3½ in. over the neck). The wheelbase was 3 ft. 2 in., they stood 4 ft. 8½ in. from rail and were 2 ft. 8 in. wide. The only survivor, No. 50 (in the Narrow Gauge Museum, Tywyn) has outside bearings but it seems likely all the original stock began life with them inside. Like other iron-bodied stock, number plates were seldom carried, details being painted on in white characters. (The original series had wooden bodies).

Covered Vans (earliest types were converted opens, built at Boston Lodge, 1862–4) XIII XIV

There were three types, the earliest having a narrow body, inside bearings and vertical planking. It was a covered version of the first opens. An 1897 type with a much larger body had a sliding door on one side, but the third and largest variety of c. 1875 was a covered companion to the large coal wagons, and had brakes, sprung buffers and end doors. A few vans are still in existence.

The illustration of No. 7 on Creuau curve shows the ninth wagon with a gable roof whilst that of old Dinas Junction about 1887 shows a van of the second type as the third vehicle in the train.

Cattle Vans Nos. 101 and 104

Nothing is known about these two vehicles, save that both were converted to covered vans.

Goods Brake Vans XV

The Festiniog never had much use for brake vans as they were exempt from attaching brake vans to goods trains and they rarely ran any goods trains! Apart from gravity trains, most others ran mixed. The brake vans were used principally by returning brakesmen travelling back up the line after they had worked a Down gravity train. The vans were small, with a balcony at each end (mainly because these were likely to work over the triangle at Glan-y-Pwll and become turned) and a brake pillar in the centre of the body. The running gear was identical with the last type of quarrymen's coaches. They were so small that when standing on the balcony an average man could look over the roof without difficulty. There was no room for a stove, and the fire risk would be rather high. Some were built from quarrymen's coaches.

To enable signalmen and others to ensure that the train was complete a large oval plate reading 'LAST VEHICLE' in white on a red ground, was hung from the last vehicle (in the case of most Up trains this vehicle

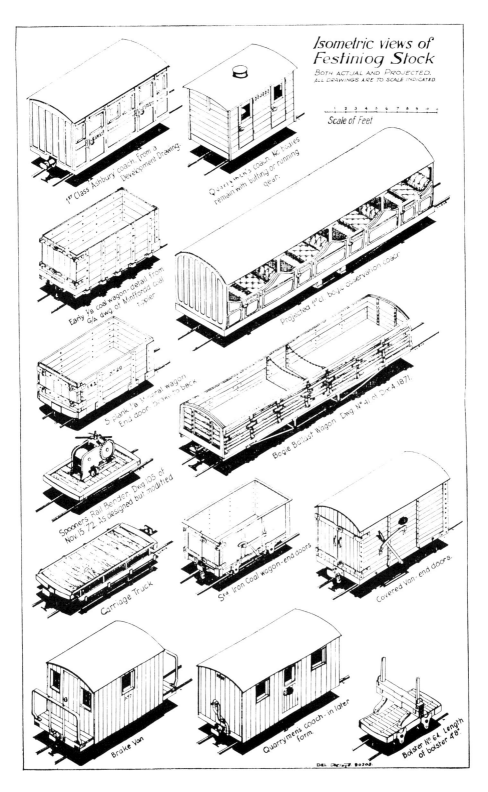

Isometric views of Festiniog Stock

BOTH ACTUAL AND PROJECTED.
ALL DRAWINGS ARE TO SCALE INDICATED

Scale of Feet

1ˢᵀ Class Ashbury coach, from a Development Drawing.

Quarrymen's coach. No bodies remain with buffing or running gear.

Early ⅛ coal wagon- detail from G/A dwg of Minffordd coal Tippler

Projected 1ˢᵗ cl. bogie observation coach

5 plank ⅛ Mineral wagon End door brake to back

Bogie Ballast Wagon. Dwg Nº 41 of Dec 4. 1871.

Spooner's Rail Bender. Dwg 105 of Nov. 15 '72. As designed but modified

Carriage Truck

Stᵈ Iron Coal wagon- end doors.

Covered Van- end doors.

Brake Van

Quarrymens coach - in later form.

Bolster Nº 64. Length of bolster 48".

DEL. ꓕꓥꓵꓦ 80303.

was usually an empty slate wagon). Another similar iron plate was in use, reading 'SPECIAL FOLLOWS'.

In 1946 survivors were: No. 5 in Carpenters' Shop, No. 6 in Loco Yard, No. 7 in Top Yard (damaged); all Boston Lodge.

Rail-bending Trolley

This resembled a large clothes mangle on wheels and was designed by Spooner as a mobile rail-bending machine. It is recorded that it once formed part of the make-up of a test train during the trials, and travelling at speed it must have looked a remarkable sight! It was last in use as a capstan wagon at a quarry. When first made it was described in the engineering journals of the time.

Side-tipping Wagons

These were sheet-iron bodies with hinged side-discharge door built up experimentally on steel chassis. Two appear to have been made for Groby Granite traffic but were not high enough to unload into main line wagons.

Breakdown Van

No breakdown train was in use. A van was fitted up with tools, jacks and bars for rerailing but most casualties could be dealt with by a few lusty men. There were double doors each end; the body had vertical planking, brake one side, cant-rail level side ventilators and inside bearings. (In existence 1946.)

Painting (generalisation)

The goods brake vans, larger mineral wagons, wooden 2-ton slate wagons, wooden open wagons, and large vans were usually brick red with black ironwork, grey roofs and white lettering.

The mass of small four-wheel stock was:
1895—Framework: brick red.
   Floor and running gear: black.
   Numbering: white.
   Brake handles: white.
1925—All vehicles dark grey or black.
   Some dark grey frames; remainder, black.
   Numbering: white.
Wooden stock tended to be painted brick red at all times.

Bogie Open Wagons

Among some early drawings which survive is one for a bogie open wagon. This has an overall length of 22 ft. and the width inside the body is 4 ft. 6 in. The framing is part timber, part steel, the solebars being supported by 'T' section girders running beneath them. The truss rods with stretchers are built up in rodding and the cross stretchers are diagonally braced. The bogies are arranged for springing though springs are not shown; the bogie is carried in a half-sphere bearing, such as was first used on the coaches. The buffer is unsprung and the coupling is pivoted from the bogie stretcher but has no springing either. Drop-side doors are fitted the length of the vehicle which is described as a Ballast Car. The drawing is dated 4 December 1871.

A 'Double Bogie Coal Truck' [*sic*] of 13 May 1875 embodied many improvements over the drawings of 1871. The bogies were identical with those under coaches 15 and 16, the combined buffer-couplers were sprung and brakes were fitted to all wheels. The bodies were of the same type as the large 4-wheeled coal wagons, and the design suggests that this was to be a bogie version of them. A wooden underframe is shown and the brakes were applied by a large hand-wheel which protruded at solebar level on one side only. In the centre of the sides were two opening doors, vertically hinged. To prevent the sides from bulging outwards under load, four heavy chains connected their tops. The body was to be 20 ft. 5 in. long, 5 ft. wide and 5 ft. 6½ in. high from rail level. Two large steps are shown at each end, possibly to enable men to pass between the vehicles

Even this magnificent vehicle seems fated never to have been built; however, two bogie opens did appear, in 1874. There were modifications in the side discharging doors and the brake handle was mounted on a vertical pillar which was probably not a bad thing when some of the side clearances left a good deal to be desired. They were officially described as 'Ballast Wagons' and bore this title on the side, with a tare weight of 4½ tons; they could carry 12 tons of ballast or '8 tons of Corn in sacks' [*sic*] and extra side boards could be added to give them a carrying capacity of 10 tons of coal. Their final use was for loco coal between Minffordd Yard and the sheds. These wagons were in use in the early 1880s but were taken into the Works before the First War for 'conversion' (into what is not known). Nothing was ever developed from them, but they were 'cannibalised' for parts in the early 1920s. Brake van No. 3 had the 'half worn wheels off one of the old Bogie Coal Trucks lying in the yard'. It will be noted from the engraving (plate 20R) that the bogies each differed in pattern. They had Beuther's Patent No. 7 axle box covers XVI

Some long truss rods were recently unearthed at Boston Lodge which may have come from these wagons. (One may have been used by the Shell Factory and fitted with vacuum brake; alternatively this may have been a W.D. vehicle belonging to the Factory.★)

One further bogie vehicle deserves reference at this stage; this is a steel-bodied bogie open wagon shown in Vignes' book of 1877. It is a

★ Reference *F.R. Magazine*, No. 30, p. 27.

development of the single steel-bodied open wagon No. 8, which is
carried on six wheels on the Cleminson principle. The bogie development shown by Vignes possibly never reached the working drawing
stage, but it was a logical outcome of the six-wheeled version.

ex-W.D. Bogie Wagons XVII

Five 5-ton open wagons were delivered in March 1926 for Brookes'
stone traffic to Blaenau. All were disused by 1930 (see also under
Carriages Nos. 37–42); they were numbered 1B–5B.

Brookes also owned a number of ex-German bogie wagons which
could be used to Blaenau: they carried plates thus:

> Franz Méguin & Co.
> A.G.
> 1916 (1917 or 1918)
> Dillingen—Saar.

Cranes

There was a travelling hand-crane of 'to lift 1 ton 10 cwt.' mounted
on a four-wheel wagon. It was a simple affair used around the Works
and elsewhere, but not for derailments. It was acquired by the Shell
Factory during the First War (ref: Chapter Ten, p. 185) but the Railway
found its use limited.

A second crane came through Colonel Stephens in 1926 (ref: Chapter Eleven, p. 226) which proved almost as useless as the earlier one!

Water Wagons

A mobile water tank for the Oakeley salt-water bath existed in
1871–84. A second one was built before 1880, capacity 2 tons. It had an
iron tank with manhole cover, four-wheel chassis and Thompson's
Patent buffers. It ended its days on top of a sleeper tower as a locomotive
water tank at Pont Croesor on the Welsh Highland. (First noted in
Report for 30 June 1879.)

Other Stock

Boston Lodge repaired Brookes' steam crane in December 1918. A
man was injured during the unloading at the Works. During its passage
through Moelwyn Tunnel the jib struck a rock projection which broke
it. The Works' foreman protested it was only a heap of scrap and not
worth repair, but it *was* repaired at considerable expense and Brookes
forthwith consigned it to their Conway quarry, much to the Works'
annoyance.

Adaptations of existing wagons to carry special loads were not usually required but Brookes again had a large boiler for delivery and it was brought down from the L.N.W.R. yard to the quarry on a specially-fitted wagon. (*Welsh Pony* was derailed in the quarry premises whilst working this consignment: a quarry employee changed the points under the engine.) This working was carried out on a Sunday in June 1918, the boiler loaded on to the F.R. by the L.N.W.R. yard crane and all the low footbridges between there and the Moelwyn Tunnel were raised at Brookes' expense. A trial run using a wooden frame was made on 1 June: the strengthened and adapted wagon was the carriage truck. Additional expense incurred by Hugh Hughes in the trial run was 'Tea for two persons at Tanybwlch paid by Hughes £– 1s. 0d.'

Boston Lodge made wagon stock for other railways (e.g. the Gorseddau) and the quarries. In 1919 twenty-eight rubbish wagon bodies were built for Greaves (Llechwedd) Quarry at £29 10s. 0d. each.

Brookes never received sufficient Boston Lodge conversions—they leased 24 ex-L.N.W.R. slate wagons from the L.M.S. in March 1924.

Passenger Stock

Before public traffic began the Boston Lodge accounts of 1859 reveal the existence of:

1 Railway Carriage	Value £12
1 Small do	Value £6
Harness & Cushions of the Company's Passenger Carriage	Value £9 6s. 6d.

These two vehicles survived to June 1865 at least, when further vehicles were obtained, viz:

1 Workmen do	Value £8

and under 'New Work' in the same month:

8 'Passengers Carriages'	Value £770 8s. 0d.
and three Luggage Vans	Value £62 5s. 0d. each

Of the two vehicles existing in 1859 no drawings exist, but possibly one of them is the carriage referred to 'as available from the Oakeley Arms Hotel'.

C. E. Spooner was in correspondence regarding carriages with Brown, Marshalls & Co. of the Britannia Railway Carriage & Wagon Works, Birmingham, laying down his broad requirements and leaving them to finalise the details. The firm tendered on 10 July 1863, this being accepted in general terms on 25 July. The Railway was to supply wheels and axles (at least) and probably buffing, etc. gear; the maker's drawing No. 1760 shows a 1st class carriage which eventually materialised in basic form, but lowered in height by 6 inches and shorn of luggage rails on

Four-wheeled Public Passenger Stock Nos. 1–14

Body Style	In 1863–4			Change By 17/4/1874	By 5/1887			1939 No.	1956 No.	Note	Notes on Latter-day Body	Seating	Present Position
	No.	Class	Built As		No.	Class	Rebuilt As						
Wide	1	1st	Closed	None	1	1st	Semi-open side Obs'n	—	—	1	2 small windows flanking centre door	12	1929 withdrawn
Wide	2	1st	as 1	*	2	1st	as 1	2	6	2	as 1	12	Extant as No. 6
Wide	3	3rd	Closed	2nd/Closed	3	3rd	—	3	3	3	2 small flanking windows of larger droplight, each side centre door (small windows original panels)	14	Extant as No. 3
Wide	4	3rd	as 3	*	4	3rd	—	4	4	4	as 3	14	Extant as No. 4
Wide	5	3rd	as 3	None	5	3rd	—	5	5	5	as 3	14	Extant as No. 5
Wide	6	3rd	as 3	None	6	3rd	—	—	—	6	as 3	14	Sept. 1931 withdrawn
Narrow	7	3rd?	Closed	*	7	3rd	—	—	—	7	Two compartments	12	1928 withdrawn
Narrow	8	3rd?	as 7	* †	8	3rd	—	—	—	8	as 7	12	pre-1922 withdrawn
Narrow	9	3rd?	as 7	*	9	3rd	—	—	—	9	as 7	12	scrapped
Narrow	10	1st	Closed	*	10	1st	—	—	—	10	Two compartments	12	scrapped
Narrow	11	3rd?	as 7	*	11	3rd	—	—	—	11	as 7	12	scrapped
Narrow	14	3rd?	as 7	*	14	3rd	—	—	—	14	as 7	12	scrapped
Wide	—	1st	Open/unroofed but no cushions	Roofed	12	1st	(see note)	11	7	12	see notes below	12?	Extant as No. 7
Wide	—	3rd	As 1st but no cushions	Roofed cushioned	13	1st	(see note)	12	—	13	see notes below	14?	Derelict

* No record of body alteration before 17 April 1874.

Nos. 1–6 by Brown, Marshalls & Co., 1863/4 (certain parts running gear from Boston Lodge).

† Nos. 7–11 and 14 by Ashbury Railway Carriage & Iron Co. (bodies only), March 1868. Into stock by Returns of 30 June 1869 at which date there were: 1st Cl. 1; 2nd Cl. 2; 3rd Cl. 3; = 6.

Notes: (1) 1st Cl. open above waist. Relegated 3rd; (2) as for 1; (3) Retains panel sides as built; (4) Sides now vertical match-boarding; (5) as 4; (6) as 4 when withdrawn; (7–11 and 14) Apparently no alterations before withdrawal; (12) Possibly un-numbered on delivery. Roof and aprons probably added by 1871. Cushioned. Rebuilt as semi-open after 1887; had become 12 at this date. Side openings glazed at first but removed by 1930 when dubbed 'Observation Carriage' and given No. 11. Parts of bowed-end semi-open left inside squared ends at 1930 rebuilding. Recently restored to 1863 condition; (13) Delivered as 12 without number, but no cushions so classed 3rd. Roof, cushions, aprons added; numbered 13 by 1887. Rebuilt 1939 as 12 and renumbered 12.

the roof. As shown, it would have fouled the loading gauge. (Spooner attempted to obtain a lower price on 22 July but the manufacturers said they had no margin for a reduction.) Correspondence from Spooner to Brown, Marshalls & Co. shows that he laid down the specification of what was wanted, and one letter contained a small sketch of the curved carriage end with a crude leaf spring set across the end as a form of buffer to go with the coupling hook; the detailed design was probably done at Birmingham.

Spooner required one 1st class and two 3rd class delivered to Caernarvon within two months, and the balance of five carriages in four months. They must all have reached the Railway by February 1864 as the accounts show the expense of transport was £48 18s. 0d. Two 1st class cost £110 each, four covered 3rd class £93 each and two 'open-class' £70 each, amounting to £713 14s. 0d. When delivered, the Company had no statutory powers to use them!

2nd class was to be provided by upgrading certain 3rds (there was a variable total of them along the years) and in April eight iron plates written 'second Class' [*sic*] were supplied. Further, brass bars were delivered in the following July, following Captain Tyler's recommendation to protect droplights (see p. 73). At the same time, eight oil lamps came, although the original drawings do not show any lighting at all. These lamps survived until the late 1920s when they were removed and electric lighting installed.

In such parts as were common to all, all the vehicles were of identical

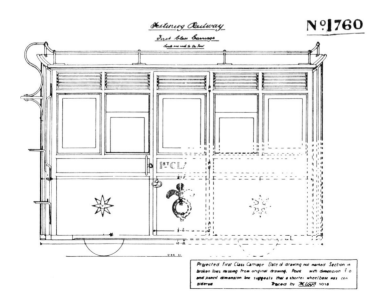

dimensions and construction. The underframe was a heavy oak affair, well suited to being placed in mixed Up trains to which numerous wagons might be attached. The body was 'hung' upon a sort of 'box' frame of great strength, carried on volute springs (replaced later by leaf springs) with running gear within the 'box'. The single buffers were above the odd-handed couplings (1 ft. 3½ in. from rail) with link one end, hook the other; a large leaf spring took up buffing and haulage strains.

Bodies were 9 ft. 3 in. over sides (and 10 ft. over bowed ends) long, 6 ft. 3 in. wide and, where roofed, 6 ft. 6 in. from rail. Wheelbase was 5 ft. and wheels spoked, 1 ft. 6 in. diameter, having plain bearings outside them. The floor was only 8 in. above the rail; inside height 5 ft. 6 in. Weight: 1 ton 6 cwt.

1st class bodies had two windows per side, flanking a central door and carrying six passengers each side on a single back-to-back seat; access to the running gear for oiling etc. was through trap doors in the seat fronts of all carriages. The other classes held seven passengers each side. So low were the bodies that the couplings projected some way up the bowed ends. Originally the couplings were unilateral, with a hook one end and a shackle at the other—these carriages were the only ones fitted with screw couplings for many years. They were upholstered in blue cloth [*sic*]; the 2nd class had a carpet runner on the seat and the 3rds were plain.

It was these coaches which caused the appearance of the balcony ends on the later bogie coaches, as they allowed people to pass through the train at stations, a feat which they could manage with difficulty in the transverse compartment stock (where the knees of travellers in 2nd and 3rd class carriages were somewhat interlocked) and which was impossible in the knifeboard coaches unless they climbed over the seat backs. This first batch were always known as 'The Birminghams' by the employees.

Two of the carriages (having no number on them as delivered) were simply a frame and seating portion having no roof or side at all, and resembling the contemporary kitchen cutlery tray with central divider-cum-handle! One had padded seat backs and cushions (1st class) and the other was bare. Clearly their use would be but limited. Passengers were strapped into the seats by longitudinal and cross-straps and their legs covered by leather aprons but this was insufficient protection so crude awnings with odd-ended curtains were fitted to them, probably the Railway's own make. The one end formed a simple observation-type window.

Vignes states bluntly that the second type of carriage to be introduced was '*beaucoup préférable*'! He refers to the two-compartment carriages resembling the four-wheelers of the day, and carrying three classes of passenger. (Nos. 7–11 and 14 built March 1868.) There were no complete partitions and they cost slightly less than the 'knifeboards'. Each carriage held twelve passengers, three on each seat. (The Festiniog & Blaenau carriages were near-relatives of this variety.) The Ashbury Railway Carriage and Iron Co. built the whole of them he claims, but F.R. records show them to be of their own make. Probably Ashbury supplied bodies and Boston Lodge the rest. All disappeared during the 1920s. These vehicles were more conventional in dimension and seating; the 'low-slung' appearance was discarded at the expense of spaciousness, being more narrow-bodied in consequence.

The Engineer for 29 April 1870 shows a 2nd/3rd class coach as 9 ft. 9 in. in length and 4 ft. 10½ in. in width over body, a 5 ft. 6 in. wheelbase and only 4 ft. 9 in. headroom inside. From rail to roof they were 6 ft. 7 in. high (the other dimensions in the same article confuse Brown, Marshalls and Ashbury vehicles). Some ended their days as store sheds at Welsh Highland stations, where the above dimensions were confirmed save that wheelbases were 5 ft. *The Mining Journal* of 9 April 1870 preferred to say 'New carriages are being constructed 5 feet 4 inches wide the floor more elevated and the wheels underneath'. (One might think they felt the early carriages had the wheels elsewhere!)

A reference to the smallness of the carriages suggests it was usual to hand-shunt them and in discussing vehicles of longer length says they would 'be inconvenient for moving about at stations'.

The Engineer for November 1869 has some unusual statistics; a train of twenty carriages—which must have included some quarrymen's carriages as there were only fourteen public vehicles—would be 250 ft. long: it would carry 230 passengers or one passenger per 1·04 foot-run of train: the air space surrounding each passenger would be 27·33 cu. ft. compared with 31·5 cu. ft. in a standard gauge carriage!

It was not long before changes in the stock were made. Certain 3rds were upgraded to 2nds, and downgraded again as warranted by traffic. Statistics show 2nd class passengers were never numerous. Of the six Ashburys, they remained as delivered in June 1869 viz: one 1st class; two 2nd class; three 3rd class but the numbers carried by the 2nds and 3rds cannot be confirmed. By June 1872 so many interiors of all four-wheeled stock had been altered that the picture had become three 1st class (covered); two 1st class (open sides/aprons); three 2nd class; six 3rd class = 14.

Four-wheeled Carriages for Quarrymen

The carriage of quarrymen was an important part of the Festiniog's traffic. Most of these men lived in the Portmadoc district and lodged in barracks at the quarry during the week. The original weekly early morning train was therefore a 'Mondays Only' special which ran for many years and its complementary Down train ran at noon on Saturdays.

According to season, the morning train left Portmadoc at varying times, albeit before daylight in the winter. Many men walked miles from their homes to pick up the train at stations en route. It is clear that at the end of 1866 the Company was prepared to carry workmen but only in the existing slate wagons.* 'Quarry Labourers' they were termed. The Board of Trade refused to allow this and the Company was informed the men must be carried in 'properly constructed passenger carriages'.

The service began with a primitive form of four-wheeler, probably in February 1867; the men were charged 4d. 'for the whole distance'.

In later years the habits of the quarrymen began to change and many of the married men travelled every day, preferring this to the primitive barracks at the quarry. In course of time the quarrymen's trains ran every day and a special carriage shed was built at Duffws where the train was stored during the daytime.

The first vehicles provided (Type 1a) were very precarious open four-wheelers; these appear behind *Little Wonder* on plate 8R and it is clear that the men were almost *on* them rather than *in* them, so pokey were they. Vignes has an illustration (reproduced) of the form as roofed and with sides and ends in the 1870s (Type 1b), the contour of the roofs varying in curve somewhat. (20 August 1873—Minute to cover at least '28 quarrymen's trucks at first'.) There was a cast-iron plate on the side denoting the number and that it was a quarrymen's carriage; these plates were transferred to later vehicles. Length 8 ft. 6 in.; width 4 ft. 7 in.; wheelbase 4 ft. 6 in.; height of body 5 ft. 6 in. at centre line.

In the 1870s a second variety (Type 2) was built to replace Type 1b; it was one of these which was rebuilt into the hearse van, whilst the remains of another survives near Plas Halt, as a P.W. hut: the latter has had doors with windows fitted into it at a later date. In the hearse van, doors without windows fill the entry spaces. In an Accident Report of 1881 it is learned that this Type was in use on Mondays and Saturdays only. It had a 'covered wooden body—open window and door *spaces*'. It seated 12 men and weighed about 11 cwt. Wheels, frames and axles were much the same as used on the slate wagons—there were no springs or conventional axle boxes, the axles running in plain bushes. The wheels were of cast iron 1 ft. 6 in. diameter on axles supplied by Caine & Kitchen of Liverpool (who supplied many axles at this time). The vehicle in this Report had involved the workmen's train in a derailment due to a fractured axle. It was the absence of springing which caused the derailment, the coach having run on three wheels and when traversing the curve at Dinas Junction where there was a low outside rail for 2 ft. with a drop of $\frac{1}{4}$ inch, a wheel ran over the top of the rail and the axle broke. Major Marindin utterly condemned this form of carriage in the October: '(they) are nothing better than slate wagons with covers to

* And the practice was probably being followed even then . . . unofficially.

FESTINIOG RAILWAY.

NEW QUARRYMEN'S CARRIAGE.

FR 1655

them and I am not aware that any Parliamentary or other sanction has been given to the conveyance of passengers, even at reduced fares, in such vehicles, which are undoubtedly less safe than the 3rd class passenger carriages in use on this line'.

The coaches were also found to be unstable on curves where the super-elevation was considerable, and drivers were instructed to pull up gradually on a curve as when the tension came off the couplings, the vehicles had a tendency to keel over!

The costing records show that these early vehicles had sides and ends covered in between December 1872 and August 1874. Length, 9 ft. 0 in.; width, 5 ft. 2 in.

Type 2 had simple entry openings with safety bars at first; doors and windows in them followed by arrangement between the Company and the Quarrymen's Guaranteeing Committee (Chapter Eight, p. 140). By 1887 they had been given numbers 19–33, all being built between January and March 1875—a considerable production.

From the late 1880s the Type 2s were replaced by Type 3, the last. Nos. 1–18 were supplied from Boston Lodge in 1885–7, Nos. 19–33 being the Type 2 just noted; 'These were being gradually replaced by carriages similar to No. 1 to 18'. Type 3 had perimeter seating, spring bearings, glazed windows and was oil lit. (The lighting and other features were later to be the subject of complaint.) The earlier Types had candle lighting, the spike being hung from the roof; the men provided their own candles, as they did down the quarry. By 1896 all 34 carriages had received oil lights; all were removed during the First War and restored in 1921.

In 1901 the maximum number of 44 in 1895 had been reduced to 36; they carried numbers 1–36. Nos. 15, 18 and 20 were off their running gear and stood at Duffws and Minffordd as shelter for the slate loaders; many earlier withdrawals became P.W. huts. Despite their primitiveness, they were used in public trains if there was a coach shortage. Some of Type 3 were converted; to goods brake vans Nos. 5, 6, 7; to W.H.R. meat van No. 1; as W.H.R. dual-brake-fitted van, No. 4. The 36 carriages available in 1901 had cost £1,895 14*s.* 8*d.* including the fitting of brakes.*

There was a bi-lingual warning notice in each carriage, especially with regard to damage of doors.

There was no exact uniformity amongst Type 3: the Company's drawing No. 1655 of 4 March 1885 has length of body, 11 ft.; the 1887 stock list gives 11 ft. 2 in. while a sketch of 1906 gives 11 ft. 1 in. Personal measurement of No. 9 in 1940 gave 10 ft. 8 in. with only a 5 ft. wheelbase. An average might give 11 ft. length, 7 ft. from rail to rooftop,

---

* A note of late 1918 says there were '24 in good order and 8 at Works for rebuilding'.

5 ft. 6 in. wheelbase and widths between 5 ft. 1 in. and 5 ft. 3 in. Each carried 16 passengers and tared 1¼ tons.

In an estimate for boarding-in and covering the Type 1a of the early 1870s, 'brown paint' was mentioned. The surviving Type 2 at Plas and all the Type 3 were certainly in the brick red during living memory. Colonel Stephens objected to the coaches being taken into the Works for painting 'sufficient . . . with one coat lead colour . . . the carpenter's boy can do this'.

Bogie Carriages

C. E. Spooner began designing bogie coaches about 1870, and there are a number of various drawings for coaches preserved in the Company's records. Some of these were to be built on a standard underframe which would also be used for open wagon bodies, covered vans, etc. Two massive types are dated 1870 and are astounding in their immense length (about 40 feet, though no dimensions are shown) and another body fits into an enormous well-frame, whilst the bogies are but insignificant appurtenances appended to each end! In this design the wheelbases of the bogies are so short that the flanges of the bogie wheels almost touch; the bearings are simply the ordinary slate-wagon type with no springing. Another drawing dated 1872 shows a much more conventional bogie carriage of a type which the Company did not acquire until 1897–8, and besides the above there are several designs for wagon and coach bogies all of which reveal the line of thought which the Spooners were pursuing. Charles was responsible for the earliest designs, whilst Percival designed the later ones under his father's watchful eye. The vehicles appear to have evolved from ideas for very short wheelbase unsprung conceptions of about 1870, leading to the first more-sophisticated bogie coaches of 1872; the 'curly-roofed' vans and bogie open wagons followed, each showing a touch of the whimsy from G. P. Spooner!

No. 15 Bogie Composite Carriage. Length, 35 ft. 9 in.; Width, 5 ft. 9½ in.; Height, 7 ft. 8 in.; Wheelbase, 27 ft. Built 1872, Brown, Marshalls & Co. (body and frame only). Wrought iron frames. (Arrangement: 3rd/3rd/3rd/1st/2nd/3rd/3rd. Later 3rd/3rd/3rd/1st/3rd/3rd/3rd.) Tare 6 tons. 48 passengers.

No. 16. Exactly as for No. 15. Seating in the second period was arranged with only one seat in the ex-2nd class compartment.

No. 17 Bogie Composite Carriage. Length, 32 ft. 3 in.; Width, 6 ft. 0 in.; Height, 7 ft. 8 in.; Wheelbase, 26 ft. 6 in. Built 1876, Brown, Marshalls & Co. (body and frame only). Wrought iron frames. (Arrangement: 3rd/3rd/1st/2nd/3rd/3rd. Later 3rd/3rd/1st/3rd/3rd/3rd.) 44 passengers.

No. 18. Exactly as for No. 17.

No. 19 Bogie Composite Carriage. Length, 34 ft. 6 in.; Width, 6 ft. 0 in.;
Wheelbase, 24 ft. 4 in. Built 1879, Gloster Wagon Co. (body and
frame only). Wrought iron frames. (Arrangement: 3rd/2nd/1st/1st/
2nd/3rd. Later 3rd/3rd/1st/1st/3rd/3rd.)

No. 20. Exactly as for No. 19 except in second stage of seating arrangement, one 1st class derated to 2nd.

The above have end balconies; only 1st and 2nd classes were divided
by compartment partitions reaching to the roof.

No. 21 Bogie Composite Carriage. Length, 29 ft. 11½ in.; Width, 6 ft.
0 in.; Height, 7 ft. 8 in. Designed and built, Ashbury Railway Carriage
& Iron Co., 1896, complete with running gear and continuous brake.
Seven compartments, all 3rd, with floor-roof partition dividing the
body into three and four compartments open above the waist inside.
48 passengers. Relegated to quarrymen's trains, 1925.

No. 22. Exactly as for No. 21.

The above have no end balconies.

(Numbers 23–36 were later given to passenger stock of the Welsh
Highland Railway.)

No. 23. Became part of F.R. stock in exchange for ex-W.D. bogie
wagons (three sent for Beddgelert coal traffic.*)

Nos. 15 and 16

In late 1872 the first of two bodies with frames were delivered from
the Birmingham firm of Brown, Marshalls & Co., the details being their
own, but the general design being Spooner's. They were the first
revenue-earning bogie coaches in the British Isles and with wrought-
iron frames. The frames were of considerable strength, in order to take
the strain of a train passing through reverse curves of short radius, and
to haul strings of empty wagons behind. The bogie centres and bolsters
were of oak sandwiched between cross girders. The two vehicles had
seven compartments, which accommodated three classes (though the
three contemporary descriptions of them cannot agree on their arrangement!). Vignes describes the coaches as having a 1st class compartment
upholstered in blue broadcloth, holding six passengers, 2nd class fitted
out in plain cloth, holding eight persons and with 3rd class seating for
24 on wooden seats with no intermediate partitions. The total seating
capacity was 50. Running and buffing gear was added at Boston Lodge.

The end compartments which were situated over the bogies were of
diminished height, in consequence of the vehicles being slung very low.
Their floors were raised to clear the running gear; as built they had
movable benches across the side doors and entry was generally made
from end balconies, there being a gangway across the ends of these
carriages with suitable steps each side. They seated three per side and

* Ref.: NARROW GAUGE RAILWAYS IN SOUTH CAERNARVONSHIRE, p. 398.

were described as being 'for servants and baggage'. The end compartments had their windows removed later. Wooden boards replaced
them, and the compartments were used for luggage. They probably
entered traffic in January 1873.

The bodies of teak were 32 ft. 9 in. long, the longest on the system:
the seven compartment arrangement was not used for further stock.
The bogies were built in Boston Lodge shops with wheelbase 3 ft. 6 in.
At first iron wheels of 1 ft. 6 in. diameter were used, but steel wheels
with integral tyres replaced these later when the standard wheel diameter
for all stock became 1 ft. $7\frac{1}{8}$ in. The original bogie mountings gave
trouble through an unusual cause and many of them were not modified
until the First War period. This was because the pivot was a spherical
mounting on which the body rested only by virtue of its own weight.
As a result there were a number of instances of coaches blowing off their
bogies when crossing the Embankment during a gale. Vignes describes
the bogies in the greatest detail, as they were a novelty at that time:
'Springing is on the Thompson System and the grease boxes on the
Beuther System . . .'.*

The original coupling gear was modified by a patent described in a
paper published by G. P. Spooner dated 22 January 1874, and the old
drop-hooks, shaped like the head of a pike, were replaced. The hook
was furthermore pivoted on an eccentric on the end of whose axle hung
a weighted pendulum. When coupling together the weighted arm was
raised to the horizontal and the hook moved forward on the eccentric;
when engaged the hook was drawn back into the buffing socket when
the pendulum fell down by its own weight. Of those couplings William
Williams wrote:

I am fully aware of all the difficulties . . . the precious time it takes to couple
. . . the present coupler [i.e. replacement of Spooner type—Author] is a
thoroughly safe one (but) it takes too long to uncouple . . . I remember years
ago the eccentric had a balance weight on . . . this was a failure, the inventor
Mr. Spooner allowed me for safety to put the present right and left coupling
on . . .

This system has been widely used on other varieties of the central buffer-
coupler or 'Norwegian' coupler system. The coupling springs were on
the short side and somewhat insensitive; in consequence, it was usual to
attach the train engine to one of the four-wheel carriages as these had
substantial springs and the advantage of screw-link couplings. It was not

* Originally patented in Germany by E. A. H. Beuther. The patent was
taken out in this country by M. Neuhaus who states formally that he is not the
inventor but has the invention by communication from Beuther. [Patent 806,
24 March 1871.] According to *The Mining Journal*, 26 April 1873, a company
was incorporated under the name 'Beuther's Patent Railway Axle Box Co. Ltd'
to acquire the patent.

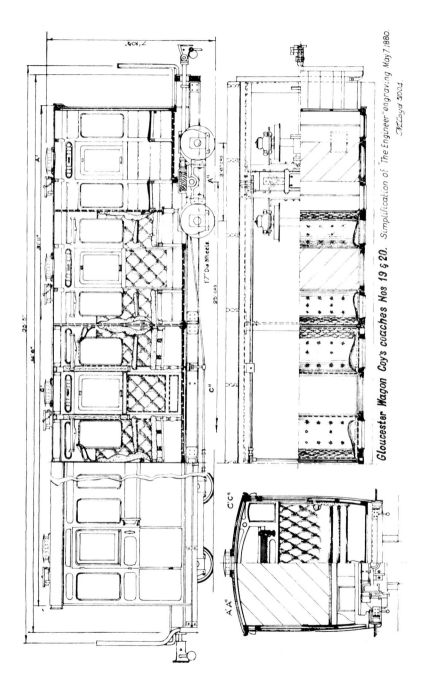

Gloucester Wagon Coy's coaches Nos 19 & 20. Simplification of "The Engineer" engraving May 7, 1880.

until the end of the First War that trains were run with the engine coupled direct to bogie passenger carriages.

When these bogie coaches first went through the Moelwyn Tunnel they emerged with their lamp tops knocked off; this was due to a projecting lump of rock which had to be removed.

At first oil lighting was in use. Later, acetylene gas took its place; the generator was in the guard's van. Finally the coaches were electrically lit by secondary cells placed in the guard's van; these were charged by a plant at Boston Lodge.

The body is built around a frame running along the cant-rails and across the body at compartment partitions.*

Nos. 17 and 18

Two further bogie coaches followed in 1876, to G. P. Spooner's designs, the bodies being again by Brown, Marshalls and the running gear from Boston Lodge. This time only six compartments were used, the bodies being raised so as to increase the height in the end compartments. Unlike the early coaches, the sides were waisted-in at the bottoms.

Nos. 19 and 20

Two more coaches, of the same overall dimensions and similar (but not identical) external appearance as 17 and 18, came from the Gloster Wagon Company in November 1879, their Order 282. Here again, improvements were carried out; one 2nd class compartment was derated to 3rd before 1887. With the exception of No. 19, partitions in all coaches (where existing between 3rd class compartments) were taken out. Detail variations may be noted in many points, including window bars, ventilators and panelling. Evidence of class changes are reflected by variations between widths of doors, and between compartment widths and panels dividing windows.

On 19 and 20 the bodies were arranged to stand one inch above the underframes, being mounted on indiarubber blocks. Frames are officially described as being of wrought-iron girders.

Spooner's Patent buffers were fitted; the outer timber was teak and the inner deal. The 1st class had an oil-cloth floor covering and central carpet; a time-table and vanity mirrors were displayed in mahogany frames, two per compartment. The 2nds had stuffed horse-hair seats covered by 'dark repp'. (Ref.: *The Engineer.*)

It may be noted that whilst the two earliest carriages had lights arranged so that the 1st class compartment had one to itself and the 2nd and 3rd class had to share lights which hung centrally above the dividing partition, all later examples had individual lights for each compartment.

* *F.R. Magazine*, No. 31, p. 16 has details of body construction.

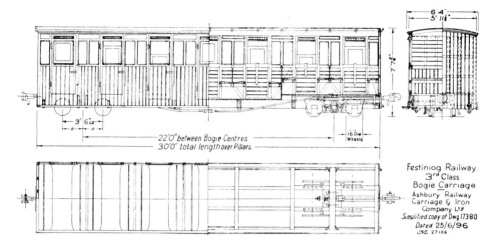

Festiniog Railway.
3ʳᵈ Class
Bogie Carriage
Ashbury Railway
Carriage & Iron
Company Ltᵈ
Simplified copy of Dwg 17380
Dated 25/6/96

The bodies were painted in one colour (the lighter upper panels being abandoned) and had the F.R. monogram on the upper panel.

Nos. 21 and 22

The growth of the passenger traffic was a very satisfactory feature of the 'nineties, and in 1897 a new bogie carriage, vacuum fitted, was placed in traffic in the autumn. It was No. 21, a seven compartment all-third-class coach, with matchboard sides and no end balconies. There was only one partition above the seats, dividing the carriage into two unequal parts, and the length was 30 feet over the body. Accommodation was nominally 56 seats, giving it the largest capacity of any carriage on the line. The builders were the Ashbury Railway Carriage & Iron Co. of Belle Vue, Manchester, who about this same period had supplied carriages to the North Wales Narrow Gauge Railways. In spring 1898 a second identical carriage was delivered, both being financed by the issue of $4\frac{1}{2}\%$ Preference Shares. They cost £305 12s. 8d. and £308 1s. 4d. respectively, and were not satisfactory. Firstly the wheels were found to be of contractors' specifications and unsuitable for high speed and main line work, but the suppliers (Hadfield's of Sheffield) maintained that they were of the type which they always supplied to the Festiniog. This was true enough, but they had only been used for wagons! Ashbury further maintained that this was the best wheel they could afford within the price of the coach. Lastly, Williams at Boston Lodge averred that for hanging trains of empty slate wagons on the rear coupling, the main frames were far too lightly constructed and the bogies set at centres which were too far apart. For good measure Williams added that they were top-heavy and too high for safety, being actually dangerous in a train which was 'making up time'. Some passengers swore that they left the rails and jumped back on again with alarming regularity. Whatever the true facts, they certainly hit the roof of the tunnel in places and in 1901 were withdrawn from passenger trains as their reputation was such that regular passengers boycotted them completely.

Williams recommended that their height be cut down by at least six inches.

Finally, the brake gear was inefficiently designed in the rodding and soon became so badly corroded by the sea air that it jammed in any position.

Against Williams' advice, Boston Lodge was instructed to use the wheels from the bogie open coal wagons and this was carried out; the objection to these was that having separate tyres, they worked loose due to heat from the brake blocks, on the Down journey. Coil springs were added outside the bogie frames to stop rolling, and the bodies lowered a further two inches on to the bogies. No attempt was made to reduce the height by lowering the roofs. These two coaches, despite the alterations carried out, never went into passenger trains except in case of emergency. They were often marshalled into the workmen's trains where they must have seemed a luxury. They were known as the 'Yellow Coaches'; the period of their appearance in this livery is pre-1914.

In 1953 No. 21 had original Ashbury bogies at one end with cast iron wheels; wheels cast at Works and fitted *circa* 1937: No. 22 had F.R. pattern bogies.

Nos. 37 to 42

Shortage of coaching stock led the Company, in July 1923, to purchase six War Department design open bogie carriages which were built by Robert Hudson Ltd. of Leeds. They were open above the waist, and had no doors. Hudson had supplied similar carriages for use on military lines during the First World War and in fact the Festiniog's first idea was to purchase ex-W.D. bogie wagons and convert these into carriages themselves. When it was found that Robert Hudson would build new carriages to the military design for £155 each, fitted with vacuum brake and deliver in three weeks, second thoughts prevailed! The seating was 30 passengers of one class and they were known by the staff as 'The Toastracks'. To save time in delivery they arrived in primer grey paint but were ultimately painted 'lake' (official). Delivery began on 13 August 1923; as a precautionary measure additional safety chains were put across the entrances before they went into traffic; not all of them were used during that year. They carried numbers 37–42.

These carriages had a short life, four of them being converted into flat wagons during the period 1926–8 and in May 1929 the unconverted ones, 37 and 42, lay in the Works bereft of their running gear. Nevertheless, this was later restored and both coaches were in use until 1939 when passenger services ceased. (They were ultimately stripped of their upper-works in 1955 and used for P.W. and other work of reconstruction.) It appears that being interchangeable with the open wagons running on the Welsh Highland, it was the practice in the 'twenties to cannibalise the running gear off them to keep the 'opens' running; the 'opens' were better revenue-earners than the carriages as there was a year-round coal traffic, especially to a merchant at Beddgelert.

Although it was intended originally to cover the cost of these carriages between the two companies, the Festiniog in fact paid the whole amount. They were used by both systems, however.

Their fate was fairly swift:

No. 37. Derelict 1929. Later returned to service: Stored 1939.
No. 38. Converted to flat wagon, 1926.
No. 39. Converted to flat wagon, 1928.
No. 40. Converted to flat wagon, 1926.
No. 41. Converted to flat wagon, 1928.
No. 42. Derelict 1929. Later returned to service: Stored 1939.

Parts were interchangeable with four ex-W.D. bogie open wagons bought by Colonel Stephens from Honeywill Bros. of Ashford in October 1925, for coal traffic on the Welsh Highland. Five similar wagons, alleged 'new', were delivered March 1926, of five tons capacity, for Brookes' Quarry traffic into Blaenau. (These are thought to have included some German-built wagons used by this quarry.) These wagons had to go into Works for turning of wheel profiles due to derailments. Numbers 1B–5B.

These later wagons were F.R. property and assuming three of them were interchangeable with the ex-W.D. type, these three were sent to the Welsh Highland for the Beddgelert coal traffic (making nine in all on this work) in exchange for carriage No. 23 (ex N.W.N.G.Rlys.) an Ashbury-built 'Summer Coach' of 1894 carrying No. 11 on that system.

Four survive as flat wagons, one being used as a weedkilling vehicle. (Additionally four similar drop-side wagons were purchased in winter 1960 from Smith's Crisps Potato Farm, Nocton.)

Coach interiors tended to carry notices in mahogany frames such as 'Passengers are requested not to lean over, or put their feet outside the Carriage, or on the Cushions, nor throw out Empty Bottles'. But they did.

Might-have-beens

One other bogie vehicle, which is unlikely to have been constructed, was a Bogie Saloon Observation Car which, by its sheer magnificence, could only have been intended for the use of the directors and their

18L   *The first double-engine*, Little Wonder, *at Duffws c. 1876 (Note early wagons carrying ballast, behind).*   *(National Library of Wales)*

19L   *Maker's photograph of* Taliesin *1876. (The cab was altered in autumn 1876). The first single-engine—see Plate 22 for the second double-engine,* James Spooner, *of 1872.*   *(Vulcan Foundry)*

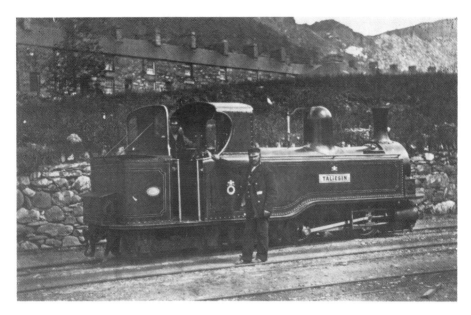

20L   Taliesin *with modified cab to clear tunnels and bridges, at Duffws c. 1877.*
(J. I. C. Boyd)

21L   Taliesin *about 1900 after fitting of new boiler, enlarged cab, side tanks etc. At*
Portmadoc.   *(L.P. Co.)*

22L James Spooner *as first put into traffic, in old Harbour station 1874.* *(J. I. C. Boyd)*

23L James Spooner, *bells and whistles removed, on the head-shunt Duffws c. 1876. Note the Type 2 Quarrymen's stock behind in the shelter, and wheel sprag on the loaded slate wagon made from discarded T rail.* *(National Library of Wales)*

24L Little Wonder *on an Up train on the curve where Tan-y-Bwlch station was to be sited later. The train make-up is the customary form of mineral wagons followed by coaches, with empty slate wagons behind. The track has been relaid with double-*

headed rails. The third and fourth wagons are former Dandy Wagons converted for coal carrying; the pole at the extreme right is the site of the 'laying of the first stone' 26 February 1833. This is one of the few illustrations to show the early mineral stock. 1871. (F.R. Co.)

25L   James Spooner *with Neilson parallel boiler of 1889. Harbour, pre-1908.*

(L.P. Co.)

26L   Livingston Thompson; *an 'official' view on The Cob, 1887.*

(F.R. Co.)

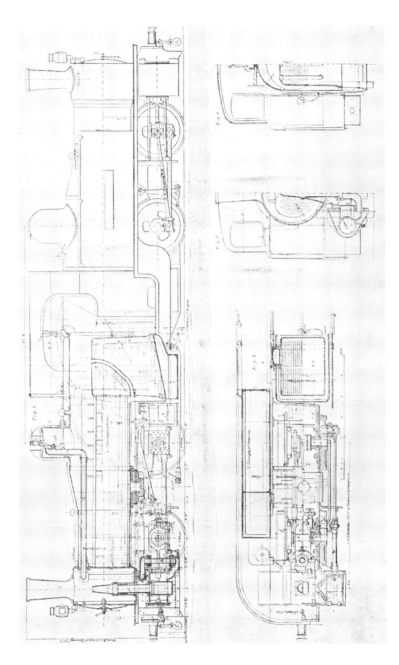

27L   *Working Drawings of Merddin Emrys. Central cab roof not fitted when first put to traffic.*

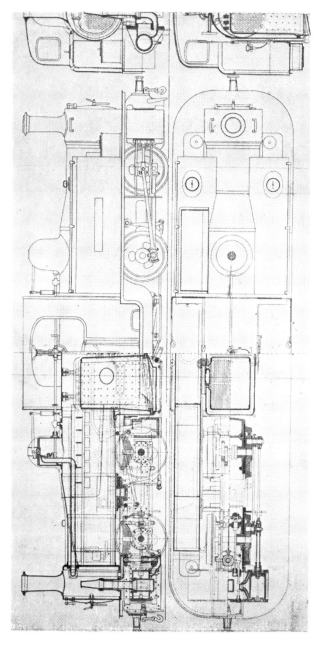

28L   Working Drawings of Livingston Thompson, showing Patent Regulators and non-standard sand-boxes and smokebox handrails. These were not as built. Subsequently, the chimneys were shorter and the domes were taller.

families on the finest of days. The coach was a development of the open-above-waist observation cars, and may even have preceded them; the drawing is undated. There are four sections to the car, each being a compartment fully upholstered with maroon material stuffed with horse-hair, and having a carpet on the floor with the Company's crest thereon. In view of the fact that the sides of each compartment were bowed downwards to meet the tops of the waist-high doors which were level, a good percentage of the elements was likely to enter the carriage and ruin such sumptuous upholstery and fittings, not to mention the occupants who might complain of rheumatism caused by sitting on damp carriage seats. Indeed, the car would have had to have been kept in a heated shed to maintain it in good order and, if for no other reason than that the drawing, though coloured, is unfinished as regards details of the bogies or buffing gear and carries no date, it may be regarded as a form of 'Spoonerism' of the railway variety. The designer has amused himself by planning an extravagant luxury observation car—perhaps to carry the Duke of Sutherland and members of his party at the trials, who knows?

It is possible that this magnificent vehicle was designed before the open wagon referred to previously, as the underframe is entirely of timber.

There is little doubt that Spooner was advocating bogie vehicles for use on wider gauges (he produced specifications and plans for them in his book, *Narrow Gauge Railways*) before 1870.

Vignes shows an intriguing 6-wheel coach in his Atlas—perhaps a Festiniog version of the basic six-wheelers on the North Wales Narrow Gauge Railways?

Four-wheel and Bogie Brake Vans for Passenger Traffic

It will be apparent that to satisfy the Board of Trade some efficient braking vehicles had to be supplied. There were three and details of them have not survived. Old photographs show them to have been four-wheeled vans with a single balcony at the Down end, having a sentry-box affair in which the brakesman sheltered from down-grade slipstream! The hand-screw was conveniently placed on the balcony and the picture does not reveal any access from it into the van, proper, which was presumably used for luggage, etc. Apparently they were built at Boston Lodge, classed as 'Luggage Vans' and valued at £62 5s. 0d. each in June 1865. They did not survive by 1883.*

These vans were superseded when bogie coaches were introduced in 1872–5, and three bogie vans took their place. A distinguishing feature

---

* *F.R. Magazine*, No. 31, p. 21, contains drawings and notes on four-wheeled passenger stock.

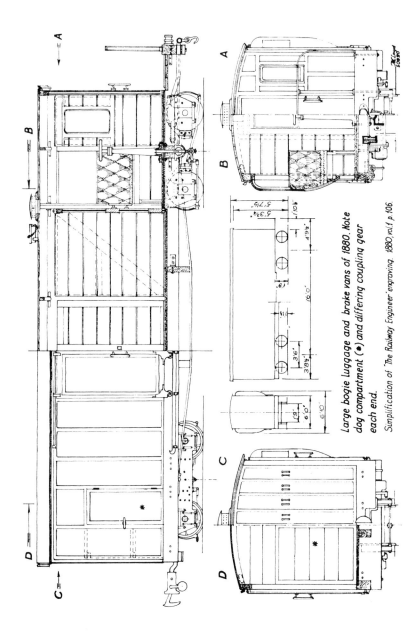

Large bogie luggage and brake vans of 1880. Note dog compartment (∗) and differing coupling gear each end.

Simplification of 'The Railway Engineer' engraving, 1880, vol.1, p.106.

of these vehicles was their roof outline. The dates of construction were No. 1, April 1873; No. 2, September 1873; No. 3, February 1876. An illustration of No. 1 as new shows Beuther's Patent axle boxes with 'No. 7 1874' cast on the covers. The roofs suggest the hand of G. P. Spooner. There was a hand screw for the balcony end bogie. There were two large sliding doors in the sides, lookout windows with side seats between and an end door on to the balcony. At the non-balcony end was a compartment, suitably labelled on the outside, 'Dogs'. The door to this compartment lifted up from the bottom.

It will be noted that the bogies were not set equally from the ends of the vehicle.

Two much larger vans were added in 1880 to G. P. Spooner's design. They were intended for carrying luggage and were made up with vertically planked sides and an end balcony. They were numbered 4 and 5. They had guard's lookouts, large sliding doors, and brakes to each bogie. Internally they were divided into three compartments, for guards, luggage and dogs—the latter compartment contained a seat and was entered by midget doors (3 ft. 6 in. high) each side, quite unlike the 'dog' doors of the smaller vans. The balcony end had a hook and chain coupling for attaching to goods wagons, etc., the other end having a 'Norwegian' coupler. Despite previous trends the frames were of timber —pitchpine. *The Railway Engineer* described the painting as 'lower part a chocolate tint, the upper part black'.

No. 1 Bogie Luggage Brake Van. Length, 20 ft. 8 in.; Width, 5 ft. 8 in.; Height, 7 ft. 8 in.; Wheelbase, 11 ft. 11 in.; Tare, 4 tons 2 cwt. as built. 16 passengers. Dismantled 1921 owing to rotten frame.* Number given to Welsh Highland van (four-wheeled) rebuilt from Festiniog quarrymen's coach.

No. 2 (New Series No. 10) Bogie Luggage Brake Van. Dimensions exactly as for No. 1. Rebuilt at Boston Lodge, 1921, with new body incorporating guard's and two 3rd compartments. [In service again from 1954, for service purposes only.]

No. 3 Bogie Luggage Brake Van. Dimensions exactly as for No. 1. Stood out in the open during the years following 1939 passenger service cessation, and was beyond repair when railway reopened.

No. 4 (New Series No. 11) Bogie Luggage Brake Van. Length, 24 ft. 6 in.; Width, 6 ft. 3 in.; Height, 7 ft. 3 in.; Wheelbase, 15 ft. 6 in.; Tare, 4 tons 10 cwt. as built. 30 passengers.

Rebuilt at Boston Lodge, 1928/9, with new body incorporating guard's, one 1st and two 3rd compartments. [In service again from 1956. Rebuilt, Boston Lodge, 1957/8, as observation car after intermediate period of running van-to-van with No. 12 (New Series)

* The van lay in the yard in 1920 with 'woodwork in a bad state'. The rotted frame was then unsuspected.

connected by fall-plates for use of staff working between them en route.]

No. 5 (New Series No. 12) Bogie Luggage Brake Van. Dimensions exactly as for No. 4. Rebuilt at Boston Lodge, 1929/30, with new body incorporating guard's, observation section with longitudinal seat, and two 3rd compartments. [In service again from 1955, being the first ex-Festiniog passenger coach to return to normal traffic. Rebuilt, Boston Lodge, 1956/7, by removing observation section and installing buffet counter and side corridor, during 1956 being run van-to-van with No. 11 (above).]

The builders of vehicles Nos. 1–5 were Brown, Marshalls & Co.

Private Vehicles

'*The Boat*'. Gravity cars were early to the fore. The Spooner family had one shaped like a boat, having a long-pointed prow said to open the various gates across the line in early days (or stick any sheep wandering on the line). It was known as 'The Boat' and carried the inscription 'Ni l'un, Ni l'autre'.

It appears that it was fitted with a sail. A further reference in A. G. Crick's diary for 12 February 1886 says that 'The Boat' was smashed to pieces whilst conveying Mr. Spooner and friends on a gravity run and coming into head-on collision with an Up train.

The Oakeley Carriage. The Oakeley family went one better. They had a twelve-seater model with a brakesman as extra. Like the Spooner 'Boat' it was attached to Up trains, but detached at Tan-y-Bwlch. When convenient, the brakesman let it roll down to the private Plas station (suitably protected by carrying the single line staff) either to unload a special party there, or to pick one up. The vehicle then continued by gravity to Boston Lodge. It was usually stored in the paint shop.

Permanent Way Inspector's Trolley. This was a very light four-seater type distinguished by having enormous wheels. It was light enough to be lifted off the track at convenient points. It is seen in the photograph of Tan-y-Bwlch, plate 33H.

Miscellaneous Stock not Numbered in Goods Stock

No. 1. Four-wheeled goods and parcels van built 1910 from converted quarrymen's coach. Sliding doors. Disintegrated by 1950. Length 11ft. 2 in.; Width, 5 ft. 1 in.; Height, 5 ft. 6 in.; Wheelhouse, 5 ft. 6 in.; Paint, grey; Vacuum brake (piped). [One of two similar vehicles.]

No. 2. (Not known.)

No. 3. (Not known.)

No. 4. Four-wheeled brake van built from converted quarrymen's coach dual brake fitted, for Welsh Highland, September 1922. Scrapped. (This van had no balconies at all.)

No. 5. Four-wheeled brake van for Brookes' Quarry traffic, built from converted quarrymen's coach. (New Series No. 2.) Extant. (Carried 'No. 8' 1940–54.)

No. 6. Four-wheeled goods brake van. Probably converted quarrymen's coach using chassis with new body. Built 1908 at Vaughan's instructions. (New Series No. 1.) Extant.

No. 7. Four-wheeled goods brake van. Probably converted quarrymen's coach using chassis with new body. Built 1910 (as for No. 6). Scrapped.

Lighting—to 1953

By 1909 all the Festiniog coaches had been lit by acetylene gas and the N.W.N.G. by Colza oil; the latter was extremely poor. The Festiniog bogie carriages were converted to six-volt electric light by 1926 using accumulators stored in the guard's van. These were taken from the van into the Works for charging but were a constant source of trouble. The accumulators were not understood by all the guards and often became 'lost'; being 'found' working some employee's wireless set, or down in the town at the local electricians for charging, as the Works plant had broken down! Ultimately the Highland stock was fitted similarly.

Painting

1st class carriages were probably given Royal Purple panelling and ends, and the mouldings and lettering were picked out in gold. Undergear was black and roofs probably white. 2nd and 3rd class livery was probably the Indian Red which lasted for the whole life of many carriages; lining and lettering was yellow.

At first the 1st class carried the Company crest on the centre panel, a star on each side; the significance of the latter might simply be a form of identification among a public, not all of whom could read; the class was spelled out in lettering on the door panels. The vehicle number was carried once or even twice on each side, according to type of body and period of painting. In later years it appears a carriage might be taken into the Works for a quick and elementary coat of (latterly green) paint, more as a precaution against weather or, as one contemporary enthusiast put it, 'to hold the decaying woodwork together' and it would appear at the last minute for the peak season, without number or any identification at all. Many of the carriages shown in pictures of the late 1930s cannot be identified by number, though at the time of the Welsh Highland/Festiniog merger, they all received black numbers put on with stencils; body colours varied at this time (see NARROW GAUGE RAILWAYS IN SOUTH CAERNARVONSHIRE, p. 339).

Goods and Mineral Rolling Stock to 1946
(Excluding slate wagons)

Wagon No.	Type	Tons Weight Load	Note	Wagon No.	Type	Tons Weight Load	Note	Wagon No.	Type	Tons Weight Load	Note
1	W	1		56	W	2		111	S		16
2	W	2		57	W	3		112	V	4	
3	W	2	13	58	W	3		113	W	4	
4	W	3	20	59	W	3		114	W	4	
5	W	2		60	S	1		115	W	4	
6			2	61	S	1		116	V	4 sidedoor	
7	W	2		62	S	1	11	117	W	4	
8		6	3	63	V	4	12	118	W	4	
9	W	2		64	WB	2		119	W	4	
10	W	2		65	WB	2		120	W	4	17
11			4	66	WB	2		121	W	4	
12	W	2		67	WB	2		122	W	4	
13	S	1		68	WB	2		123	W	4	
14	W	2		69	WB	2		124	W	4	
15	W	2		70	WB	2		125	V	4	25
16	W	2	5	71	WB	2		126	W	4	
17	W	2		72	WB	2		127	W	4	
18	IC	2	x	73	WB	2		128	W	4	
19	W	2		74	WB	2		129	V	4	26
20	W	2		75	WB	2		130	W	4	
21	W	2		76	WB	2		131	W	4	
22	W	2		77	WB	2		132	V	4	26
23	W	2		78	V	4	24	133	W	4	18
24	W	2		79	W	4	28	134	W	4	
25	IC	2	x	80	W	4		135	V	4 sidedoor	
26	V	4		81	W	4		136	IC	2	
27	S	1		82	WB	2		137	IC	2	
28	W	2		83	WB	2		138	IC	2	
29	S	1		84	WB	2		139	IC	2	
30	S	1		85	WB	2		140	IC	2	
31	S	1		86	WB	2		141	IC	2	
32	S	1		87	WB	2		142	IC	2	
33	S	1		88	BO	8	1	143	IC	2	
34	S	1		89	W	4		144	IC	2	
35	S	1		90	W	3		145	IC	2	
36	W	2	6	91	W	3		146	IC	2	
37	W	2		92	W	3		147	IC	2	
38	IC	2	x	93	W	4		148	IC	2	
39	W	3		94	W	4		149	IC	2	
40	W	2		95	W	4		150	IC	2	
41	IHB	1	7	96	V	4	19, 24	151	IC	2	
42	IC	2	x	97	W	4		152	IC	2	
43	IC	2	x	98	W	4		153	IC	2	
44	IC	2	x	99	W	4		154	IC	2	
45	IC	2	x	100	W	4		155	IC	2	
46	IC	2	x	101	V	4	14	1	PC		8
47	IC	2	x	102	W	4		2	PC		8
48	IC	2	x	103	WB	2		3	PC		8
49	IC	2	x	104	WB	2		4	PC		8
50	IHB	1	21	105	BO	8	1	1	V		9
51	IC	2	x	106	WB	2		1	ST		
52	S		22	107	WB	2		2	ST		
53	W	2		108	WB	2		3	ST		
54	W	2		109	WB	2		4	ST		29
55			10	110	S		15				

The 1863–1939 painting can be summarised:

1863—(Probably) 1st class: Royal Purple.
   (Probably) 2nd and 3rd class: Indian Red.
   Roofs: white.
   Gilt lining and lettering.

1875—Upper panels: white, black lining.
   Lower panels: chocolate, yellow lining.
   Roofs: white.
   Class in full, gilt lettering below door light.
   Black solebars and running gear.

1885—Brick red bodies, some had panels.
   Window and door lights picked out in yellow, red lining.
   Roofs: grey.
   Class in yellow figures below door light, viz: '1st', '3rd'.
   Black solebars and running gear.

1925—Dark green bodies similar used Colonel Stephens elsewhere
   ('Kentish Green' with red oxide ends).
   Roofs: white or grey.
   Lettering: yellow.
   Black or brick red solebars.
   Enamel plates to show class.

1934-7—Some vehicles in pink, yellow, etc.
   Hudson Body: grey.
   Roof: white.
   Ironwork, etc.; black.

The Festiniog Railway

Wagon No.	Type	Tons Weight Load	Note	Wagon No.	Type	Tons Weight Load	Note	Wagon No.	Type	Tons Weight Load	Note
1	IB	2		9	IB	2		Oddments with assorted			
2	IB	2	27	10	IB	2		numbers:			
3	IB	2		11	IB	2		37 'Iron Slave Wagons'			
4	IB	2		12	IB	2	27	38 'Iron Slave Wagons'			
5	IB	2						37 'Wooden Sledge'			
6	IB	2		40	DS	2		A 'Iron Slave'			
7	IB	2		41	DS	2					
8	IB	2		42	DS	2					

Original No.	Original Type	Weight Tons	Later No.	Later type where rebuilt	Note
12	IF	2			
13	IF	2			
14	IF	2			
15	IF	2	38	IC	23
16	IF	2			
19	IF	2			
20	IF	2	18	IC	23
21	IF	2			
22	IF	2			
23	IF	2	42	IC	23
24	IF	2	45	IC	23
25	IF	2			
26	IF	2	49	IC	23
27	IF	2	47	IC	23
28	IF	2			
29	IF	2	25	IC	23
30	IF	2	48	IC	23
31	IF	2	51	IC	23
32	IF	2	43	IC	23
34	IF	2			
35	IF	2	44	IC	23
36	IF	2	46	IC	23
37	IF	2			
38	IF	2			

W	Wooden Open*		IHB	Iron Horse Box (Dandy) Coal Wagon
S	Sack Truck		PC	Pig/Calf Truck
ST	Stone Truck		IB	Iron Bolster
BO	Bogie Open		V	Covered Van
WB	Wood Bolster		DS	Donkey Vertical Slab Trucks
IC	Iron Coal		IF	Iron Flat Slab Wagons (Originally 1-42 separate series)

* The small open wagons with drop side doors were those used for mussel traffic between Portmadoc and Blaenau.

NOTES

1 Dismantled by 1910
2 Scrap 1887
3 Cleminson 6-wheel Open
4 Stone Truck No. 1 converted to 1 ton Open, March 1921, and numbered 11
5 Loco Shed Coal Wagon
6 Number carried by two wagons
7 'Slave' Wagon in Works, converted from Dandy, July 1901 and not renumbered
8 Small Open Wagons
9 Parcel Van
10 Blank
11 Converted to Ballast Wagon, 1906
12 Built to replace Pig and Calf Truck No. 4
13 Number carried by two wagons. Rebuilt as 2-ton High Side End Door Wagon from 1-ton Open
14 Converted from Cattle Van, 1904
15 Converted to Ballast Wagon, 1906
16 Converted to Ballast Wagon, 1906

17 Dismantled by 1910
18 Converted to Goods Van, 1905
19 Converted from Open Wagon, 1904
20 Number carried by two wagons (also 3-ton Open)
21 Dandy rated as '1 ton Iron Wagon'
22 Number also carried by 1 ton Wood Open
23 Converted to Iron Coal before 1898
24 Actually Hipped Roof Covered Wagon, converted before 1898
25 Converted from Open Wagon, 1900
26 Originally Open Wagons, converted to Vans, 1900
27 Runners only ('sledges')
28 4 ton Opens formerly rated 5 ton
x Converted from Iron Slab Trucks before 1897 (IF numbers alongside)
29 Ex-original Van No. 63

Note.—The foregoing list has been prepared from miscellaneous sources as no Official List exists. It should be used in the knowledge of this reservation.

Carrying no Number:	*Number in Service (1910)*
a. Breakdown Appliance Van	1
b. Fuel Supplier's Wagon	1
c. Oakeley Water Truck	1 2-ton
d. Loco Shed Coal Wagon	1 (in addition to No. 16)
e. Coke Wagon	1 1-ton
f. Tan-y-Bwlch Flour Truck	1

The low numbers in the series tended to be re-utilised as their vehicles were withdrawn; e.g. 4, 5, 6, 7, 10 and 21 were bolsters in 1934; 14, 16 and 34 were covered vans; 18, 25 and 33 were 'slab trucks' (etc.).

Boyd/Mackearth Survey 1939–51

Ref.	Body Length Ft.	In.	Body Width Ft.	In.	Body Height from rail Ft.	In.	Wheelbase Ft.	In.	Load Tons of Body	Material of Body	Purpose	Official Tare Weight
I	5	3	2	7	3	2	2	11	2	Wood	Small slate: slat sides	10½ cwt. ⎫
II	6	0	3	4	3	2	3	1	2	Iron	Small slate: slat sides	to
III	7	6	4	0	3	2	4	1	3	Iron	Large slate: slat sides	1 ton 2 cwt. ⎬
IV	8	0	3	3	1	7	5	0	3	Iron	Flat: slab	15 cwt.
V	7	8	3	9	4	6	4	0	1	Wood	Small: coal open	17 cwt. (1)
VI	8	9	4	3	4	8	5	6	3	Wood	Small: coal end door open	(2)
VII	9	6*	4	10	5	3	4	9	4	Wood	Large: mineral (or) open	to
VIII	8	0	3	10	4	8	4	5	2	Iron	Small: coal open	1 ton 9 cwt. (3)
IX	14	8	5	0	5	3	10	0		Iron	Six-wheel: open	(4)
X	6	4	3	2	1	10	3	0	5 pair	Wood	Bolster. (Bolster 4 ft. 9 in. long)	3 ton 2 cwt. (5)
XI	5	8	3	4	1	8	3	4		Wood	Gangers' flat wagon	13 cwt. each (7)
XII	6	0	3	0	5	0				Iron	Gunpowder van	
XIII	10	3	4	10	7	0	5	0	4	Wood	Covered van: side door	
XIV	10	0†	4	10	7	2	4	9	4	Wood	Covered van: end doors	
XV	11	0	5	2	7	0	6	3		Wood	Brake van: end balconies	
XVI	21	3	4	9	3	10	18	6		Wood	Bogie ballast open	(6)
XVII	17	8	5	0	platform					Wood		

* Some 10 ft. 0 in. or 9 ft. 0 in.

† Varies between 9 ft. 7 in. and 10 ft. 3 in.

(1) 3-plank Fixed sides and ends; 2 vertical frames (wood) each side body; inside bearings; flush soles.
   2-plank Length, 8 ft.; Width, 4 ft. 6 in.; Height, 4 ft. 6 in.

(2) Single door one end; various buffing gear; 2 vertical frames (wood or iron) each side; flush soles; inside or outside bearings.
   (A smaller variation was 3 ft. 10 in. high.)

(3) 3 varieties door(s) one end; flush soles; sprung buffers; inside or outside bearings.

(4) Double doors one end. Some had very elementary bearing pillars.

(5) Double doors one end. Cleminson's Patent Wheelbase.

(6) Bogies 3 ft. wheelbase; truss depth 1 ft. 3 in.

(7) Maximum load length, 60 ft.

CHAPTER SIXTEEN

FENCING AND PERMANENT WAY 1836–1953

Brief mention of the earliest form of track—recommended by Robert Stephenson, disliked by James Spooner and criticised as inadequate by contemporary engineers—has already been made. Messrs. Jevons Sons & Co. of Liverpool supplied the wrought-iron rails weighing 16 lb. per yard, with fish-bellies to give strength between the chair supports and costing about £9 per ton. Messrs. Thomas Jones of Caernarvon, iron founders, put up a small foundry in Portmadoc to execute the order for chairs, amounting to 50,000 in all; these weighed 5–6 lb. each. Jones' business passed to his son John, becoming the well-known Glaslyn Foundry; they charged 15s. per cwt. for the chairs.

The rails were secured in the chairs by iron wedges or keys and in turn, the chairs either to granite blocks of about 9 in. cube, or to slate slabs of about 9×9 in. surface area.* Examples of this early format survived around the Works to be unearthed in the mid-1950s; the rail section varied somewhat and one drawing of a 16 lb. section appeared in *Verhandlung des Gewerbfleisses Vereins* 13, 1834 (Plate XIX) 'Archer, Engineer'. On the Cob, wooden sleepers were used but elsewhere each chair was carried on its individual slab or granite block except at joints where a single slab carried the chairs for both rails.† The rails were slightly flattened at the ends, and butt-jointed within a slightly larger and heavier chair, the key holding the joint fast. It is quite possible that materials varied somewhat along the length of the line, at this first stage ... and as they were to do for quite different reasons forever afterwards.

There was no question of the sleepers being used to tie the rails into gauge in the modern sense, and they were often quarried at some suitable site near where they might be laid, and drilled only when required. Recently it was found that dam works used in connection with the Moelwyn Incline were constructed in portion by using blocks probably intended for trackwork, but not drilled; the drilling was for plugging the resultant hole with an oak peg (17s. 6d. per thousand), the borers being given 3s. 6d. per dozen; the chairs were spiked to the sleeper with an iron pin (6d. per dozen) driven into the oak peg. Iron pegs and chair wedges came from the local nailer. *Engineering* of 26 September 1884 described the rail section as 'oval', which was very misleading.

* Typical granite cubes were 1 ft. 4 in.
† Typical joint sleeper 2 ft. 9 in. long, 1 ft. 6 in. wide and 3 in. deep.

Approx. Year of Introduction	Section	§ Length	Weight/Yard	Material	Joints
1832	Fishbelly T section	*18 ft.	16 lb.	W./Iron	Butt type in special large chair.
1842	Parallel T section	18 ft.	16 lb.	ditto	ditto
1846	ditto	21 ft.	30 lb. (from 1852 42 lb.)	ditto	At first as above: after 1868 a fore-runner of Spooner & Huddart clamp type fishplate.
1868	Double-head reversible	24 ft.	46 ll. (later 48½ lb.) By 1896— 50 lb.	ditto Steel	Spooner & Huddart Patent evolved from the 1868 pattern. 24 lb. a pair
1878	Bull-head	24 ft. and 30 ft.	50 lb.	Steel†	Plain fishplate some with lower cranked extension piece. Mainly 4 bolt; 2 bolt introduced late 1930s

PHASE I. from 1832. Fish-belly T section rail, 16 lb in 18 foot lengths, pitch 30" approx.* Possibly used for original Cob tramway.

PHASE II. from 1842 Chairs. 9/1 weight 5 lb (intermediate) as ph.I. Rail W/1. parallel 'T' section 16 lb.. *
* Rail section approximate ~ measurement from rusted samples

PHASE IIIA. 1846 ~ '52 approx. 21 ft W/1 in 30 lb section.
Intermediate (10·7 lb) & Joint (16·38 lb) chairs remained unchanged. Both shown.

PHASE IIIB. 1852 approx - 1868 approx. 21 ft. W/1 in 42 lb section.
FROM F.R. DRAWING.

MID-SECTION

Development

| Sleepers | Chairs | | | Ballast |
	Material	Key	Fastening	
At joints; slab carrying joint chairs for both rails. Intermediate granite or slab blocks carrying one chair only	W./Iron 5 lb. intermediate	Iron Peg, later wood	2 Iron Pegs	Ship's ballast
ditto		ditto		ditto
Wood, conventional	W./Iron 10·7 lb. intermediate 13 lb. (later 16·38 lb.) at joints	Iron, later wood	2 Iron Pegs	ditto, especially River Elbe stone.
Larch wood—local sources. Half round or rectangular sections 4 ft. 6 in. long × 9 in. wide × 4½ in. deep (10 in. × 5 in. at joints)	Cast Iron 'S' base 15½ lb.	Wood (Oak)	2 W./Iron Pegs 4½ in. × ⅝ in.	Elbe stone and later, granite chips locally.
As for above: later creosoted Pine or standard gauge cut to half length Lair at 2 ft. 9 in. centres: 2 ft. at joints	Cast Iron Various Patterns Rectangular base ⁺/⁻	Wood (Oak)	2, 3 or 4 steel pegs according to chair. Some bolts in use	As above. (Packed 6 in. deep under sleepers, 12 in. at side. Width at sleeper level 6 ft.)

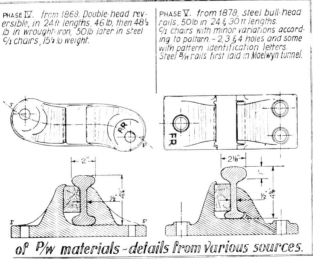

PHASE IV. from 1868. Double-head reversible, in 24 ft lengths, 46 lb, then 48½ lb in wrought-iron, 50 lb later in steel S/1 chairs, 15½ lb weight.

PHASE V. from 1878, steel bull-head rails, 50 lb in 24 & 30 ft lengths. S/1 chairs with minor variations according to pattern. – 2, 3 & 4 holes and some with pattern identification letters. Steel B/h rails first laid in Moelwyn tunnel.

of P/w materials – details from various sources.

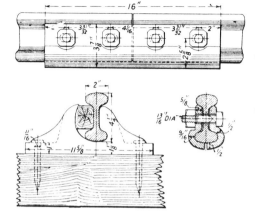

Drawing reproduced from 'The Railway Engineer' of May 1883, showing Spooner & Huddart's Patent rail-joint in its final form, double-headed rail and spike chair fastenings

Points were of a pattern then widely favoured, having a frog-section cast in one piece weighing about 1 cwt. The moving parts were the wrought-iron blades which were mounted each on a smaller casting having a chair-shaped support outside the stock rail. This 'chair' carried a pin which supported the blade vertically at its heel. When these pins became bent, the blade would not properly engage with the stock rail, and when locomotive haulage began, the Inspector recommended these pins to be removed.

Official figures for the rail gauge have varied along the years. C. E. Spooner advised Mr. Kinnan of Dublin on 18 April 1856 that it was 2 ft. 1 in. centre rail to centre rail, this giving a gauge over the inside of the existing rail-faces of 1 ft. 11¼ in. This was probably the 1836 figure and has varied as the rail section differed.

Ultimately the stone and granite blocks were displaced by wood and found their way into walls, some for instance, forming the portals of the Garnedd Tunnel. They must have been a useful local source of material when the original fencing needed urgent replacement. From the surviving material it is noted that the spacing of chair holes varies from 3 in. upwards, according to the type of material they were carrying.

In the Company's archives are some undated drawings of developments for track, probably prepared on the realisation that the existing materials were deteriorating. There are some curious sections including a type of bull-head with a flattened inner running face and another, developed from a later period when 42 lb. 'T' rails were in use, shows developments from this. The drawings suggest one weakness of the early rails was the butt-joint which tended to collapse. One method of treatment was a fishplated joint held within a chair and using bolts screwed through the chair into the rail. One dated drawing (28 May 1863) shows 30 lb. 'T' rails using the aforementioned screwed rails but carried in the existing chair of this time. The original concept of a centre-centre gauge of 2 ft. 1 in. is preserved throughout, no matter what rail. None of these proposals took form, though possibly the Spooner & Huddart Patent fishplate (q.v.) was developed from them. The drawings also take the narrative well beyond the period just discussed.

A nice discovery brought to attention was the unearthing in 1965 on the northwest side of High Street, Portmadoc, of a section of fish-bellied track twelve feet to the west of and parallel to High Street. It was two feet below the present surface level and possibly below that of the nearby Croesor Tramway. No siding at this situation is shown on early records, and its date is not known. Some connection with the reincarnated Cob Tramway, or the clearance of an area using old F.R. materials, may be discovered by a later historian!

From 1846, a heavier form of track was laid using parallel section 'T' rails—sometimes known as Heel rail from the stiffening bulb along one side of its lower edge—the rails weighing 30 lb. (and later 42 lb.) per yard and the new chairs 10 and 13 lb. each. A Minute of 1846 reads 'Rails having now commenced to wear out, it is proposed to renew, a heavier Rail to be adopted'. Two miles of it had been relaid by 1848 and it was expected the new material would enable the twelve men engaged on track maintenance to be reduced to four. Relaying was complete by 1855. Rail lengths varied between 18 and 21 feet, and the chairs were spiked to wooden sleepers. It was over this track, still without fishplates, that the first steam engines worked. A few sidings survived in the material at Boston Lodge, Tan-y-Bwlch and on the Dinas branch until the mid-1950s; it was to this form that Spooner & Huddart Patent plates were ultimately fitted most having a recess-shaped slab under them to support the fishplate.

In 1850 chairs were being cast in the new foundry at Boston Lodge; by that time only three miles of the original track survived. To safeguard level crossings, signs were put up on the railway side 'Put on the brake' and on the road side, 'Beware of Trains'.

In order to improve the crude joint in the single chair, a heavy fish-plate was evolved in 1867 for clamping the 'T' section rails where locomotive running was in force. This fitting comprised two different and separate plates, each having five bolt-and-nut fixings. The inner plate was of 'D' section and extremely thick; the outer plate was of customary pattern. The plates were extended downwards below and under the rail, so as to clasp it underneath, and were joined by a single bolt and nut in the centre of the downward projection, immediately under the joint itself. This arrangement was a simple forerunner of the Spooner & Huddart Patent plate, used on the later double-headed rails and in general service by 1868. In that year 46 lb. double-headed rails first came into use.

Of the oldest track, the Accounts show disposals including:

23 August 1847	Old rails, wheels and chairs app. 3¾ tons @ 126/–
30 June 1848	Old rails to Shelton & Greaves
	Llechwedd & Maenyfferam (1 ton) @ 126/–
30 September 1848	(as 30 June)
30 December 1849	Old rails, Shelton & Greaves
9 October 1849	10 tons old rails, chairs 'at different
	times up to this date' Cwmorthin
	Slate Co. @ 100/–
31 March 1851	Old rails, etc., Hafodty Slate Co.

(There are no further entries after this date; a recent survey of all quarries in the Ffestiniog district—when most of them had been cleared of scrap metal—shows the Rhosydd group, Cwm Orthin, Wrysgan and Oakeley workings together with all workings north and east of these, contain old Festiniog Railway materials; some survive in tracks but much is found in wall-bars, stone steps, building material or stockyard piles. Underground at New Rhosydd, some track survives.)

By 1867 the Annual Report said it was advisable to relay the whole line 'it is in many places much worn'. Rail weighing 48 lb. with fished joints was recommended at £6,600 to be spread over four years. It was completed by 1870 save for a short length near Duffws, a branch which was always behindhand for relaying; its original 1836 materials were not replaced until 1861 by the heavier 'T' rails. This was due to the light traffic over it for many years.

The new rails were double-headed, weighing 46 lb. (later 48·66 lb.) and were fishplated from the first. Though not strictly *designed* to be used twice, when the head was worn, they were turned over and the bottoms used for the running surface. It was found that due to hammer blow, the rails became pitted where the chairs supported them so that the lower face had to be planed before it could be used as a running surface. As an economy measure, the track on the Embankment was thus relaid in 1884, the saving being £396 per mile.

The chairs were larger and heavier than previously, having the form of main line chairs of the present day: various types have been evolved over the years, fastening with two, three or four pins or bolts. The early patterns had an 'S' outline base, popular at the time. A later type had a lower inner jaw which did not strike the flanges of passing wheels whose tyres were badly worn . . . a very useful feature of the between-the-wars-period when maintenance was bad. At this period too, fish-plate bolt heads suffered seriously from blows by deep flanges. On sharp curves a special chair with thickened base was used to carry the outer rail.

The Patent Fishplate evolved by C. E. Spooner and George Augustus Huddart was dubbed the 'Double Socket-joint Girder Plate' one of each of which was placed round the web and foot at rail joints, the deep flange projecting below the assembly where the plates were joined by steel clips or bolts. (Patent No. 1487 of 14 May 1869.) As with many Spooner enterprises, the Railway formed a convenient 'Test Bed' for such ideas. The Patent Schedule, with drawings for many types of rail and gauges, is dated 1868–9 as from Bron-y-Garth, Port Madoc.

In addition to fishplates of the above or other pattern, two longitudinal sleepers were placed under the adjacent sleepers, so that the whole joint assembly rested as a bed of rectangular timbers in the ballast. The Patent fishplates were not a success with the double-headed track as when the rails were reversed, the fishplate holes, owing to rail wear, were not central for the reversed rail. The Board of Trade referred to the fishplate as of Clip Type.

For the double-headed rails, the sleepers were renewed. The standard form was in larch, 4 ft. 6 in. long, 9 in. wide and 4½ in. deep, spaced at 2 ft. 4 in. (later 3 ft.) centres. At joints they were 1 ft. 6 in. (later 2 ft.) centres. In certain locations in the past (e.g. at Rhiw Plas Bridge) special sleepers of less depth were used to suit the solid rock beneath the track and the thinner ballast bed there used.

The rails in the Moelwyn Tunnel were always a problem, due to the wet; nine years was the expected life for them there. The tunnel was selected as a venue for the first steel rails (1878), these coming from the Dowlais Iron Works (who had rolled the first steel rails ever made by the Bessemer Process in 1856). They received the order in 1877. By 1893 all the main line was laid in steel rails. In the interim it contained a mixture of iron and steel. It was over the period 1896–1904 that relaying next took place in the Moelwyn Tunnel.

In the complete renewal of the track in the late 1860s and early 1870s, all curves were relaid as true parabolas, and super-elevation given for the first time. Until 1884—and possibly later—specimens of early track were kept in a small Museum in the draughtsman's office; by this date most of the surviving double-head rails would be in steel. Super-elevation reached considerable heights (3 inches is recorded) before being reduced on Board of Trade instructions. *The Illustrated Guide to, and Popular History of North Wales* of the 1888 period contains a short section on the Railway, and noticing the Board of Trade withdrawal of the 12 m.p.h. speed limit, maintains that 30 m.p.h. was 'not uncommon' and that the *James Spooner* had run a measured mile at 45 m.p.h. So perhaps the super-elevation was considered prudent!

As to ballast, the Railway was fortunate in having access to ships' ballast brought into Portmadoc, much of it from the river Elbe and known to the Company as 'Hamburg Ballast'. When shipping fell away, the cost of bringing in stone from elsewhere brought a sharp decline in the standards of the track, but even ships' ballast declined in quality and by 1906 was considered to be too poor to use.

Between the wars the last of a phase of using half-round sleepers came to an end; these too were condemned by the Board of Trade but the last had lingered on the Mineral Line until this time. Special sleeper orders were no longer placed; the cheap source from the abandoned P.B. & S.S. Railway venture will have been noted—prior to the First War, and now cut-down standard gauge sleepers, bought second-hand, came into use. Some Patent Fishplates might still be found, but plain four-bolt plates were in the majority. Copying London, Midland & Scottish Railway practice, some of the latter were cut in half, the joint sleepers brought closer together and the fastening made in a two-bolt plate. Major relaying, as had been practised throughout the life of the Railway, ceased in 1925 and when the Second War came, the line was laid in a mixture of materials none of which had received the maintenance they needed for some time. By Talyllyn Railway (and other minor railway standards of the day) the track was still of substantial order, though down-at heel. Many who might have known better pronounced it would be the Achilles' Heel of the undertaking. They were wrong.

The narrow gauge interchange yards where the standard gauge railways inter-twined their tracks with the narrow were places of great interest as the narrow gauge was often built up in standard gauge materials. It had a massive appearance. The track at the Zinc Mine, Moelwyn, survived until the 1946 closure and, save for some track on the Dinas branch, contained some of the only flat-bottomed rails on the line. It must be said that the Newborough Slate Mills branch of early 1879 had 3¾ tons in 24 ft. lengths in this material when laid down, and a siding near 'Smith's Box' was laid in them. These must have been of odd section and very light, as they were reported as being '12–14 lb. f.b. rails large section' and were lying at Boston Lodge in case they might be re-used, in February 1902. They were quite unsuitable for the locomotives, of course.*

In the 1940s the bull-head steel rails latterly employed were 30 ft. long and nominally 50 lb. per yard. The steel-railed points were of double-blade pattern with conventional fixed frogs. Special chairs for blades, slide chairs, frog angles, together with all running line chairs, and point levers, were cast and made up at Boston Lodge. At the dead end of Portmadoc Harbour station was a three-way stub point, the only one on the line (currently on Glan-y-Mor). The drawing for it is dated 22 April 1879. On the main line there were two diamond crossings, first

---

* In a letter from Spooner to Greaves' Quarry dated July 1883, he offers them 30 tons steel f.b. rails 40 lb. per yard at £3 10s. 0d. per ton 'recently taken from the tunnel, and fishplates'. This suggests an early small experiment to use f.b. rails. The letter brought no reply. He wrote again '. . . not long in service . . . water pitted . . . suitable for contractor's purposes'.

laid in iron. That at the Loop Line was relaid in steel in late 1880.

Originally the ballast was brought up to the level of the rail running surface, but B.O.T. Inspectors found it hid faults in the track and the practice ceased. The use of Boston Lodge became less intensive as years passed, and latterly many bull-head rail chairs were supplied by outside contractors. By 1922, it was stated the average life of rail was 20 years, that of sleepers 15 years.

The fencing of the line was done originally in wooden materials; these were last installed in 1864. Some wooden fences were on top of existing stone walls and were not tall; they required extensive maintenance. When stone sleepers became available, almost all the line was given stone walling surmounted by iron post and wire fence to replace the wood. In certain places there was (and is) no walling at all. In others iron railings have sufficed, particularly near housing.

Finally, though 'T', double-head and bull-head rails were used in the main line, clearly this did not rule out other sections where engines did not enter sidings. For instance, it is recorded that 3 tons of bridge rail ($2\frac{1}{2}$ in. high and in this case therefore, of suitable section for locomotives) were used in the Powder Magazines' sidings near Tunnel Cottage; they were lifted before the turn of the century.

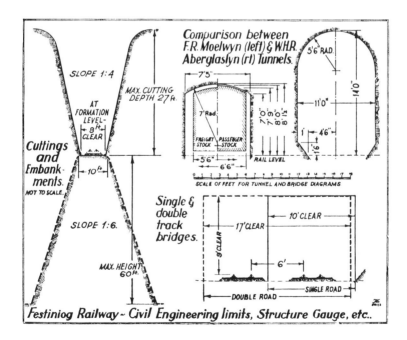

CHAPTER SEVENTEEN

TRAFFIC AND OPERATION 1836–1953

Signals—Telegraph—Telephone—Single line working—
Train operation—Accidents.

As is to be expected on such a singular system, the signalling employed was not similar to that used by any other railway company. The original equipment, in the main, was not replaced by more up-to-date fittings as the years went by, and even today old disc signals are still standing beside the line. The signalling system was of historic interest for many years before the line closed.

It has proved extraordinarily difficult to record the signalling with exactitude; some of the remaining documentary evidence is conflicting and there is no proof that certain planned improvements were carried into effect.

The signalling system began to fall out of use when the line was scheduled as a Light Railway in 1923, though certain signals had already been dismantled by that date. The three cabins in Blaenau were closed in 1923 and ground frames substituted.* On the other hand, the three-arm bracket signal on the Embankment installed in 1929 to replace a former double-arm semaphore with a new McKenzie & Holland arm added below it, was used as a 'calling on' signal for locos working from Boston Lodge until recently.

The basic signalling system was a simple scheme—each station (including Rhiw Goch and Hafod-y-Llyn) had a single wooden post at approximately the mid-point of the station. This post had twin arms, one each side of the post and each applying to one direction of running. These signals served as stopping signals. There were no starting signals, the authority to proceed being possession of the single line staff by the driver, and the 'Right-away' from the guard. At either end of the station was a distant signal in the form of a disc on a post. Although complicated by additional signalling this layout of posts, discs and semaphore remained in use throughout the life of the signalling system.

The semaphore signals at through stations had double arms pivoted upon a common pivot at the top of the post. The arms fell into a com-

* No. 2 survived for some years as Shunting Cabin for the G.W.R. who built a new central box to replace the two former ones and brought it into use 28 September 1926.

mon slot. The post was surmounted by a lamp with a fixed case; as the arms moved a spectacle glass within the case rotated to the appropriate indication. The arms had rounded ends, often painted to give a square appearance. The arms were worked by handles at the foot of the post. At first the left-hand arm was painted red whilst the right-hand arm (presenting the rear aspect to an oncoming train), was painted white: after about 1887 the right-hand became red instead of the left. The Rule Book of 1864 reads: 'the signal is invariably made on the left side of the post . . .'. It was the practice of the Company to use the right-hand loop for passing trains so about 1887 the arms were re-painted with the right-hand face in red, etc. The Harbour station signal was said to have been used in three positions (Accident Report, 1881).

Originally, these semaphores gave a three-aspect signal: 'All Right' [*sic*] by means of the arm within the post (or a white light); 'Caution' [*sic*] by the arm raised at 45 degrees to the post (or a green light); 'Danger' [*sic*] by the arm in the horizontal position (or by a red light). Later the more common two aspects were adopted with the arm at 45 degrees for 'All Right'.

The disc signals consisted of a three-foot diameter disc mounted on a fluted cast-iron column. On top of the disc was a lamp of normal pattern. The disc revolved through a right angle and was worked by a twin-wire running to a capstan in the station centre. Each station had two capstans, one for each of its disc signals. On top of the capstan was a small disc repeating the position of the signal proper. The two aspects were: Danger—the disc face towards the train; All Right—the disc turned edge-on to the train. Discs were sometimes used as stop signals outside station limits, e.g. Glan-y-Pwll until 1896.

Flag signals followed the colour scheme outlined for semaphore lamps; it was the practice of signalmen to give an additional white flag indication. Signalmen were employed at every station where signals were located and no form of shelter was at first provided for them. As there were no lever frames, signal boxes were unnecessary except as once installed at Blacnau Festiniog and Boston Lodge—and the latter only contained instruments. Although there were no other uses for the semaphore signals already described, the disc signals were used also as auxiliary signals. Thus, although it was permissible to pass a disc signal used as a distant signal, it was not permissible to pass a disc signal in use as an auxiliary.

There were other special signals (not forgetting the semaphore to stop trains at the private Plas station), namely for use at Penrhyn level crossing and the Moelwyn Tunnel, the former 12 ft. high with a 15-in. diameter lamp signal on top and fixed arm 2 ft. 3 in. long: the whole revolved. The latter at the Moelwyn Tunnel was probably the first place where any form of signalling was sited. Brown, Marshalls & Co. provided a set of bells, 2 signals and lamps showing red, green and white in Spring 1864. The signals were square boards and appear to have been used, like the lamps, in three positions; the illustration of the south end shows the board at caution (plate 8R)—this is likely to have been an end-on position rather than the apparent diagonal as shown, the other two aspects being, like the lamp with which the post was normally surmounted, at right-angles to each other. Besides these, there were two varieties of point signal. The first was a point indicator semaphore, mounted on a fluted cast-iron post ten feet tall, with an arm falling into a slot at the top. It was pivoted at the top and surmounted by a lamp which was fixed but a spectacle, red at the front and white at the rear, was connected to the arm and moved with it. The arm only rose on one side of the post; when within the post the points were set for the main line and when extended the arm pointed the direction in which the point was set. Lugs fixed to the post allowed the signalman to climb up and remove the lamp. The second type was generally used at points not actually giving access to the main line but over which locomotives were wont to pass. It consisted of a lamp with discs on opposite faces. The lamp was fixed but a spectacle glass rotated with it as the point blades moved. These point discs were occasionally mounted on posts, six feet tall, to give a clearer indication.

At Tan-y-Grisiau there was for a time an additional disc Home signal just before the Down loop points; this served as a repeater to the disc Home itself which was hidden by earthworks.*

The original signalling equipment of 1864 was supplied by Messrs. Brown, Marshalls & Co. of Birmingham and comprised:

9 April 1864   2 disc signals with bells and lamps complete
               2 lamps and sockets for Tunnel to show red, white and green
25 July 1864   7 semaphore signals and lamps complete
               16 disc signals and lamps complete

The point/semaphore indicators probably were born of need and possibly made locally; they are first seen in pictures of the mid-1870s. The disc type on posts were likely to be McKenzie & Holland pattern installed during replacement of the original signalling.

The growth of traffic at Blaenau Festiniog, together with the arrival of the Festiniog & Blaenau Railway, the London & North Western Railway, and the inadequacy of the old station at Duffws, led to considerable changes in layout, extension of facilities and tracks, establishment of exchange sidings and the resiting of the line leading to the Duffws branch. These changes were made from 1869, and at intervals since that date. Messrs. McKenzie & Holland of Worcester were given

_____

* There was also a small signal cabin with disc signals to protect the Dolrhedyn level crossing nearby. All was removed when a bridge was substituted, 1900.

the task of completely resignalling the line from old Dinas Junction to Duffws, on modern lines. This dated from Autumn 1878.

The section eastwards from old Dinas Junction was divided up into three-block sections. The first commenced at old Dinas Junction, passed Glan-y-Pwll Junction (in the apex of which the first signal box was situated), and the L.N.W.R. Exchange station, finishing at but not including the junction points for the L.N.W.R. yard.

The second section controlled the L.N.W.R. yard points, the junction for the Festiniog & Blaenau Railway known as Dòlgarreg-Ddu Junction (laid out with full signalling in 1878, the cost being shared), as far as but not including the crossover just short of the Queen's Bridge.

The third section controlled the remainder of the line.

The three signal boxes ('cabins' was the official term) controlling this complete section were of timber, clad in horizontal shiplap with sliding windows, slated roof and access by porch from a stairway. They had lockers and stoves; No. 3 was 12 ft. × 11 ft. × 15 ft. high. Dolgarreg-Ddu Junction (or Duffws Junction or No. 2 cabin) was similarly built but with a floor only 2 ft. 6 in. above the rails (more in the nature of a ground-frame hut), stove, desk, locker, etc.

No. 1. Glan-y-Pwll Junction. This was built in 1880 and resited in 1899 immediately east of the Glan-y-Pwll Road level crossing so as to give a better view of the L.N.W.R. Exchange station: it was then designated Glan-y-Pwll No. 3. (Originally known as Dinas Junction Box No. 3.) (19 levers.)

No. 2. F.R. & G.W. Joint No. 2. (Situated at the west end of the interchange platform, G.W.R.) This box was known as Duffws in 1880, when it controlled Dolgarreg-Ddu Junction; at this time it lay between the Newborough Slate Mill branch junction and the F. & B.R. junction. (23 levers.) In 1883 the box was rebuilt, the physical junction with the F. & B.R. having been abandoned with the re-gauging of the F. & B.R. Two frames were then installed, the one for the Festiniog and the other for the Great Western line (as it was to become). The frames were sited back to back (but adjoining) and manned by a Festiniog signalman, the main line company contributing towards wages and upkeep of the box. At first the box was known as Duffws Junction (although there was by then no actual junction) but the ultimate name was adopted later.

No. 3. Duffws Station No. 1. (Situated on the north side of the line on site of a former coal yard under the west wall of the Queen's Bridge.) (14 levers.)

Some locking of points and semaphores was done at Portmadoc in 1880 but a more thorough resignalling for which both McKenzie &

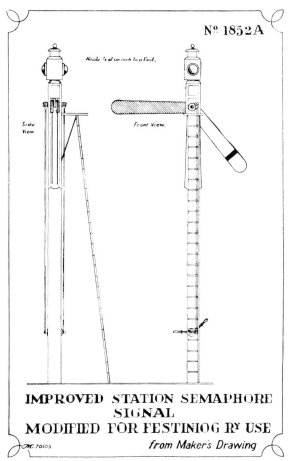

Nᵒ 1852A

Scale ⅛ of an inch to a Foot,

Side
View

Front View.

IMPROVED STATION SEMAPHORE
SIGNAL
MODIFIED FOR FESTINIOG Rʸ USE

from Maker's Drawing

Holland and Gloster Wagon Co. Ltd.—Signal Department, tendered
in 1879 and 1880 was shelved.

The semaphores installed by McKenzie & Holland were of modern
appearance; a drawing is reproduced on plate 3S. The same lamp
colours were in use as with the early semaphores; at Danger a single
red spectacle was before the lamp and when the arm was lowered this
spectacle moved away and a single white light shone for All Right.
There was a rear spectacle plate giving green when the arm was 'on',
blanked off for 'time' and white for 'off'.

The signalling of the 'Duffws Branch' is known only by the map of
June 1864 showing that disc signals at first controlled the crossing at
Glan-y-Pwll Road. A disc signal protected the Queen [*sic*] Hotel level
crossing (the main street through Blaenau) and its complementary

signal was a single-armed semaphore with a slotted post which served a double purpose, being the starting signal for Down trains from the Duffws terminus.

The later signalling arrangements (McKenzie & Holland) started with alterations at Glan-y-Pwll Junction and resulted from the abandonment of Dinas as a passenger station. It will be seen from the diagrams that although the line was formerly double from Glan-y-Pwll Junction to the terminus, the tracks were not used for Up and Down running. Rather, they were two independent single tracks; at first the south line was designated the mineral line, and this enabled Festiniog & Blaenau trains to work on to the Festiniog without fouling the passenger line. On the other hand, it was necessary for Down passenger trains to cross the mineral line when leaving Duffws, and vice versa; they also had to cross the connection to the L.N.W.R. yard. They passed finally on to the main line at Glan-y-Pwll Junction, where the track singled. Catch points were installed at suitable places to prevent wagons running away and fouling the passenger line—it must be remembered that the whole system was on a considerable gradient.

Though to avoid confusion the terms have not been reversed here, for the period of physical connection to the F. & B.R., Portmadoc–Llan Ffestiniog became Down working, and vice versa.

Shortly after the abandonment of the Festiniog & Blaenau Railway with its physical connection, the north track was converted into the mineral line. To enable passenger trains to reach the G.W.R. exchange platform they used the cross-over at the west end of the platform.

Due to these changes, both in junction connections and the resultant alterations to passenger and mineral lines, the signalling underwent drastic changes. The diagrams to illustrate track layouts and signalling in connection with these modifications have been prepared with the help of the limited amount of documentary evidence which survives, and the assistance of recollections of old employees.

Schemes for modernising the signalling at Penrhyn, Tan-y-Bwlch and the Tunnel (north end) were prepared in early 1890 in consequence of the 1889 Act, the Worcester firms of Dutton & Co. and McKenzie & Holland submitting schemes. Elementary interlocking using the existing disc and semaphore signals sufficed and no re-signalling was done. It is regrettable that all plans and documents belonging to Messrs. McKenzie & Holland were destroyed when their successors were evacuated hurriedly from London during the early years of the last war.

Extracts from the 1876 Rule Book in connection with Signalling

Certain of the signalling regulations are worth quoting in full:

124a. The Stop Blocks on the Main Line at Duffws and Dinas, below the lowest Points, to be fixed in place immediately after the arrival

of every Train, Engine or Truck at the Stations, and immediately
after the passing of any Train, Engine or Truck out of the Stations,
the Stop Blocks are to be re-fixed in their respective places.

This rule also applies to the Glan-y-Pwll Junction.

The Signalman and Porters also to take care that all Trains or
Trucks are Stop Blocked when standing in the Sidings.

39. On a train approaching the long tunnel, the signalman next the
train will telegraph to the man at the other end of the tunnel, which
will be answered by the latter, when, if the tunnel is clear, the 'All
Right' signal must, under the Rules specially provided for working
the tunnel, be shewn to the approaching train . . .

When the line is under repair, the lamps in the tunnel to be kept
lighted . . .

[Author's Note: The above applies to the special semaphore signals controlling the tunnel, already mentioned. At the north end, the instruments were
kept in Tunnel Cottage, and at the south end in a small cabin near the tunnel
mouth.]

43. When a train is stopping at a Station, or when there is any obstruction thereat, the Main and Auxiliary or Distant Signals must be at
Danger, and any coming Engine or Train must be brought to a
stand at the Auxiliary Signal, when the Engineman will open his
whistle and afterwards proceed with caution towards the Station.

45. Engines with Passenger Trains or Passenger Trains without
Engines, must carry a White Light on in front by night and in foggy
weather; and every Cattle, Slate, Merchandise, or Coal Train, with
or without an Engine, a Green Light in front of it.

[Author's Note: Once again the Up trains with engines attached, as against
the gravity-only Down trains with engines running light, are provided for. See
Rule 46 also.]

46. At night and in foggy weather Detached Engines must carry a
White Light on the buffer plank, and a Red tail light.

122/9. These rules refer to the duties of pointsmen, policemen and
signalmen, among which is a rule directing that engines working on
the branch line, etc. must come to a dead stand in foggy weather
before crossing the junction points. At this time there were no catch
points fitted at junctions, only stop blocks. (A detachable quadrant
placed on one rail and curved to receive a wheel: Vignes Fig. 16.)

131/9. Rules applying to gatemen and maintenance of gate signals.

161. This rule lays down that enginemen must pay immediate attention
to the state of the signals whether the cause of their position is
known to them or not, but adds the following rider: '. . . the enginemen must not, however, trust to signals, but on all occasions to be
vigilant and cautious . . .'

Board of Trade Return dated 31 December 1882

	Distance worked by Absolute Block System in addition to Train Staff	
Absolute Block	Miles	Chains
Boston Lodge Box–Minffordd	1	1
South End Tunnel Box–North End Tunnel Box	0	41
Tan-y-Grisiau–Dinas Junction	0	74
Dinas Junction–Festiniog & Blaenau Junction	0	36
Festiniog & Blaenau Junction–Duffws	0	12
	3 m	5 c

Single Lines of Railway (not included in foregoing) worked under the *Train Staff System;*

Portmadoc–Boston Lodge Box	1	8
Minffordd–Tan-y-Bwlch	5	44
Tan-y-Bwlch–S. End Tunnel Box	2	44
N. End Tunnel Box–Tan-y-Grisiau	0	79
	10 m	15 c

Board of Trade Return dated 31 December 1889

Absolute Block
(As above but second line reads;)

Dduallt–North End Tunnel Box	0	76
(Total)	3 m	40 c

Single Lines (as above)
(As above but third line reads:)

Tan-y-Bwlch–Dduallt	2	19
(Total)	9 m	60 c

The locomotives were fitted with two whistles of different size. The England engines had them on the tank top, and the double engines at one end of the cab. When shunting wagons into either the Great Western or London & North Western yards, the junction points were moved from No. 2 signal box. Three blasts on the small whistle instructed the signalman to change the points for the G.W. yard: three on the large the L.N.W.R. yard. On 11 October 1920 the small whistle failed on *Prince* and the driver, thinking that the signalman could see him despite a thick mist, gave three blasts on his L.N.W.R. whistle, intending to enter the G.W.R. yard. The engine started forward, propelling its wagons but the signalman changed the L.N.W.R. junction points under the train and derailed the slate wagons. These caught the engine under the buffer beam and threw it on its side. Fortunately the men escaped with a shaking.

As early as 2 October 1860 Joseph Morton of Liverpool sent an

Block Signalling Diagram 1893.
INCORPORATING A SKETCH BY J.E. WHITTALL, SIGNAL ENG.

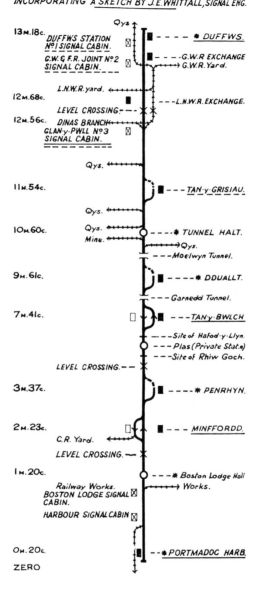

Qys.

13 M.18c.   DUFFWS STATION ⊠ ■ — — — ✱ DUFFWS.
No 1 SIGNAL CABIN.

G.W. & F.R. JOINT No 2 ⊠ ■ — — — G.W.R EXCHANGE
SIGNAL CABIN.   →→ G.W.R. Yard.

L.N.W.R. yard. ←←←←←

12 M.68c.   ■ — — — L.N.W.R. EXCHANGE.

LEVEL CROSSING — — ✕✕

12 M.56c.   DINAS BRANCH ←←←
GLAN-y-PWLL No 3 ⊠
SIGNAL CABIN.

Qys. ←←←←←←←

11 M.54c.   ■ — — — TAN-y-GRISIAU.

Qys. ←←←←←←←

10 M.60c.   Qys. ←←←←← ○ — — — — ✱ TUNNEL HALT.
Mine. ←←←←←←←
→→ Qys.

— — Moelwyn Tunnel.

9 M.61c.   ■ — — — — ✱ DDUALLT.

— — Garnedd Tunnel.

7 M.41c.   □ ■ — — — TAN-y-BWLCH

— — Site of Hafod-y-Llyn.
○ — — — Plas (Private Stat.n)
— — — Site of Rhiw Goch.

LEVEL CROSSING — — ✕

3 M.37c.   ■ — — — — ✱ PENRHYN.

2 M.23c.   □ ■ — — — MINFFORDD.

C.R. Yard. ←←←←←

LEVEL CROSSING. — ✕

1 M.20c.   ○ — — — ✱ Boston Lodge Hall
Railway Works.   →→→→→ Works.
BOSTON LODGE SIGNAL ⊠
CABIN.

HARBOUR SIGNAL CABIN ⊠

0 M.20c.   ■ — — ✱ PORTMADOC HARB.

ZERO

STATION & JUNCTION NAMES WITH SOLID UNDERLINES ARE BLOCK
POSTS FOR PASSENGER TRAINS CROSSING.
PLACES WITH BROKEN UNDERLINES ARE BLOCK POSTS FOR LIGHT
ENGINE OR MINERAL TRAINS CROSSING.
✱ DENOTES NON CROSSING BLOCK POSTS.

estimate for installing Single Needle Telegraph Instruments along the whole line, the wires to be carried over the Tunnel, for £227 3*s*. 7*d*. Instead, the Tunnel only was later fitted out for £130.

At the insistence of the B.O.T. Inspector, Spagnoletti's Telegraph had been put into Moelwyn Tunnel by 4 February 1865 and there was bell telegraph over Wrysgan and Cwm Orthin Inclines. On 27 October previously the Inspector complained that an existing system of bells through the Tunnel 'do not work well'.

The stations were connected by telegraph in 1869–71 and before Tyer's instruments were in use the arrival of a train at a station was telegraphed back to the preceding station by the signalman. 'Train started' was telegraphed to the next forward station when the train moved off. By 1889 the single needle telegraph linked:

Boston Lodge–Minffordd
Dduallt–Tunnel North
Tan-y-Grisiau–Duffws

By 1883 only part of the railway had been equipped with block telegraph, for which Tyer's two position semaphore instruments were used. Most of them survived until the block signalling fell into disuse, and as the spelling of the Welsh station names was rather beyond the makers of the brass plates which they carried, some extraordinary place names resulted.

Owing to the heavy traffic in slate, etc., moving on the section between Minffordd and the Harbour, the following rule was in force:

254. No passenger train and no slate train to be started from the Minford [*sic*] station and Minford Weighing Office for the Port without first telegraphing Is Line Clear? to the Telegraph Signalman at Signal Box, Boston Lodge, at South end of Embankment, and not to start the Passenger Train or Slate Train till receiving a reply Line Clear from the Boston Lodge Signal Box.

Until 1912 when part of the line had the Electric Train Staff installed and the existing Block Telegraph System removed, the single line working was controlled by staff and ticket. There were five sections: Portmadoc/Boston Lodge: Boston Lodge/Minffordd: Minffordd/Tan-y-Bwlch: Tan-y-Bwlch/Tan-y-Grisiau: Tan-y-Grisiau/Cabin No. 3. Except at Boston Lodge and Cabin No. 3, the instruments were installed in the station buildings or (as at Minffordd and Tan-y-Bwlch) in the small outbuildings forming part of the station premises. On the closure of Cabin No. 3, the instruments there were removed to the booking office of the L.M.S.R. Exchange station; this took place in 1925. Up to 1912 the tickets were printed blue. The staffs were robust tokens of wood, about 15 in. long and 2 in. diameter, having a brass

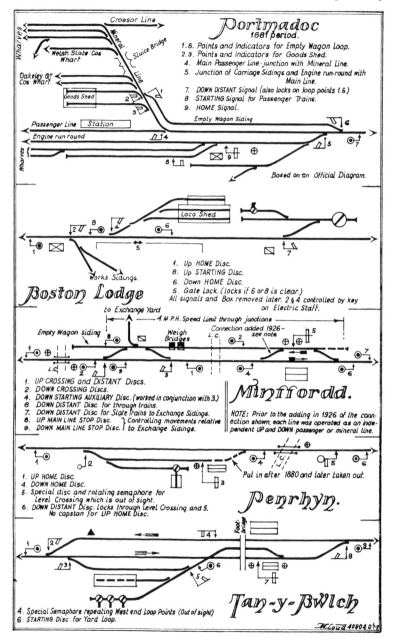

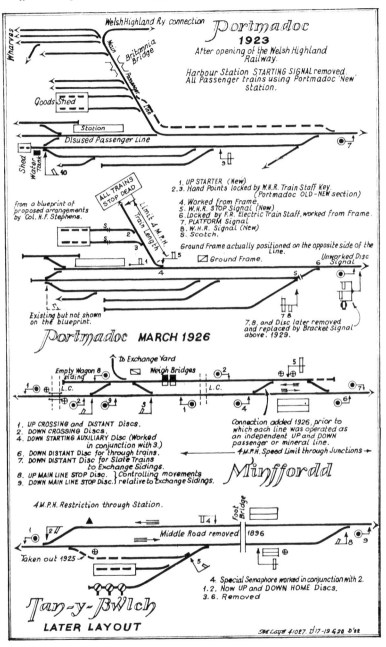

Portmadoc 1923
After opening of the Welsh Highland Railway.

Harbour Station STARTING SIGNAL removed.
All Passenger trains using Portmadoc 'New' station.

Welsh Highland Ry connection

Wharves

Britannia Bridge

Main

Passenger Line

Goods Shed

Station

Disused Passenger Line

Shed   Water Tank   40

from a blueprint of proposed arrangements by Col. H.F. Stephens.

ALL TRAINS STOP DEAD

Limit 4 M.P.H. Train Length

1. UP STARTER (New)
2.3. Hand Points locked by W.H.R. Train Staff Key. (Portmadoc OLD-NEW section)
4. Worked from Frame.
5. W.H.R. STOP Signal (New)
6. Locked by F.R. Electric Train Staff, worked from Frame.
7. PLATFORM Signal
8. W.H.R. Signal (New)
S. Scotch.

Ground Frame actually positioned on the opposite side of the Line.
☐ Ground Frame.

Unworked Disc Signal

Existing but not shown on the blueprint.

7.8, and Disc later removed and replaced by Bracket Signal above. 1929.

Portmadoc MARCH 1926

to Exchange Yard

Empty Wagon & siding   Weigh Bridges

L.C.   L.C.

1. UP CROSSING and DISTANT Discs.
2. DOWN CROSSING Discs.
4. DOWN STARTING AUXILIARY Disc (Worked in conjunction with 3.)
6. DOWN DISTANT Disc for through trains.
7. DOWN DISTANT Disc for Slate Trains to Exchange Sidings.
8. UP MAIN LINE STOP Disc. } Controlling movements
9. DOWN MAIN LINE STOP Disc. } relative to Exchange Sidings.

Connection added 1926, prior to which each line was operated as an independent UP and DOWN passenger or mineral line.
← 4 M.P.H. Speed Limit through Junctions →

Minffordd

4 M.P.H. Restriction through Station.

Foot Bridge

Middle Road removed | 1896

Taken out 1925

4. Special Semaphore worked in conjunction with 2.
1.2. Now UP and DOWN HOME Discs.
3.6. Removed

Tan-y-Bwlch
LATER LAYOUT

M Layt 41027. D 17-19 & 28 D'22

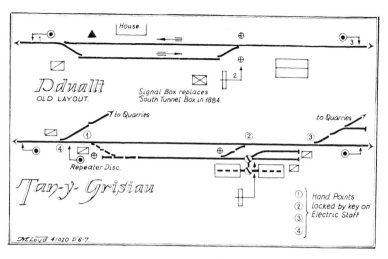

Dduallt
OLD LAYOUT.

House

Signal Box replaces
South Tunnel Box in 1884.

to Quarries

to Quarries

Tan-y-Grisiau

Repeater Disc.

① ⎫
② ⎬ Hand Points
③ ⎬ locked by key on
④ ⎭ Electric Staff

M.Lloyd. 41020 D'6·7.

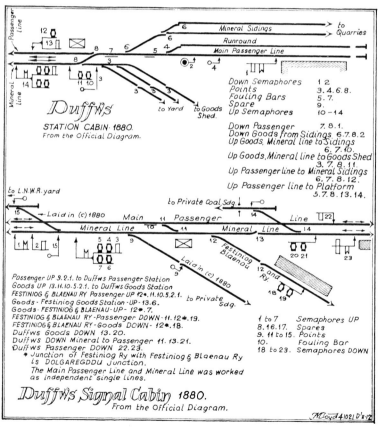

Passenger line

Mineral Siding

to Quarries

Mineral Sidings

Runround

Main Passenger Line

Mineral line

Duffws

STATION CABIN · 1880.
From the Official Diagram.

to Yard

to Goods
Shed.

Down Semaphores   1 2
Points   3. 4. 6. 8.
Fouling Bars   5. 7.
Spare   9.
Up Semaphores   10 – 14

Down Passenger   7. 8. 1.
Down Goods from Sidings 6. 7. 8. 2
Up Goods, Mineral line to Sidings
                             6. 7. 10.
Up Goods, Mineral line to Goods Shed
                           3. 7. 8. 11.
Up Passenger line to Mineral Sidings
                           6. 7. 8. 12.
Up Passenger line to Platform
                           5. 7. 8. 13. 14.

to L.N.W.R. yard

Laid in (c) 1880

Main   Passenger   Line

to Private Coal Sdg.

Mineral Line

Mineral   Line

Laid in (c) 1880

to Private
Sdg.

Festiniog and
Blaenau Ry.

Passenger UP 9.2.1. to Duffws Passenger Station
Goods UP 13.11.10.5.2.1. to Duffws Goods Station
FESTINIOG & BLAENAU RY Passenger UP 12*.11.10.5.2.1.
Goods - Festiniog Goods Station - UP - 13.6.
Goods - FESTINIOG & BLAENAU - UP - 12*.7.
FESTINIOG & BLAENAU RY - Passenger DOWN - 11.12*.19.
FESTINIOG & BLAENAU RY - Goods DOWN - 12*.18.
Duffws Goods DOWN 13. 20.
Duffws DOWN Mineral to Passenger 11. 13. 21.
Duffws Passenger DOWN 22. 23.
    * Junction of Festiniog Ry with Festiniog & Blaenau Ry
    is DOLGAREGDDU Junction.
    The Main Passenger Line and Mineral Line was worked
    as independent single lines.

1 to 7   Semaphores UP
8. 16. 17.   Spares
9. 11 to 15. Points
10.   Fouling Bar
18 to 23.   Semaphores DOWN

Duffws Signal Cabin 1880.
From the Official Diagram.

M.Lloyd 41021 D'11·12

1R *Top left: Early wooden slate wagon—inside bearings, No. 390.*   (*J. I. C. Boyd*)

Top right: Iron coal wagon, Harbour 1943.   (*J. I. C. Boyd*)

Middle left: Large bolster wagons., G.W. yard 1944.   (*J. I. C. Boyd*)

Middle right: Various wagons at Portmadoc wharves, including gunpowder and small bolsters; open No. 20.   (*J. Richards*)

Bottom left: No. 5 Brakevan (converted from Quarrymen's coach), Glan-y-Pwll 1939.
(*J. I. C. Boyd*)

Bottom right: 'Col. Stephen's Crane', Boston Lodge 1929.   (*J. I. C. Boyd*)

2R   *Small open wagon (inside bearings) and iron ex Horse Dandy No. 50, Harbour, 1943.*
(J. I. C. Boyd)

3R   *3 Ton slate wagon from 'Official' Spooner Album collection of 1887. Not a very typical specimen; ratchet brake fitting and sprung buffing gear not common. Probably built 1871.*   *(F.R. Co.)*

4R   *Early fixed low-side open wagon, probably used for cask etc. traffic. Note sprung buffers, inside bearings and Baines' loco turntable beneath.*   *(F.R. Co.)*

5R Boston Lodge Yard with (right to left) No. 27, 1 Ton sack truck; No. 3, 2 Ton high side wagon; No. 314, wooden slate wagon; a flat wagon; No. 8, 6-wheeled open as roofed.   (J. I. C. Boyd)

6R Open wagon for coal, etc., traffic, with side discharging doors and pillar brake screw. Cob, 1887.   (F.R. Co.)

7R Cleminson 6-wheeled wagon and Hearse Van (former Quarrymen's coach). Boston Lodge 1956.   (J. I. C. Boyd)

8R *Down Saturdays Only Quarrymen's train at Creuau in 1871, with 30 of the 3*
existing Type 1 Quarrymen's vehicles in the rake. Train stands on site of Tan-y-Bwlch

9R Palmerston *at Harbour in the 1920s; winter train formation.*   *(J. I. C. Boyd)*

ion, not then built. 'First Stone' Site extreme right. (*J. Owen*)

10R *Plate 8R shows the earliest passenger stock; this austere vehicle was one of a batch supplied by Robert Hudson Ltd in 1923, known as 'Toastracks'.* (*Robt. Hudson Ltd.*)

11R No. 11 Open Class and No. 1 semi-enclosed First Class coaches on Cob, 1887. (Coach on left originally without roof and ends; by 1887 was designated Third Class). Screw couplings, with hooks Up end only. (F.R. Co.)

12R No. 1 (see above) awaiting scrap at Boston Lodge 1932. Note; Vacuum brake piping, safety mesh and 'Observation Car'. (H. C. Casserley)

13R No. 6 on Cob in 1929. Small windows and boarded sides have replaced earlier panelling. (R. W. Kidner)

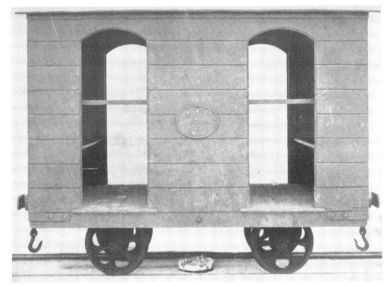

14R   *Official Photograph of Type 2 Quarrymen's vehicle.*   (F.R. Co.)

15R   *Covered Type 1 and Type 2 Quarrymen's stock behind* Merddin Emrys *(no centre roof to cab) Duffws c. 1876.*   (J. I. C. Boyd)

16R   *Rebuilt small bogie van No. 2. Harbour 1936.*   (G. F. Parker)

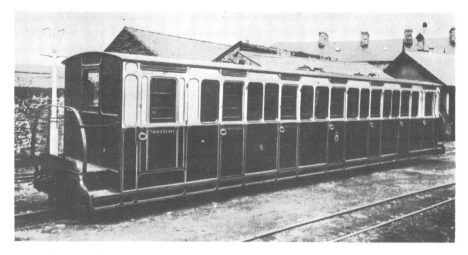

17R   *No. 16 at Harbour 1874.*   *(F.R. Co.)*

18R   *No. 20 of 1879 after conversion of one Second Class compartment to Third. (F.R. Co.)*

19R   *Harbour in the mid-1930s with typical passenger train formation.*   *(R. W. Kidner)*

cap each end on one of which there was a short chain to which was attached the key for the ticket box. A brass plate was affixed, one example reading: 'Tan-y-Bwlch and . . .'. As the other block point is not stated it is assumed the staffs were painted to designate them as applying to the section either Up or Down of the issuing station. The staff boxes were of the large cumbersome pattern associated with this type of staff, and from surviving drawings, it appears that the Company made their own instruments and staffs. (The portion of the Welsh Highland not equipped with Wise's staff used similar equipment.) New staff boxes were made in 1893 and new staffs in 1900. Miniature Electric Staff between Tan-y-Bwlch and Glan-y-Pwll was not put in until 1919, and it was applied to the remainder of the system in 1921–2.

Copies of correspondence of the period 1900–1 between Saunders & Co. and the Company contain information on the telegraph system; single needle telegraph instruments were installed at Portmadoc, Minffordd station, Penrhyn, Tan-y-Bwlch, Dduallt, Tunnel, Tan-y-Grisiau, No. 3 Cabin, Blaenau and Duffws (these names are copied from an official list). The instruments were connected by single wire, with earth return. In addition there was a Phonophone circuit with instruments at Portmadoc, Boston Lodge Box, Boston Lodge Office and Minffordd Weigh Bridge; this was used in connection with working slate wagons by the Bottom Shunting Engine. The telephone replaced the original single needle telegraph and connected Portmadoc, Minffordd station, Penrhyn, Tan-y-Bwlch, Dduallt, Tunnel Cottage, Tan-y-Grisiau, No. 3 Cabin, Blaenau and Duffws (names as given in 1901 list). At this same period, the block telegraph instruments between Dduallt and Duffws No. 1 were of the single needle type with single stroke bells—Saunders were suggesting that they could be replaced by Tyer's instruments as they had recently been offered a number '. . . quite equal to new for practical purposes'. The first telephone of 1890 was a direct line between the Harbour station and Minffordd weighbridge.

The special repeating signal in connection with the gates at Penrhyn level crossing, was erected in December 1900 at the express wish of the gravity train crews. A month prior to this, the Down repeating signal at Tan-y-Bwlch supplied by McKenzie & Holland was taken down. The reason for its removal was that the post was rotten and unsafe, but it is curious that a new post was not fitted.

The signalmen at the small Boston Lodge cabin (which was more of a 'bothy' than a signal cabin, the three signal quadrants being outside anyway) worked in two shifts: 5.20 a.m.–2.20 p.m. and 12 noon–9 p.m. (one hour being deducted for meals). The signalman also assisted with shunting and turning locos; the afternoon shift included two hours daily labour at the Works.*

* See also *F.R. Magazine*, No. 39, p. 3.

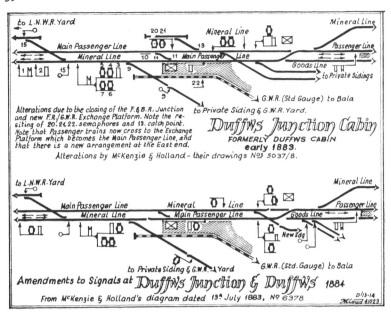

to L.N.W.R.Yard

Alterations due to the closing of the F.&B.R. Junction and new F.R./G.W.R. Exchange Platform. Note the re-siting of 20.21.22. semaphores and 13. catch point. Note that Passenger trains now cross to the Exchange Platform which becomes the Main Passenger Line, and that there is a new arrangement at the East end.
Alterations by McKenzie & Holland - their drawings Nºs 5037/8.

Duffws Junction Cabin
FORMERLY DUFFWS CABIN
early 1883.

Amendments to Signals at Duffws Junction & Duffws 1884
From McKenzie & Holland's diagram dated 13ᵗʰ July 1883, Nº 6378

    Simplification of signalling under the Light Railway Order was complete by 1926 and inspected on 6–7 October that year by the Board of Trade but even before the Order was granted the Company had taken steps 'to do away with all signalling . . .' (which was a most irregular move).
    Prior to the Order Tan-y-Grisiau had been relegated to a Train-Following station, where passenger trains could not pass each other, but a passenger and a goods, or two goods trains could do so. This avoided putting a second passenger train 'inside' the loop. East of Blaenau (L.M.S. Exchange) the Miniature Electric Staff system was not extended, instead, simple staff and ticket working survived. As all cabins had been removed, two-lever ground frames (supplied by The Railway Signal Company) locked by the staff took their place though the loops at Minffordd and Tan-y-Bwlch retained hand-worked weighted levers set for directing traffic into their loop lines. By Autumn 1926 there were eight new situations where ground frames were locked by the staff, in addition to seven existing sites. At places where gated crossings existed, these were retained, together with 'the old fashioned signals' [*sic*] which were not interlocked, however. On Glan-y-Pwll Cabin No. 3 being dispensed with, the gates were now worked by a gatekeeper and, in view of the bad sighting, a speed restriction of 5 m.p.h. was imposed.
    At the west end of the line, 'Portmadoc Old Station' lost its existing home and starting signals, and a ground frame of six levers (one spare)

was installed. This worked the junction points with the Welsh High-land. Four McKenzie & Holland semaphores were retained here, the old double-arm semaphore with one of these arms on the post below it finally disappearing in 1929 when replaced by a three-arm bracket signal. The old disc distant was retained, unworked, until then also. The sidings loop line from which several wharf lines emanated, was connected at the south end by a point with a single lever ground frame.

At Boston Lodge there was an occupation instrument; this was removed. The three junctions were given a ground frame each. The Inspector insisted that the staff be kept at Portmadoc or Minffordd overnight and fetched when it was required to bring an engine from Works or Shed . . . a recommendation which was honoured in the breach.

At the Cwm Orthin Quarry junction, a single lever ground frame existed; this also controlled a scotch on the siding which was a danger in itself, plus a trap on the loop. Incline working was carried out under the supervision of the Tan-y-Grisiau station master.

The simplified yard at Duffws and the pointwork between passenger and mineral lines hereabouts was all done by hand-worked levers which the Government Inspector did not like. Colonel Stephens revised these arrangements.

A speed limit of 15 m.p.h. was imposed over the whole railway, with a 5 m.p.h. limit over loop points.

From 1922 the main developments can be summarised:

July: G.W.R. agree to pay half costs of No. 2 cabin, Blaenau Festiniog.
October: Special signals at north end of Tunnel removed.
December: Proposal to dispense with gatekeeper at Minffordd and install warning bells. Not proceeded with on account of cost.
1923
March: J. B. Saunders & Co. taken over by G.W.R. thus ending F.R. maintenance contract of 28 November 1918, and N.W.N.G. Rlys. contract of 16 September 1912. After this, F.R. and W.H.R. appoint own linesmen.
May: Col. Stephens unfamiliar with Festiniog signalling, asks Tyrwhitt for a description and receives reply: '. . . in the section Tan-y-Grisiau to Portmadoc inclusive the signalling is much the same type that the *Rocket* worked by . . .'.
June: M.O.T. agrees to signals being removed Portmadoc/Tan-y-Grisiau but not to cattle guards at Glan-y-Pwll.
August: Proposed put in new passing loop on west side north of Tunnel mouth. Not proceeded with.
October: Boston Lodge cabin closed. Staff section becomes Harbour/Minffordd and if staff not on engine when in shed, necessity to walk

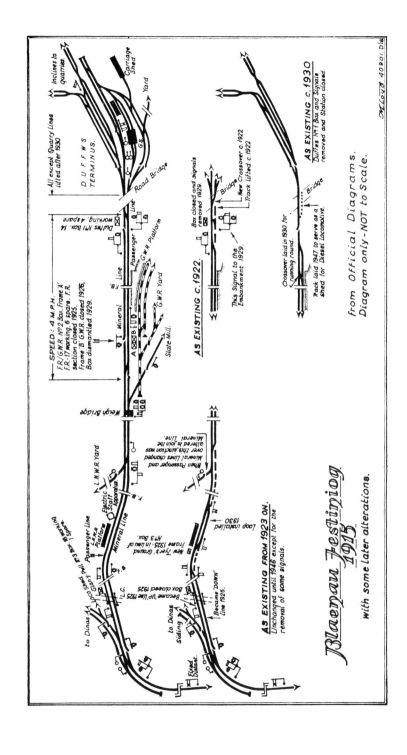

Blaenau Festiniog
1915
with some later alterations.

from Official Diagrams.
Diagram only - NOT to Scale.

AS EXISTING FROM 1923 ON.
Unchanged until 1946 except for the
removal of some signals.

AS EXISTING c.1922.

AS EXISTING c.1930
Duffws Nº1 Box and Signals
removed and Station closed.

DUFFWS TERMINUS.

Carriage Shed

Inclines to quarries

All except Quarry Lines
lifted after 1930

Road Bridge

G.S.

Yard

SPEED : 4 M.P.H.
F.R./G.W.R. Nº2 Box. Frame 'A'
F.R.-17 working 6 spare. F.R.
section closed 1925.
Frame 'B' G.W.R. closed 1926,
Box dismantled 1929.

Duffws Nº1 Box. 14
working, 4 spare

Passenger Line

G.W.R. Platform

Mineral Line

F.R. Line

A B C

G.W.R. Yard

Slate Mill.

Weigh Bridge

Box closed and signals
removed 1929.

This Signal to the
Embankment 1929.

Bridge

New Crossover c.1922
Track lifted 1922

Crossover laid in 1930 for
running round.

Track laid 1947 to serve as a
shed for Diesel Locomotive.

Bridge

When Passenger and
Mineral Lines changed
over this junction was
altered to join the
Mineral Line.

L.N.W.R. Yard

Electric Staff
Apparatus

to Dinas

Loco Shed

L.N.W.R.
Platform

Passenger Line

Mineral Line

Nº3 Box & Spare
working

L.C.

to Dinas
Siding

Became 'UP' Line 1925.

Box closed 1925.

Became 'DOWN'
Line 1925.

Loop installed
1930

New Tyer's Ground
Frame 1925, in lieu of
Nº3 Box.

Fixed
Distant.

The Lloyd 40901. D/6

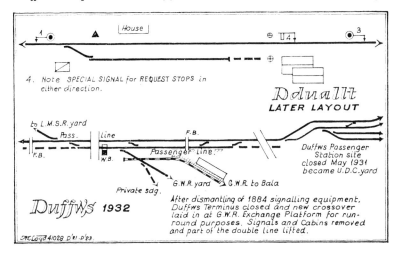

to either of these stations to fetch it. Proposed that Company buy a push bike for this purpose!

December: Sections as follows:

Harbour/Minffordd	Miniature Electric Train Staff.
Minffordd/Penrhyn	⌠ Becomes one section Minffordd/
Penrhyn/Tan-y-Bwlch	⌡ Tan-y-Bwlch 4 December 1923.
	Miniature Electric Train Staff.
Tan-y-Bwlch/Tan-y-Grisiau	⌠ Becomes one section Tan-y-Bwlch/
Tan-y-Grisiau/No. 3 Cabin	⌡ No. 3 Cabin 21 January 1924.
	Miniature Electric Train Staff.

1924

May: Capt. May (Superintendent) discovers the old ticket boxes and staffs used prior to 1912 and suggests economy would result if M.O.T. were to give permission for railway to revert to these in place of M.E.T.S. Colonel Stephens tells Jack exactly what he thinks of Captain May and his suggestion!

June: All signals at Blaenau to go: Glan-y-Pwll cabin to close.

December: Private phone in box at Plas private station removed.

1925

June: 5-lever Tyer's ground frame for Blaenau Festiniog (L.M.S.R. Exchange) station, delivered. Type B5. To replace No. 3 Cabin.

August: M.E.T.S. instruments and phone from No. 3 Cabin removed to Exchange station building.

September: No. 3 Cabin closed; signals disconnected and Glan-y-Pwll gates now worked by crossing-keeper. Locos to give 3 whistles on Up trains when $\frac{1}{4}$ mile from crossing and 2 whistles when on Down trains about to leave L.M.S.R. Exchange. Revised arrangements of running lines as follows:

'Trains will work along old mineral line between new points worked by new 5-lever ground frame and the bottom of No. 12 points, Glan-y-Pwll. No train to pass along section until signals connected to 5-lever frame are off.'

October: Staff and ticket working inaugurated between L.M.S.R. Exchange and Duffws station. This the result of lax working on the section; in previous month two engines had been working in section, neither carrying staff. One had run down to Glan-y-Pwll shed to turn and had reached L.M.S.R. Exchange when it saw Up train approaching; it was obliged to reverse at once and run into a siding. Staff and ticket introduced as drivers all refused to work without a staff when on Top Shunting Engine; prior to this the acceptance of an Up train depended on the No. 3 Cabin signalman knowing the whereabouts of the Top Shunter and putting it in a siding. Drivers refused to work by this system after the above experience.

During 1925 the back-to-back, interlocked frames of No. 2 Cabin were disconnected from each other and the Festiniog signals dismantled. Festiniog points were connected to local frames. Thereafter the G.W.R. frame (actually a 13-lever ground frame) was used for shunting movements only. A new central signal box was erected by the G.W.R. (the latterday structure) and brought into use 28 September 1926. This combined two original boxes, one being the No. 2 Cabin. This cabin released a ground frame operating Festiniog points leading to a diamond crossing of Festiniog and standard gauge metals; this layout was amended later and the crossing removed.

G.W.R. removed their frame from No. 2 Cabin in January 1929 and the Festiniog their own in April. (The cabin had thus lain out of use for four years, so far as the Festiniog was concerned.) Demolition was completed by late April. The cost of working this cabin was £61 in 1913 and £295 in 1921.

1926

July: Banking engine staff installed by Railway Signal Co. at Tan-y-Grisiau. Did not come into use until January 1928. Was source of considerable trouble to certain Festiniog personnel: Top Shunter would work down to Brookes' Quarry with it and returning, forget to return the staff to the instrument, completely locking-in the next Up train as a result. Harbour station signalling renewed.

1927

June: Portmadoc (Harbour)/Portmadoc (New) provided with new Tyer's staffs and ticket boxes sanctioned by Colonel Mount's inspection of May 1923.

1929

January to May: No. 1 Cabin and signalling at Duffws dismantled. Three-arm bracket signal (ex-Duffws) on Cob as calling-on signal to bring engines and trains into Harbour station or to Highland line.

Operating

For the first nine months the railway was worked by day labour, and from then, let out by contract—a convenient way of avoiding the expense of stables, horses and manpower which the Company would have had to meet had they provided their own haulage.

The earliest contract to survive is one dated 6 November 1838, and gives Morgan Jones of Rhiw Goch the right to work traffic over the railway. James Spooner signs for the Railway Company with Thomas Pritchard as witness. Morgan Jones makes 'his mark'. In this agreement Jones undertakes to find horses and carters [*sic*] 'to convey all slates raised . . . at the Rhiwbryfdir Slate Quarries . . . from the Quays opposite Rhiwbryfdir House to the Quays at Port Madoc at the rate of seven pence per Ton, and to carry all back carriage at a rate of two and six pence per Ton . . . the Railway Coy. to undertake to find all waggons or trucks and keep the same in repair except the broken rails of the Rail Waggons which shall be subject to a fine hereafter mentioned . . . also to . . . oil all the waggons and clean same, the aforesaid Morgan Jones furnishing the oil at his own cost for doing so and the waggons to be oiled at each end of the journey . . .

. . . for locking the wheels by break or breaks with cord, chain, or any other material or using any other contrivance than the Hand for applying the same and for stopping the train by anything than the Break . . .' Jones would be fined 5s. There were also fines for blocking tracks near points, taking wagons off the rails to unload them, persons removing wagons from trains, and other causes. The time allowed for the carriage of Down slate was eighteen daylight hours from the time of loading.

Jones held this contract for a period and on 31 March 1849 a rather different contract was let out to Robert Roberts of Pensyflog. Here the rate was 5d. per ton, and he had to make the journey in two and a half hours. (This was amended in the Agreement from two hours.)

Under an Agreement between the Welsh Slate Co. and the Railway in 1841, the Quarry was to have the first opportunity of refusal if the haulage was let out (presumably if a fresh contractor had to be found and the W.S.Co. was left without means of moving its traffic).

Roberts was re-empowered by successive renewals, and a typical one is dated 10 February 1855: in this the contractor undertakes the haulage and carriage 'from the Railway Terminus at the quarries to portmadoc' (not given a capital letter) 'of all slates and slabs at a rate of sixpence per

ton . . . and starting and arrival of trains shall be regulated by the said
James Spooner . . . the time allowed for the arrival of the train being
two hours after its departure and eight hours after it leaves the quays
at portmadoc . . . Robert Roberts shall be answerable for all the
Bushes as also for the damage to the wheels by an improper application
of the break or by any other means which entirely prevents the wheels
from turning round . . .'. He was responsible for the Back Carriage
(i.e. Up traffic) and was given a shed at Glan-y-Pwll as an office, etc.

Other clauses forbade Roberts to carry hay or straw in trains, but
allowed the Company to carry up to half a ton of materials in any train
for track repairs, for carriage of which Roberts was not payable. Roberts
had also to provide 'Sheat tin cases' in which to carry the weigh bills,
and straps to suspend these tins from the driver's shoulders. Roberts
was liable to a fine if the weigh bills were forgotten, mislaid, not delivered
or not carried in the correct tin. From this last note it seems that each
quarry had its own tins for the bills.

Four horses were used for each stage of the journey; each train
comprised twenty-five wagons.

The earliest timetable at present known relates to the period when
Roberts would be working this traffic (see Timetable 1). The table was
laid out in peculiar form. After passenger services began tables set out
under the heading of each station were used in the preparation of small
card timetables in the manner of the modern pocket timetable, which
were presumably for the convenience of operating staff and purely
applicable to arrivals and departures at their own place of working. No
workings are shown beyond Boston Lodge (the weigh-house point), and
tolerance of five minutes over and above that shown in the table was not
permissible except in case of accidents. Trains were to take at least
eighteen minutes between stations and not exceed ten miles an hour on
Down runs; wagon trains were numbered but the unconventional
timetable layout meant the number changed en route.

Some curiosities of this timetable include the apparent printing error
whereby Down Train No. 1 was timed to arrive and depart from the
Tunnel at 7.48 a.m. leaving no time for a change of horses. In the Up
table the departure of Train No. 6 from Hafod-y-Llyn at 6.28 a.m. and
the next one from Cae Ednyfed at 5.54 a.m. should be noted. This is
more likely to have arisen from a convenient arrangement for both
horses and men in relation to their sleeping accommodation, etc.,
rather than some complexity of train operating. Again, the trains in
the last Down column are two quite separate workings and it is possible
that the 5.04 a.m. from Boston Lodge became train No. 6 of the Up
table. There is no evidence today of the amount of stable accommodation at either Rhiw Goch or Hafod-y-Llyn and they had no smithies;
Boston Lodge and Cae Ednyfed at the bottom end, and Quarry Terminus

at the top end, were the largest stables where a smithy and a good proportion of the available horses would be kept; it could be that some of the more curious workings were connected with trains which did not carry slate but men, fodder, horses or stores. There was a small stable near Tafarn Trip used by a local driver.

TIMETABLE No. 1   16 September 1856

DOWN TRAINS		6	1 a.m.	2	3	4 p.m.	5	6
Quarry		....	7.30	9.28	11.16	1.14	3.12	5.10
Tunnel	arr.	....	7.48	9.36	11.34	1.32	3.30	5.28
	dep.	....	7.48	9.46	11.44	1.42	3.40	5.38
Hafod-y-Llyn	arr.	....	8.06	10.04	12.02	2.00	3.58	5.56
	dep.	....	8.16	10.14	12.12	2.10	4.08	6.06
Rhiw Goch	arr.	....	8.34	10.32	12.30	2.28	4.26	6.24
	dep.	6.46	8.44	10.42	12.40	2.38	4.36	★
Cae Ednyfed		....	....	....	....	....	....	....
Boston Lodge		7.04	9.02	11.00	12.58	2.56	4.54	....

UP TRAINS		6	1	2	3	4	5	6	7
Boston Lodge	dep.	....	....	7.14	9.12	11.10	1.08	3.06	5.04
Cae Ednyfed		....	5.54	....	....	p.m.	....	....	5.34
Rhiw Goch	arr.	....	....	8.34	10.32	12.30	2.28	4.26	....
	dep.	....	6.46	8.44	10.42 p.m.	12.40	2.38	4.36	6.34
Hafod-y-Llyn	arr.		8.06	10.04	12.02	2.00	3.58	5.56	7.54
	dep.	6.28†	8.16	10.14	12.12	2.10	4.08	6.06	....
Tunnel	arr.	....	9.36	11.34	1.32	3.30	5.28	7.26	....
	dep.	7.58	9.46	11.44 p.m.	1.42	3.40	5.38	....	....
Quarry		9.18	11.06	1.04	3.02	5.00	6.58	....	....

   ★ Stops at Cae Ednyfed overnight and becomes 6.46 a.m. morning train.
   † Empty wagon working.
   (The table is a modern layout of the original.)

It will be noted that trains were booked to pass each other at Tunnel, Hafod-y-Llyn and Cae Ednyfed; ten minutes were allowed for the change-over between Up and Down trains at loops. In this event, horses would merely walk from the head of the Up train to the Dandies in the rear of the Down train which, of course, would be standing at the same end of the loop. At the same time those horses which had rested in the Dandies as the Down train descended, would walk across and be attached to the Up train. This process would be repeated at each 'station'.

The horse-changing stations (as opposed to the points in the time-table where trains passed each other) would be:

Tunnel (south end); Hafod-y-Llyn; Rhiw Goch; Boston Lodge and the foregoing arrangement broke the line into four sections of roughly the same length. These were:

Quarry–Tunnel (south)
Tunnel (south)–Hafod-y-Llyn
Hafod-y-Llyn–Rhiw Goch
Rhiw Goch–Boston Lodge
Boston Lodge–Harbour

Summarising this procedure, as traffic grew a Down train would require up to four horses for each stage or section—as already mentioned—or sixteen horses for the full length of line; it seems that the stable at Tafarn Trip (between Hafod-y-Llyn and Tunnel (south)) provided horses for the changing points at these two places; and the stable at Cae Ednyfed (Minffordd) supplied Boston Lodge and Rhiw Goch. The availabilities were clearly operated variously as required.*

There was some anxiety felt when the changeover from horses to locomotives was made, as the services of the contractor had been dispensed with, and the locomotives had not proved efficient on trial. However, at the eleventh hour the locomotives were put into a reliable condition. The actual table concerned would be put into operation during the second week in August 1863, if it is assumed that locomotive working began on the anticipated date. However, the form this took is not known, although Timetable No. 2 shows the arrangements adopted for October 1863.

TIMETABLE NO. 2							October 1863
UP TRAINS							
Portmadoc		7.00	9.00	11.00	1.00	3.00	5.00
Penrhyn	arr.	7.20	9.20	11.20	1.20	3.20	5.20
	dep.	7.25	9.25	11.25	1.25	3.25	5.25
Hafod-y-Llyn	arr.	7.50	9.50	11.50	1.50	3.50	5.50
	dep.	8.00	10.00	12.00	2.00	4.00	6.00
Tan-y-Grisiau	arr.	8.35	10.35	12.35	2.35	4.35	6.35
	dep.	8.40	10.40	12.40	2.40	4.40	6.40
Rhiw		8.50	10.50	12.50	2.50	4.50	6.50

* See also *F.R. Magazine*, No. 44, p. 16.

DOWN TRAINS

Rhiw		7.00	9.00	11.00	1.00	3.00	5.00
Tan-y-Grisiau	arr.	7.10	9.10	11.10	1.10	3.10	5.10
	dep.	7.15	9.15	11.15	1.15	3.15	5.15
Hafod-y-Llyn	arr.	7.50	9.50	11.50	1.50	3.50	5.50
	dep.	8.00	10.00	12.00	2.00	4.00	6.00
Penrhyn	arr.	8.25	10.25	12.25	2.25	4.25	6.25
	dep.	8.30	10.30	12.30	2.30	4.30	6.30
Portmadoc		8.50	10.50	12.50	2.50	4.50	6.50

The clean and inversely proportional timings of this arrangement are most unusual, as is also the layout, which is not as set out above but is divided into two parts numbered No. 1 and No. 2. The upper part relates to both Up and Down trains as between Portmadoc and Hafod-y-Llyn only, and the lower to the Hafod-y-Llyn and Rhiw section. This suggests the engines were shedded at each end of the line and the railway operated in two halves, one engine having ten minutes at the terminus of its section to change trains, take coal and water, etc. The arrangement would therefore call for smart working and turnround.

The same table was used as a basis for a new timetable which seems to have come into force in April 1864 and lasted until the next September. Thereafter there is a footnote that it would continue in force until March 1865 with only five trains each day (times not stated) running one hour twelve minutes later and ending one hour twelve minutes later each day as compared with its predecessor. The table beginning April 1864 has additional longhand notes inserted of some significance. The first train from Portmadoc now runs at 6.00 a.m. and its counterpart from Rhiw at 6.05 a.m. Running times both Up and Down are the same as formerly but the over-all speed must have been increased as two additional stops are inserted, one at 'R' of three minutes and one at 'Dtt' of three minutes. These are clearly abbreviations for Rhiw Goch and Dduallt and though the addenda is wrongly shown in one place as if Rhiw Goch lay between Penrhyn arrival and Penrhyn departure (the times are correctly given, just the same) no other explanation will fit the circumstances. This being so, the appearance of Rhiw Goch as a 'station' on the 1869 Plans would be explained although as a horse exchange point it would not have survived. It is possible that there was a water tank at Rhiw Goch which would be conveniently sited along the route of the engine working the lower half of the line; similarly there is no doubt that the timetable amendments mark the date of the installation of the Dduallt water tank to which the three minute stop for the upper engine would apply.

From April 1864 therefore trains left Portmadoc at 6.00 a.m., 8.25 a.m., 10.50 a.m., 1.15 p.m., 3.40 p.m. and 6.05 p.m.; from Rhiw trains left at 6.05 a.m., 8.30 a.m., 10.55 a.m., 1.20 p.m., 3.45 p.m. and 6.10 p.m. Though the inverse character of the first table is not as well maintained, the principle is still there. In connection again with the first table, what better example of time interval running such as has been more widely introduced today, than this early example?

A reminder is again given that Down trains were not headed by their engines at this period, but that the locomotive followed down behind the wagons 'at a respectable distance' (see pp. 84–5).

There is no copy of the Working Timetable for January 1865 when passenger trains were introduced, but the passenger services were as Timetable No. 3.

TIMETABLE No. 3			1 January 1865 (Weekdays only)		
UP TRAINS					
Port Madoc	6.57	9.15	11.33	2.01	4.19
Penrhyn	7.15	9.33	11.51	2.19	4.37
Hafod-y-Llyn	7.45	10.03	12.21	2.49	5.07
Dinas	8.32	10.50	1.08	3.36	5.54
DOWN TRAINS					
Dinas	7.05	9.23	11.41	2.09	4.27
Hafod-y-Llyn	7.45	10.03	12.21	2.49	5.07
Penrhyn	8.22	10.40	12.58	3.26	5.54
Port Madoc	8.47	11.05	1.23	3.51	6.09

Here again, in considering the Down trains it must be recalled that they ran in three parts, and the amount of time taken by the engine for water would not affect the passenger train times. Just why the last train should require so much extra time between Hafod-y-Llyn and Penrhyn is not clear, unless the engine was attached for the final run and water taken at Rhiw Goch, though this is not a likely explanation. In all the foregoing cases of horse or locomotive haulage, Down trains would be hauled across the Cob.

In the timetables which are given in the Appendices, due allowance must be made for the following limitations which had either a temporary or permanent effect on traffic:

1. Growing slate traffic and the handling of loaded gravity trains and empty wagons.
2. The working of the Top and Bottom shunting engines in connection with their duties and the growth of traffic.
3. The hindrances due to shunting at Portmadoc Harbour, Welsh Highland trains and coaling up on the connecting line at Portmadoc; the working of wagons in and out of the exchange yard at Minffordd and the attaching of empty wagons to Up trains both here and at Portmadoc Harbour; special

stops at Plas private station; hand-operated crossing gates in four places (latterly three) i.e. Minffordd, Penrhyn, Tan-y-Grisiau, Glan-y-Pwll; the extended movements of the Top shunting engine between the north end of the tunnel for Brookes' traffic, Festiniog Granite Co., the L.N.W.R. yard, the G.W.R. yard and the Dinas branch; the passing of trains (principally at Tan-y-Bwlch).

4. The necessity for passenger trains to make connections at Minffordd for the Cambrian, Blaenau Festiniog Junction for the L.N.W.R. and at the Great Western station there for Bala trains; at a later date, the necessity for prompt through working on and off the Welsh Highland to ensure connections on adjacent systems.

5. The checking of tickets and the locking of carriage doors which increased the times of station working. Tickets were latterly collected at Tan-y-Bwlch (Up) and Minffordd (Down); it was originally Tan-y-Grisiau for the Up run. Ticket inspection and punching took place at Portmadoc and Blaenau before trains left.

6. The vagaries of Down gravity trains which were subject not only to loading and weather conditions, but which might not run freely and require the assistance of an engine to push, either using the Top shunting engine or one detached from an Up passenger train for the work.

7. The crewling of wagons at the foot of inclines adjacent to the main line which frequently blocked the section.

8. The limitations of locomotive power, usually associated with the economic difficulties of the Company, i.e. the sheer inability to raise sufficient money for labour or materials to keep and maintain enough engines in traffic.

9. The limitations of locomotive power associated with poor coal, a frequent cause of delays resulting in passengers having to continue their journeys in hired road vehicles and probably to miss standard gauge connections.
   (a) Varying times of Quarrymen's trains to suit changing hours of quarry work and (b) the repercussions if Up Quarrymen's trains were late.

10. The failure of rolling stock leading to accidents; these occurred especially to gravity trains and in particular between Tan-y-Bwlch and Tyler's Cutting. Causes would include the following:
    (a) Lack of springing on wagons would cause riding on three wheels and derail a vehicle at a low joint or point switch rail.
    (b) Loose tyres on slate wagons.
    (c) Slate wagon bearing bolts becoming loose and the bearings falling off.
    (d) Wagon wheels sliding along axles.
    (e) Sheep, etc., on the line derailing trains.
    (f) Telephone wires or fallen trees, forest fires, etc., detaining and/or derailing trains.
    (g) Incorrect setting of hand-points, leading to derailments. (There being only a limited amount of interlocking with the signals.)
    (h) Insecure loading of wagons with merchandise, especially in vans which were often loaded clumsily and too high, resulting in sacks, etc., shifting en route so that the vans fell over on their sides when traversing a well super-elevated curve.
    (i) Worn tyres causing flanges to strike chairs which in turn broke off pieces of the flange which, if the tyre was thin would probably also be thin and deep. This would ultimately cause derailment.

Between the wars irregularities in timetable working were extremely frequent and seldom a day would pass without some impasse of major or minor import; unlocked carriage doors would fly open en route and be smashed against the cutting walls; sheep would get inside the Moelwyn Tunnel; slate wagons coming down from Dinas under the control of the shunter would slide on icy rails so that the brakes became ineffective and the shunter would be unable to catch them before they fell into the river; undetected fractures in slate wagon tyres would derail a whole train; faulty chains on the couplings of slate wagons would fracture on a quarry incline and bring work on that incline to a halt until the damage was cleared; station staff would oversleep and so the single line staff for the section could not be released by the previous station and the first Up train would be delayed; the over-night cleaner at Boston Lodge would stifle the fire of the double engine by putting on too much of the latest load of 'cheap' coal, so that it was not ready for the morning train . . . these were among the every-day worries of a Traffic Superintendent; working under the stress of slate quarries clamouring for empty wagons and ship loaders complaining they could not work until wagons arrived, the Festiniog was prey to them all and an easy prey to failures with its limited resources, single line and critical position. In general, if circumstances caused a cessation of services—as they often did—no attempt was made to run the timetable as laid down; a whole series of trains was cancelled outright and the workings taken up again in the timetable from a point where traffic could conveniently be resumed.

Among the accident reports which occurred from these causes the following extracts are typical:

. . . an accident occurred to the 10.50 a.m. Up train at Hafodllyn. Covered goods wagon No. 132 loaded to the top with flour, etc., and which was noticed to oscillate a good deal on the curves on the way up left the rails on the curve under the old farmhouse at Hafodllyn and immediately fell over on its side and into the field under the line and dragged over iron coal wagon 147 loaded with lime and 5 ton goods wagon 121 with some bags of potatoes, also 5 empty slate wagons, whilst 7 more were thrown together in a heap off the rails . . . The traffic was disorganised for the day . . . the cause of the accident was the loose state of the bushes on the van allowing inches of play in the wheels. William Roberts, Signal Inspector, who was sitting on a wagon next the van had a most miraculous escape as the wagon he was sitting on with his fencing material went over into the field, and he only saved himself by clinging to the handrail of the van . . .

. . . Accident to 3.30 p.m. Up train from Portmadoc . . . at Hafod-y-Llyn . . . a goods van No. 129 loaded to the roof overturned clean off the rails and fell into the field under the line, the coupling bar snapped and the passenger portion of the train and some other loaded wagons went on without stopping. One 5 ton wagon loaded with flour, 1 lime wagon and 16 slate wagons were hurled into a heap 20 yards across.

In this accident, 19 wagons came off the line.

Loaded covered vans were often off the line on this curve; it was said they were unstable when overloaded.

... as the 10.50 a.m. Up from Portmadoc was running into Tan-y-Bwlch yesterday, the axle of iron goods wagon No. 150 broke, it left the rails causing two other wagons to get off, besides damaging the end of the guard's van. The empties had to be left behind and were sent forward by special engine at 2 p.m.

... at 2.30 p.m. yesterday, 3 loaded slate wagons from Votty Quarry for L.N.W.R. yard were standing in Duffws siding ready to be taken away—the guard took out the peg from the wheel before coupling them to the engine with the result they ran away. Smith at No. 2 Box noticed them coming and turned them off the line at the points leading to L.N.W. yard ...

Mr. Jones Morris thought fit to address himself to the Chairman and wrote thus from his solicitors' office in Ffestiniog:

... I travelled up with the 10.30 train this morning when the accident occurred on Tan-y-Bwlch curve and you will pardon my calling your attention to what I have for a long time considered to be a very objectionable practice of hooking empty trucks and especially timber trucks and vans and trucks of goods on to the passenger train. The condition of the permanent way is to me perceptibly out of repair and either the permanent way must in future be kept in a better state of repair, etc., etc. . . . that there will be no occasion to call the attention of the Board of Trade to it.

Amongst other Reports will be found:

...a passenger with a party travelling up to Blaenau yesterday says that he never experienced anything like going through the tunnel. The smoke with the heat being fearful and he suggested that notices be put up in the carriages to have the windows closed before entering the tunnel. Being strangers he did not know anything about it.

... to derive the best means of relieving a passenger train imprisoned in the long tunnel through any part of the machinery of a loco engine breaking down or the bursting of a tube therein, I have this case under consideration which is surrounded by many difficulties. It is an easy matter to detach a train from the engine anywhere except in the tunnel so the experiment should be tried with the actual running train in a place where: 1st, one would be nearly suffocated with sulphurous smoke; 2nd, how to get the driver and stoker off their engine when there is not room for a man's hand scarcely anywhere; 3rd, to get at the vacuum pipe valves and all in total darkness ... the frequent bursting of tubes makes it a matter of serious consideration.

... I wish to report to you that whilst bringing down a slate train from Greaves Quarry on Saturday, its numbers being 25 upon which were 4 brakes, 1 spring and 3 cordbrakes, I asked the oilman, if he saw the slate train starting at too great a speed, to put in a pin; well, he had three pins at hand and was at the first end of the slate train. When starting I asked him to put a pin in but he did not; he could have had three chances. Down it went at great speed, the brake wheels were sliding it being wet rails and slippery, my only expectation was to stop before going to Dinas or to attract some one's notice to put some sand on the rails there being a large heap of sand and fine gravel at the shed there; it being stormy weather there was no one about. After this I did my utmost to check it in coming to the junction. I found that a slate train composed of four wagons and 3 empty C wagons behind which I had brought down about nine o'clock on Saturday had been left there unnoticed by the brakesman at 10.15 a.m. Seeing that a collision was inevitable I jumped off the slate train within a chain length of the standing slate train so I managed to escape with slight injuries . . .

The slate train and passenger train had a narrow escape this morning owing to the great blizzard at the top blowing down three telegraph poles and wires below the tunnel. The slate train ran right through two of the poles and the men had a narrow escape; they only had just time to jump off and the slate train cut through one of them. The men managed to catch the last wagon and got on again. The passenger train was kept at Minffordd until 12 o'clock and ran into another pole going up . . .

. . . slate train was delayed through carelessness at Tan-y-Grisiau, no one there attending to the signals and stopped the slate train, being Saturday there was no engine up and it had to be pushed by hand to the Tunnel.

Shunting Guard G. W. Pugh reports that he ran into a horse and trap belonging to Mr. O. Owens, Penybont, Bl. Festiniog at the Dinas crossing at the Bottom of the new incline on Sat. Morning Mar. 30th while going up to Dinas with a train of empty waggons, the trap was thrown over on its side and one of the wheels smashed to pieces all the spokes being broken. . . .

Some horse shunting was practised by the quarries up the Dinas branch. Occasionally one would walk up from the Dinas level crossing, along F.R. tracks to its place of work. On 19 June 1905 one horse fell through the decking of the 'Middle Bridge' into the river.

Train working with poor coal was common. Sulphurous coal would make it very unpleasant for passengers in Up trains through the Moelwyn Tunnel, and bad steaming would cause brakes to leak on. Some coals were found to burn the tube ends and burst tubes were more frequently a source of engine failure when on the road than any other cause.

None of the locomotives was fitted with sanding gear, a surprising omission it might seem in view of the steep gradients and the wet climate. There is evidence that in early days engines were fitted with sanding gear having indiarubber delivery pipes; these are mentioned in renewals lists. The drawback to it was that it would often shut imperfectly, resulting in a dribble of sand being left along the running rail. This was sufficient to bring the Down gravity train to a stand. The gear was removed and the only method was then for the fireman to ride on the front of the engine and lift sand out of the pots by hand, dropping it over the front on to the rail as best he could. In the Moelwyn Tunnel, the best position was found by lining up with the vacuum brake pipe! Should a double engine stall in the tunnel and the fireman not be sanding at the time, the wretched man was obliged to crawl out through one of the spectacle glasses (which were suitably large for this eventuality) and find his way along the tank and boiler top to the front of the engine. On the England engines there was room to walk along a small beading below the edge of the water tank. If in doubt, firemen preferred to make their way on to the front of double engines before the tunnel was reached!

Regarding the handling of locomotives, the following notes were made by a driver who manned the engines before the Second War. They describe the engines as then running:

Oiling was done on the shed before running across the Cob for the stock which was already at the Harbour, and also at Tan-y-Bwlch on the Up journey; on the Down it was carried out at Minffordd whilst tickets were being examined. Steaming was easier on *Taliesin* than *Merddin Emrys*. The former would steam especially well when heavily loaded; *Merddin Emrys* was a slow engine to move away from rest.

Riding on the double engines was luxury compared with the small type. After a few minutes run on an England engine, visiting drivers from the standard gauge would wonder how the men stuck the confined cabs and the rough behaviour of the engine.

Injectors were on the driver's side, the stoker having the additional work of sanding and therefore, not being always on the footplate. The Fairlies had two injectors, also the England engines with the exception of *Princess* and *Little Giant* which had only one.

Bargoed coal was found to be most suitable; other types burned the tubes and smokebox. Firing was done in rounds of three shovelfuls, on a double engine this meant three per box in this order—back, mid-feather and the last under the tubeplate.

Shortage of footplatemen affected locomotive handling too. Often a double engine was not available for the Monday quarrymen's train. This meant two England engines and double crews. In the 'twenties when the Company had no extra men, firemen were promoted to work England engines . . . and *Prince*'s lead plug was melted on the morning train as a result. Hugh Hughes, the former driver and now Locomotive Foreman, took the train more than once after this mishap. The N.U.R. members among the footplate employees made formal complaint to their headquarters about Hughes—the Company's reply did not mince its words either.

Prince, by the way, was so badly needed by the Traffic Department when it re-entered service after rebuilding in September 1920 that it went straight into use as Bottom Shunter without trimmings or paint; it ran like this until the following year when the work was finished, allowing official records to give 1921 as the year of completion!

Taliesin (the Single Fairlie) was a very popular engine with the men. She was of just that calibre which was badly needed at times—something in between the under-powered and rough riding England engines, and the other extreme in the double bogie engines with two fire-boxes to fill. She was fast, moderately powerful and a very steady runner, and was particularly suitable for medium passenger work, mail trains, etc. Unfortunately, like the double engines, she was unsuitable for yard work, and would not pass into any of the exchange sidings. It would sometimes happen that she was used on Special Trains which required breaking up on arrival at Festiniog; here she was very unpopular as no work could be done without the conventional Top Shunter.

Those Up passenger trains which attached empty slate wagons at Minffordd would run into Minffordd station and reverse immediately, dropping back on to the slate wagons in the empties siding (this line held about 50 wagons). It was usual to draw forward into the station again for passenger purposes; occasionally the operation was reversed.

Since 1902 (as a result of a B.O.T. investigation), all Down gravity trains finished their journeys at Minffordd where the loads were checked and weighed on the weighbridge. The wagons were then split up by the Bottom Shunting Engine, those for Minffordd being drawn back and pushed down the steep curve into the Cambrian Yard, and those for the Harbour being taken as a train at a later stage. The maximum loading for this engine between Minffordd and the Harbour—on a dry day—was 200 loaded wagons . . . an impressive sight across the Embankment.

Although the work for a shunting engine at Blaenau was sufficient to employ one engine, in earlier times two engines were required to work 13 hours on six days to clear the traffic.

On Saturdays the 11.10 a.m. passenger train which took up the empty slate wagons, would not have its wagons distributed to the various quarries by the Top Shunter as on other weekdays; instead these would be left at Duffws station until the next Monday. The Top Shunter would work the 1.0 p.m. Down passenger on Saturdays. On Mondays, wagons for the Dinas branch would not be taken by the Top Shunter until after the arrival of the 9.15 a.m. Up train with further empties.

On the Down journey ticket collection was made at Minffordd. Down quarrymen's trains had their tickets checked at Tan-y-Grisiau and for this reason certain ordinary travellers took advantage of the situation; it was in May 1902 that some honest ordinary travellers, arriving by a Down train which had quarrymen's carriages in it, gave up their tickets at Portmadoc. They had travelled from Penrhyn and because there was no room in the train, had travelled with the quarry-men in a quarrymen's coach. As quarrymen's tickets had been examined at Tan-y-Grisiau, these carriages were not checked at Minffordd; hence the honest passengers had given up their tickets at Portmadoc. When the position was examined, it was found that no one at Minffordd had ever thought that ordinary passengers might ride, unnoticed, in the quarrymen's coaches, and so a certain clientele had enjoyed free travel for a considerable period of time!

Goods trains proper used to leave Portmadoc at 6.0 a.m. and return from Blaenau Festiniog at 9.45 a.m. Additional goods trains were run if required.

Before the morning train, and after stormy conditions, the length-man for both Penrhyn and Moelwyn Tunnel sections was required to patrol the line and report obstructions.

After the curtailment of the all-year passenger services, during winter only quarrymen's and slate trains were run. The morning Up train (still nicknamed 'the Parliamentary' although no longer justifying this classification) would trail the empty slate wagons and still run double-headed with a double engine as train engine and an England engine as pilot, the latter becoming the Top Shunter for the day. One typical table for this period is given:

2 October 1933 until further notice.		(Saturdays excepted.)	
Portmadoc Harbour	5.20 a.m.	B. Festiniog (GWR)	4.20 p.m.
Minffordd	5.30	B. Festiniog (LMS)	4.23
Penrhyn	5.35	Tan-y-Grisiau	4.28
Tan-y-Bwlch	5·55	Moelwyn Halt	A
Dduallt	A	Dduallt	A
Moelwyn Halt	A	Tan-y-Bwlch	4.48
Tan-y-Grisiau	6.15	Penrhyn	5.10
B. Festiniog (LMS)	6.20	Minffordd	5.17
B. Festiniog (GWR)	6.23	Portmadoc Harbour	5.27

A—Stops if required.

At this time the Bottom Shunter would be a tractor, and during the winter tabled above, only *Welsh Pony* and *Taliesin* (double engine) were in use.

A broader survey of operating may now be given, with reference to the Rule Book of 1876 and the march of events during the period, the latter effecting a gradual change over the traffic of the railway and, therefore, of its operating characteristics.

The operation of the line could be divided into four categories:

1. Gravity slate trains. (Down only.)

2. Passenger and goods trains, both Up and Down, locomotive hauled.

3. Return of empty slate wagons, Up only, locomotive hauled.

4. Shunting duties.

1. *Gravity slate trains.* Locomotives were not required on any portion of this work, save for the ultimate splitting up of trains at Minffordd or Portmadoc Harbour; this falls into category 4.

For giving warning whilst *en route*, the head breaksman [*sic*] was given a horn; this later became a whistle. When the Rule Book was issued, only two brakesmen worked per train and they were to

arrange the breaks on every train before starting down the line, bracing them up in such a way that the train can be controlled ... any breaksman who shall be seen or found locking the break wheels by tightening too much and allowing the wheels to slide along the rails, will be liable to fine or dismissal. . . .

The brakesman was to keep strictly to the timetable laid down and not take sharp curves at speed.

The operating of gravity trains, though covered by the rules, was undoubtedly of high risk and it is a wonder there were not more personal accidents; at 'Gelliwenog Bridge', near Dduallt, the shunting guard, William Pugh—an elderly man—acting as brakesman on the front portion of 59 loaded wagons (he being in charge of the first four fitted with brakes) failed to notice the oncoming bridge, and whilst jumping from one wagon to another at speed, was knocked down and severely injured. From this time light overhead gantries were erected with ropes suspended from them to remind men of approaching bridges, and the Board of Trade ruled that no old men should 'be employed on such dangerous duty'.

2. *Up and Down Passenger and Goods trains*. These were ultimately locomotive worked in all cases. Only on special occasions was goods traffic sent by an individual train, it being sufficient to add wagons to passenger trains when necessary. Passenger trains (and slate quarry-men's trains) in every case travelled between the termini of the system, the carriage shed for quarrymen's vehicles being at Duffws and for ordinary stock at Boston Lodge (formerly the Harbour).

3. *Return of empty slate wagons*. These were attached to the rear of any convenient Up passenger train, the early morning workmen's train being the most important example. In the case of Up trains picking up empties at both the Harbour and Minffordd, it was necessary to set back to attach them. On approaching Glan-y-Pwll the engine driver shut off steam and slackened the couplings; the guard of the passenger train would pull on a light chain hung on the rear of his van. This lifted the coupling hook of the leading empty slate wagon which was thus detached from the train. After giving a flag signal to the driver who would put on speed, the train drew clear of the slate empties still following, and the facing points were thrown in front of the empties to allow them to roll into the mineral line.

4. *Shunting Duties*. A shunting engine was stabled at Blaenau through the week, and worked on the head of the Monday Up slate quarrymen's train as a pilot engine. It collected and sorted loaded and empty wagons from the various quarries between the Moelwyn Tunnel and Duffws; this involved the branches leading to other concerns (slate-mills, granite workings, etc.). Loaded slate wagons were assembled on the mineral line for formation into gravity trains. This was the Top Shunting Engine and its crew lived in the hostel at Glan-y-Pwll for the week. The engine used Blaenau shed for the period.

The Bottom Shunting Engine worked from Boston Lodge shed and its duties ranged from Minffordd branch and yard, to the Harbour and wharves around it. Unlike the top engine, it worked at the Up end of its train. At Minffordd the empty wagons had to be hauled out of the yard and dropped back into the empty wagon siding to await an Up passenger train. Wagons going down into the yard did not need a locomotive as the branch fell steeply.

In early times the impetus would carry the slate train over the Cob to the Harbour, but the Bottom Shunting Engine would lurk at Boston Lodge ready to push if need be. Latterly, the movement was controlled and the engine propelled the train over the Cob. Irregularities in operation brought in a new rule that the train must be stopped at Boston Lodge. If this could be done whilst the enginemen were having dinner, the youngest fitter could be put to cleaning out the engine's fire. The working was made twice daily. It was a well-remembered feature of gravity trains running through the Harbour sidings, the brakesmen neatly detaching rakes of wagons for various quays and the remainder ending at Greaves' Wharf . . . almost in Borth-y-Gest! A later practice was to allot a brakesman to each portion, the men available being the shunting guard, or gravity train brakesmen or Portmadoc station signalman. This was the practice by 1880. In an irregular practice the engine would lie in the Boston Lodge siding beside the shore until the gravity train dashed past at an awe-inspiring rate, careening round the sharp curve outside the works. It would then start up after the train which, moving on the slight downhill grade, made excellent progress because of its tremendous impetus. In wet weather the train frequently ran over the whole Cob before the engine could catch up with it, and the fireman, riding on the front, could drop a hook on to the last slate wagon.

The shunting engines were always of the England type, whilst the heavy duties were taken by the double engines.

Apart from the ordinary rules of the day which were common to most railway companies of the times, the Festiniog had certain special regulations.

72. Carriages and Waggons are never to be allowed to remain on the main line, but must be placed on a siding, the wheels securely scotched and breaks applied and the stop block locked across the line or siding, and not allow crawling* on the inclined planes of the Cwmorthin and Moelwyn Inclines adjoining the railway at times when . . . trains are expected to pass between Duffws and the tunnel.

75. . . . all carriage doors are carefully fastened and locked on both sides going Up and Down. . . .

78. . . . when it is necessary to detain a person, such detention shall not continue for a longer period than is absolutely necessary, and the party shall be conveyed before a magistrate with as little delay as possible.

A reflection of the early method of working goods Up the line from Portmadoc, by making every train Mixed, is found in 80a. . . .

* The vernacular was 'crewling'.

As soon as the goods have been weighed, loaded . . . are to be put on the turnout or under the shed near the office, until the next Up train for forwarding on. A certain number of trucks of goods and parcels to be forwarded by every Up train. . . .

Under Rule 102 the wagon inspector was required to inspect all wagons before the train left Portmadoc, and to tap all wheels, checking coupling hooks, etc., at the same time. He was also to see that no railway company wagons went up the inclines containing goods, and to keep a record of the wagon numbers going up the inclines and returning from the quarries. Wagon Inspectors at Dinas and Duffws were, in fact, the Company's agents, looking after their interests as regards the use of its wagons by the quarry companies.

In Rule 127 pointsmen are enjoined to inspect their points after the passage of every train to see that no

coke, coal, gravel or dirt has dropped within the points to prevent them from closing. . . .

151. Every engineman to regulate the speed of his engine . . . never exceed . . . 17 miles an hour (except when ordered to do so).

It would obviously be difficult to estimate such an odd figure with exactitude! Rule 161 states that sharp curves must be taken at not more than 6 miles an hour.

In cases of danger three short sharp whistles are to be given and repeated by any other engines in the train. All engines are to be reversed at once and the guard is to apply his break [*sic*], Rule 166.

175. . . . to pass Boston Lodge, weighing offices, Dolgaregddu Junction (for the F. & B.R.) at no more than 6 m.p.h. . . .

A later insertion enforces a speed restriction between cabins Nos. 2 and 3, Blaenau Festiniog, of 12 m.p.h.

Guards are concerned with Rule 196:

Persons in charge of the Company Police, deserters and persons afflicted with insanity must never be placed with other passengers. . . .

Special regulations affected working through the Molewyn Tunnel, which no train might enter until permission was given by the special signalmen at each mouth. (In the case of the south end, the control of entry was later moved back to Dduallt.)

205a. . . . In the case of an accident taking place when running Up the gradient from any truck coming off the line below the passenger carriages, the first truck next the carriages or next to the truck off the line, is to be immediately uncoupled, so as to enable the passengers to proceed on through the tunnel, and on to Duffws. . . .

Wherever possible the derailed vehicles were to be uncoupled and the engine to draw the remainder of the train from the tunnel.

... In the event of the engine of a passenger train running off the line when going up the gradient, the carriages or truck next the engine must be uncoupled and the train taken down to the lower end of the tunnel. If such should take place with the train on going Down the gradient through the tunnel, the passenger train must be uncoupled next the engine and the passenger coaches must be pushed back through the tunnel by the Guard in charge and officials accompanying the train, and also to obtain, if possible, the assistance from the passengers to push the train back to the top end of the tunnel. ...

Under the Railway Employment (Prevention of Accidents) Act 1900 the Company was permitted various exceptions as a result of two inspectors sent by the Board of Trade in October 1901. The inspectors agreed that to fit brake levers on each side of wagons was impossible as they would have fouled each other on the inclines, and having regard to the safe working of the line 'for over 60 years' they permitted certain exemptions. However, on gravity trains 1 in 5 wagons must have a brake, be in charge of an experienced man; each train to have two brakesmen save with more than 80 wagons when 3 men must be in charge. No train should exceed 120 wagons and it must be marshalled so that no brakesman has to move 'an undue distance between the breaked [*sic*] wagons under his control' (1902). A special set of Regulations in addition to the operating rules was brought out by the Company in 1902, and these are mentioned again later.

Penrhyn Derailment—28 August 1896

On 28 August 1896 the 10 a.m. passenger train from Portmadoc left the rails whilst approaching Penrhyn station. The engine *Princess* and the first two carriages left the track and ran along the ballast for about 24 yards before the train stopped. Luckily the rest of the train remained on the rails and both the derailed carriages were empty. No one was injured. Details of the accident reveal the make-up of trains at that time, and give particulars of the permanent way. The train consisted of the engine and tender, Workmen's carriage, a Third Class, a First Class (both four-wheeled), two composites (bogie), and a brake van (bogie). The Board of Trade report quotes the gauge as 1 ft. 11¼ in. except on curves, where it was 1 ft. 11½ in. The rails were double-headed steel rails weighing 50 lb. per yard, 24 ft. in length and fastened in chairs weighing 18½ lb. each, spiked to half-round sleepers, nine to each rail length.

The train derailed on a right-hand seven-chain curve, mounting the left-hand rail; the engine struck a low wall on the left side of the line and then turned obliquely across the rails and came to rest leaning against the right-hand side of a low cutting. Part of the curve had been resleepered but not the portion where the derailment occurred; this work was pending.

At the enquiry the driver, Jarrett Davies, then 22 years of age, blamed the track about which he had complained the day previously. The fireman was only 17 years of age. The Guard referred to the unsteady riding of the small engines compared with the bogie engines, and how he had unlocked the compartments to allow passengers to alight after the accident.

The Inspecting Officer pointed out what terrible consequences might have ensued if the derailment had occurred on many other points along the railway, and blamed the state of the track for the accident. He emphasised the unsteadiness of this type of engine and that because of the narrowness of the gauge, the bearing area of the sleepers on the ballast was much reduced. The report ends: '. . . I feel it incumbent on me to draw attention to the extreme youth of the engineman in charge of this train. The driver said he was 22 years old and the fireman 17, but neither of them looked their age . . . it does not seem right to entrust passenger trains . . . to lads of so little experience.'

Glan-y-Pwll Junction (No. 3 Cabin) Head-on collision—23 July 1897

The 10.5 a.m. Down Passenger (double Fairlie engine, three bogie and four four-wheel carriages) was held on the passenger line at the Down Home signal 2, whilst an Up Mineral train (England engine, 22 wagons) came through from Tan-y-Grisiau, carrying the Staff for the Tan-y-Grisiau to Glan-y-Pwll section. This train, a special, was due to enter the Mineral line at Dinas Junction and so run past the Passenger. When the Mineral train arrived it had held the Passenger for 15 minutes. The signalman lowered the Up Distant, Outer Home and Inner Home signals, forgetting that the Down Passenger was standing on the Passenger line. When the Mineral was 60 yards from the box the signalman threw the Inner Home to danger 'because it was travelling too fast for the curve and I wished to check it' but the driver was unable to stop and the points being set for the Passenger line, there was a head-on collision. Fortunately the Mineral train had already reduced speed and the collision was not a severe one. The signalman was clearly to blame.

During the enquiry it transpired that the signalman did not keep the Tickets in the Ticket Box in order to draw them out one at a time with the Staff Key—rather, he drew a quantity in the morning of each day and used them as required, handing them to drivers through the window who accepted them without being shown the Staff for the section which was not, at the time the Ticket was handed over, in the cabin at all. Even in this instance the signalman had a Ticket all ready to give the driver of the Mineral train, though he had not possession of the Staff. Apparently the drivers were reckless enough to accept Tickets under these circumstances and in fact the Company's Rules did not lay down the conditions under which Tickets might be issued and received.

One other point emerged. The two parallel tracks, one for passenger and one for mineral traffic, were treated as one line and the Staff & Ticket as applying to either line. The Inspecting Officer pointed out the danger of this and that the Passenger line should be classed as the main line and the Mineral line worked under special operating regulations.

The locking frame was arranged so that 12 could not be pulled off unless either 10 or 11 was pulled first; a recommendation that this be altered so that 12 could be lowered independently of 10 or 11, and also that the Up Distant 1 be made to apply to the Passenger line only and not to the Mineral line, was made. In this way Up trains would be brought under control before they passed the signal box, if necessary. These alterations were not in fact carried into effect, as the whole layout was shortly swept away by alterations to the Junction.

The Inspector wrote: 'the Festiniog does not practice Rules for single line working—and especially those relating to Tickets—accepted by the Association of Railway Companies'.

In October 1900 a Down gravity train was thrown off the line at the bottom end of Tan-y-Bwlch station. The signals were at 'clear' but there being no interlocking between signalling and pointwork at this location, the semaphores gave no protection from wrongly set points. It was the custom of the Porter to hold the points for the Up passenger train and to return to the points again when he had lowered the Down signals after the passenger train had come to a stand. On this occasion he returned to the points 'only to find them padlocked'* and still set for the Up passenger which had recently passed and was still in his station. It was too late to do anything before the gravity train hit the points in the trailing direction. Luckily almost all the wagons remained on the right-of-way whilst crossing the road bridge, but 14 wagons were thrown down the embankment, some on to the road, others into the stream and the remainder into the woods. The derailment took place at 11 a.m. and the line was not cleared until 11 p.m. It was months before all the wagons and broken slate were lifted up again.

Among other types of accident which, although fortunately not incurring personal injury, nevertheless occurred from time to time, were derailments to slate gravity trains. These were sometimes caused by obstructions on the line, whether animal, vegetable, or mineral (trees blown down, telegraph wires blown down and straying sheep were all common causes of them). There exists a photograph of an impressive accident to a gravity train which took place in the woods

* According to the Station Master's report.

near Dduallt water tank. This was caused by a broken axle or wheel and resulted in the train being hurled all over the place, some wagons into trees and others over the side of the embankment into the fields below where they fell a considerable distance. For a number of years there was an upturned slate wagon with one pair of wheels missing, lying at the south mouth of the Moelwyn Tunnel; this wagon had brought a slate train to grief in the tunnel. There were other similar cripples along the route, and at the foot of several inclines on the feeder lines it was quite usual to find a small mortuary of old wagon parts, whilst a little exploration would disclose others in a nearby river bed and sometimes a pair of wheels on their axle hanging from a tree. In connection with these trains and especially their operation, extracts from the Special Rules (previously mentioned) under which they ran and dated 1902, are pertinent.

2. . . . the brakes of every wagon must be carefully examined . . . and the brakes securely applied but not so as to skid the wheels . . .

4. The slate train from Rhiw* must be brought to a stand on the main line below Glan-y-Pwll Junction so as to be clear for the slate train from Duffws being connected to it. Sufficient brakes must be put down to do this.

5. The slate train from Duffws must have the brakes pinned down so as to stop easily and smoothly to connect behind the slate train from Rhiw.

6. . . . in no case shall a train run without 2 Brakesmen . . . over 80 wagons there shall be 3 Brakesmen . . . no train shall consist of more than 120 wagons . . . train shall be marshalled as to prevent Brakesmen from having to travel an undue distance on a train between the braked wagons under their control.

7. . . . see that there is 1 braked wagon to every 5 unbraked wagons . . .

8. . . . regulate working so as to prevent breakage of wagon couplings . . .

9. . . . keep a good look out . . . in case of broken axle or wheel . . . when one Brakesman wants to draw attention of the others he must blow his horn twice.

10. . . . keep train under complete control . . . to bring it to a stand above the Weigh Office at Minffordd.

11. . . . keep a sharp look out . . . signals approaching Glan-y-Pwll Junction . . . and different stations and level crossings . . . give notice of the approach of train by blowing horn three times.

12. During the winter months a hanging white lamp must be fixed on the first wagon and a red light behind the last wagon.

13. . . . speed not to be exceeded on sharp curves . . .

14. Head Brakesman responsible . . . that train does not start from Glan-y-Pwll Junction without Staff or Ticket from . . . No. 3 Box and that he gets the Staff or Ticket from the different Staff Stations along the way.

A number of accidents were due to goods wagons derailing: for instance, two vans overturned at Tan-y-Bwlch on 30 June 1902, they were attached to the 2.15 p.m. Portmadoc–Blaenau Festiniog train and the accident occurred, approaching Tan-y-Bwlch, due to overplay in

* i.e., the Dinas branch line.

an axlebox. A loaded van was dragged off next and six empty slate wagons followed. The coupling broke and the passenger train ran ahead unaware of the derailment.

On 2 August 1901 a load shifted in a wagon behind a passenger train which jumped the track between Penrhyn and Tan-y-Bwlch, pulling off fifteen empty slate wagons behind it; the front (passenger) portion continued as the coupling broke.

Another incident noted by the Board of Trade was on 19 August 1901 when a covered wagon and four others (behind the passenger train) left the rails below Tan-y-Bwlch, the causes being the bushes of the axleboxes were worn causing too much sideplay and the wagon was overloaded to the top with bags of flour.

These three occurrences made the B.O.T. look again at mixed train operation on the line and there was some pointed correspondence, the Board re-emphasising their Order R11993/90 under the 1889 Act (Part III) 'when the Company was treated with exceptional liberality' as to the number of unfitted wagons which could be attached to passenger trains on the railway (i.e. 'that only one unfitted vehicle is to be attached to passenger trains' (1893) . . . 'four unbraked wagons rank as one vehicle'). The Company was obviously stretching its luck! (See also Chapter Nine, p. 174.)

The running of private trains for special personages, or for the Oakeley family, has already been noticed, but such events were not, apparently, the preserve of the gentry; there is a nice little tale in the Minutes of Evidence of the Royal Commission on Land in Wales & Monmouthshire 16 September 1893, the witness being a farm tenant at Tan-y-Grisiau Isaf, one William C. Williams, Jnr. He was asked 'Am I to understand there was no road here, or that there was not at the time when the Williamses were tenants of the farm?' The reply: 'No, not at all, only the narrow gauge railroad. Of course, we were allowed to take anything down along the narrow gauge after the trains stopped at night. They took the wagons down and shunted into a siding. Of course, that was nothing but permission from the railway company'. '. . . What was done before the railway was built?' 'I do not know.'

As to the respect which the local population paid to the Railway and its property, one is left with the impression that the nearer the line came to Blaenau, the more they cared not a damn for it! It was footpath, conveyance or convenience as they chose.

Robert Jones of Tan-y-Grisiau was killed by a train on 23 October 1901; at the inquest attention was drawn to the fact that through the village, no part of the railway was fenced.

The *Mining Journal* of April 1879 wrote: 'Accidents have been of rare occurrence on the Festiniog Narrow Gauge Railway but on Wednesday last (9th April) a loaded slate train ran off the rails near

Portmadoc. Happily no lives were lost but the wagons and slates were much damaged'—and for another two years the line was free of tragedy.

The major accidents since the line was opened, all resulting in Board of Trade enquiries, occurred in the span 1881–1908, there being no serious accident involving death to a passenger or a public passenger train before or after these years—a significant pronouncement on the safety record of a line which is potentially dangerous in certain aspects not usually found on standard gauge or minor railways of any description.

Date	Place	Note
4 March 1881	Portmadoc Goods Shed	Gravity train diverted into goods shed, striking stationary wagons therein and crushing Wesley, who attended to the clocks on Fridays, to death (he was employed by Richard Banner Thomas, the clock-maintenance contractor). This accident was due to the points being left in the wrong position and the speed of the train being too high for the Bottom Shunter to catch up with it. There was a manslaughter charge in consequence.
15 October 1881	Dinas Junction	Down passenger from Duffws including a number of quarrymen's coaches in the rake, derailed along the train. Caused by fractured coach axle and low spot in outer rail on curve. First accident to a passenger train. Four men injured.
28 August 1896	Approaching Penrhyn	Up passenger train from Portmadoc derailed.
23 July 1897	Dinas Junction	Head-on collision between passenger and mineral trains.
4 October 1901	Coed-y-Bleddiau	Down 6.15 p.m. passenger train completely derailed on curve. Caused by faulty track and too much super-elevation on curve.
10 December 1908	Near Dduallt	Gravity train brakesman knocked down by overbridge.

A defective wagon link on the Extension Railway's No. 1 Incline caused a runaway and settlement for £85 with Mr. Bowton (16 September 1905). (See illustration *History of N. Wales Slate Industry*, p. 154.)

In February 1893 a runaway platelayer's trolley hit two children crossing the line at Penrhyn; one was seriously hurt.

Among the lesser events which have more recently been recalled was the loss of a left-hand driving wheel to the engine of an Up passenger train in August 1900 which left the engine leaning up against the rock face and the derailment in Dduallt cutting of a South Wales miners' Special on its way Up for the Blaenau Ffestiniog Eisteddfod; the latter was due to a sow jammed under the train and it was found on enquiry that the owner had placed her on the line.

The mention of *Prince*'s derailment at Blaenau (described earlier in this chapter) is still vivid in memory; the moving blades under the revolving wheels, threw the slate wagons off the road; catching under the buffer beam, they then threw *Prince* on its side. Will Williams the driver recalls, 'The engine stood right up on end and rolled over as gentle as a ball. But the gauge glass broke and what with the steam the fireman got a bit excited and kept treading on me. . . .'

This same driver had previously gone through the stone wall at the end of Glan-y-Pwll turntable with *Princess* when the handbrake failed. He was also the first driver of the several Board of Trade specials to inspect the Welsh Highland, also driving the last public train over the Portmadoc–Rhydd-Ddu section of that line. (Other incidents from his life on the Railway are recorded in the *Festiniog Magazine*, No. 29, p. 2.)

The overturning of *Prince* was recalled by an elderly inhabitant of Blaenau who, being one of a number of young men who helped to right the engine quite quickly, was highly amused when the gang arrived from Boston Lodge and found they had little left to do.

Crick's diary gives fuller details of the demise of The Boat on 12 February 1886; '. . . when Mr. Spooner came down today met with an accident . . . Mr. Spooner went up with the 10.30 train today with Miss Tidderman, Mr. & Miss Robinson and started down without the staff and consequently came into collision with the up passenger train near the tunnel causing the boat to smash to pieces and Mr. Spooner and Miss Robinson badly hurt. Miss Tidderman and Mr. Robinson came off luckily. Parkins driving the up train did his best to stop the train but unsuccessfully. They were bandaged up and are now laid up in beds—damage to engine, slight.'

(Appendix 1 contains a summary of accidents for the period 1872–1922 taken from the Parliamentary Sessional Papers.)

The paper-printed notices shown on p. 424 were affixed to portable wooden boards which were hung in the various Block Posts. The date of the above is immediately pre-First War, but not completely decipherable owing to damp damage. There were in addition, twelve other codes of standard Railway Clearing House format appearing in the list; apart from certain Codes whose interpretation had been amended to suit Festiniog traffic (the most important being 'Goods Train or Slate Train' above), there was nothing especially individual about the Railway's Bell Code.

The Great Western Railway issued a special Bell Code and a set of 12 Rules to cover shunting movements at Blaenau Festiniog where their headshunt from the platform loop was crossed on the level by the F.R. Exchange Yard access. A notice of January 1897 is signed; T. I. Allen (Great Western Railway) and J. S. Hughes (Festiniog Railway) and contains 14 special codes for use between the North (F.R.) Box and South (G.W.R.) Box, the G.W.R. Lines between the two Boxes being called—'Main Line—Loop Line and Goods Line'. It is unlikely that any other British railway would have gone to the same lengths, but this was a Great Western tradition!

FESTINIOG RAILWAY

Code of terms for Train Signalling on Festiniog Railway worked on Electric and Train Staff Block System.

Bell Signals		*Beats on Bell*	*How to be given*		
Call Attention		1	1		
Is Line Clear for	Ordinary Passenger Train	4	3 pause 1		
	Shunting Engine	4	1	3	
	Empty Coaching Stock Train	5	2	2 pause 1	
	Light Engine, Light Engines (coupled together) or Engine and Brake	5	2	3	
	Ballast Train or Wagons	5	5 consecutively		
	Goods Train or Slate Train	3	3 consecutively		
	Shunting Engine or Ballast Train requiring to stop in section	5	1	2	2
	Train entering section	2	2 consecutively		
	Train out of section, or Obstruction removed	3	2	1	
	Obstruction Danger	6	6 consecutively		
Portmadoc		A. G. Crick			
		Traffic Superintendent.			

CHAPTER EIGHTEEN

PUBLICITY AND TICKETS

In general terms, the main publicity was directed at the holidaymaker and so covered an area reached roughly by the Cambrian and L.N.W.R. in the district. As far back as the 1870s (when incoming visitors used the Minffordd exchange station) the district has been much sought after as a tourist centre and railways played their biggest role in this traffic during the 1930s, a period which has already been discussed.

For the project, the Company produced small card timetables; for window and hotel display, there were cards which could be hung. There only appears to have been the one 1910-issue large poster whose Dantéesque qualities were said to have put more people off a ride than encouraged one.

It is difficult to say at what period the Railway began to publicise its passenger services or extol the virtues of its scenic attractions, but evidence points to the time when it must have appeared obvious that the slate trade was past its zenith and other forms of income must be built up. Certainly by the late 1880s a few well-defined channels were being exploited but more might have been done if money had been available. Nothing approaching the publicity of the 1930s had been attempted in the past, and like many other small railways, the line relied on more indirect approaches to whet the public appetite. Guide Books then formed a far more important place in the literature of the aspiring tourist, who had no cinema or travel books to advise him. There were over fifty Guides covering North Wales alone in those days, many of them published in the Principality. At first, the natural beauties of the district were extolled, but eventually capital was made of the Railway's unique character; the narrow gauge, its age, 'first ever made', Faery Glens and Toy Railway treatments came into vogue. Accuracy went by the board and in its publicity the Railway acquired for itself some amazing distinctions and achievements. On many of the L.N.W.R., G.W.R. and Cambrian stations there were poster boards and frames of photographs. Comprehensive inter-facilities for travel and ticket booking were arranged off and on to these lines by the Festiniog.

Locally, publicity was strong and both management and employees were given opportunity for promoting traffic. Football, concerts, eisteddfodau, Sunday School outings, the Company was ready for them all and matched the occasion with special trains. The great publicity feature of all railways of the pre-Second War era was the handbill, a feature which has almost disappeared. The Festiniog's were printed locally (albeit often crudely) in vast quantities and sent to all local standard gauge stations for public attention.

For tourists with little local knowledge, interest in the Railway and the scenery through which it ran was created mainly through folded brochures costing one penny each. In this respect one wishes the Company had shown as much imagination as they did on the engineering side; apart from an occasional break into colour, the same somewhat drab views and out-of-date maps appeared for almost fifty years; black and purple in print, they were perhaps after all no more dismal than their competing contemporaries. Almost every form of advertising contained 'This celebrated Miniature Line, the original TOY RAILWAY, and the world-renowned pioneer of narrow gauge railways ...'. Whilst Fairlie and Spooner had used the line to trumpet their praises, later publicity preferred the softer touch of emphasising its bijou qualities—in the words of one leaflet '. . . it . . . is well termed by its admirers, the "Faery Line" '.

From the late 1890s there seems to have been little done to promote local traffic by publicity. Occasionally newspaper advertisements appeared but already by then there was widespread antagonism to the facilities, as witnessed by the repeated efforts of quarrymen to better their service. Like so many other services with a touch of the 'suburban' about them—for there was always commuter traffic between Blaenau and Portmadoc—the local users of the line were quick to use other means of transport when they became available. There seems little evidence of goodwill or rapport between local public and the Company.

A few large poster boards remained on stations like Holyhead, Penmaenmawr, and Afon Wen until the 1960s, still headed in cast iron characters FESTINIOG TOY RAILWAY but by then put to other uses. These were products of the 1930s and it is unlikely the Festiniog owned large poster boards before this time. The term Toy Railway however, is used in the 1882 Edition of *Hanes Plwyf Ffestiniog*; this is the first note of it.

For a time in the early part of the century a triple-fold brochure was available for summer seasons with the timetable on it; most publicity avoided having a timetable which made the material useless for another season. At this time a paragraph on technicalities was included '. . . It has great interest from its Engineering features, with its gauge of less than 2 feet, and its sharp curves and gradients, which have drawn to its study scientific people from all nations. It is laid with heavy steel rails, was the first line in the country to be fitted with clip-fishplates, Bogie Engines, Bogie Passenger Carriages and open Observation Cars with centre couplings. The whole being fitted with Automatic Brakes working with the greatest safety'.

Leaflets using existing blocks were widely distributed in varying colours; they first appeared in 1911 and amended, survived for almost thirty years.

Fares

The original average fares per mile in the period 1865 to 1867 were:

	1st Class	*2nd Class*	*3rd Class*
1865	2.80d.	1.87d.	1.27d.
1866	1.97d.	1.47d.	1.26d.
1867	1.97d.	1.47d.	1.04d.

It seems that, for the first year at any rate, there was an 'open class' in addition to the three classes; presumably this was for travel on the open four-wheelers. There was no Parliamentary rate at this time.

A rough list of proposed fares for 1 November 1867 onwards shows:

	1st Class	*2nd Class*	*3rd Class (covered or open)*	
Single	2s.	1s. 9d.	1s. 2d.	whole distance
Return	3s. 4d.	2s. 11d.	not quoted	(return same day only)

From pencilled notes alongside it seems these were adopted, save the returns which became 3s. 2d. and 2s. 6d. instead of those proposed.

There were rough calculations on quarrymen's tickets showing that an increase of 1½d. week to 6d. journey on 400 tickets would increase earnings, but these only indicate the way management was thinking and the figures alone are unhelpful.

It was at this time intended to keep a fare differential of '1st single at 3d. more than 2nd, and 2nd single 6d. more than 3rd; 1st return 5d. more than 2nd return, 2nd return 7d. more than two 3rd singles'.

The fares list at Hafod-y-Llyn for 1873 shows:

Rates	1st Class	2¼d. per mile single; 1½d. per mile return.
	2nd Class	1¾d. per mile single; 1¼d. per mile return.
	3rd Class	1¼d. per mile single; ¾d. per mile return.
	Quarrymen	4d. flat rate (no return fare)

In 1916 passenger rates were (per mile): 1st, 2·36d.; 3rd, 1·43d.; Parliamentary, 1d.; Workmen, 0·17d. Goods rates were: slate, 1·71d.; coal, 2·08d.; general merchandise, 2·59d.–4·66d. per ton per mile. Trans-shipment costs per ton: minerals, ¾d.; general merchandise, 1½d.–3d.

From 31 May 1923, a surcharge of 6d. was put on Observation Car travel. Parliamentary fares ceased after 31 March 1924.

Tickets

The tickets of the Railway covering the last century are a subject in itself so large that only the most interesting and important features can be selected from the period.

Like many another mid-Victorian railway, the Company placed its initial order for printing of the tickets with the old-established Quaker concern of John B. Edmondson of Manchester. As was customary, they would probably have supplied the date presses and storage cabinets too: Waterlow & Co. became their suppliers until 1921 when Edmondson's came back into the picture with his characteristic 'negative-type' numerals, to remain supplier until 1939, apart from the Stephens era, when they were characteristic of all tickets printed at Tonbridge.

Surviving accounts of April 1865 are the earliest to be found concerning tickets, though presumably there must have been an earlier order in the late autumn of 1864. For reference purposes the stations of this early time were each given a number: 1 Portmadoc, 2 Penrhyn, 3 Dinas and 4 Hafod-y-llyn [*sic*], the last number suggesting that perhaps a passenger station at Hafod-y-Llyn was a late decision.

Countless thousands of early tickets survived down the years and were indeed still issued in 1975 in a few limited cases, but nothing earlier than 1875 has survived. Unfortunately too, tickets showing either of the oldest stations at Dinas or Hafod-y-Llyn do not exist.

Ultimately, but not originally, the everyday colour form of Festiniog tickets became standard with the Railway Clearing House colour scheme, to which its ordinary 1st, 2nd and 3rd Class tickets conformed for many years. These were: (the colours of 1865 follow in brackets)

		1st	*2nd*	*3rd & Parliamentary*
Single		White (Red)	Red (Yellow)	Green (Green)
Return	Out	White (White)	Red (Red)	Green (Green)
	Return	Yellow (Yellow)	Blue (Blue)	Buff (Buff)

Aside from the regimentation of the above, the Company's other issues were often lavish and gaily coloured. Most reflected the somewhat special services the line provided for which the Clearing House had no guide lines. In the 'Tourist Era' (1920s–1930s) there was possibly greater variation from 'the standard' than could be found on most other major lines.

When 2nd Class ceased on 1st October 1908 the surplus ticket stocks were put into store at the Harbour station where they remained for the ensuing forty-six years . . . longer than they had been available. Parliamentary fares (single only), were available on the first Up and first Down trains each day except Sundays; they appear to have been discontinued in 1922/23 when ordinary fares settled down to some sort of stabilisation following a very high level just after the First War.

The earliest surviving tickets are very neat and concise in appearance and seldom suffer the printers' errors of later years. Fares were usually shown on the face of all Classes except Parliamentary. As traffic developed and railways came into the district from various directions, a great variety of through bookings to places off the Festiniog developed; these were available on to the L.N.W.R., G.W.R. and Cambrian Railways by means of the various interchange points en route. Such tickets to 'foreign' destinations were the most colourful and assorted of any. Printed tickets were stocked for such destinations as Bangor, Aberystwyth, Llangollen and Rhyl, and through bookings could be made to Liverpool and Manchester from Portmadoc. For these latter destinations blank cards or simply paper tickets were used.

The greatest number of persons travelling over the line were quarrymen and workmen. Tickets for these were provided in considerable variety, varying from singles and day tickets to weeklies. Even Four-Day tickets were printed and, as presumably these were for a short working week, one may ask if other Companies ever printed workmen's tickets for customers' poor trading conditions? In this series tickets for youths were overprinted LAD and each ticket of each variety was endorsed 'Available in Workmens/Quarrymens train and carriage only' and on the reverse appeared extensive conditions together with a clause limiting the Company's liability to £25 in the case of accident. Portmadoc issued a weekly ticket in this series to Boston Lodge; the modest price was 4*d*., whilst many other issues of the like rarely exceeded ⅓*d*. per mile.

When the Welsh Highland opened in 1923 the number of printed tickets to 'foreign' stations increased greatly and through fares were available off the F.R. to Nantmor, Beddgelert, South Snowdon and Dinas. By comparison with the tickets over the standard gauge lines this new series was somewhat insipid, being given to all-green or green and buff. An unusual printer's error of this series was the ticket 3rd single Dinas–Blaenau Festiniog which was headed Festiniog Railway.

The Five Valleys Tour which was so much a feature of the period between the wars was decimated with the closing of the Welsh Highland in September 1936. In following seasons passengers had to make their way from Portmadoc to Caernarvon by Crosville bus, supplementary tickets being given at Blaenau marked 'Via Crosville Motor Services' plus a special 3rd class single pink ticket to cover the section on the F.R. At this time too, holders of L.M.S. Holiday Runabout Tickets travelling between Afon Wen and Blaenau and vice versa could obtain specially reduced fares and in the reverse direction there were facilities to extend the journey to Pwllheli. The return half of this latter ticket, though headed 'Festiniog Railway' was in fact for a journey over G.W.R. metals from Pwllheli to Afon Wen only: the bulk of the holders of these runabout tickets travelled clockwise from the coastal resorts east of the Conway, and returned thence via Caernarvon and Bangor.

In the years immediately before the Second War Sunday School outings from Blaenau and Tan-y-Grisiau to places off the line (Barmouth and Pwllheli, for instance) became very popular and special tickets were printed for them. One such issue is dated 22 July 1939 and headed 'Jerusalem Sunday School'. The guaranteed sum payable for a special over the full railway was £5.

When passenger services first began, each station issued its own tickets. On Dduallt being reduced to unstaffed status it seems that tickets were issued by the train guard, as a printed ticket marked Dduallt is dated 26 February 1924. Tickets issued from Penrhyn and Tan-y-Grisiau after 1934 became less common suggesting both a slump in traffic originating from either and irregular manning of the booking offices there, which step was taken as an economy measure.

No printed tickets issued at either Boston Lodge or Moelwyn Halts have survived, and probably they were never printed. On the other hand, workmen's tickets were available to both these Halts. In connection with the latter, and to references about special trains for Brookes' Siding nearby, an interesting sidelight on a little-documented service is provided by carbon copies of the Tan-y-Grisiau Excess Fare Receipt Book; in this some entries for 1930 refer to workmen's fares from Moelwyn Halt by the '4.0 p.m. Brookes' Special', apparently a special short working for employees at Brookes' granite quarry returning to Tan-y-Grisiau and Blaenau.

All four stations in Blaenau issued tickets during their lifetime save for that at Duffws where the openings and closings for intermittent periods after 1920 have made it difficult to determine if the re-opened phase coincided with re-opening of booking facilities also. On the G.W.R. Exchange station the ticket stocks were at first housed in a small hut at the end of the interchange platform, later moving to the G.W.R. booking office. Whilst tickets stating 'Blaenau Festiniog G.W.R.' commonly survive none is dated pre 1922, suggesting that at no time were tickets issued both at Duffws and the G.W.R. Exchange simultaneously. Certainly up until the cessation of passenger trains in 1939 it was still possible to purchase a ticket for the Up journey whereon Duffws was shown as the terminus, and conversely Down journeys begun at the G.W.R. could be made on tickets marked Duffws. Such economy in using old stocks was laudatory, but it becomes worthless when on the other hand it is noted that in late July and during August 1939 almost 7,000 new tickets were ordered and delivered from Edmondson's, these being among the almost half-million tickets found in stock when the new regime prepared to re-open for business.

The Author is indebted to A. Michael Davies for most of the information detailed above, and the basis of the Table which follows.

TICKETS

[PRE-1955 SERIES ONLY.]

		1ST	2ND	3RD
Ordinary Ticket	Single	All White	All Pink	All Green (a minority Pink) Pink were special cheap issues
	Return	Out: Yellow Ret.: White	Out: Blue Ret.: Red	Out: Buff (some all Green) Ret.: Green or Grey/Green (some Out: Buff Ret.: Khaki)
Privilege Ticket (Out half: avail. 1 week. Ret. half avail. 1 week or 1 month overprint red 'R'.)	Single	All White	All Pink	All Green
	Return	Out: White Ret.: Yellow	Out: Blue Ret.: Red	Out: Buff Ret.: Green Some all Green
Day Excursion Ticket	Single	Not issued	Not issued	Not issued
	Return	Out: Yellow Ret.: White 3 narrow Blue stripes across length on some	Out: Blue Ret.: Red 2 Blue horizontal bands	Out: Buff or Brown Ret.: Green 3 narrow Blue or Green stripes across length on some. Special trains all Green
Half Day Excursion Ticket	Return	No record	No record	Both halves Slate Grey or Light Blue
Special Excursion Ticket *Cheap One Day* (Issued to points off F.R.)	Return	No record	No record	All Green 3 diagonal thin Red stripes on return half
Cheap Week-end Ticket (Issued to points off F.R.)	Return			Out: Buff Ret.: Dark Green overprint 'W' in Dark Blue
Parliamentary Ticket	Single			All Green: '3rd Parly . . .' or 'PARLIAMENTARY'
Excess Tickets	Single	3rd–1st White	2nd–1st White	3rd–2nd Pink

TYPE	Available in	COLOUR, ETC.
Police Officer on duty at ¾ ordinary fare	3rd class	Out: Buff Ret.: Green
7 day Return to places off the F.R. ('Available 7 days, Sundays not counted.')	3rd class	All Dark Green. Return half overprinted 7 in Red. (Another series has Out: half Yellow with 2d. overprint in Red. Return half as usual.) (A third series was Out: Buff. Ret.: Green with Blue circle.)

(1st class similar is Yellow Out and White Return with Blue circle on it.)

10 days Return to places off the F.R. ('Available 10 days including day of issue.')	3rd class	Out: Buff Ret.: Green—10 in Red overprint on each half.

Also 1st. Out: Yellow; Return: White; then as 3rd.

Through Quarrymen's Ticket to points off F.R. (Standard gauge only.)	Quarrymen's Carriage	All Buff. Return half overprint R. in Red. 'Available on Quarrymen's Carriage only.'
Quarryman's Daily Ticket	Quarrymen's Carriage	Single: All Buff, or Orange (in the 1930s the Orange type was used).
Quarryman's Weekly Ticket	Quarrymen's Carriage	All White or Buff or all Yellow; 2 broad Red vertical bands at each end.

This ticket printed similar to Return ticket and described '3rd class' stations: 'X to Y and back'. Left half states: 'Available in Quarrymen's train and carriage only one journey daily each way up to Saturday in the week of issue.' Up to 30 Nov. 1925, issued as one-piece ticket. After 1 Dec. 1925, two-piece ticket with week number impressed.

Quarryman's 4 day Ticket	'Quarrymen's train and carriage only.'	All Buff, large Red 'four' thus ⊬ (horizontally).
Quarryman's Excess Ticket	Quarrymen's Carriage	Single: Dark Blue with 2 thin Red vertical bands.
Daily Workmen's Ticket	Workmen's Carriage	Return: All Orange or Red or all Stone. Return half overprint R. in Red. 'Available in Workmen's train and carriage only.'
Daily Workmen's Ticket (Excess)	Workmen's Carriage	Return: Out: Buff Ret.: Green
Workmen's Weekly Ticket. Portmadoc–Boston Lodge (4d.)		Single: Mauve, Black 'W' overprint.

TYPE	Available in	COLOUR, ETC.
Workmen's Weekly Ticket	Workmen's Carriage	All Yellow, with four broad Pink vertical stripes. Printed like Single ticket, with station names, e.g. 'Duffws & Tunnel Halt'. 'Available in Workmen's train and carriage only.' Earlier issue printed like ordinary Return 3rd.

Another variety: Colour as 2nd class single overprinted 'W' in Black.

Receipt for Excess Fare Ticket, e.g. Minffordd—Harbour: all Dark Blue.

Pram Ticket	'Single' type	White
Dog Ticket	'Single' type	Tomato
Cycle Ticket	'Single' type	Blue/Grey. Some—'not exceeding 25 miles'.
Observation Car	'Single' type	Some Dark Blue with broad purple band across centre; others all Pink.
Tour Tickets		(In connection with advertised tours, tickets printed, e.g. 'Special Series. Tour No. 16. Third class F.R. issue') All Pink. All Single. Some 'via Crosville Motor Service' (in place W.H.R., 1938).
Holiday Contracts Series Ticket (Issued to points off F.R.)		Some headed 'Holiday Contract Series', others 'Special Series: issued in connection with L.M. & S. Railway. Holiday Contract Ticket.' Single: All Green. Return: Out: Buff ⎫ one thin Red band Ret.: Green ⎭ down each half. Available one day only.
Festiniog and London & North Western Railways Excursion Ticket (Available 3 days.) Issued to stations on the L.N.W.R.		Return: Out: Buff. Ret.: Green—early series with thin Blue diagonal line: later series overprint '3 days' in Red.

CHILDREN: Early issues have 'Child's Ticket under 12 years' additionally printed on them. Later issues 'CHILD' overprint in Red.

LADS: Reduced fares in Quarrymen's train—word 'LAD' overprinted in Red on daily and weekly Quarrymen's tickets.

TYPE	COLOUR, ETC.
First Class—Season Ticket.	Small card folder, Yellow cover.
Third Class—Season Ticket.	Small card folder, Red cover.
First Class—Free Pass.	Small card folder, plain White back, sometimes having thin Red stripe. Company's name not printed on cover.
Third Class—Free Pass.	Small card folder, Green or Blue cover. Company's name not printed on cover.
First Class Pass. (Issued to Directors of adjacent Railway Companies, etc.)	Folding card of oval shape, backed white leather with red stripe running down outer cover. Outer cover lettered, e.g. 'FREE PASS. FIRST CLASS 1910 FESTINIOG RAILWAY' in Gilt characters.

All the above signed by the Managing Director.

Welsh Highland & Festiniog Railway. (Introduced 1923.)	Third Class—Fortnightly Season Ticket available between all stations. Small card folder with titles of both companies printed on Green cover.

Above signed by the General Manager.

'Welsh Highland & Festiniog Railways.' (Free Ticket.)	First Class. Free Ticket. 'From .... To .... and back Mr.................................,' Signed H. F. Stephens. All White. Corner tear off.

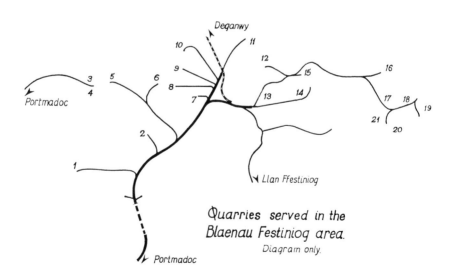

Quarries served in the
Blaenau Festiniog area.
Diagram only.

CHAPTER NINETEEN

QUARRY CUSTOMERS AND THEIR FEEDER BRANCHES

(including summarised histories of each quarry site connected with Festiniog Railway)

Slate Quarries served directly by Festiniog Railway

1. Moelwyn
2. Wrysgan
*3. Rhosydd
*4. New Rhosydd
5. Conclog
6. Cwm Orthin
7. Glan-y-Pwll
8. Cesail   ⎫
9. Rhiwbryfdir ⎬ (becomes) Oakeley ⎰ Upper
10. Welsh Slate Co. ⎭   ⎨ Middle
                                        ⎱ Lower
11. Llechwedd
12. Votty
13. Bowydd (later Votty & Bowydd)
14. Diphwys Casson
15. Maenofferen
16. Cwt-y-Bugail
17. Blaen-y-Cwm
18. Frudd
19. Rhiwbach
20. Bwlch-y-Slater (later New Manod)
21. New Manod (quarrying site)
*22. ⎱ North & South Pole Quarries with, immediately west, Craig Ddu with,
*23. ⎰ to its south, original Manod (each in very close proximity when started)
*24. Dwr Oer
*25. Penmachno
*26. Morgan Drum

Brynglas, Foel Gron and Croes Ddwyafon in the Pont-yr-afon-Gam area, carted to the F. & B.R. at Llan Ffestiniog; these small quarries, each having a tramway to the nearest road, are not shown.

* Exceptions; never used F.R. directly.

The Festiniog Railway was the last of the great Welsh narrow gauge slate lines. The first was Lord Penrhyn's private railway; the second was built by Thomas Assheton-Smith and the third was a statutory undertaking known as the Nantlle Railway (these three undertakings are due for description in a companion volume). The three had been built, emulating each other, between 1799 and 1828. Between them they served all the major slate quarrying areas of North Wales except

Ffestiniog. By 1820 if not sooner, every quarry operator was aware that the costs of extracting slate were roughly equal wherever the site or whatever the method, but that cost of transporting output to shipside was the critical factor in his competitiveness. In consequence, quarry owners at Ffestiniog looked with dismay upon the advantages of their competitors for, as early as 1783 the quarries of the areas where the first two-named lines were to run, were producing 57% of total North Wales tonnage.

Yet it was not solely quarry interests which brought the Festiniog Railway into existence, but rather an amalgam of land-owners, share-pushers, capitalists and quarry-owners—transport for the slate quarries existent and potential being their common cause. On completion of the Railway in 1836, one might have felt that the Ffestiniog quarries would be thankful to compete at last on equal terms with other North Wales quarries which had long enjoyed good rail transport. But were they? Instead of taking immediate advantage of the Railway, for a number of reasons including the thought that they considered slate rates too high, they boycotted it in the hope of bringing the Railway Company to the brink. However, the Railway obtained Samuel Holland's traffic immediately and were saved from financial crisis by a mortgage from Sir Joseph Huddart. So though some quarries hung back, they were ultimately obliged to come to terms and make physical connection with the Railway.

At Ffestiniog it was soon discovered that the above-ground method of quarrying as practised elsewhere, could not win slate, and it was necessary to abandon the above-ground gallery method of working in many sites in favour of inclined adits below ground. Mining was done in chambers which collectively honeycombed the sub-surface, the chambers being connected with each other by horizontal tunnelled levels, or underground Inclines. From about 1825 these underground connections were laid out with tramways, the first being in the Bowydd Quarry.

Not all the landlords in the Ffestiniog area lived locally and only occasionally did they quarry themselves. Seldom did they or their lessees speak Welsh. The leases given were often too short to make the site worth while. Some lessees only paid a nominal rent, but the landlord benefited by a royalty on output, so that their personal interest in the success of their lessees was keen, and in slate transport (often through their lands) was profound. Often they appointed qualified agents to supervise efficient working of quarries on their estates, these posts sometimes involving Festiniog Railway administrators, acting in quite a separate role, it must be understood. For the same reason, certain quarry owners and lessees were from time to time to be found on the Board of the Railway Company.

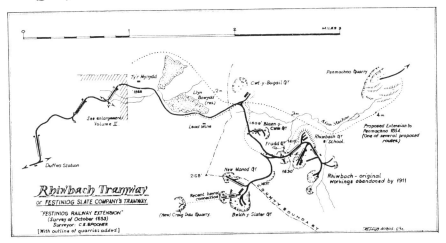

The Railway passed from a time of monopoly and, at the end of one hundred years came to the point where it had to advise its quarry customers that if they did not use it, it would close its freight services and become a tourist railway. This never happened, but when costs became too high and with falling quarry tonnages the line appeared uneconomical in future prospect, it was closed. Today, in 1975, it might appear inconceivable that those vast piles of debris around Blaenau, with their empty water-filled Chambers below, should have ever been begotten to the Railway, and in turn of the screw, the Railway should have become essential to them. The trade and prosperity of the Railway varied with the fortunes of the slate industry and the effectiveness of its export trade. Success came only whilst Portmadoc was a thriving port; when challenged by Deganwy it lost much business. The Railway tried to make good the loss at Portmadoc by offloading into the Cambrian at Minffordd, but to the quarry owners the very keen costs of using this route were offset by the shorter standard-gauge routes when they became available. These standard-gauge routes enjoyed the overriding advantage of having a reasonably straightforward administration—when the Festiniog wanted to consider costs, it had land-owners en route. The Tremadoc Estate, the Harbour Board and diverse quarry interests to satisfy. One or other was always a stumbling block.

Peak tonnages were carried over the line in the 1870s (approximately 127,000 tons per annum). The national output was 504,000 tons representing an eleven-fold increase in eighteen years. It then became irregular until the great Penrhyn Quarry dispute of 1900–3. This brought a small boom to some but spelled the death-knell of the slate trade as other roofing material was devised to take its place. 1898 was the peak year of quarry employment at Blaenau; matters declined until the First War, resumed in hope during the 1920s and then slipped away. Today, only a handful of men are at work and nothing is taken from the district by rail. A few larger sites have worked continuously since opening but the summarised histories which follow will show how spasmodic has been the life of most. Very little information remains about them, in contrast to the story of the Railway Company which is plentifully chronicled. The smaller sites especially blossomed and faded under successive titles (a title sometimes being used repeatedly) and liquidations were commonplace. Speculation lost thousands of pounds to the unwary, yet a few made vast fortunes. The Railway Accounts show the extreme fluctuation in tonnages, how slates were stocked at quarry and port during slack times (the Railway's wagons being inconsiderately used as mobile warehouses!) and the effect of strikes, roof falls and weather . . . dry weather stopped the water-powered machinery and wet weather flooded the workings. There were prejudices against slate colour, foreign taxes and, by quarry owners, a constant complaint about the failings of the traffic department to supply empty wagons or quote keen rates.

Against this background of supplier/customer relations, a special relationship survived for many years between Railway Management and quarry owners. It may still be detected in the visual reminders of James, or Charles E. Spooner or J. S. Hughes acting as agents for landowners, consulting engineers to quarries, or surveyors on boundary disputes; outside business there was social connection (there were few English gentry in the district at the time), interchange of the same residences, the link through the Church—as opposed to the Chapel—and the probability that some families knew each other before they went to Wales, coming from nearby English localities. St. John's Church, Portmadoc, contains memorials to the names of Spooners and quarry owners alike.

By 1800 the following district quarries had begun work; Cwm Bowydd (in 1801 only), Diphwys, Hafodty and Manod. The last-named was within the quarry now known as Craig Ddu and was never connected to the F.R. The first-named three were ultimately connected. By 1820 the following were also working; Holland's Rhiwbryfdir (sold 1825), Cwm Orthin, Moelwyn, Rhiwbach. By 1830 Holland had sold Rhiwbryfdir to the Welsh Slate Company, and had opened his own Cesail Quarry in 1828. The lower levels of Rhiw (as it is usually abbreviated) were not worked by the W.S.Co., and it became Mathew's Quarry in 1833, after the lessees' name. Except for Rhiwbach, the foregoing also connected with the Railway shortly afterwards.

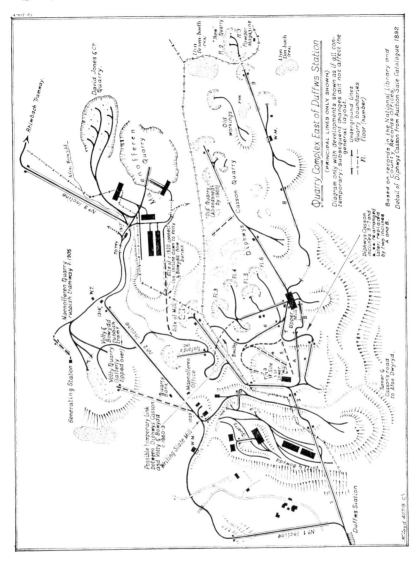

Blaen-y-Cwm (or Pen-y-Ffridd or Frudd) No. 17 on Reference Plan.

1820   By date, said to be open; auctioned 1826.

1855   Unconfirmed suggestion that the site may be working.

1876   Festiniog records show traffic passing.

1877   Listed by D. C. Davies as an open working (i.e. not under-ground).

By 1896 Closed.

1899 Blaen-y-Cwm Quarry Co. Ltd. incorporated.

1911 By date, operators were Blaen-y-Cwm Slate Quarry Co. of Salem House, Tan-y-Grisiau (residence of agent: John Pugh).

Not listed in Returns 1893 but working in period 1899–1902. Years of working before 1893 probably minimal. In 1911 employed 13 men—6 below ground.

Bowydd (or Cwm Bowydd or Lord's or Bowydd-Percival's) No. 13 on Reference Plan.

This site lay to the west-south-west of Diphwys Casson on Lord Newborough's land. At first its boundary with Diphwys Casson was not defined. Underground workings passed below Maenofferen Quarry.

1800 Working on a small scale, but closed during 1801 by his Lordship.

1823 By date, for a second time under control of Lord Newborough's brother, who sold to John Roberts of Caernarvon in 1828. Meanwhile it had become the second largest quarry in the district and in 1825 the first with tramways (Glynrhonwy Quarry at Llanberis, introduced them the same year); tonnages for the year were 2,978 compared with Diphwys Casson 5,673 and W.S.Co. 683 tons.

1833 After five-year search for additional slate rock, Roberts bankrupt. He had spent £30,000. Quarry closed for 366 days.

1834 Edwin Shelton and John Whitehead Greaves (already working Glynrhonwy for four years) take lease.

1846 Shelton closed the partnership due to ill-health, and Greaves ended lease alone; he did not renew.

late 1840s Lease taken by Frederick Samuel Percival of Northampton, along with a second site known as Hafodty, or sometimes Fotty or Votty (q.v.).

1850 Lease for 40 years by Morris Jones (labourer) of field called Blaen-Bowydd and farm Cwm Bowydd. 'New Vein' discovered.

1854 Connection to Festiniog Railway at Duffws station by its own Incline and a second Incline later to become No. 1 Incline of the Festiniog Extension Railway. Connection shared with Votty Quarry (above).* Accounts for carriage with both quarries opened September.

---

* It also appears that when Diphwys Casson Quarry first began to use the Railway (being the last major quarry so to do) they carted their slate by horse to the head of the No. 1 Incline. C. E. Spooner took a wagon census in June 1862 and D.C. wagons were standing on the Extension Railway at the time. D.C.'s own Incline to Duffws was not ready until 1864, owing to the illness of C. E. Spooner who was Engineer to both Quarry and Railway at this period. For about three years therefore, Bowydd, Votty and D.C. were sharing this one outlet to Duffws.

1860 Wayleave given to the Festiniog Slate Quarry Co. Ltd. for building of a tramway (the Rhiwbach Tramway or Festiniog Railway Extension), and on 26 December, lease from Lord Newborough for 21 years of land at Cwm Bowydd and Maenofferen. Concern now becomes a partnership of members of Percival family (F. S. Percival now of Bodawen, Portmadoc).

1868 Agreement with Railway following arrangement by Percival with Festiniog Slate Co. to transport his output from 1861 at 3*s*. 9*d*. ton to Portmadoc. This arrangement ended 1866, Percival giving the necessary three months' notice to F.R.Co. He then used the F.R. for three years at 3*s*. 3*d*. ton, but failed to advise F.R. he had concluded his arrangement with F.S.Co.; F.R. on learning of this, cancelled the Agreement.

1870 Formal amalgamation with Votty Quarry, combined concern now being styled Votty & Bowydd Quarries (q.v.).
Manager 1850: William Rowlands.

Bwlch-y-Slater (tr. Pass of Slates) Neighbouring concern; Manod Slate Quarries Ltd. No. 20 on Reference Plan.

Rail connection between the concerns at the title existed, outlet being via Bwlch-y-Slater.

1824 May As part of Manod Quarry, leased by John Evans to John Pritchard and then part to James Smart.

1835 Re-opened by Messrs. Hudson and Magnes.

? Worked for seven years by Company from Manchester (Manchester & Festiniog Slate Co. ?).

? Worked for period by James Meyrick who became indebted for £60 and lost lease. (The March 1851 Census shows he was from Bristol, and then living at Woodbine Cottage, Ffestiniog.)

? Worked by Edward Jones (Meyrick's Manager) of Teliau Bach, Llan Ffestiniog, who sold balance of lease to Williams of Bennar Fawr, Dyffryn, who spent £10,000 on the site.

1866 Account opened with Festiniog Railway in name of Bwlch-y-Slater Slate Co. but traffic passes for this year only.

1873 Productive again.

1877 D. C. Davies states quarry is currently worked above ground (which it was at a later period also).

1882 Worked by Uriah Bramley and — Wright as The Bwlch-y-Slater Slate Co.

1883 Bwlch-y-Slater Quarry Co. Ltd., registered in Chester—sometime styled Manod Quarries Ltd.

1896 Re-opened after period of closure.

1908 Richard Bowton & Co., agents to quarry, take wharf at Minffordd Yard. (Bowton was later to be a director of the Railway.)

1911 By this date styled Manod Quarries Ltd. of Blaenau Ffestiniog.

1913 Working suspended.

1919 By this date work resumed (work done at Boston Lodge on behalf of).

1937 Working as Manod Slate Quarries Ltd.; closed by 1960.

There was no output in 1882 and only two employees. By 1884 output was 1,058 tons for the year with forty employees; forty-nine were employed at closure in 1913. This quarry was one of a few using the Car Gwyllt, mentioned later in the chapter in connection with an accident.

Part of the workings are currently in use, trading as Cwt-y-Bugail Slate Qys. Co. Ltd. During the Second War, part of the National Treasures was stored here and the L.M.S. Railway's Derby Works built some special stock to 2 ft. gauge for underground transport. Today, the whole complex is collectively known as Manod and the quarry of the heading simply gives access to Craig Ddu Quarry.

Cesail (tr. Armpit) (S. Holland & Co., or Samuel & Charles Holland) No. 8 on Reference Plan.

Landowner—Oakeley or Tan-y-Bwlch Estate, being originally per W. E. Oakeley and from 11 October 1835, per Mrs. Louisa Jane Oakeley on the death of her husband. At her death to W. G. Oakeley to whom the quarry reverted at the end of the lease. The land was that part of the original Rhiwbryfdir Farm lease taken out by Samuel Holland, Senr. in 1819 and retained when the remainder was sold to the Welsh Slate Copper & Lead Mining Co. in March 1825. Holland, Senr. was not interested in working the balance following the sale; firstly there was recession in the industry and secondly some uncertainty about ownership of certain Crown Lands adjacent to the property but to which Oakeley established his right after litigation. As a result, Holland, Jnr. (who had meanwhile occupied himself on more distant projects) returned to Cesail and persuaded his father to let him work the site. Accordingly;

1827 Holland, Jnr. takes over balance of lease from Oakeley.*

1833 Lease expired but renewed to 1839.

1836 Railway opens with Holland the only customer. Further trouble between Holland and W.S.Co. after Holland and Archer had agreed over an Incline; W.S.Co. successfully prevent Holland connecting

---

* Without wasting any time, Holland had driven an underground tunnel but W.S.Co. sent men to prevent him from proceeding, claiming the land was theirs. Litigation began in May 1827; Oakeley reckoned the boundary was not in question and the matter ultimately settled in favour of Holland who began to open out the quarry. Palmerston maintained that if he had known the facts, he would not have proceeded against Holland.

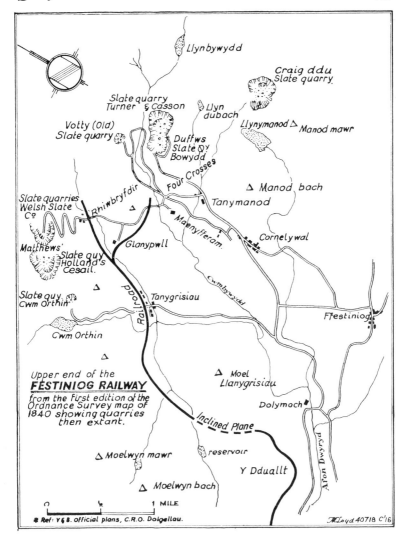

Upper end of the
FESTINIOG RAILWAY
from the first edition of the
Ordnance Survey map of
1840 showing quarries
then extant.

with F.R. (1836). His Incline being prevented from completion, he carted slate to the Dinas terminus of the Railway and trans-shipped there.

1839 Agreement with F.R. re building of an Incline and rates for carriage of slate 18 March. New lease of quarry from Mrs. Oakeley, extending to 1870. Incline completed and opened.

1853 23 August. New Agreement with F.R. over rates, much to

Holland's annoyance. From this date he was to take initiative to break monopoly of F.R.

1856   Quarry lit by gas; some piping survives. Completed by 1875.

1863   9,169 tons passes over F.R. Another Agreement against Holland's judgement, but he had no option. Charges now 2*s*. 6*d*. for whole distance, against 3*s*. 3*d*. of 1853 Agreement. New rate subject to all quarries consigning annual total of more than 110,000 tons.

1870   Lease ended, but occupation continues on annual tenancy. W. E. Oakeley attempts to persuade Holland to amalgamate with his neighbours (Mathews and W.S.Co. beneath him) to enable Oakeley to put all three tenants on same footing. Holland senses Oakeley aim to take over whole premises and is no longer interested in a long-term venture.

1877   Oakeley re-enters the property; it becomes his Upper Quarry and in 1882, part of Oakeley Slate Quarries Co. Ltd. (q.v.).

Peak output 1873 = 18,494 tons; 'about 500 employees'. Oakeley royalty 3*s*. ton. Holland's latter-day Manager was Rees Roberts; in 1877 he continued for Oakeley, going to the Middle Quarry (ex-Mathews) in 1883, succeeding Robert Roberts there.

Conclog (north portion worked as Glyn Ffestiniog *c*. 1896; opened up 1879 but closed long periods until 1895) No. 5 on Reference Plan.

Situate at the head of Cwm Orthin, to which a tramway (leading at first only to Cwm Orthin Quarry) was extended in 1874 using ex-F.R. track materials as available. There was a barracks stable and slate mill at the head of the Cwm; adit level gained by a short Incline which crossed the footpath leading to New Rhosydd Quarry, situated on the ridge and watershed to its west. Wayleave over Cwm Orthin tramway.

1872   Site leased by two Devonshire men, one Matthews.

1873   March. Conclog Slate & Slab Co. Ltd. incorporated; £40,000 capital. Directors; T. M. Matthews (of Rhiwbryfdir Quarry) and Joseph Kellow (of Portmadoc and Croesor Quarry).

1874   August. Reported that £1,000 would cover extension of Cwm Orthin tramway to Conclog. Tramway built by October.

1881   April. Company wound up.

1882   March. New Conclog Slate & Slab Co. Ltd. incorporated.

1896–1909   North part worked as Glyn Ffestiniog Slate & Slab Quarry. 15 employees. [Also for copper—1897.]

1904   New Conclog S. & S. Co. Ltd. wound up. October.

1913   Working suspended in Glyn Ffestiniog portion; 23 August owners declared bankrupt.

1919   25-in. plans show site as being 'New Welsh Slate Co.'. F.R. monthly account opened with J. J. Riley, Deganwy.

There appears to have been no production since the early 1920s.

Annual Returns show 200–400 tons output 1882–4; 17–20 employees; 1893 'not worked'; 1896–7 Glyn Ffestiniog tonnages 226 and 131 tons.

Cwm Orthin (colloquially 'The Slaughter House') No. 6 on Reference Plan.

Site situated on Lord Newborough's Peniarth Estate on west side of range being worked by Oakeley's tenants from the east side. Underground connections with Oakeley at two levels in due course. Land at outlet of Cwm tenanted by Samuel Holland, Senr.; became site of Tan-y-Grisiau village, Holland giving sites for school, church, etc. Holland built road down lower end of valley which crossed F.R. at Dol-Rhedyn and caused much dispute; its level crossing replaced by by underbridge in 1900. At first Holland's road used by slate carts and trans-shipment made at Dinas terminal; later, F.R. provided siding on site of later Tan-y-Grisiau station. By 1850 a tramway (mentioned in Cliffe's *The Book of North Wales*, 1850 Edition) had been built by the F.R. to serve this quarry, being extended in the early 1870s to Conclog (q.v.). To give outlet for Rhosydd Quarry (which had had plans of its own to build a connecting railway) agreement was given by Holland to use the valley road and reach Tan-y-Grisiau siding.* This traffic ceased when the Croesor Tramway was built and Rhosydd connected to it.

Conditions of work in this mine were dreadful. Chambers' roofs fell down. Winding engines and boiler houses underground filled workings with fumes. There was six inches of soot and carbon caked on roofs and walls of the chambers. A man, boy and horse were sent to open up the workings after a period of closure and fumes from chambers long closed up overcame them. All died. There was no proper ventilation and the nickname was well-earned. Local people would not work there and men from Caernarvon, unfamiliar with conditions therein, would stay only a short time—being used anyway, to above-ground quarrying. Even in times of hardship, this quarry failed because of working conditions.

1810–20 Thomas Casson (one of the brothers Casson) together with Lloyd (Pwllheli) and Evans (Tyn-y-Coed) worked it as an open site. Called Casson's Pit. Casson improved Holland's road.

1830 Quarry abandoned.

1840 Changed hands twice; first to John Edwards of Teiliau Bach, and Magnes (see Bwlch-y-Slater): second to W. B. Chorley of London.

184– Estimate and section prepared for tramway: to cost £1,407 19s. 0d.

1845 Account opened with F.R. but only in connection with back carriage and materials used for opening up quarry.

1847 Liverpool agent appointed.

* Cwm Orthin Quarry prevented Rhosydd using *wheeled vehicles* however, setting up Toll Bar shortly above the F.R. level crossing; Rhosydd was restricted to using horses or mules as pack animals to its own siding.

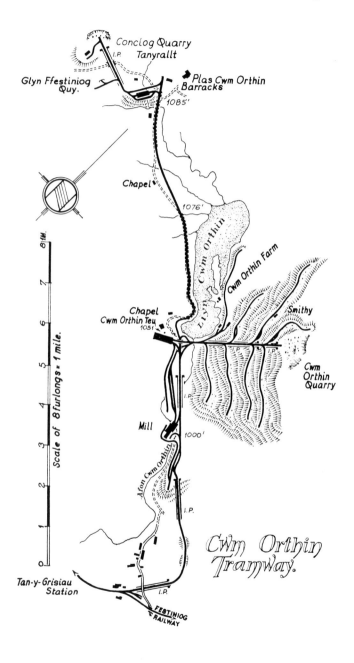

Conclog Quarry
Tanyrallt
I.P.
Glyn Ffestiniog
Quy.
Plas Cwm Orthin
Barracks
1085'
Chapel
1076'
Llyn Cwm Orthin
Cwm Orthin Farm
Smithy
Chapel
Cwm Orthin Teu
1051'
Cwm
Orthin
Quarry
I.P.
Mill
1000'
Afon Cwm Orthin
I.P.
Cwm Orthin
Tramway.
Tan-y-Grisiau
Station
I.P.
FESTINIOG
RAILWAY

8M.
7
6
5
4
3
2
1
0
Scale of 8 furlongs = 1 mile.

1849   Working on larger scale commences, managed by Allen Searell from 1844 (living in the Manager's house, ref. March 1851 Census).*

1850   30 June. F.R. Accounts show first output passing down line. Inclines and branch railway completed, with storage sidings alongside F.R. Existing siding taken out.

1857–60   No traffic passing over F.R. Chorley's interest ends.

1859   Leased to Rhosydd Slate Co. Ltd. (Incorporated 1856) (q.v.) by Chorley (ref. Longueville 901–2) and scale of working intensified.

1861   June. Cwm Orthin Slate Co. Ltd. incorporated. Capital £100,000. Built wharf at Portmadoc, later shared with other quarries.

1863   728 tons passes over F.R.

1864   B.O.T. Inspector objects to connection of Incline with F.R. there being no safety traps. New regulations requiring Distant Signals on F.R., telegraph connection with Incline Summit and no passing trains on F.R. when Incline in use.

1869   Evidence given by J. W. Greaves at House of Commons Enquiry, shows quarry is not working.

1873   Quarry valuation (cost £120) by Charles E. Spooner. Working again.

1875   Sims *v* Evans test case under Metalliferous Mines Act 1872— an underground slate quarry is a mine within the meaning of the Act (re inspection).

1876   Company in liquidation.

1879   Undertaking subject of another test case as to whether quarry or mine Jones *v* Cwm Orthin Slate Co. Ruled that in the matter of profit assessment, it was a quarry not a mine.

1888   June. Winding-up order. August. In liquidation. Sold for £83,000.

1889   May. New Welsh Slate Co. Ltd. incorporated. Capital £65,000. Directors include Hon. Evelyn Ashley (of W.S.Co.) and Joseph Howard, M.P.

1897   290 employees (153 underground).

1900   In voluntary liquidation; wound up 1902. Undertaking passes to W. E. Oakeley as part of Oakeley Slate Quarries. Railway dispute with Oakeley over use of level crossing; underbridge then built. Worked intermittently but out of use for years at a time; 1914 quarry closed.

1930   Working resumed on very reduced scale, partly by new access tunnel driven from main Oakeley Quarry.

1933   Amalgamation with Votty & Bowydd.

1936–7 Oakeley records show renewals on main Quarry Incline and F.R. feeder tramway.

* See NARROW GAUGE RAILWAYS IN SOUTH CAERNARVONSHIRE for Allen Searell.

The lowest floors have flooded recently (1970) when Oakeley stopped work and pumping ceased.

1873, 320 men. Year of maximum employment 1878 (526 employees). Maximum tonnage 13,590 in 1880. Tonnages fell afterwards; output 1937 less than 700 tons.

First tunnel link to Oakeley was 1877 under Herbert Kirkhouse management (he gave name to small quarry opposite Cwm Orthin). After Simms (appointed 1873), Andreas Roberts was Manager for two periods; he had begun in Cesail age 10, afterwards working in Dublin. Owned 6,045 yds. overground and 4,192 yds. underground tramways, plus 168 rubbish wagons in 1873.

Cwt-y-Bugail (tr. The Shepherd's Hut) No. 16 on Reference Plan.

A remote working, partly above and partly below ground served only by bridle path and later, by Rhiwbach Tramway. A medium-sized quarry, much prey to the weather which closed it for long periods in the winter. On the Peniarth Estate. Last distant user of Rhiwbach Tramway, all of which was lifted from foot of No. 3 Incline when the quarry ceased in 1961.

1835   Working begun by Gregory.

1853   'Hanes Plwf Ffestiniog' remarks that concern was flourishing.

1861   Agreement with Rhiwbach Quarry for use of tramway to Duffws at 1s. 4d. ton.

1862   Lease arranged for period 1864–88.

1863   April. Cwt-y-Bugail Slate Co. Ltd., incorporated. Capital £50,000. Chairman; Hugh Beaver Roberts (Plas Llandoget, Llanrwst) and four others, three of whom were also directors of the George Hotel Co., Bangor. By 1869, Samuel Palmer, the Reading biscuit manufacturer, was on the board.

1867   Account opened with the Railway.

1875   January. Company wound up; subsequently sold same year for £11,900.

1875   April. The Bugail Slate Co. Ltd. incorporated. Capital £71,000. (Roberts had sold out by 1880; latterly composed of Scottish and Irish interests only.)

1891   July. Company wound up.

1893   August. Bugail Slate Quarry Co. Ltd. incorporated £4,000 Capital—a quarrymen's undertaking.

1909   F.R. take legal steps to obtain arrears of payment from B.S.Q. Co. Ltd., but it goes into liquidation June.

1911   New Welsh Slate Quarry Co. Ltd. (third time use of title) ('proprietors of Bugail Mine') incorporated under aegis of Cadwalladr Pierce—and shown in possession on 25-in. plan of 1920.

1913   Working suspended.

1921   Working resumed.

1923   Lease given to Cwt-y-Bugail Slate Quarries Co. Ltd., mainly a private concern run by Tudor Roberts who also owned the Glan-y-Pwll Saw Mills (ex F.R. Loco Shed).

1939   Working ceased; about forty employees.

1947   Re-opened under existing style heading but with new owners. Working consistently until

1961 and spasmodically thereafter. The site is presently one of a group of quarries worked by this Company.

Not worked in recent years. Probably the last quarry to use the Rhiwbach Tramway lifting of which began in 1956. Until the early 1960s slate was taken along its surviving length and a leased upper section of the F.R. (then closed and isolated at Duffws) from Duffws to the ex L.M.S.R. yard at Blaenau.

Output for 1882 was 2,549 tons with 73 employees. After 1883 the Returns show 'Mine not working' and tonnage fell though stocks were sold. An average of 30 was employed 1883–92. Peak employment of 116 in 1873, and output 3,669 tons 1874. Under the Bugail Slate Co. Ltd., Evan Evans left to manage the Bryneglwys Quarry at Abergynolwyn (Talyllyn Railway), during McConnel's time.

Diphwys (Turner & Casson or Diphwys Casson) No. 14 on Reference Plan.

Situated on Lord Newborough's Peniarth Estate; the first quarry at Ffestiniog. Owned considerable fleet of brigs based on Portmadoc. Slate is close to the surface and can be worked in the open.

1760–70   Opened by Methusalem Jones, a quarryman from Cilgwyn Quarry, and five colleagues. One of these was William Morris, the first man to be killed in a Ffestiniog Quarry accident; 1794 small company formed.

1799   Acquired for £14,000 by William Turner, William and Thomas Casson, the foremost fleeing from mining ventures in Co. Wicklow due to riots there in 1798. They formed the first formalised quarrying in the area, bringing men from Cilgwyn and changing their skills to meet local conditions.

1847   March. Festiniog Slate Quarries Co. formed to purchase and work 'Turner Casson & Co's' slate quarries. Became Limited Company July 1853 but with different objectives, the original not having been achieved. Capital £50,000. Board includes men later prominent in other local ventures, e.g. H. B. Roberts. Prospectus of 11 March 1847 describes quarry as having '23 cottages . . . all necessary iron tramroads . . . output 5,000–6,000 tons per annum . . . employing about 180 men'. (Later objectives included purchase of the Tyddyn-bychan Estate, Penmachno, 'to make a tramway to the Festiniog &

Portmadoc Railway at Diffwys, to purchase from Robert Owen Mousdale' etc.)

1848 Turner & Co. offered £235 per year by F.R. towards costs of taking slate to the Railway until his Incline was ready. (The quarry was not using the Railway, having its own road to the river. The F.R. offer was not taken up.)

1860 Account with F.R. opened at year's end in name 'Wm. Turner & Co'; last major quarry to start using Railway.

1863 Diphwys Casson Slate Co. Ltd. incorporated when quarry sold for £120,000 on death of George Casson. Capital £200,000. Own Incline to Duffws contemplated; heretofore since beginning to use F.R., slate carted to head of Rhiwbach No. 1 Incline and then put into D.C. earmarked wagons. In this way 4,999 tons had passed over F.R. Last shipments made from Dwyryd wharves.

Chairman; Thomas Barnes, M.P. (of The Quinta, Oswestry)—see Glyn Valley Tramway interests—Deputy Chairman: Thomas Savin (Railway Contractor).* Engineer: Charles E. Spooner. Secretary: John Sylvester Hughes (at this time not connected with the F.R.). Bankers; Casson & Co., Portmadoc. Plans for Duffws Incline ready by June.

1864–5 Company's Engineer ill; work on Incline not yet commenced 'owing to a protracted illness'. Incline construction postponed. When it would be ready 'horse labour would be saved' says shareholder at meeting. Incline ready during 1865.

1873 By date, all quarry machinery is steam powered (cf. Llechwedd which had none at this time).

1887 William Galley Casson, grandson of first partner, 'still working the quarry'. Railway want to make extra charges in view of the many Inclines in the quarry.

1892 January. Concern liquidated. 24 May; auction at Queens Hotel, Blaenau Ffestiniog. On sale, title amended to Diphwys Casson Slate Quarries Co. Ltd.

1897 Re-arrangement of Duffws Incline at upper end, allowing it to pass through Votty & Bowydd premises; alteration to layout at top end also (ref. Votty & Bowydd Collection, Dolgellau Record Office) 30 December. Ownership of Incline to pass to Votty & Bowydd provided whoever is the owner, he is bound to carry D.C. products 'at 1½d. ton royalty to Lord Newborough and not more than 4d. to the owner of the tram . . .' '. . . as to the extension of the Diphwys Casson tram to join the Incline at the top'. 155 employees (77 underground).

1917 Closed for remainder of war.

1919 Worked as Diphwys Slate Quarry Co. Ltd. for part of year only.

* Also connected with Brynfferam Slate Quarries, nr. Llangollen.

1927   Closed.
1936   Acquired and worked by Oakeley Slate Quarries Co. Ltd., for this year only.
1955   Closed for last time.
1972   Purchased by J. W. Greaves & Sons Ltd.
Output in 1825, when the largest quarry in the area, was 5,673 tons. In 1882 it was 6,363 tons with 222 employees and thereafter declined. Little work has been done since 1926.

Evan Parry Jones, Manager appointed for the new owners in 1864, had started work in the quarry age 12: 270 were employed in 1870.

Glan-y-Pwll (or Nidd-y-Gigfran) (tr. Raven or Griffin's Nest) No. 7 on Reference Plan.

Located up on the mountain face above Glan-y-Pwll, Blaenau Ffestiniog, a once notoriously evil swamp thought to be the origin of much local ill-health.

1840s   Opened by Thomas Evan James, a miner from Ruthin who worked for a short time on a small scale. Known as 'Evan James' Quarry'.
1861   August. Glan-y-Pwll Slate & Slab Co. Ltd. incorporated. Capital £30,000. Possibly little work done until 1867 when about this time an Incline was built to the Festiniog Railway. The upper portion of it terminated at a rock-face platform from which probably a series of ropeways were carried to each of several adit entrances in the rock wall, each with its loading platform.
1867   30 September. Account opened with Railway.
1870   Working ceased.
1872   August. Company in liquidation.
1877   Lease terminated.
1882   At time of publication 'Hanes Plwyf Ffestiniog' working was suspended.
At a much later date the workings were linked underground with Oakeley Slate Quarries Co. Ltd., and worked for a short time; connection was via the Cesail level.

There was a slab mill at Glan-dwr, operated from a water wheel. Litigation between Tan-y-Bwlch (Oakeley) and Glan-y-Pwll Estates closed down the undertaking Mrs. Oakeley clashing with the Trustees of Richard Parry as to ownership of the quarry. Mrs. Oakeley prevented work being continued and a case heard at Chester went in her favour, a stone boundary wall being built in consequence. Trespassers faced a £10,000 fine upon conviction.

A recent survey shows 3 or 4 chambers and a small open quarry, with the remains of a timber-built winding house above the latter.

Peak output 1867, 387 tons. Maenofferen Quarry wharf was used for shipments. (In 1866 there existed a Tan-y-Grisiau Slate Co. which had an account with the F.R. for that year only. Tradition has it that this concern worked part or all the site for that year only.)

Hafodty (or Votty or Fotty) (Shown on some statutory material as Jozzy or Jolly) No. 12 on Reference Plan.

A small working shown on the 1-in. First Edition Map of 1836, lying to the north of Bowydd Quarry, on Lord Newborough's Estate. Not shown in F.R. Accounts after 1860, but 'Bowydd Lower Mill' first appears in March 1864.

1801 Worked by this date by a small group of local men, largely for local roofing requirements.

1846 'Revived' (ref. D. C. Davies) by F. S. Percival of Northampton at the same time as he took a lease of the adjacent Bowydd Quarry.

1851 Account opened with Railway 31 March for a few weeks only.

1854 Account re-opened with Railway 30 September, at same period as that with Bowydd opened (see opening note about closing of Account). Linked by tramway to Bowydd (see under Bowydd for detail now and later), using part of the later Rhiwbach Tramway or Festiniog Extension Railway.

1870 From this date, Percival worked Votty and Bowydd Quarries as one concern (q.v.).

pre-1905 After workings abandoned, a new tramway extending from Votty & Bowydd Quarry ran north and west, passed under Rhiwbach Tramway No. 2 Incline, and enabled the derelict workings to be filled with V. & B. rubbish.

c. 1905 At an early date this century, a tramway was extended westwards from the foot of No. 3 Incline Rhiwbach Tramway, leading into the top of the abandoned Hafodty workings. This enabled Maenofferen Quarry to tip rubbish into the old workings also. Thus at two levels, the old quarry was used as a slate rubbish tip, both Votty & Bowydd and Maenofferen being unable to find adjacent room for more tipping. The latter branch still exists (1975) and has a short tunnel on it.

Part of the old quarry was also used as a reservoir, abandoned chambers being allowed to fill to supply a pumping station for Votty & Bowydd. In consequence, very little of the original concern can be discerned today.

Llechwedd (or Llechwedd-y-Cyd or Greaves') No. 11 on Reference Plan.

Originated and worked entirely by the Greaves family, trading latterly as J. W. Greaves & Sons Ltd. The most northerly of the major local quarries. Partly on Oakeley land until the mid-1930s, when the freehold was bought.

1846 Opened by John Whitehead Greaves who left Bowydd Quarry at the end of his tenancy: his son A. Ernest Greaves was Manager.

1847 Desperate search to find the Old Vein rewarded; Greaves given £235 per annum by Railway to bring his slates to the line until his Incline was complete.

1848 Incline completed and account opened 30 June.

1851 Offices moved from Quarry to Portmadoc: output *c.* 2,900 tons.

1853 Wharf opened at Portmadoc. Agreement with Railway over Rates and as offered to other Railway users 23 August.

1863 7,620 tons passes over Railway.

1873 Quarry still worked by various water-wheels—no steam power.

1890 Quarry turns over to electric operation—the earliest in Ffestiniog.

1897 Three month strike affects F.R. traffic very considerably. 533 employees (245 underground).

1899 Becomes Limited Liability concern.

1904 Quarry fitted out for hydro-electric operation.

1934 Final purchase of land to acquire freehold of property.

1972 Purchased site of Diphwys Casson Quarry.

Employees in 1872 were 330 men and boys.

Output figures show 1884 as the heaviest tonnage; 23,788 tons with 513 employees, and the third largest quarry in the district. By the end of the century, only about one-third of product was shipped from Portmadoc. By the middle 1930s, output was about the same as 1863.

A Railway Company breakdown of traffic from the quarry has interest;

1935 To Portmadoc for shipment 5,585 tons; to Minffordd 4,907 tons; To L.M.S. Nil; To G.W.R. (B.Ff.) 3 tons.

1937 To Portmadoc for shipment 3,433 tons; to Minffordd 4,028 tons; To L.M.S. Nil; To G.W.R. (B.Ff.) Nil.

demonstrating that standard gauge wharf at Blaenau was not in use, the quarry supporting the F.R.

Maenofferen (tr. Sacrificial Stone) (or Maenofferen Slate Co.) No. 15 on Reference Plan.

This site was known as Fridd-y-Gelli in far-off days where owing to a fault in the strata, brick clay could be found. There was a tradition of finding copper there before men from Diphwys Quarry began to work slate shortly after 1800. At unspecified date Lord Newborough's agent, John Hughes, appointed Morgan Jones of Dyr Mynydd to work the site. Morgan cleaned up the clay slant (it becoming 'Morgan's Level') and built a shaft. It then passed to Roberts of Caernarvon (see also Bowydd Quarry), later becoming a small interest of Shelton and Greaves following Roberts. Slate found to be too brittle. A better level in the 'Old Vein' above came too near Diphwys Quarry to be pursued. There was clearly some success as the chronology shows.

1848 F.R. Accounts show 'Maenyfferran (Shelton & Greaves)' tonnages for 1848 and against J. W. Greaves only for 1848–9. Thereafter
traffic ceased.

1855 D. C. Davies states quarry open at this time.

1857 Traffic over Railway this year only; more traffic follows but not
in 1858 or 1865, otherwise flow was consistent. Probably using
Bowydd Quarry Incline of 1854 to reach Duffws station.

1859 Company formed by Messrs. Allen Searell, David Jones (of Cwm
Orthin) and Lewis Thomas (of The Shop, Maenofferen). Later
owners were Sir William Cooke and others who ultimately sold it in
1861 to form new Company.

The above notes apply to a small northern part of the site known as
the David Jones & Co., or 'Two and a Half' Quarry (referring to the
levels) which is now abandoned but has interesting specimens of
machine tunnelling to be seen. Loaded wagons were lifted a short way
on to the main incline for Duffws.

1861 Maenofferen Slate Quarry Co. Ltd. incorporated 12 June.
Capital £50,000; (later £70,000) usually styled on the leases 'David
Jones & Others'. Several minor changes of ownership and title
follow; shareholders largely in the south of England. Output at this
time *c.* 400 tons. Directors include W. F. Cooke; C. B. Skinner;
W. S. Percival a subscriber. William Owen, Manager.

1862 Portmadoc wharf leased January.

1863 181 tons passes over Railway.

1877 May. Overdue Railway account put in lawyer's hands.

1881 Boundaries surveyed and determined by James Brunton and
Charles E. Spooner (J. S. Hughes a witness to the document).

1882 Operating company styled Maenofferen Co. Ltd. in F.R.
Accounts, but altered shortly to Maenofferen Slate Quarry Co. Ltd.

1897 429 employees (209 underground).

1908 Turntables and sidings put in at Minffordd yard.

1920 November. Additional empty wagon siding put in at Duffws
station. New Incline and tramway link built between Mills and Votty
& Bowydd enabling Company to use Votty & Bowydd Incline into
Duffws station, so avoiding use of, and new high charges on, the
Rhiwbach Tramway. Boston Lodge supplied the point work for the
foot of the Incline (September) (see map).

1928 Purchase of Rhiwbach Quarry, which was worked until 1953.

1962 Last use of Duffws—ex L.M.S.R. trans-shipment yard at
Blaenau section of F.R. by Quarry for slate coming off Rhiwbach
Tramway (by this time owned by Maenofferen (see 1928)). Quarry
goes over to road transport, for removal of finished products. Retains
rail transport and part of Rhiwbach Tramway.

1975 Transport position as in 1962: Company still trading.

Output rose to 14,065 tons in 1897 and the highest number employed was 450 in 1911. For many years this was the fifth largest quarry in the district. The 1930s breakdown was:

1935   To Portmadoc for shipping 228 tons; Minffordd 8,825 tons; L.M.S. 24 tons; G.W. 146 tons.

The Mining Journal for 16 April 1870 has an 'Advertisement To Miners and Quarrymen' seeking tenders for sinking a shaft 47 yards × 14 ft. × 12 ft.

*Matthews** (or Rhiwbryfdir Slate Co.) No. 9 on Reference Plan.

This was the middle 'layer' of the three concerns quarrying at this place, in Oakeley property. It lay partly under Cesail, and partly over Welsh Slate Co. workings. Part of it is said to have been worked as early as 1800.

1825   Formed part of W.S.Co. purchase of Rhiwbryfdir from Samuel Holland, Senr. This Company did not consider the time opportune to develop the portion, and left it standing.

1833   Estate leases re-set, and one assigned to Nathaniel Matthews (of Wern, Tremadoc) G. H. Huddart (of Brynkir) and others, who did some trial explorations in view of shortness of lease.

1839   New lease obtained, and trading commenced as Rhiwbryfdir Slate Co. following year.

1842   Agreement with F.R. made 1 January in the name of John Richards and account opened the same month. Incline assumed to be complete at this date, but no record available. The exact position location of the Incline is not known, and it appears to have been destroyed in 1870 (q.v.).

1853   23 August. New Agreement with Railway over rates, citing Edward Windus Matthews, Geoffrey Windus and (Captain) Nathaniel Matthews.

1863   11,179 tons passes over F.R.

1869   After opposing F.R. Bill of 1869, Matthews alters opinion in favour of Railway, fearful his Company might 'have to build a wagon fleet (at cost of £12.20 each)' if the Bill failed. Significant that Andrew Durham is on Board of both Railway and Quarry at this time, and that Samuel Holland is a director of Rhiwbryfdir at the period.

1870   F.R. Minutes record building of new Incline to R.S.Co., possibly to improve on first one and make provision for tipping of rubbish. The new tramway at its foot passed through Rhiwbryfdir hamlet but this arrangement was later altered to continue the

* Spelt as 'Mathews' in earlier years.

Incline foot to a lower point and meet the F.R. alongside the south-west corner of the W.S.Co.'s viaduct.*

1871   Lease expired, but annual tenancy continued until December 1877 when Oakeley re-entered the property and worked it himself (see Oakeley).

A royalty of 4s. ton was paid to Oakeley.

In 1854 Captain Edward Windus Matthews invented the first mechanical slate dressing machine, so displacing the hand knife. By 1856 a stationary steam engine drove these machines at the quarry. [J. W. Greaves also produced a slate-cutting machine.]

Moelwyn (or Moelwyn Mawr or Great Moelwyn Slate Mine or Quarry) No. 1 on Reference Plan. (On Crown Lands.)

A lofty remote site of 356 acres, high on the slopes of Moelwyn Mawr, worked intermittently over many years and connected to the F.R. by a series of seven inclines, falling to a junction at the north end of the Moelwyn Tunnel. A part of the Cwm Orthin wharf was leased at Portmadoc.

1826   Site explored by Rothschild's Royal Cambrian Co.

1828   Royal Cambrian Co. withdraw.

1841   Traditionally opened by this date under Humphrey Jones a lawyer of Ruthin and at times subsequently after long years of inactivity.

1860   Great Moelwyn Slate Co. Ltd. incorporated January: to purchase from Thomas Cooper Smith for £9,890.

1865   Great Moelwyn Slate Co. Ltd. re-constituted, quarry re-opened. Capital £50,000. Four London and one Oxford directors, Engineer James Wright of London.

1866   Welsh Slate Co. specifically engage one Philips from Festiniog Slate Co. 'to manage also the Moelwyn Mawr' July (ref. W.S.Co.'s records). No other apparent links between G.M.S.Co. and W.S.Co. Inclines to F.R. had been completed by this date.

1867   March. Account opened with F.R.

1869   According to J. W. Greaves' evidence at House of Commons Enquiry on F.R. Bill, the quarry was closed.

---

* After amalgamation into the Oakeley Quarries this 1870 Incline was ultimately abandoned in the interests of simplifying the quarry track layouts and the tipping of further rubbish. As the Welsh Slate Co. had also become part of the Oakeley concern, Matthews' was connected to W.S.Co. by internal quarry Incline and all their combined products came to the F.R. by means of the original W.S.C. Incline, was displaced in favour of a more appropriate site. The internal Incline was the largest on the Oakeley site, and all machinery for it was supplied by De Winton & Co., Caernarvon.

Highest employment in 1880 (390) and tonnage 20,728 in last year of Matthews' lease.

1870   Quarry plant and lease auctioned in London 27 September, through Manchester firm. Did not reach reserve.

1871   14 April re-auctioned; items include '10 iron rail trucks—all nearly new'. Prices obtained high in view inaccessibility (says *Mining Journal*). The quarry itself was on offer from Messrs. Clear & Cheffins, London, E.C. and James Wright, and bought by Messrs. T. E. Pemberton, C. E. Flavell and C. J. Allison all of Birmingham under a lease for 21 years from the Crown dated 30 November; for £17,000 to the above, the undertaking was sold in 1873 to

1873   The Union Slate Co. Ltd.* then incorporated to work the site. Capital £40,000. All machinery, tramways, etc. had to be re-installed and it was resolved on 21 May '. . . contract between Mr. Arthur Wade and the Company for the execution of the tramway, saws, water wheel . . .'† Company advertising for 45 tons of 20 lb. rails (March).

1874   F.R. receive enquiry from William Popham David (manager) for rates of carriage 25 February but there are no further references. 45 men employed then. Quarry working.

1875   Company in liquidation (final winding up 1891).

1879–80   List of plant prepared for auction (quoted *Mining Journal*, 20 December 1879).

1891   February. J. Solomon Jones of Moelwyn Slate Co. given Free Pass over Railway. Quarry is operative until 1897.

1900   Officially recorded as disused.

Few output figures are available. There is only one set of Returns at the Department of Mines.

The site was never recognised locally as a successful working.

Oakeley (Oakeley Slate Co. later, Oakeley Slate Quarries Co. Ltd.) Nos. 8, 9, 10 on Reference Plan.

Formed when Oakeley re-entered the three quarries on the Reference Plan (q.v.).

1878   Oakeley Slate Co. formed to work the three previous undertakings (including Cesail and Matthews whose leases had terminated), henceforward known as Upper and Middle Quarries.

1881   Curious reference in Dunlop's field book (agent to Oakeley) reads '30 July; met Robert Owen and Robert Roberts at Welsh Slate

---

* There was a Company of this title formed in September 1859: a William Tuxford was one director; it purchased the Great Welsh Union Slate Co. Ltd.'s four quarries but none was in Ffestiniog. (The G.W.U.S.C.L. was incorporated in April 1857.) There appears to be no continuous link between the Union Co. of 1859 and this of 1873.

† Arthur Wade was of 24 Waterloo Street, Birmingham in 1874 and may have been related to Julia Wade who became the wife of James Spooner. He failed to complete the tramway and works by 1 December 1873.

Co's Bridge re crossing rails from L.N.W.R. siding'. (Owen and Roberts were the respective quarry managers; entry suggests a L.N.W.R. trans-shipment siding was provided from the time of opening of their branch line. To which it was made is not yet clear.)

1882 Oakeley Slate Quarries Co. Ltd. formed (see *Journal* of Merioneths. Historical & Record Society, Vol. VI, p. 198 for method of financing). Both set of workings affected by enormous collapse of Welsh Slate Co. workings beneath them, resulting in Oakeley taking his case to arbitration and receiving judgement in his favour, Welsh Slate Co. is unable to meet the cost. Their lease is surrendered in consequence.

1888 Oakeley re-enters W.S.Co. quarry, working it as part of combined operation. Known thereafter as Lower Quarry.

1897 Oakeley Estate mortgaged to Rock Life Assurance Co. 1,647 employees (669 underground).

1900 Cwm Orthin Quarry acquired.

1930 Pen-y-Bont Incline built to make direct connection with L.M.S. yard to develop a container traffic for slate. This led from Pen-y-Bont Mill to a new standard-gauge siding and wharf. L.M.S. rates proved too high, and wharf little used at first.

1933 Votty & Bowydd Quarry acquired; Company reformed (after liquidation) under 1882 title.

1936 Diphwys Casson Quarry acquired.

1946 Pen-y-Bont Incline comes fully into use and tramway extended beyond 1930 wharf to trans-shipment wharf in L.M.S. yard (north side), following closure of F.R. in August. Considerable new trackage in narrow gauge.

1970 14 October. Quarry closed by owners.

1971 1 July. Company wound up.

The quarry is now re-opened on a limited scale under new management. Output goes by road. This was the largest underground slate mine. There were 50 miles of underground tracks. Slate was worked on five veins, each running for about 2 miles inside the mountain. There were 26 floors over a vertical difference of 1,400 ft., 26 tunnels for the removal of rubbish; 7 floors were drowned when pumping ceased and those below the water table were flooded.

1882 Middle 13,414 tons, 363 employees;* Upper 13,753 tons, 524 employees.

1893 (whole undertaking) 56,589 tons (*c.* 14,000 shipped), *c.* 800 employees.

1935 Portmadoc for shipping 1,309 tons; Minffordd 5,427 tons; L.M.S.R. 4,192 tons; G.W.R. Nil.

* Before the Great Fall (see above) 1881 output was 36,103 tons with *c.* 800 employees at Welsh Slate Co.—not then part of Oakeley.

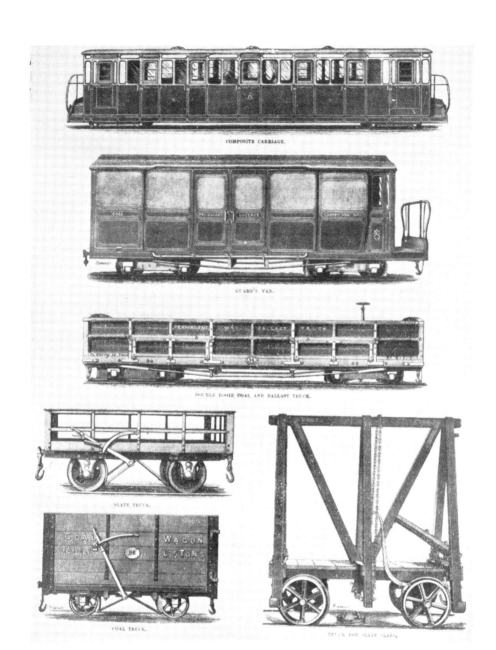

COMPOSITE CARRIAGE.

GUARD'S VAN.

DOUBLE BOGIE COAL AND BALLAST TRUCK.

SLATE TRUCK.

COAL TRUCK.

TRUCK FOR SLATE SLABS.

20R   *Contemporary engraving of rolling stock from 'Engineering' 26 September 1884.*

21R   *Renovated carriages at Harbour, July 1958. Left to right; Nos. 23, 22, and 18.*

(*J. I. C. Boyd*)

22R   *Morning Up train, with empty slate wagons on rear of passenger coaches, crosses the Cei Mawr, 1932.*   (*Fox Photos*)

23R   *Private vehicle, thought to be the latter-day Oakeley 'coach', at Boston Lodge 1923.*
(Photomatic)

24R   *Renovating No. 11 inside Boston Lodge, after rebuilding a second time, on this occasion with an observation end. (Formerly No. 4.)*   *(J. I. C. Boyd)*

25R *Large open mineral wagon with end door, brake one side and sprung buffing gear. One of several forms. 1887.* (F.R. Co.)

26R *Stock initially restored forms the Harbour–Boston Lodge train with* Prince, *August 1955. Pen Cob.* (J. I. C. Boyd)

27R *Penrhyn–Harbour working with gangway-connected vehicles behind* Taliesin, *approaching Minffordd. July 1957.* (J. I. C. Boyd)

1S   *Double slotted-post semaphore; disc; McKenzie & Holland signals. 1936.*   *(C. E. Lee)*

2S   *Train Staff Tickets; Welsh Highland Railway (left), Festiniog Railway (right).*
      (J. I. C. Boyd)

Welsh Highland Railway.

TRAIN STAFF TICKET.

TRAIN No. _____ (UP)

To the ENGINE DRIVER or BRAKESMAN

You are authorised, after seeing the Train Staff colored **Red** for the Section, to proceed from

Beddgelert to Croesor Jnct.

and the Train Staff will follow.

Signature of person in charge ....

Date............................. 19   (over)

FESTINIOG RAILWAY.

TRAIN STAFF TICKET.

TRAIN No. _____ (DOWN)

To the **Engine Driver** or **Brakesman**

You are authorised, after seeing the Train Staff colored **Blue** for the Section, to proceed from

Duffws to Bl. Festiniog.

and the Train Staff will follow.

Signature of person in charge.............................

Date.......................19   (over)

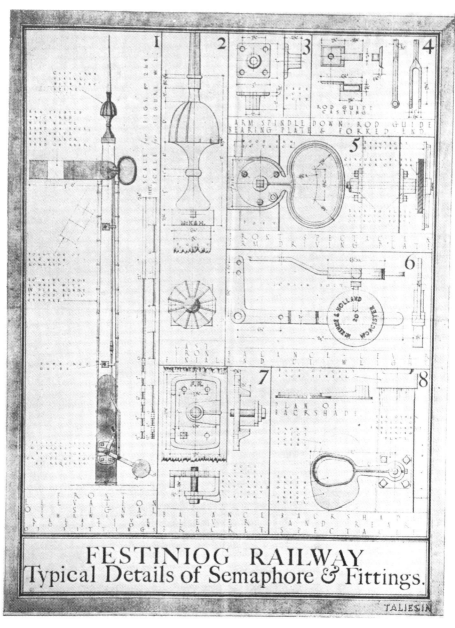

FESTINIOG RAILWAY
Typical Details of Semaphore & Fittings.

3S   *McKenzie & Holland's signal fittings as used on the Railway.*   *(J. I. C. Boyd)*

1T   *Early fish-bellied track in Boston Lodge, 1956.*   *(G. E. Baddeley)*

2T   *Chair joining two differing sections of T rail. (This was not a proper joint chair.) Tan - y - Bwlch 1943.*
            (J. I. C. Boyd)

3T   *Forerunner of Spooner & Huddart Patent fishplate. Dinas branch 1947.*
            (J. I. C. Boyd)

1G   *Gravity working; early style with Horse Dandy in rear.*   *(C. E. Lee)*

2G   *Gravity working; later style train passing through Dduallt 1924.*   *(J. I. C. Boyd)*

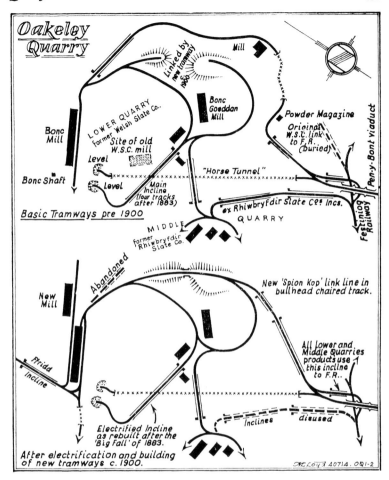

Exceptionally, this Quarry, as successor to the Welsh Slate Company which appears to have had Agreement to run its own wagons over the F.R. from earliest times, owned its own Coal Wagons which worked over the Railway at cost to the Quarry. One of these wagons has been preserved in the Narrow Gauge Railway Museum, Towyn, and may be of F.R. origin.

Rhiwbach (tr. The Little Hill) (or Festiniog Slate Co.) No. 19 on Reference Plan.

This remote working lay almost four miles east of Duffws, on Lord Newborough's land. It was ultimately two separate quarries, Rhiwbach

Old and Rhiwbach No. 1. The site was traditionally the place where, for three centuries, local people had gone to win materials for roofing. Latterly, it was a complete and isolated hamlet, with chapel, school and shop. Apart from rough road, its only link with the outside world was the Rhiwbach Tramway. Several cottages and other properties in the Machno valley were owned. The quarry was never worked extensively at any time. A Prospectus by H. Humphries I.M.M.E. about 1902 (undated) states it was still operated part above and part below ground then. One engine at the main incline foot (the quarry lay below the level of the Rhiwbach Tramway) worked all other inclines (four) in the quarry by means of a system of pulleys. The original four boilers, put in during the late 1870s, were then replaced by one Babcock boiler.

A new phase of the working had begun in 1898 with an inclined drainage tunnel 350 feet below surface level. From its end there ran a 600 yard tunnel (level) with tramway to the foot of the mountain near Penmachno village; its main function was a drain. Shells of old boilers were used to line the tunnel where brittle. This tunnel, its exit collapsed, is still visible (1975) and spewing out water; the tramway appears intact also. Several modern developments were contemplated or tried out here; one was a transport system using White's Patent Aerial Ropeway instead of surface tramway links.

1812 *et seq.* Started by two men from Penmachno and Yspytty Ifan; later enlarged by — Owen (of Mela) who (according to 'Hanes Plwyf Ffestiniog') apparently defaulted and was displaced by — Pugh, possibly representing the wronged party. After litigation, Owen re-entered the property. For a time there was a five-man partnership. About 1849 it was purchased by Robert Owen Mousdale of Bryn-dyffryn, Llanrwst, and worked by John Hughes and — Griffiths (of Amnodd) on his behalf.

1852 December. Rhiw Bach Slate Quarries Co. incorporated in Manchester. (Probably a consortium of ten local working directors.) Civil Engineer: Charles Edward Cawley, 41 John Dalton Street, Manchester. Quarry to be commercially exploited.

1855 By this time being worked by the Cambrian Slate Quarrying Company.

1856 February. Manchester & Ffestiniog Slate & Slab Co. Ltd. formed to purchase quarry from the Cambrian S.Q.Co. for £28,000 in part exchange. Registered Office: 13 Corporation Street, Manchester.

1858 July. Festiniog Slate Quarry Co. Ltd. incorporated. Capital £100,000, the Board consisting of certain directors of the 1853 Festiniog Slate Quarrying Co. Ltd. (see Diphwys Casson) with similar objectives.

1860 Agreement between Festiniog Railway and quarry company over rates; meanwhile F.R. Agreement to build Extension Railway, thereafter supplying stock for 21 years (27 November).

1860–2   Connected to the extended (minerals only) section of F.R. by end-on junction with existing head of incline serving Bowydd Quarry (q.v.), existing incline then becoming No. 1 Incline of Extension Railway. Wharf built Portmadoc 1861.

1863   31 March. Account opened with F.R. Probably denoting completion of tramway, 3,964 tons pass.

1877   Company wound up in order to re-constitute as Festiniog Slate Co. Ltd. (same capital).

1882   On behalf of existing Company, worked by Rev. J. Philips and Griffiths Jones (of Bangor).

1890   Working suspended.

1891   Company into liquidation; final meeting January 1892. Meanwhile, operation re-commenced by arrangement, trading as 'Rhiw Bach Quarry Owners' of Blaenau Ffestiniog, H. Humphries—lessee (1894).

1908   Two wharves taken at Minffordd through Humphries; marked wagons requested.

1911   Old Rhiwbach abandoned by this date.

1896: 95 employees (28 underground).

1913   Company wound up and quarry closed.

1918   Though officially closed (additionally by wartime legislation over labour) F.R. records show slate passing—possibly removal of existing stocks on hand?

1919   Festiniog Slate Quarries Co. Ltd. incorporated.

1920   Working resumed; new lessees impose extortionate charges on other users of Rhiwbach Tramway, most of whose slate had been carried along it for a charge of 1s. 4d. ton by previous Rhiwbach owners. New owners want £3 ton (!!) (The House of Commons Enquiry of 1869 quotes 2s. 1d. ton as the probable true-costed Rhiwbach Tramway rate and sought to show how much more competitive it was than the existing F.R. rates—a rather futile comparison). Most other users now obliged to find other means of transporting output, e.g. Maenofferen built new Incline down into Votty & Bowydd quarry and so by means of their Incline to Duffws direct, avoided the use of the Rhiwbach Tramway. Income from this source for R.S.Q.C.L. fell drastically and parts of the tramway were never used again after this.

Monthly account opened with F.R., April.

1928   Sold to Maenofferen, who relaid portions of tramway.

1953   Working suspended; quarry closed; tramway dismantled between Rhiwbach and Cwt-y-Bugail.

In practice, the quarry was only worked for five years between

1883–92. Output maximum 1867 = 6,668 tons. Employment; maximum *c.* 1873 = 160 men (1887 = 147).

Rhiwbach Old was apparently part abandoned as early as 1884 as all produce in that year came from No. 1.

In 1935 1,083 tons passed over the G.W.R. from Blaenau Ffestiniog, only 446 tons going to Minffordd.

Thomas Williams, Manager to 1865, went to Croesor Quarry; Robert Owen, foreman and then Manager 1862–6, went to Welsh Slate Co. Principal character was James George Tuxford, Civil Engineer (of Portmadoc), agent for Festiniog Slate Co. and Secretary to the earlier concerns; he became Engineer & Manager in 1866, serving until 1883. His services were widely used by all quarries (he surveyed Welsh Slate Co. workings in 1866). His name was at first given to No. 1 Incline of the Extension Railway (probably it was rebuilt to his requirements when the Extension Railway was built) but later the nickname 'Tuxford's' passed to a considerable Incline which he engineered for Votty & Bowydd, being their principal internal haulage Incline. It may still be seen.

Rhiwbryfdir (or Rhiwbryfdir Fawr or The Company's or Palmerston's or Welsh Slate Co.) No. 10 on Reference Plan.

Part of Oakeley Estate, and the undermost of three quarries worked on this site. Said to have been first worked by Robert Morris about 1814 and Richard Thomas of Penmachno in 1816; by Oakeley himself, wastefully. Taken by Samuel Holland, Senr. in 1819 who took Rhiwbryfdir Farm site for trial three-year period, the rent being £120, £150, £150 for each year, the lease with Oakeley to expire 1835. Holland took a wharf at Portmadoc in 1824.

1825 Purchased by Welsh Slate Copper & Lead Mining Co. for £28,000; current output 683 tons.

1833 Expired lease renewed to 1839; Oakeley royalty 4*s.* 6*d.* ton.

1838 Doubts about future of quarry and renewal of lease are ended when new lease offered. In consequence, Incline built to F.R. *This was the first quarry to make direct connection.*

1840 Profits shown for first time. Partnership made of Company (now Welsh Slate Company).

1842 10 January. Earliest surviving entry with F.R. According to Agreement, quarry may use its own wagons on F.R. main line. Quarry company pays first dividend.

1853 23 August. New slate rates Agreement with Railway.

1854 Quarry carpenter builds wooden viaduct to connect new tipping site at Pen-y-Bont (across valley) with Horse Tunnel. Glan-y-Don Mill built later on the resultant tip. All level route from this Mill, over viaduct and through the Horse Tunnel, giving direct access from the workings; traditionally at the sound of the end-of-day Hooter, horses would stop work and make their own way to their stable. Viaduct rebuilt later in brick and steel, and one span filled in with rubbish; from then its local name became Pont Goch (Red Bridge) (Details; Tracing P.R.O. MT6/300/9 shows bridge, etc.) [Dismantled 1970.]

1863   New lease of wharf at Portmadoc, and Agreement to use portion of Railway free of charges. 20,607 tons pass over F.R.

1864   Profit on working quarry alleged to be £40,000 for this year.

1866   Working Moelwyn Quarry (q.v.) for at least part of year. Death of first of the four shareholders, Lord Palmerston. In January a very severe roof fall, the first major catastrophe in a Ffestiniog mine.

1871   New lease proposed; to expire 26 December 1890 with option to renew until 1910. Oakeley royalty on 'first' slates to be 7s. 9d. ton. Not taken up.

1873   Steam locomotive at work by this date: the first in a local quarry.

1877   20 December. Lease of 1839 expires; renewed to 26 December 1890.

1878   Further serious falls of roof and pillars continues. . . .

1880   June. Considerable roof fall, and further falls anticipated.

1882   6 December. The Great Fall commences and continues to a climax on 16 February 1883 when 5–6 million tons of rock were estimated to have fallen, right through from ground surface above and submerging most of the working chambers. Estimated that 20 years would be required to clear the site, but in fact, much of the rubbish still lies over it in 1975. Oakeley took Company to arbitration October 1884 and on losing the case, the Company surrendered its lease, being unable to meet damages.

1888   Oakeley commences to work the quarry himself (see Oakeley Slate Quarries).

In 1871, Dunlop's diary (agent to Oakeley) records in December . . . 'I settled Incline with the L.N.W.R. with Mr. Oakeley at the quarries.' This was likely to be a new Incline on the north side of Pen-y-Bont viaduct to replace the original Incline which heretofore had its foot at the Zero termination of the F.R., i.e. the first Incline connection to the F.R. of any quarry, dating from 1838. (Its site is now covered by rubbish.) This new Incline was possibly built in anticipation of the Bettws & Festiniog Railway Act of 1872 with its proposals for physical junction with the F.R. in this vicinity.

This quarry was the largest underground mine in the district. The Company had a capital of £500,000 in Feb. 1827; it took over Pen-Trwyn-y-Garnedd Wharf from Holland and shipped from there to Portmadoc at first. It suffered then from the high price paid to Holland for the site; it was some years before becoming profitable and became notoriously bad at paying the men's wages. Its wage rates were the worst in the district. It had the reputation of very poor employer/labour relations and there were personal feuds at Board and lower levels. After Palmerston's death it was managed by a Committee from London and relied on local Management as a link. This proved its undoing, though it was the most prosperous of the local quarries.

Output figures are hard to obtain as the concern kept its returns very closely. In 1851 they were *c*. 19,000 tons, in 1865 22,670, in 1869 46,502, in 1873 63,805, the last-named said to be the best year's production. Roof falls made output irregular, but tonnage over the F.R. was a very significant part of that Company's traffic. Employees in 1873 = 700 men.

George W. Chessell, a member of a Cardiff family who came to the district, was its most notable Manager; he died in September 1873. A predecessor of his in earliest times was in 1835, George Homfray, a member of the South Wales ironmasters' family. Before the hamlet was abandoned, his residence was Rhiwbryfdir House, for many years the seat of management.

Rhosydd No. 3 on Reference Plan.

This quarry was worked at later date by the owners of *New Rhosydd* quarry, physically connected and adjacent to the north. Underground tramways ran a mile from one end of the workings to the other.

This site lay to the north west of Tan-y-Grisiau, over the top of a col from that village, which separates Cwm Orthin from Cwm Croesor. It stood many feet above the head of Cwm Croesor and because of lack of transport along that valley, took its slate down Holland's Cwm Orthin road to the F.R. siding at Tan-y-Grisiau. It was thus a customer of the F.R. before June 1864 when it was connected to the new Croesor Tramway.

(The New Rhosydd Quarry was never a customer of the F.R. It was incorporated in October 1874 with capital £80,000 and had three members of the Casson family on its board; the Croesor Tramway was available to it from the start.)

Charles E. Spooner was one of the prime movers of the rejuvenated project of 1856, and used as Consultant thereafter.

Of special interest in both quarries' workings is the amount of ex F.R. track material which still survives therein; entries for the consignment of this material appear in the surviving Croesor Tramway accounts.

Pre-1833 Opened by — Cadwalladr (of Croesor) and rebuilt by — Roberts (of Llety) who found additional slate-bearing veins. Later Meredydd Jones (of Maenofferen—a part of Ffestiniog, not the quarry of that name) found the original trial levels and opened them out. Ormesby-Gore, the land-owner, claimed the workings as his own but later lost claim to the site. (There is an amusing legend about fox-hunting and this matter in 'Hanes Plwyf Ffestiniog'.)

?1833 Worked by William Turner (of Turner & Co.) who sold out to Ormsby-Gore.

? Continued by Matthews (of Aberystwyth) but working lapsed.

1851 Re-opened by Thomas Jones and — Baker (of Cwmorth-Ucha) but closed again (Baker was son of Ormesby-Gore's Agent).

1853 27 June. Rhosydd Slate Co. formed.

1854 Rhosydd Slate Co. open account with F.R. 30 September. No traffic passes in 1855 or 1865–6 but otherwise is continuous up to 1867 and intermittently thereafter. Proposal for F.R. to build connecting branch tramway (2 miles) and work it.

1855 Notice in *London Gazette*, November stating intention to apply for Act to build railway between Tan-y-Grisiau and Rhosydd Quarry, by the Festiniog Railway Company (not proceeded with). To serve also Cwm Orthin and Wrysgan quarries. '. . . wanting to obviate expense of application to Parliament.'

1856 Rhosydd Slate Co. Ltd. incorporated. Capital £50,000. F.R. directors on its Board, including G. A. Huddart. Agreement with Samuel Holland 20 January enabling Company to use cart road to Tan-y-Grisiau siding. Cwm Orthin allows no wheeled vehicles.

1859–61 Leased Cwm Orthin Quarry, after which it raised more capital on its own account.

1863 1,121 tons passes over F.R.

1864 New capital raised to build connection to Croesor Tramway for £5,000.

1873 Company wound up.

1874 Site leased to William Davies (of Caerblaidd), William Casson (of Sandbach) and Dr. R. Roberts (of Ffestiniog) all being members of the New Rhosydd Slate Co. Ltd. incorporated that year with the objective of purchasing the Rhosydd Quarry, which was done. Capital £80,000.

1921 July. Company wound up, but quarry worked at odd times subsequently by arrangement until 1930.

F.R. Accounts show slate carried from Tan-y-Grisiau in 1854, 1856–64 and 1867. Only occasional use thereafter—presumably when Croesor line unsuited.

In 1882 output was 5,616 tons with 192 employees; in 1874 there were only 83 employees.

The quarry is of interest in view of its close personal ties with the Festiniog Railway. Manager in 1872 was Oliver; at the time 100 men were there.

There were two Rhosydd Railway surveys by C. E. Spooner; the first connected the east side of the quarry by a half-mile tunnel linked with their Floor 5. It fell into Cwm Orthin by four Inclines. The second (of 1860) took advantage of the short-period lease to the Cwm Orthin Quarry, and used that concern's Inclines to the F.R. The latter plan was considered again in June 1862 when links with either F.R. or Croesor Tramway were being considered.

Votty & Bowydd (or Percival's) No. 13 on Reference Plan.

1861   Account under this heading opened with F.R., though no formal amalgamation as yet.

1863   7,089 tons passes over F.R.

1868   Agreement with F.R. over haulage terms, Percival being the last owner to agree on common terms. August.

1870   Formed by amalgamation of Percival's Votty and Cwm Bowydd quarries (q.v.).

1874   22 December. Votty & Bowydd Slate Quarries Co. Ltd. incorporated, but title later amended to the singular. Percival and Mathews families main shareholders.

1880   Agreement with Lord Newborough to have use of Diphwys Casson quarry tramway and incline to Duffws station, 30 October.

1883   Title re-amended to that of 1874. Lease taken for 30 years.

1897   Quarry property purchased outright, plus lease of other lands to 1 July 1957. 479 employees (258 underground.)

1899   All steam plant redundant; converted to electric power. Connection begun with Yale Electric Power Co. Ltd.

1912   Valuation by Moses Kellow of Croesor; leasing now enables landowner to one-third market value of output.

1919   Board of three includes Richard Bowton (Festiniog Railway).

1933   Taken over by Oakeley Slate Quarries Co. Ltd.

1957   Lease expires.

1962   5 October. Quarry closed and later dismantled. 3 November. Last use of Duffws Incline and line to ex L.M.S.R. yard for transshipment. Thereafter this isolated section of F.R. derelict.

1964   March. Liquidator appointed.

Output rose from 1882, 12,092 tons and 344 employees; to 17,231 tons in 1897. Maximum employment in the early 1890s, *c.* 475 men. 1873 = 310 men.

	1935	1937
To Portmadoc	153 tons	265 tons
To Minffordd	4,329 tons	4,781 tons
To L.M.S.	2,343 tons	1,168 tons
To G.W.	38 tons	6 tons

Wrysgan (or Rhysgan) No. 2 on Reference Plan.

Part Ormesby-Gore, part Oakeley Estates. Boundaries not properly set out until 1855. A quarry on the west side of Cwm Orthin and opposite the quarry of that title. Its first three chambers were on Cwm Orthin land leased, and slate therefrom attracted royalty for the lessors. For two miles beyond here, land was leased from Ormesby-Gore. The quarry history is typical of the small workings of the district —obscure, intermittent and complex. Some records of it give conflicting evidence. When first opened, it was on land owned by Samuel Holland, Junr., a legacy of his father's estate. There is no record of continuous working.

1830s Opened by William Roberts (of Coed-y-Bleddiau). Sold to — Constable who later failed. (Everyone at this time lost money whilst trying to work the quarry.) It remained idle for some years.

Re-opened by a second Methusalem Jones who formed a Company, but most of the capital was lost and the workings closed down. Apparently Jones was not bankrupted as the Census Returns of March 1851 show his as living at Dropol, Ffestiniog, age 43 and a 'quarry agent'. Like many another local man, he came from Llandegai, Caernarvon.

1844 — Barnard and some colleagues took over, but it bankrupted them. They hailed from Bristol. They begun to build an Incline down to the Railway; this was the cause of their undoing.

c. 1850 Wrysgan Slate & Slab Quarries Co. Ltd. incorporated.

1851 Incline appears to have been completed, at cost of £5,000 with siding. Account with F.R. opened 30 September, rate 3*s*. ton. Figures show quarry productive in 1851, 1853–6 and 1858 only in account name of 'David Roberts'. Lease for 90 years from 1 January given by Mrs. Ormesby-Gore at £100 for quarry and £50 for Incline. Not worked 1856–7 but again by David Roberts 1858 and again from 1874.

1854 Leased by Thomas Wilkinson (purser to the W.S. & S.Q. Co. Ltd.); who continued to trade as 1850 title. Shortage of capital; problems over title.

1857 Company into liquidation, May. Wound up 5 June 1860.

1859 Chancery Court action re failure to register new owner shares. 'The various phases of absurdity which these cases present are without number, and it is a marvel how any man in his senses can risk his money by becoming a member of these companies . . .'

1863 Spooner refers to Railway's stock of Contingent Wagons 'for occasional supply of Wrysgan Quarry now in small produce . . .'

Quarry now working under licence from Ormesby-Gore to Thomas Tovey Barnard May (a member of the Barnard family who seem to have acted as managers or custodians of the property between bouts of operation).

1864 Bell Telegraph installed at foot of Incline.

1867 Traffic re-commences over F.R. Rate reduced 1/13 basis less distance of Ffestiniog quarries.

1869 Quarry auctioned in Manchester 9 March by Barnard Thomas & Co. of Bristol; not taken. Auctioned again in London 21 June. Stated to have 'two powerful water wheels and a steam engine'.

1872 Leased to James Clarke; Ormesby-Gore giving separate lease for Incline 'this being coterminous with the Wrysgan lease' ... 'this Incline enables us to put our produce on the Festiniog Railway at 4*d.* ton cost of transit from the quarry'.

This is probably a renewal; the Plan on the lease is prepared by C. E. Spooner.

1874 Part of workings leased from Cwm Orthin for 21 years. Now worked by William Davies (also of Rhosydd Quarry), David Roberts (of Garth Villa, Portmadoc) and George Henry Birch (of Handsworth, Birmingham). Traded as Wrysgan Slate Co., Portmadoc.

1875 Account re-opened with Railway.

1879 Welsh Slate Co. inspect with view to purchase. Price required £36,000.

1880 Quarry for sale.

1881 Purchased by David Davies (contractor of Llandinam) and son Edward A. Davies (of Bryntirion, Towyn). Losses shown thereafter and Davies's sue sellers for misrepresentation; High Court action 14 July 1882.

1884 December. Wrysgan Slate Quarry Co. Ltd. incorporated. Capital £25,000. Directors include David Roberts, William Davies and G. H. Birch (all of 1874) plus Randall Casson (Solicitor).

1891 Company liquidated with purpose of re-forming August, using same title and Capital. Board list gives Birch as Colliery Owner, includes Richard Davies (slate merchant of Portmadoc) and Randall Casson (of Bron-y-Garth—moving in after C. E. Spooner's death 1889).

1893/1894/1900/1907/1909 Evidence of quarry being operational at least during these years. [1897: 100 employees (54 underground).]

1912 August. Company into liquidation.

1913 Incline lifted.

1923 At some prior date, New Wrysgan Slate Quarry Ltd. formed. February. Incline relaid with new siding at foot. Inspected by B.O.T. 7 October 1926.

1924 January. Traffic over F.R. again.

? Quarry closed and Incline dismantled before 1940.

By 1940 Quarry open on limited scale, worked by T. O. Williams (ex

Braich Goch and Hendre Ddu Quarries) until his death 1946. Incline relaid in single track, as original double-acting Incline was never satisfactory, the topmost length proving too much for ascending wagons to overcome. Various stationary steam units or ex road lorry engines used to assist working over the years.

1946 Quarry closed; subsequently dismantled.

Note: A somewhat variable claim to this property exists; ownership was claimed by Ellis Humphries of Gellilydan through various wills made by him to his son of the same name, and his brother. Ellis Humphries, Jnr. failed to sign a lease of 1850 and there were further lettings to Joseph H. Holdsworth in February 1850 (probably the same who was author of an article on the Geology of Merioneth in *The Mining Journal* of 1849), W. H. Rawlings and Mary A. Poole in March 1850, the latter mortgaging to William Griffiths in 1852. Adolfo Tosan, Richard Thomas, and Thomas Williams were also concerned with leases in the period 1853–4.

Output of the quarry at the turn of the century was worked to Minffordd by the Down morning gravity train and involved special problems. The quarry would phone Duffws the previous night if traffic was available. Duffws would display a card in the station window 'Wrysgan ready'. The gravity would stop and collect wagons but the Top Shunting Engine would have to follow it down and push to re-start. On occasions the card would be forgotten and the gravity would be stopped by the Tan-y-Grisiau signal—it proving the quarry had forgotten to phone. By then the Top Shunter had gone about its work and nothing would re-start the gravity. Blame usually passed between Tan-y-Grisiau station, the quarry and Duffws booking clerk. Subsequent delays held up the Up 10.15 passenger train at Tan-y-Bwlch and a barrage of complaints followed from late passengers at Blaenau. This train would also be held up when quarries failed to crewl the previous night, and the gravity waited on their pleasure. Occasionally an inadvertent stop was made by the gravity at Tan-y-Grisiau or Wrysgan at times when the Top Shunter was not available. No one has recorded the aftermath!

Output for 1882 was 2,078 tons with 96 employees, falling sharply to 441 tons in 1884. 1897 tonnage was 3,485 (the highest figure available) and in 1902 762 tons was shipped from Portmadoc.

Quarry Agreements

Over the years the Railway drew up many Agreements, usually involving rates and tonnage. The first to survive is that with Welsh Slate Co. of 1841. A typical one was with Votty & Bowydd, for 21 years from 1 January 1868 (*inter alia*). The Railway Company was to provide a sufficient number of wagons within 30 daylight or working hours or in default pay 1*d*. per wagon per hour for any number short of the required total.

It would charge demurrage on wagons kept over 12 daylight hours from the time of leaving the foot of the lowest Incline . . . or 6 hours at the lower terminus, Portmadoc . . . 'at 1*d*. per waggon per hour'.

It would carry the wagons from the foot of the lowest Incline to the lower terminus in 18 daylight and working hours after receiving a weigh-bill and in default of 1*d*. per ton per hour . . . unless the delay was occasioned by storm or other unavoidable obstacle.

It was not compelled to carry more than 15 tons per time 'or more than 1/100th of a make of preceding year in one day'.

The Quarry Company was not to put more than 4 tons in each wagon including the weight of the wagon.

It must pay for wagon damage after a valuation had been made.

It must keep its Inclines in good order and not use F.R. wagons for anything but their specific purpose.

Quarry Relationships

These were usually abrasive. Written complaints were much reduced after the quarry–Portmadoc station telephone link was installed. One typical letter between C. E. Spooner and F. S. Percival (Votty & Bowydd) dated 20 July 1875 reads:

I beg to call your attention to the injury that is being caused by your crewlers and others using the grease out of the Railway Company's wagon bushes for greasing points and crossings at your quarries.

Greasing the points and crossings has a dangerous effect on the transit down the Line, rendering the brake wheels slipping and retarding brake action, and hence being a cause of great danger—also, much damage is done from the wagons being thrown over on their sides, instead of your men taking the trouble to run through the nearest turnout—a must request your attention to these matters as also to a third complaint—that is I find wagons are not filled from only it both the Railway Company and yourselves suffer and should be 'remedied'.

I am Dear Sir,
Yours truly,

(the last sentence is quoted as written).

Quarry Feeder Branches

(Figures of length and number of inclines taken from F.R. statistics 1876 where given: lengths were always the full distance from the main line, disregarding changes in ownership of feeder along its length.)

Blaen-y-Cwm. Served by a branch tramway from off the main Rhiwbach Tramway, the junction was about 2½ miles from the F.R. terminal milepost at Duffws and about halfway between the branches for Cwt-y-Bugail and Bwlch-y-Slater quarries. The junction height was 1,614 ft., the short branch descending by incline to the mill area; the quarry itself was a little south of this, being part above and part below ground. The winding equipment differed from the customary, having a sloped near-horizontal wheel on top of a pillar. Haulage was by endless rope and steam winding engine at the incline foot. Braking was by wooden shoes bearing on the top winding wheel. (Length: 2 miles 1,440 yd. via Rhiwbach Tramway. 4 inclines.)

Buardd Melyn. This small sett quarry was usually spelt Buarth Melyn, a form which still survives. Its connection with the main line must have been brief and no detail of the arrangement or operating particulars has yet come to notice.

Bwlch-y-Slater. Connected by a branch to the Rhiwbach Tramway from a junction at $2\frac{3}{8}$ miles, just over a bridge at the south end of the Blaen-y-Cwm workings at 1,626 ft. elevation. A connecting tramway reversed into a neck on the hillside and then ran steeply forward (south), climbing to about 1,670 ft. to cross the watershed and fall to the quarry premises. Here, an incline climbed to the north west with the Manod workings at its summit. (Length: 3 miles 80 yd. via Rhiwbach Tramway. 3 inclines.)

Cesail. Original incline connection from the Lower Mill at its summit, falling north east to a junction behind Dinas station (as later provided) where a sharp curve connected it with the F.R. (Length: 998 yd. 2 inclines.)

Conclog. The Cwm Orthin Tramway was extended to the head of the valley by Oct. 1874 to serve this and Glyn Ffestiniog quarries. It commenced at a point where the Cwm Orthin Tramway swung north along the east shore of Cwm Orthin lake (1,045 ft.) and taking a clockwise curve round a swamp patch, the extension passed the barracks and a chapel, then running alongside the road. It thus climbed gradually, the lake falling away to the right; the valley being a typical Welsh 'cwm', it ends abruptly—first there is a derelict chapel on the left and then the ruins of Plas Cwm Orthin and a quarry barracks are seen ahead. At the valley head, the tramway formed a headshunt, reversing sharply to the west and leaving the road. It passed beside Conclog Quarry Mill (with its waterwheel at Tan-yr-Allt) and curving again, climbed by incline up over the path to New Rhosydd Quarry (whose rubbish tips tower above), the mine adit being behind the incline summit. Off the incline, another branch led to an adit beneath the Rhosydd path. All work was done underground. The tramway was intact in the early 1950s, consisting mainly of ex F.R. horse-period track placed on wooden sleepers, the light 'T' rail varying in section. A few sections survive in 1975. (Length: 1 mile 1,360 yd. 3 inclines.)

Cwm Orthin. (Also serving Conclog (q.v.).) The branch junction lay a little on the Up side of Tan-y-Grisiau station, where there were transfer sidings and signalling put in to the dictates of the B.O.T. Inspector. The incline foot was very close to the F.R. main line and its trains were never adequately protected from a runaway on the Incline the foot of which was the scene of a fatal accident, but not involving a train. The quarry road passed over the Incline near its summit and there followed a short level section of tramway involving some embankment work and a short cutting of considerable depth through a spur in the hillside. A second Incline took the tramway into the Cwm Orthin level and then under its rubbish tips into the narrow mouth of the valley. Wrysgan Quarry is clearly seen across the valley on the west side; Cwm Orthin Mill yard is also on this far bank of the stream, there being suitable bridges connecting it with the quarry. A rich variety of old rails did duty among the former stock yard there. The main tramway continued with a long passing loop to climb a final Incline—not steep—to the lake shore at the foot of the rubbish tips; the shore line of the lake itself has been obliterated by tipping into the lake itself. In the Quarry, one great Incline was used; tramways for levels and tips reached out on either hand from it.

Like the Conclog extension, the track remained *in situ* until 1952, in the hope of a quarry re-opening. The line between F.R. and quarry had had its old F.R. chaired materials replaced by a sound 30 lb. flat bottomed rail; here and there at this time, a number of F.R. wagons were still left standing on the branch, mainly as balancing vehicles should the Inclines be re-used. (Length: 1,566 yd. 3 inclines.)

Cwt-y-Bugail. Served by a short spur off the Rhiwbach Tramway, it left the main line where it crossed the county boundary; possibly at some stage this may have formed an elementary triangular junction. The branch ended in front of the main Mill, about 1,598 ft. above sea level. (Length: 2 miles 820 yd. per Rhiwbach Tramway. 3 inclines.)

Diphwys. This was the last quarry to make connection with the Railway and when first using the F.R., its output was routed down the ex Bowydd or No. 1 Incline of the Extension Railway—as it became. At one period, the quarry had no less than nine internal Inclines, due to the age of the workings and the use of tramways at a late stage. In more recent years, some rationalisation of Inclines took place, reducing their number. (Length: 1,495 yd.)

Glan-y-Pwll. A short branch led off through a gated wall-opening to the west, close by the original Glan-y-Pwll Junction. From here an extremely steep Incline led to a platform about two-thirds up the escarpment. Although certain Oakeley Quarry Plans show a further Incline to the summit from here, fieldwork confirms this never existed. It is suggested the various adit mouths on the mountainside above were connected to the summit platform by wire ropeway.

Hafodty. The original connection to this old quarry (now completely buried by rubbish from Votty & Bowydd and Maenofferen quarries) was by an Incline of the 1850s running roughly north and south to fall into the Bowydd premises and so pass to the head of their Duffws Incline. When the Extension Railway was built, the foot of this Incline was connected by a short track to it, just near the foot of the Extension's No. 2 Incline. About seventy years ago the Maenofferen Quarry (q.v.) was permitted to build a tramway into this quarry; this also led off an indirect connection from the Extension Railway. This tip line still exists, with tunnel, remains of loco shed, water tank with, near the engine shed, a disused adit entrance. (Length; see Votty & Bowydd.)

Llechwedd. The original terminus of the F.R. was extended northwards, past Rhiwbryfdir hamlet; here it forked, the left-hand curve serving the foot of the Welsh Slate Co. Incline, the right hand the Llechwedd Quarry. The junction was on the south bank of the river and the branch immediately crossed the stream and, becoming a double line, entered a stone vertical-walled cutting on a right-hand curve, to pass under the 'Crimea Road' just beyond Pont Pant-yr-Afon, to the foot of the main Incline running north-west up to the Mills. The days when much of the surviving traffic on the F.R. was from Greaves' are well remembered, and the Top Shunter would lie snugly inside this cutting, somewhat protected from the blustery winds which funnel up between the slate tips, and remain thus (so it was for one anxious to see the engine at work), until crewling had produced sufficient wagons to pull out the rake. To a childhood enthusiast whose first duty on emerging from the tunnel in the L.M.S. train was to look where the F.R. engine stood, it was disappointing to say the least to find only chimney top and cab roof visible as he went by. Near the foot of the branch there still survives the boundary post reading 'FR/JWG'. (Length: 100 yd. 1 incline and 3 principal internal inclines.)

Maenofferen. At first this quarry had no branch of its own, connection being made to the Rhiwbach Tramway just outside the Mill by means of a reversing neck running into the former David Jones' quarry. An alternative independent outlet was provided to avoid using the Rhiwbach line in the 1920s (see p. 454) but has recently been tipped over. This concern still uses the Rhiwbach Tramway (now its own property) from the Mills, down the former No. 2 Incline to road access at the Incline foot; this road was built in the 1930s. (Length: 1 mile 130 yd. via Rhiwbach Tramway. 2 inclines.)

Matthews'. The site of the first Incline connection is not precisely known. The later connections are discussed on p. 455 under the historical summary. (Length: 696 yd. 2 inclines in second phase.)

Moelwyn. A long-abandoned branch consisting of seven Inclines with short near-level connecting sections. The date of origin remains uncon- firmed, but it existed by the 1860s. The junction with the F.R. was on the now-submerged section north of Moelwyn Tunnel, on the west side of the line and between Buardd Melyn and Aelgoch, beyond the later Moelwyn Mines Siding. It was fully protected by signals and made a trailing junction to Up traffic. The first four Inclines were close together, climbing the Camfa Derw with the valley of the Afon Stwlan running parallel on the north hand. To locate it at a place of adequate water power, the Mill was part-way along the tramway and not at the quarry (as on the Gorseddau line), on the level between Nos. 4 and 5 Inclines. The quarry underground workings were adjacent to those of Pant Mawr Quarry, served by the Croesor Tramway on the other side of the ridge. (Length: 1,685 yd. 4 inclines (official—as some were counted as singles).)

Oakeley. For some time after formation, Cesail, Welsh Slate and Matthews' original Inclines continued in use. In 1905 a considerable Incline opened on the west side of the valley above the former Dinas station and ran upwards northwest to the Middle Level, allowing Matthews' Incline to be discontinued and tipped over also burying the Baltic and Commercial Hotels. Similarly, Cesail Incline, which connected to the F.R. at the same place, was abandoned. All remaining habitations hereabouts were then buried. In the quarry itself, and at its north end, a new connecting tramway was built along the top of a new curved embankment. It connected the Mills at this end of the quarry with a new Incline which fell to the summit of the short 1872 Incline on the north side of the Pen-y-Bont viaduct. This useful connection eliminated older tip lines, the 1839 Incline, a complete Mill area and tramway tunnel from it; it was dubbed the 'Spion Kop' line, being built at the turn of the century. This line was also linked by a short spur to the track over Pen-y-Bont. When the 1930 Pen-y-Bont Incline was made (see quarry history, p. 458) the 1905 Incline to Dinas was to be superceded; costs with the L.M.S. proving unacceptable, Pen-y-Bont Incline remained largely out of use until after 1946 when, with the F.R. closed, a line was extended from its foot to the L.M.S. yard and outlet made thereon. The 1905 Incline tracks were then lifted. (Length: the feeders were less than 1,000 yd. long and have varied due to the alterations above-mentioned. Relaying of Oakeley internal tramways is the subject of a separate diagram.)

Rhiwbach. This quarry had virtually no road access and relied on a tramway. It lay 860 ft. above Duffws terminus and approximately 1,560 ft. above sea level, on a moorland plateau. It was over three miles east of the town sited in an especially bleak and desolate upland where winter work was carried on in very difficult conditions which often stopped production. Rhiwbach, like Rhiwbryfdir and to a lesser extent, Cwt-y-Bugail, was a community itself. The circuitous tramway route from Blaenau was lifted by three Inclines to summit level, and fell by a fourth to the quarry; the four Inclines totalled $1\frac{1}{4}$ miles length. Bridge rails were used at the start, a heavier section replacing the originals as traffic grew. The terrain appears unsuitable for gravity working though a 1898 report states it was used, with horses for the return. Operation was in sections between Inclines, that between the third and fourth requiring 2 or 3 horses when business was brisk. Gradients varied between 1 in 60 and 1 in 200. Latterly a small wooden shed was erected at the top of No. 3 Incline and a rail tractor kept therein. In the 1920s and 1930s, a workmen's train of sorts worked between here and Cwt-y-Bugail, running beyond when required. On this upper section the track was improved by inserting light flat-bottomed rails and in places, a heavier bridge rail with soleplates, but the tractor was always too heavy for the material. At one period the tractor only took empty wagons eastwards from the Incline head, men and slate returning at each day's end by gravity.

No. 1 Incline was marked with a F.R. boundary post at its foot; the tramway then ascended the first-named 'Tuxford' Incline (not that later so named within the Votty & Bowydd Quarry) the scene of a spectacular run-away on 16 September 1905 when a loaded wagon broke away due to a defective coupling link. A photograph of the spilled wagon shows the Incline as then constructed with baulk timber longitudinal sleepers under squat flat-bottomed rails (similar in section to those used on parts of the Festiniog & Blaenau Railway) and wooden cable rollers—a feature not noted elsewhere. At the Incline summit there is a nice little piece of narrow gauge civil engineering, involving cutting and some stone embankment running through a gully of craggy rocks with such remote undertones it is difficult to imagine the proximity of a town only a short way below. The embankment which follows is quite up to the current standard of the F.R. works. Then to the left stood a small engine shed, followed by the remains of an overbridge carrying a tramway to a rubbish tip (Maenofferen property). This bridge was the centre of a legal action as it was built without giving adequate clearance for Rhiwbach traffic. Turning east and north, there was a weighing machine and the Votty & Bowydd workings now spread out on the right hand, but much below, a complex of galleries, sheds and Inclines. Beyond, the backcloth is an immense pile of slate rubbish reaching up to the skyline, with an occasional chimney or Mill building identifiable; the distant workings are those of Diphwys Casson. There is no means of separating one concern from another by inspection.

To the right was a short Incline connecting the tramway with Votty & Bowydd's most northerly Mill; it was driven by waterwheel along-side the Incline and produced school writing-slates. Beyond it was a small engine shed. To the left now comes the abandoned connection to the foot of Votty Quarry Incline. Nearby is the ruin of 'Quarry Bank' where the Votty Manager lived. Opposite, to the right of the tramway, the Maenofferen offices survive; other buildings in the vicinity including a barracks, are almost gone without trace. No. 2 Incline commences at 1,026 ft. and it lifts the line to 1,316 ft. Beneath it runs a tipping tram-way from Votty & Bowydd to old Votty Quarry, now forming an im-mense heap of rubbish on the left. At the summit, the line turns along a ledge to the south-east, with the Maenofferen tipping line parallel to, and above it. Presently the valley closes in, the existing Mills of Maenofferen come alongside on the further slope and this currently-used section of the tramway ends in the Mill area.

Under a boundary bridge marking the line between Maenofferen and other properties, the track passed another boundary post, followed by No. 3 Incline. At the top the line is brought out on to a tongue of slab to form the head; it forms a landmark for miles. The tramway turns east at the top; passes the old tractor shed and heads off over swampy ground high above the lush valley below. Llyn Bowydd is passed on the left, its exit being crossed on a wooden bridge carried on stone abutments; it was built into a reservoir to form part of a hydro-electric scheme. There now comes an uninteresting length until the lake shore is reached again and the line skirts it on a stone embankment, followed by shore-line rock-cuttings. The scene is reminiscent of such sea-shore locations on former narrow gauge lines in western Ireland. The summit of the line beyond the lake is in shallow cutting (1,612 ft.) and here it crosses the county boundary. There are the remains of a small lead mine nearby. The track now turns south, over the watershed, with a fine view down the valley of the Machno ahead, and upland mountain-scape on every hand; it passes the junction for Cwt-y-Bugail, through a series of rock cuttings and then onto the open mountain side. The steep rise of the Cwt-y-Bugail branch to the junction may be noted;

the rail tractor was limited to two loaded wagons.

The Blaen-y-Cwm branch comes next, with Incline and workings below to the left. The main tramway is now 1,614 ft. and has fallen somewhat; it now climbs again and beginning a curve of a quarter circle to the west, passes over the open workings of Frudd Quarry and the site of Bwlch-y-Slater Quarry junction. The course of the branch may be followed up to its reversing neck. The main tramway ends on an outcrop of hill, a superb point to 'launch off' the ultimate Incline down to Rhiwbach itself. Rhiwbach itself is desecrated; the older part of the workings are connected by a further Incline to the south and east. Absence of Incline drums will be noted—an unusual feature. The lowest point in Rhiwbach is about 1,410 ft. above sea level. At this point the tramway extinguished. (Length; 3 miles 440 yd. 4 inclines.)

(The entire tramway was built by Gellin Owen Jones of Penmachno, a local civil engineering contractor of some note. He is said to have made a handsome profit from this well-built extension. A stone mason by trade, among other work he built a church in Bettws-y-Coed.)

The Inclines in the quarry were operated by a single central steam engine, cables being carried above-ground by pulleys supported on wooden pylons where necessary.

Rhiwbryfdir (Welsh Slate Co.). See summarised history of quarry and under Oakeley. (Length: 1,314 yd. 3 inclines.) *Carnarvon & Denbigh Herald* reports on steam locomotive in use February 1873. Possibly *Mole?*

Rhosydd. No physical connection with F.R., though a user of it for a time.

Votty & Bowydd. Via Diphwys Casson Incline to Duffws station (q.v.).

Wrysgan. A direct Incline between quarry and Railway, there being a short siding at the foot and, much later, a storage shed. Connection with the F.R. was at the south end of the 'double embankment' near Tan-y-Grisiau. An unusual feature was the tunnel at the incline summit, and the cutting with winding machinery beyond it. The single tracked tramway on it was operated by former lorry engine on the occasion of a visit in 1942, when the daily goods train left three empty wagons at the incline foot. (Length: 1,070 yd. 2 inclines.)

Other customers. The foregoing comprised the larger slate producers having connections to the Railway. There were a number of lesser customers, some being merchants only; among them were to be found: R. & J. Williams—early 1850s.

Catherine & Jane Consols Lead Mining Co., Cei Mawr—lead, had a siding connection; first used F.R. 1856 and then intermittently until 1875 when wound up.

Bwlch-y-Plwm Mining Co.—lead, incorporated 1863; first used F.R. 1864.*

New Craig Ddu Slate Co. Ltd.—1865 onwards; later per Festiniog & Blaenau Railway, a physical connection of its own with F.R.† This quarry first connected with the F. & B.R. in autumn 1869 (evidence of manager Thomas Jarman re F.R. 1869 Bill. He stated the quarry was making connection with the F.R. at Duffws but did not clarify this was via the F. & B.R.; at the time (July) they had 300 yards of incline at the foot to finish). There is a photograph showing men completing this last length at Tan-y-Manod, late 1869. The quarry had been worked since 1840; New Craig Ddu Slate Co. Ltd., incorporated 1864/5; Craigddu Slate Co. Ltd., incorporated 1880; later, Craigddu Manod Slate Co. Ltd., and after First War, Craigddu Slate Quarries Co. Ltd.

William Griffith, Ffestiniog—lead, from 1866.

Pant-y-Wrach Mining Co.—copper, from 1866.

Morgan Drum Slate Quarry Co.—opened 1840; from 1868 via F. & B.R.

The foregoing comprised all the minor customers to be found in the accounts 1836–67.

Use of the harbour lines owned by the Railway was practised by both Croesor- and Gorseddau-borne traffic. During 1852–5, slate from Penmachno was carted to Blaenau and loaded on the Railway.

At later date, other minerals were carried on the line. See pp. 480–81.

Working on these feeder lines, especially the Inclines, exposed employees to many risks. Some of these are included in the Reports of Inspectors of Metalliferous Mines. In 1875 a fatal accident came to notice: 'The deceased was employed at the foot of an Incline by which slates are brought down from the Cwmorthin slate mine to the railway . . . it was the duty of the deceased to hook and unhook the waggons by which the slates are conveyed, and to place the loaded ones on a siding in readiness for a train for Portmadoc. While he was thus engaged a waggon came down the Incline with such rapidity that he could not get out of the way in time, and mutilated him so fearfully he must have died instantaneously. On examining the wreck of the runaway waggon it was found that the link by which it is attached to another waggon had given way while the two were being lowered by means of

---

* See *Festiniog Railway Magazine*, p. 17 for further reference.

† In 1849 Smith and Brunton were appointed advisory Engineers to the quarry and proposed building a connection to the Festiniog Railway. Site opened 1840; latterly branch to F. & B.R. having four inclines.

the break at the top of the Incline . . . The waggons are the property of the Railway Company . . . no one was appointed to examine them before sending them up to the Mines . . .' A witness said that accidents due to defective F.R. wagon coupling links were commonplace on Inclines and it was alleged that the links were not properly made. 'Another testimony to the frequence of the occurrence is a house on the other side of the main line of the railway, below the foot of the Incline at which this casualty took place. It bears yet marks on its roof of a severe riddling received from the contents of a waggon which broke loose in a similar manner some time ago. I also picked up a broken hook . . . proved in a defective state for some time before it parted . . .'

Accidents to the Car Gwyllt used on the Inclines at Bwlch-y-Slater and Craig Ddu Quarries occurred in 1897, and these are illustrated on p. 47 of the Report for that year. These were due to run-aways and hitting riders in front; more strict inspection of brakes, and the forbidding of men to borrow others' cars (or use any car for those unaccustomed to using one at all) was the result. There were no Inclines with direct access to the F.R. where Car Gwyllt were in use. It should be added that despite the tightening of the rules, and the appointment of a Captain to precede and control the down-coming cavalcade each evening, another fatal accident occurred at Craig Ddu in 1898 when due to slippery rails, 'deceased lost control of his car and it ran into that of another man who was riding in front of him. He was thrown off . . . and killed'.*

The Inclines were always dangerous to curious bystanders. As late as 1935 Votty & Bowydd wrote to the Chief Constable at Blaenau pointing out that at almost any time children might be found playing around their premises and especially on their Incline from Duffws which passed through the edge of residential property. They were just then laying their private road from the end of Lord Street adjoining the Incline, in order to take road vehicles to the office block; even tobogganing by children on it would then become their responsibility . . . 'I shall discourage (it) . . . during frosty weather . . . by laying ashes or salt on the surface'.

Children were always most likely victims of wharf or quarry Inclines or sidings. These usually lay open to access. Throughout the life of the Festiniog Railway, it appears to have been an undertaking enjoying little immunity from trespasser and accident thereto; in this respect also, it differed greatly from the average British railway whose dangers have, in the main, been recognised by the public.

It seems to have been implicit that the Railway, taking on the appellation of 'Toy' and being patently of diminutive size, would inflict personal injury or attract penalties commensurate with its physical

* See also *Festiniog Railway Magazine*, No. 16, p. 11.

Period 1868–1939

Site	Mineral	Title of working concern (usually one of several during life of site)	Date of connection (where known)
Boston Lodge			
Top Yard	(1) Sand	Sir Osmond Williams (Sandpit)	Siding 1919
Cei Mawr	Stone	(Not known—quarry east end)	c. 1888
Cei Mawr			
Bwlch-y-Plwm Mine	Lead	Bwlch-y-Plwm Lead Mining Co. (incorp. 1863) later—Penrhyndeudraeth Lead Mining Co.*	Siding: lifted by 1887
Cei Mawr			
Catherine and Jane Consols Mine	Lead	Penrallt Mining Co. (c. 1870) later—C. & J. Lead Mining Co. Ltd. (1873) later—Mereweather & Co. (from 1874)	Siding before 1873 (another enquiry for branch siding June 1906)
Ffestiniog			
Quarry	Granite	Groby Granite Co.—quarry opened 1901, later—owners Festiniog Granite Co., later—owners Festiniog Granite Quarries Ltd.	Branch April 1908. Inspected plus new sidings; April 1914
Ffestiniog			
Moelwyn No. 1	Slate	Lord Newborough—writing-slate mills	The Mills Branch 1880
Mine	Lead	Moelwyn Mining Co. Ltd. (incorp. 1893) later—M. Sinclair Stevenson Ltd. [41 employees: 1897] on behalf Ellis Pritchard	Siding and incline August 1893
	Zinc/lead	Zinc Mines of Great Britain Ltd. (1917)	Relaid 1908
	Zinc	later—Union Zinc Mining Co.—1920	Halt/sidings
Buardd Melyn			
Quarry	Setts	(Not known)—opened 1874	Short incline 1874
Moel Ystradau			
Quarry	(3) Granite	Syenite Setts Quarry Co. Ltd. (incorp. 1874)	Siding c. 1875

(2) Granite	Brookes' or Moelwyn Granite Co.	Siding on site Syenite Setts Co. siding April 1914. Junction re-sited 1918; inspected April 1919 (amendments to junction continued until 1923)
Moel Ystradau (2) Gunpowder	Elterwater Powder Co.	Using part quarry line—see Syenite Setts Co.
Portmadoc Moel-y-Gest Quarry (2) Granite	Moel-y-Gest Sett Quarry Co. (open by 1876) later—Carnarvonshire Granite Co. (in liquidation by 1903) (later owner Moel-y-Gest Granite Co. who proposed alternative new route and Glaslyn Bridge when F.R. refused to reduce rates 1905. Later owners—Caernarvonshire Granite Co. of Runcorn. Period 1922)	Using part Croesor line and F.R. to wharf near Harbour station, by August 1902

Note: See previous references for period before 1868 and that not all working titles of those concerned with working these sites have survived. Titles must be considered as a sample only.

(1) All sites closed down by early 1930s except Boston Lodge sandpit. See Chapter Eighteen for reference under 'Route'.

(2) Of the above, only Moel-y-Gest and Brookes' traffics travelled over the F.R. in the quarries' own wagons; possibly Elterwater Powder Co. owned its own stock.

(3) Syenite Setts Quarry Co. Ltd. wound up 1883 and site derelict until 1914 (Setts Company also associated with Syenite Setts Quarry Royalty Co. Ltd.).

★ *Bwlch-y-Plwm Lead Mine*. The lease of the Company formed in 1863 was held by Samuel Holland; one of the promoters of the 1863 concern was a Mr. Savin. Holland sold his lease for shares and cash, agreeing secretly to give half the proceeds to the promoters who might then enjoy the benefits of the finance raised by the remainder of the shareholders without them being aware of it! Becoming aware of this, a shareholder sought to have the Company wound up (in 1867), but was unsuccessful. (*The Law Times*: 7 December 1867, p. 235.)

The mine was advertised for sale in 1869; in 1874 it was being worked by Penrhyndeudraeth Lead Mining Co.; this concern became of limited liability the following year and also worked at Pant-y-Meusydd, Llanfrothen. No lease specifically mentions a siding with the F.R. it being stated the mine was not far from the railway. Tradition that a siding existed must be limited to the period roughly 1876-87. The P.L.M.C.L. was wound up in 1882 but continued trading until at least 1891.

The site of the mine was generally to the west of the Catherine and Jane site. In 1887 eight men were employed, produce being 12 tons 8 cwt. of ore.

stature. Such was its psychological effect; the public tended to regard it with indifference so that accidents on the feeders, in yards, on crossings or near stations (though seldom fatal) were frequent.

Correspondence

Of correspondence, it is difficult to pick out outstanding examples but most letters passing between customers and Railway were in the nature of complaint. Two are typical; one deals with the Quarrymen's Train in its earliest period, the other with shortage of wagons—perhaps the commonest source of grievance.

> Welsh Slate Company's Office,
> 19 Spring Gardens, Charing Cross,
> LONDON S.W.   Oct 3rd 1867

Dear Sir,
The Committee desire me to ask you to arrange for the Trains from Portmadoc on Monday Mornings starting at Five instead of Six O'clock, so that the Quarrymen may be able to get to their Work an hour earlier, which would be a great accommodation to the Quarries. . . .
When I was at the Quarry last Saturday I found that no empties had been received on that day until one o'clock, and the men having left at 12. no slates could be loaded, nor could any loaded waggons go down the Inclines. . . .

> I remain, My Dear Sir
> Yours truly,
> Wm Hawkins.

Charles Spooner Esqr.

> Festiniog Railway
> Traffic Manager & Accountants Office
> Portmadoc.   Sept 4 1901

Dear Sir,
The Oakeley Company are complaining again this afternoon of being short of empties, and want to know what has become of the yellow marked wagons lately used by the New Welsh Slate Co.
I find there are 17 Oakeley 'blue marked' wagons now at Boston Lodge waiting repairs.

> Yours truly,
> F. G. Crick.

J. S. Hughes Esqr.

Slate Wagons; London & North Western and Great Western Railways

The extension of these two standard gauge railways into Blaenau with the object of tapping the slate quarries' traffic, required the supply of slate wagons to put the new intruders on the same footing as the Festiniog Railway, i.e. it obviated the need for the quarries themselves to provide their own rolling stock. It also had the effect of cluttering up the quarries with wagons belonging to three owners, and it was not long before G.W.R. wagons would be used for ship-bound traffic at Portmadoc and F.R. wagons loaded in error on the transporters provided by the G.W.R. to reach the Craig Ddu outlet. Correspondence includes arguments about the wrong loading of such wagons, the quarries not being particularly concerned so long as the slate was got away!

The L.N.W.R. stock worked between the Inclines' foot and their Blaenau Ffestiniog yard. With the G.W.R., the arrangement was similar though different in that their yard in Blaenau had to deal with quarries (albeit not the major ones) which the narrow gauge Festiniog & Blaenau Railway formerly served. Whilst some of the slate traffic originating to the G.W.R. came over the F.R. tracks into their yard in the same way as L.N.W.R. traffic did, the G.W.R. catered for loaded wagons brought from their Tan-y-Manod station (and empties returning to Tan-y-Manod) on this converted narrow-gauge section. This required a pick-a-back service of flat wagons on to which loaded G.W.R. narrow gauge slate wagons were run at Tan-y-Manod and off-loaded at Blaenau; at Blaenau the slate would then be re-loaded into G.W.R. standard-gauge wagons, or sent down to Minffordd to one of the merchants there. Trouble arose when G.W.R. loaded wagons were found in Minffordd Yard, their contents being unloaded into a Cambrian wagon! This was not exceptional. After the 1923 grouping, it became an occasional practice if slate was consigned to former Cambrian depots. G.W.R.-owned wagons loaded with slate for shipment at Portmadoc—just mentioned—were seldom on legal pursuits; it was simply a matter that the supplying quarry had loaded into the next-convenient wagon, whoever the owner.

Some of the L.N.W.R.'s traffic was, in earliest times when Deganwy was being promoted, carried by running three loaded slate wagons, side by side, across the floor of specially adapted standard gauge open wagons with drop-sides. These were 15 ft. 6 in. long in body, 7 ft. 5 in. wide with 9 ft. wheelbase, rated to carry 10 tons. They appear in the L.N.W.R. Wagon Diagram Book of 1903, and were possibly built at Earlestown to meet the change in plan when it was decided not to extend to Blaenau in narrow gauge.* The exact date when this pick-a-back service ceased is not known, but it is suggested the slump in output in the early years of the century, coinciding with the fall in Deganwy tonnages, made it unrealistic, and the F.R. thereafter took the L.N.W.R. wagons to their appropriate destinations for trans-shipment to rail or ship. It is important to recall that both L.N.W.R. and G.W.R. relied on the F.R. to bring their wagons into their exchange yards, and that the L.N.W.R. only had direct access to Oakeley and Greaves'

* No photograph of these wagons has yet come to notice; the narrow gauge wagons were locked to their floors by screws. Wagon Drawing No. 7. 'Slate Truck Wagons'.

traffic (these providing the *raison-d'être* of the pick-a-back wagons), and that the G.W.R. had only the direct access of the limited traffic offered at Tan-y-Manod which they chose to bring back into Blaenau by pick-a-back.

The slate wagons themselves were of typical frame-type construction; each Company supplied two varieties, each variety showing detail differences along the years. Some of these G.W. wagons were sold and still survive in quarry use, especially at Maenofferen. L.N.W.R. examples were built in two batches in the 1880s at their Earlestown Works, and the G.W.R. originated in Swindon in 1899 and 1902.* Typical dimensions were:

	L.N.W.R. 2 ton	G.W.R. 2 ton
Length	6 ft. 3¾ in.	6 ft. 0 in.
Width	3 ft. 5 in.	3 ft. 6 in. (max)
Height from rail	3 ft. 2 in.	3 ft. 2 in.
Wheelbase	3 ft. 3 in.	3 ft. 0 in.

There was considerable variation in detail (bearings, brake gear, etc.) and in smaller measure, dimension between batches from each of the two companies.

Surviving L.N.W. wagons were sold to S. Wales for scrap in late 1965.

Working of Quarry Branches

Some notes were made in the late 1930s of impressions taken from men who had worked on some of the feeders before they closed in the slump of the early 1930s.

The Newborough Slate Mills branch led off past the former cinema, over an ungated road crossing and into the valley where the mills stood; here school slates and slate pencils were manufactured. The branch line actually entered a wharf in the mill. Most Railway traffic was concerned with taking suitable slate into the mill, the outgoing products then going mainly by road. Even at that time, a number of Welsh schools used these materials. The Top Shunter would run an occasional wagon to the mills as required.

Brookes' traffic went mainly to the ex L.N.W.R. yard. There were three or four special trips a day when traffic was at its height; the Top Shunting Engine would come down specially to work this, and the Working Timetables showed appropriate paths for working the traffic. Even at this late stage, the Shunting Engine crew lived by the week in the Glan-y-Pwll barracks; hours were 7 a.m. to 7 p.m. Latterly Brookes' workings were made at 7 a.m., noon and 4 p.m. daily.

The Groby branch, as the men called it, was at first worked by Eng-land engines. Its steep gradients required the train to rush the banks at

* There exists an official photo of No. 34 at Swindon in 1899 (Lot No. 251).

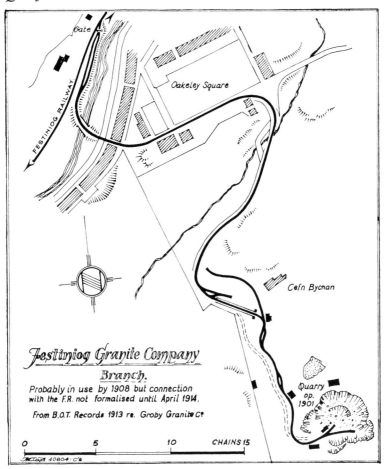

FESTINIOG RAILWAY

Gate

Oakeley Square

Cefn Bychan

Festiniog Granite Company
Branch.
Probably in use by 1908 but connection
with the F.R. not formalised until April 1914.

From B.O.T. Records 1913 re. Groby Granite C?

Quarry
op.
1901

0   5   10   CHAINS 15

20–30 m.p.h. (this was probably an exaggeration) as these were exceptionally steep. L.N.W.R. slate wagons were in use, loaded with granite setts in trains of fourteen vehicles; sometimes chippings were sent in sheet-sided wagons, four to a train. About 1930 the quarry bought petrol rail-tractors which brought shorter trains to the transfer siding, and the England engines no longer worked the line which had become unsafe for them. The quarry closed in the early 1930s. All output went to the ex L.N.W.R. yard. From 1919 the quarry provided a flagman to protect the Tan-y-Grisiau road crossing. Maximum loading was twelve 2 ton or six 4 ton wagons; heavier trains were divided at the road crossing.

The branch crossed the Tan-y-Grisiau road by ungated crossing, masked on one side by dwellings. It then curved sharply eastwards, it climbed steeply along the street in the manner of a tramway in the suburbs. At the summit there was an additional 'hump' in the line, and a sharp curve for good measure. The route then careered down a small valley away from the town by a series of short steep runs and an abundance of sharp twists, so into the quarry premises. The working of the line was an art in itself; an extra man was carried on the engine for the main road crossing. On one occasion Tom Davies, one of the two last men to work the railway, was propelling the empties hard up the street towards the quarry when a crankpin broke. The rod dropped into the ballast; the sudden snatch and halt of the engine brought the wagons on the rear into the back of the tender and shook them clear again. The jolt had uncoupled them and they ran backwards down towards the road crossing with the brakesman in chase. Luckily the road was clear and the train flew across it to mount the gradient on the other side. The brakesman could not reach the wagons in time to pin down any brakes, and they ran down across the road again in the opposite direction. All the brakesman could do was to stand in the road to warn; ultimately bystanders succeeded in holding back the train and fastening the brakes.

On another occasion the driver stalled the train at the top of the street, 'Summit Corner'; he was bringing the loaded train from the quarry. As the brakesman had walked ahead to clear the road crossing, the driver ran back towards the quarry to divide the train and take it up the hill in two parts. But he failed to properly pin down the brakes on the wagons he had detached and they began to run back towards the quarry. The driver, back on his engine and alerted by the noise, reversed and ran back after them. He was too late; the grade up into the quarry stopped them and they began to run back again. There was a horrible crash in the foot of the dip when steam, granite blocks and wagons jumped all over the place. The official explanation was that a brake failed!

Motive Power

The smaller quarries employed man and gravity power. The medium ones used horses additionally. Some of the major users of horses re-placed these with the products of De Winton & Co., Carnarvon, who built simple steam locomotives suitable to work in the rough conditions both above and below ground. Some quarries replaced these simple machines with more sophisticated products of English or Scottish builders. In their turn, steam engines were displaced by internal com-bustion or electric engines. Llechwedd and Maenofferen still use locomotives of the latter types. These engines tended to be bought, used, then sold or scrapped without much note being taken of their lifestyle. Quarry records only listed the most basic things, usually about the boilers. There is no complete list of the steam locomotives employed in these quarries, though a much more accurate picture is available of the more recent internal combustion period. The study of these quarry locomotives is a complex one, outside the present terms of reference; a list of them is a basic requirement and is based on the findings of those bodies who make special study of the subject, together with personal records.

On present knowledge the earliest steam locomotive employed was *Mole*, probably built by John Hays Wilson of J. H. Wilson & Co. Ltd., Sandhills, Liverpool which was at work—including underground and probably through the horse tunnel—at the Welsh Slate Co. in early 1873. (See also *F.R. Magazine*, No. 34, p. 15 and *Railways*, November 1951.)

Cwt-y-Bugail

—	4 wheel PM Hibberd OOU 1953. Sold 1960
—	4 wheel DM RH 223687/1944 ex Maenofferen by 1949. OOU 1967
9	4 wheel DM HE 2024/1940 ex Penmaenr, Welsh Granite, Trevor. Not used C-y-B. OOU 1967

Llechwedd

Freda	0–4–0 Vert. Br. De Winton Sold to John Corbett, Tonfanau Qy. 1898 or before
—	0–4–0 Vert. Br. De Winton Under repair 1898. Possibly then scrap or sold
Edith	0–4–0 Inv. ST Bagnall 1278/1890 Used in bldg. *The Coalition* 1930
Margaret	0–4–0 ST Bagnall 1445/1895 Used in bldg. *The Eclipse* 1927
Dorothy	0–4–0 ST Bagnall 1568/1899 Stored out of use 1963 to present day
No. 1	4 wheel BE WR 302/c. 1922
(2)	4 wheel BE WR c. 1922
'3'	4 wheel WE WR c. 1926 OOU 1964
(*Welsh Pony*)	
No. 4	
The Eclipse	0–4–0 WE MIT 5/1927
The Coalition	0–4–0 WE MIT 1930
(3)	4 wheel BE WR c. 1935
—	4 wheel PM MIT c. 1936 Bt. from Morris road lorry on rly. chassis. OOU 1964
—	4 wheel BE WR 918/c. 1936 ex Maenofferen c. 1947

Groby Granite

A number of 4 wheel rail tractors, type not known. All OOU by 1935

Maenofferen

Sanford	0–4–0 ST Bagnall 1571/1900 Sold Penrhyn Qy. 1929 per Owen Isaacs Owen, Portmadoc

Skinner	0–4–0	ST	Bagnall	1766/1906	Sold Penrhyn Qy. 1929 per Owen Isaacs Owen, Portmadoc
—	4 wheel	PM	MIT	ex Rhiwbach	
—	4 wheel	PE	MRail		
—	4 wheel	PM	Rhiwbach	Using parts of farm tractor for shunting over F.R. tracks after closure of that line. Shedded under road bridge, Duffws. Sc. 1966	
—	4 wheel	PM	Hibberd	1821	Sc. 1966
—	4 wheel	PM	Hibberd	1929	Sc. 1956
—	4 wheel	PM	MRail	1904/1920	Sc. 1966
—	4 wheel	DM	MRail	5506/1929	Sold or Sc.
—	4 wheel	BE	WR	918/c. 1936	To Llechwedd c. 1947
—	4 wheel	DM	MRail	20073/1950	From makers 1961 ex Birmingham Water Dept. OOU 1973. Sold 1974
—	4 wheel	DM	RH	174535/1936	
—	4 wheel	DM	RH	174536/1936	
—	4 wheel	DM	RH	174542/1935	ex Belgium
—	4 wheel	DM	RH	175127/1935	From Ruabon Brick by 1953. OOU 1967
—	4 wheel	DM	RH	175138/1935	ex Votty & Bowydd 1963. Sc. 1965 after falling down No. 2 Incline
—	4 wheel	DM	RH	177638/1936	ex Votty & Bowydd 1963. Dism. 1967
—	4 wheel	DM	RH	177642/1936	
—	4 wheel	DM	RH	191674/1938	Sc. 1966
—	4 wheel	DM	RH	200762/1942	Dism. 1954
—	4 wheel	DM	RH	223687/1944	ex Ministry of Supply. To Cwt-y-Bugail by 1949

Bwlch-y-Slater (inc. Manod & Ministry of the Environment)

—	4 wheel	BE	Brush	16306/1917	ex W. O. Williams, Harlech to Brockham Museum
—	4 wheel	BE	Brush	16303/1917	ex W. O. Williams, Harlech (2.75 h.p. motor)
—	4 wheel	DM	HE	1965/1939	(owner M. of S.) ex Geo. Wimpey & Son Ltd. OOU 1964

Oakeley

Mary Oakeley	0–4–0	Vert. Br.	Falcon	1884 Sc. c. 1920
William	0–4–0T	Adamson	1885	Sc.
Mary Caroline	0–4–0T	Adamson	1888	Sc. c. 1931
Edward	0–4–0T	Adamson	1888	Sc.
Algernon (ex *Mole*)	0–4–0	Geared. J. H. Wilson & Co., Sandhills, Liverpool pre-1873. Probably former Welsh Slate Co's *Mole*★ Sc.		
Charles	0–4–0T	Adamson	1890	Sc. c. 1931
Snowdon	0–4–0ST	Bagnall	1569/1899	Sc.
Eileen	0–4–0ST	Bagnall	2045/1918	ex Ministry of Munitions. Sc.
Diana	0–4–0T	Kerr Stuart	1158/1917	ex Longhurst, Kerry. To Pen-yr-Orsedd 1939
Algernon	0–4–0WT	Hudson	1028	Sc.

★ J. H. Wilson & Co. Ltd. built tugs, marine machinery, deck engines, etc. 1860–70; they changed later to cranes, winches. *Mole* appears to have been built up from suitable materials at the builders.

Clifford	0–4–0WT	Huds. Clarke	1142/1915	ex Nottingham 1924. Sc.
Kidbrooke	0–4–0ST	Bagnall	2043/1917	ex RASC, Kidbrooke. OOU 1939. Sold 1961
	0–4–0 PM	Baguley	708/1917	ex War Dept. per T. W. Ward. Sc.
(Clifford)	0–4–0 PM	Baguley	774/1919	ex Machynlleth per Oliver. OOU 1939. Sold
(Rosa)	0–4–0 PM	Baguley	779/1919	ex Kerry (as *Diana*). Dest. by fire *c.* 1937
—	4 wheel DM	Deutz		Sc. 1964
—	4 wheel DM	Bagnall	2499/1933	to Votty & Bowydd
—	4 wheel DM	RH	174139/1935	
—	4 wheel DM	RH	174540/1935	
—	4 wheel DM	RH	175405/1935	
—	4 wheel DM	RH	175986/1935	
—	4 wheel DM	RH	177598/1935	ex Egypt 1937, per Robert Hudson
—	4 wheel DM	RH	177638/1936	to Votty & Bowydd
—	4 wheel DM	RH	182137/1936	
—	4 wheel DM	RH	432652/1959	
—	4 wheel DM	RH	264252/1952	ex Votty & Bowydd *c.* 1962

Rhiwbach

—	0–4–0 PM	Baguley	731/1918	per makers 1924; ex Bicester Aerodrome. Sold or Scrap
—	4 wheel PM	MIT		to Maenofferen
—	4 wheel PM	MIT		OOU 1963

Votty & Bowydd

*Taffy**	0–4–0T	Vulcan Fdy	810/1878	Parts used for No. 8
Meirion	0–4–0ST	Manning Wardle	487/1874	ex Nuneaton. OOU 1916
Wendy	0–4–0ST	Bagnall	2091/1919	to Dorothea 3/1930
	4 wheel PM	Deutz	1912	Sc. 1963
	4 wheel PM	Deutz	1913	Parts used for the 4wh BE loco
	4 wheel PM	Deutz	1926	to Dorothea
	4 wheel PM	Deutz	1936	OOU 1951. Sc.
	4 wheel DM	Bagnall	2499/1933	ex Oakeley. Sc. *c.* 1963
No. 8	4 wheel BE	MIT	*c.* 1939	to Aberllefenni by 8/1963
	4 wheel BE	Brush		to Aberllefenni by 8/1963
	4 wheel BE	MIT		Sc.
	4 wheel BE	MIT		Sc.
	4 wheel DM	RH	175138/1935	to Maenofferen 1963
	4 wheel DM	RH	182141/1936	Sc. 1963
	4 wheel DM	RH	195773/1939	Sc. 1963
	4 wheel DM	RH	264252/1952	ex Mold. To Oakeley *c.* 1962
	4 wheel DM	RH	171902/1934	ex Rhos Qy, Capel Curig 1958. Sc. 8/1964
	4 wheel DM	RH	177638/1936	ex Oakeley *c.* 1958. To Maenofferen 1963

* See also under Appendix 2 re Spooner & Co.

Moel-y-Gest

—   0–4–0 Vert. Br. Falcon Engine *c.* 1883. Sold or scrap when quarry closed *c.* 1906. Obtained second-hand? General Repair Boston Lodge 1902

May have been a Spooner & Co. design, built by Falcon using Spooner & Co. as agents.

Quarry Tours Ltd., Llechwedd Slate Mines

No. 1	4 wheel	BE	WR	
No. 2	4 wheel	BE	WR	
—	4 wheel	BE	LMM	1053/1950
—	4 wheel	BE	LMM	1066/1950

Abbreviations used to describe foregoing:
Inv. ST = Inverted Saddle Tank
T = Side Tank
ST = Saddle Tank
Vert. Br. = Vertical Boiler & cylindered engine, carrying tank on same frame.
WT = Well Tank
DM = Diesel Mechanical
PM = Petrol Mechanical
BE = Battery Electrical
WE = Overhead wire Electrical
Geared = Geared transmission
OOU = Out of use
Dism = Dismantled
Sc. = broken up for scrap
Sold = Sold to another party

Builders' Abbreviated Titles
Brush Electrical Engineering Co. Ltd., Loughborough—Brush
E. E. Baguley Ltd., Burton-on-Trent—Baguley
Daniel Adamson & Co. Ltd., Dukinfield, Cheshire—Adamson
De Winton & Co., Caernarvon—De Winton
Motorenfabrik Deutz A.G., Cologne—Deutz
Falcon Engine & Car Works, Loughborough—Falcon Engine
F. C. Hibberd & Co. Ltd., London—Hibberd
Hudswell, Clarke & Co. Ltd., Leeds—Huds. Clarke
Robert Hudson Ltd., Leeds—Hudson
Hunslet Engine Co. Ltd., Leeds—HE
Kerr, Stuart & Co. Ltd., Stoke-on-Trent—Kerr Stuart
MIT = Built on the system on which the unit worked—MIT
Motor Rail Ltd., Simplex Works, Bedford—MRail
Manning Wardle & Co. Ltd., Hunslet, Leeds—Manning Wardle
Ruston & Hornsby Ltd., Lincoln—RH
W. G. Bagnall Ltd., Castle Engine Works, Stafford—Bagnall
Wingrove & Rogers Ltd., Southport—WR
NB: Rail tractor built 'Rhiwbach' (under Maenofferen) is thus defined—and not MIT—as it did not work on the premises where it was constructed.
All the foregoing motive power worked on a nominal 2 ft. gauge track.

1Q   *Wagon number plate— Spooner & Co.*
(J. I. C. Boyd)

2Q   *Spooner & Co-designed, Vulcan Foundry-built* Kathleen.   *(J. I. C. Boyd)*

3Q   *Spooner & Co-designed, Vulcan Foundry-built* Kelso I *and a De Winton-built engine alongside.*   *(J. I. C. Boyd)*

4Q   *Start of a journey. Loading rock onto wagons underground in the Oakeley Quarry.*
(Oakeley S.Q.C.L.)

5Q   *Moel-y-Gest Quarry loco at Harbour, 1903.*   *(L.P. Co.)*

6Q   *Looking down Votty & Bowydd incline into Duffws station. 1942. (Oakeley S.Q.C.L.)*

7Q   Mole: *probably the first steam locomotive to work in a Ffestiniog quarry. On the Welsh Slate Co.'s wharf, Portmadoc.*   *(F.R. Co.)*

8Q   *A scene in the Oakeley Quarry of one of the quarry trains coming up from below ground. Both uncut rock and rubbish is included in the load. Note the petrol tractor for working the level, and the wagon with plank seats for carrying officials on the upper incline.*
                                                                 (Oakeley S.Q.C.L.)

9Q   Edith, *one of Llechwedd Quarry's three Bagnall engines: it had an inverted saddle tank.* *(Caerns. C.R.O.)*

10Q   *Swindon-built transfer wagon for carrying slate wagons between Tan-y-Manod and the G.W.R. yard at Blaenau.* *(Photomatic)*

11Q *Runaways were frequently happening: two old slate wagons pause for a drink on the Dinas branch. 1954.*   *(J. B. Snell)*

12Q Skinner, *a Maenofferen Quarry locomotive.*

13Q The Coalition: *a converted steam engine at Llechwedd. (J. I. C. Boyd)*

1M
A derailment due to snow. (Scribner's Magazine)

THE "PRINCESS" IN DIFFICULTIES.

2M   *A derailment due to fog, Blaenau (see text for account).*   *(Thomas Davies)*

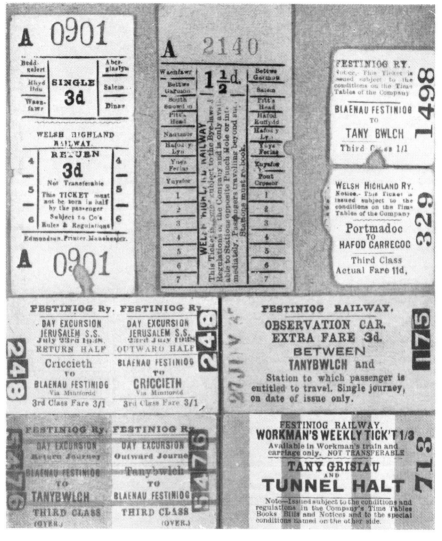

3M   *A miscellany of W.H.R. and F.R. tickets.*   (J. I. C. Boyd)

CHAPTER TWENTY

THE NEW ERA 1954–74

(*F.R.M.* references in the text refer to articles
in the *Festiniog Railway Magazine*)

1954–61
The Years Examined; an All-subject Review
1962–74
The Surviving Portion of the Original Route; The Deviation
1954–74
*Steam Locomotives—Rail Tractors—Carriages—Goods Stock
—Permanent Way and Signalling—Appraisal of the New
Era—Tickets*

1954–61

With the complete disappearance from the scene of other interested
parties, a new organisation, begun by that enthusiast whose overtures
to the Company had tended to become mixed up with those of the
1949 Group, at least had the field to itself. This body called itself 'The
(Proposed) Festiniog Railway Preservation Society'; its contacts with
the Board were now unhampered by other similar interests, but it
faced several obstacles. It was not for some time that the Board and
the organisers of this new movement saw eye to eye, and clearly the
Board were very sceptical that such a body of young men could ever
succeed. However, in the absence of anyone else, the Board were at
least being courted and those who were doing the courting were not
lacking in enthusiasm, even if they lacked financial backing. The
Society 'came into the open' when Mr. L. A. Heath Humphreys, its
founder, called a meeting in Bristol on 8 September 1951. The early
years of the Society proved very unstable, and at first its work was
focused on the details of obtaining control and the changeover from
the existing ownership.

Several large blocks of share-holdings were ultimately placed at the
Society's call, due to the appeal made through the Society to Company
members, asking for the transfer of their holdings as reasonably as they
could do so.

One problem was to find the means of raising sufficient money to
purchase these holdings, it being necessary to acquire all the Debentures,
Preference Shares and a controlling number of the Ordinary Shares in
order to take over control of the Company, including overdraft. In the

event, the Society was fortunate in being able to interest not only one who could subscribe part of the money needed to acquire these holdings, but one who was also a member of the Eastern Region Area Board of the British Transport Commission. Thus, Mr. Alan F. Pegler became the keystone of the arch which the Society had so laboriously constructed.

Although it was the intention to proceed on the same basis as the neighbouring Talyllyn Railway Preservation Society, the fact that financial assistance had to be obtained in such substantial amounts soon put the Society in a position of being beholden to those who had provided the capital to enable the take-over to be effected. This was never the case with the Talyllyn. Before long, those persons who had taken a risk and put up capital to enable the change of ownership to take place, were faced with the difficult task of reconciling their financial sacrifice with the aims of the Society: they had to choose whether to allow the Society to run the railway in the same manner as the Talyllyn Company, with the attendant risk of being unable to recoup the money they had put into the venture, or to follow up their purchase and control the Company themselves. In the outcome, the latter choice was taken. Undoubtedly this led to great disappointment among those who, having done so much laborious spadework with the idea of participating in the control of the railway, were denied it. Mr. Pegler subsequently placed his Ordinary Shares into a non-profit-making Trust, dividends on which would, if paid, not be liable for tax.

Nevertheless, the Society was to show ultimately, after forming itself into a Limited Liability Company, that it played a considerable role in the restoration of the railway. Besides contributing financially towards the many expenses which so great a refurbishing requires, labour charges to the Company have been reduced by the assistance of skilled volunteers, and also by a larger number of unskilled workers.

The Society, as a registered Company, has the power to purchase interests in the Railway Company.

The transfer of the Company to its new owners was on 24 June 1954. By October the voluntary forces of the Society had begun a planned programme to clear the track and administer emergency repairs with a view to running a train service over a limited distance during the summer of 1955. Whilst this was proceeding, more ominous tidings came from another source. The old Company had been advised, during November 1951, that part of their line lying north of the Moelwyn Tunnel would be compulsorily acquired for the purpose of making a reservoir in connection with British Electricity Authority programmes. Owing to the change of ownership, the old proprietors were no longer affected and the new possessors did not readily appreciate what was afoot until July 1954. In consequence, the Festiniog Railway Company was obliged to petition formally against a Bill which now proposed a hydro-electric scheme in a form somewhat different from an earlier one, the promoting body now being known as the Central Electricity Authority.

Counsel for the Railway Company was Mr. S. Cope Morgan, Q.C., and the evidence was taken before a Select Committee of the House of Lords on 29 March–6 April 1955.

By early summer 1953 all reclaimable materials from Brookes' Quarry were lying at Tan-y-Grisiau station with the partly-stripped tractor used for the work.

Work began on the reservoir site early in 1956 and the railway was ultimately lifted between Tan-y-Grisiau station and the tunnel mouth (north end). By March 1957 when the rails had disappeared almost to the tunnel they had been stacked where they could not be reached by any Festiniog train! Recrimination ensued between the Authority, McAlpine (the contractor) and the Railway as the materials were urgently needed for restoration. At this period the intervening earth-works had been levelled off along the railway site and the formation of the track bed was already taking on the appearance of a lake shore. Cranes, lorries and other equipment had succeeded in changing the face of the earth. The site of the line became a roadway and stone was obtained from the former Brookes' Quarry. Clogwyn Daniel, south of Tan-y-Grisiau, was blasted away to make the power station site, and parts of the line were incorporated with the side of the reservoir.

Despite this setback the Company announced its aim, in spite of the flooding of the existing course, to press on with its avowed intention of making Blaenau Festiniog its natural objective, and thus securing access to the North Wales coast traffic.

Only a small length of track had been cleared between Boston Lodge and the Cemetery when, in August 1954, Colonel McMullen visited the system and on behalf of the Ministry of Transport, gave the Company the benefit of his views and wished them luck in the venture.

The next month Morris Jones was engaged to help the skilled volunteers and with a minimum of effort the Simplex tractor came to life again. Two carriages, Nos. 2 and 17, were cleaned up and on 23 September this train ran across the Cob for the benefit of the local press. Pictures were taken and a great deal of publicity was given to the cause. Finances were still the most difficult problem as no amount of enthusiasm can overcome a shortage of money, so it was arranged that many of the derelict wagons both in Boston Lodge and those with which the Harbour station was filled, should be cut up, thus yielding revenue and giving some working space in both places.

A more melancholy event took place during the next month when the decision was made to turn over the remains of the ex-Welsh Highland engine *Moel Tryfan* to the scrap breakers. This engine had been in the midst of repairs for many years and its tanks, cab, etc., were stored in the Works yard. The boiler, resting on the driving bogie, lay in the engine shed. Many had hoped that it might be spared as suitable for future requirements. Its last journey was made behind the Simplex which towed the boiler on the bogie on a funereal journey to the Harbour station for cutting up.

One of the first tasks was the filling in of the embankment which had collapsed near the Boston Lodge turntable, and after this was done the Simplex could run Up the line; with the rails well sanded the 'well-armoured' ends of this tractor were excellent for breaking down obstructions on the track, though when Minffordd road crossing and the section by the weigh bridges higher up was reached the track had to be dug out of alluvial deposits.

Working parties, organised on the same volunteer basis as those which were working on the Talyllyn Railway, began their task as official groups in December, assisted by the Simplex whose habits were somewhat temperamental. Thus a way was cleared to milepost $5\frac{1}{2}$ where progress was impeded by large trees which had fallen across the line.

One of Colonel Stephens' trolleys, in this case off the Welsh Highland, fitted with a reversible two-stroke engine, was rebuilt by voluntary labour and returned to Portmadoc with a fresh motor unit on 22 January. This was celebrated by hauling a platelayers' trolley as far as the Moelwyn Tunnel, the first 'train' to reach this point.

By the New Year 1955 Morris Jones and an apprentice had begun to put the workshops into working condition again. A Crossley diesel engine, by then used for driving the machinery, was made to work, but as there was no water supply for cooling purposes, the engine could only run intermittently. So began the rebuilding of *Prince* which had stood dismembered for so long.

At the same time volunteers managed to clear away the last of the fallen trees so that trains could at least force a way along the line.

The immediate object was to have things ready for running a service during summer 1955. Portmadoc station was cleaned up, signs painted and erected. A station on the site of the former Boston Lodge Halt was cleared among the debris and before traffic began, both stations had a well-cared-for appearance. Boston Lodge curve was re-sleepered, followed by the track across the Cob which suffered from bad sleepers, defective rails and loose chairs.

For the service, ex-Welsh Highland carriage No. 23 and Festiniog No. 12 (ex No. 5 original series), painted green with ivory upper panels, red ends and seats, were prepared. The smart livery made a gay splash amidst so much dilapidation.

Robert Evans (60 years with the Railway) retired in early June and the new owners appointed A. G. W. Garraway, who had been working on the railway for some time, to succeed him as Manager and Engineer. The Ministry was advised that the proposed service would begin on Saturday, 23 July; but *Prince* was not yet ready, so the Simplex held the fort for a number of days. An Official Opening, presided over by Miss Janet Jones, the Welsh Tourist Queen, took place on 29 July when Miss Jones joined the train at Boston Lodge and arrived in Portmadoc.

For the initiated, the Red Letter Day was in the evening of Tuesday, 2 August when, nine years after *Princess* had last run (but not over this section), *Prince* steamed over the Cob, going into regular service three days later. From then until September 1956 when *Taliesin* went into traffic, *Prince* worked every passenger train.

The season ended on 24 September, when 20,000 passenger journeys had been made: there had been two morning and four afternoon trains per day. It was necessary to run round the train outside Boston Lodge gates, using a chain to pull the carriages clear of the engine, an awkward arrangement occasioned by there being no run round at the temporary terminus.

The following winter was devoted to the scrapping of more redundant wagons to raise money and the reconditioning of the line to Minffordd. In November Cohen's, scrap merchants, lifted the flat bottomed rails on the Dinas branch, some of them being resold for use on the Talyllyn.

Nothing had so far been done in Minffordd Exchange Yard, where the jungle still reigned. The low-level siding was eventually dug out, yielding over 50 wagons, mostly destined for scrap. From now on the coal chute was accessible, a useful feature. British Railways (Western Region) were about to lift much of their trackage in the yard but when it was apparent that the Festiniog was more alive than dead they appreciated a reminder from the Festiniog that layout alterations could only be done by mutual arrangement between the two organisations. One long standard gauge siding was thus retained.

Before the works of the Electricity Board could sever connection with Blaenau, the opportunity was taken of making several sorties there to rescue wagons earmarked for scrap.

In order to improve the rough riding of *Prince*, an articulation arrangement was devised; a small part of the weight of the rear end of the engine was carried on the tender by means of a heavy drawbar and a kingpin on the tender. The leading tender wheels were moved forward so that the kingpin was within the wheelbase. The tender brake gear was removed and a heavy plate floor fitted.

On the rolling stock side, it was agreed that *Taliesin* should be taken in hand, another engine being a necessity. To send such an engine away would have been too costly, so arrangements were made with the

Vulcan Foundry to do the work at Boston Lodge. At the same time compo-van No. 11 (ex No. 4 original series) was overhauled, the 1st class compartment being retained; it was soon found that tourists would pay for the additional distinction! No. 17 (original series) followed, going into traffic in July 1956. Its 1st class compartment was restored in all its Victorian splendour, being the only one sufficiently intact in any surviving carriage to enable this to be done.

For the 1956 season, Minffordd was the new terminus, opening on 19 May. The two morning trains ran during July and August only, and there were four afternoon trains. As an experiment, certain evening services were run. Pen Cob Halt at the south end of the Cob, was opened in May.

The telephone system, an omnibus circuit to all stations and the separate line between Portmadoc and Boston Lodge, was now taken in hand. Restoration of the Electric Train Staff began, the points at Boston Lodge and Minffordd being unlocked by the Staff Key. Instruments were being provided at Portmadoc, Boston Lodge and Minffordd initially. The former three-arm bracket signal on the Cob was given a red-painted arm with horizontal white stripe. This was strictly an elevated point signal. Minffordd road crossing gates were fitted with switches which operated green lights in special signals when the gates were open to the railway. Treadles were later fitted which would ring bells to indicate when a train was approaching. The crossovers in the main line near the weigh bridge were lifted.

Taliesin went into traffic on the evening of 4 September, a milestone in the restoration programme. When the season ended on 22 September, 39,000 passenger journeys had been made.

On the track, clearance proceeded as far as Penrhyn and a special effort was put in to enable the General Manager of British Railways (Western Region) and his party to travel behind *Taliesin* hauling a four-coach train as far as this point on 12 November.

The remaining tracks north and west of Britannia Bridge were lifted during mid-winter, and together with some rails remaining from the W.H.R. at Pitt's Head, were used for relaying on the Cob. In the spring, a start was made to lay a loop at Penrhyn station so that engines could run round trains in the ensuing summer.

In 1956, carriages Nos. 18 and 20 were removed from Glan-y-Mor Carriage Shed after a collapsed roof had been raised off No. 20.

Thus while first *Prince*, and later *Taliesin*, were used on the more spectacular passenger work, for much of the day-to-day duties the internal combustion engines were relied upon. It was the Simplex, being the more suitable to put into repair and the last unit in use with the former owners, which bore the brunt of the early reclamation work; its peculiarities soon became familiar, but as with Colonel Stephens, its new users found it most uneconomical in use. It had an insatiable thirst for petrol, and even on T.V.O., which could be used on long runs, it was scarcely less expensive. However, a Gardner 3LW engine unit was acquired and it was decided to fit this into the Baldwin petrol locomotive as its own American engine was unworthy of repair.

The Baldwin tractor, first used on August Bank Holiday 1956, soon proved itself a valuable unit. It ran up to Blaenau for telegraph poles, etc., on its maiden voyage and demonstrated clearly its potential. The Simplex was handcrank-started from the trackside (an operation which could not be performed everywhere) but the Baldwin had full electrical gear and starter, lighting and other refinements. The engine was governed and with the two gears it possessed a top speed of about 15 m.p.h.; it could not start a heavy load on a gradient. Its top speed was rarely attained due to the long heavy overhang in front of the wheel-base.

During 1957 a four-speed gearbox (Meadows) was mounted directly on to the engine with a short Layrub connection to the original main gearbox, giving a total of eight gear combinations, the lowest one being most suitable for starting heavy loads.

Up to now it had been the practice to run the Baldwin closely coupled to goods brake van No. 1 (ex No. 6 original series) to stabilise the tractor—this was an awkward arrangement when propelling the van. For the winter service, the engine was divorced from the van and modified to improve its riding by the fitting of a pony truck under the front end. This was built up from parts of one of the ex-German bogie wagons' bogie frames (Brookes' Quarry) and *Little Giant*'s connecting rods; another legacy of this engine is a part of the front buffer beam in the rear engine mounting. An ex-Welshpool & Llanfair Light Railway coupler was fitted at the front and the engine named *Moelwyn*.

In the autumn of 1957 a short-lived service of Saturday afternoon trains ran between Penrhyn and Portmadoc, but being poorly patronised, was withdrawn at Christmas.

Continuing on the repair of carriage stock, No. 12 compo-van which had gone into service during the first season in its original form, came into the Works for internal alterations. At Minffordd, a small kiosk sold refreshments, etc., but there was likely to be nowhere so suitable at other stations; it was arranged to convert this carriage, therefore, into a Buffet Car for which purpose the longitudinally seated compartment was removed, the floor lowered as far as possible and a counter with glass front installed. Corridor access was made with the rest of the coach and a door connection with the van portion. During 1956 this coach and No. 11 compo-van (No. 4 original series) were marshalled at opposite ends of the train. This was found inconvenient as trains became longer and intermediate passengers wished to load prams, for instance; the next stage lay in running these two vehicles coupled together, van to van, with fall plates and handrails forming a rudimentary 'corridor connection' between them.

For the 1957 season, both steam engines were fully painted and lined out; green was the principal colour, with red lining and black borders to the panels. For attachment to carriages the engines also were fitted with more suitable carriage couplings. A service ran at Easter this time, but the season proper commenced at Whitsuntide; again, the timetable was four trains at hourly intervals in the afternoon with two additional morning trains during July and August. Evening trains ran on four nights during the latter period. Passenger journeys for the season totalled 54,000. This season trains terminated at Penrhyn which opened on 20 April as did a new Halt at Pen-y-Bryn.

The next objective was to push on beyond Cei Mawr before winter 1957. By July, trains could work for two miles beyond Penrhyn and after a final assault had been made on that section of line which had become almost lost in a jungle of rhododendron trees, *Prince* and carriages Nos. 12 and 23 went through to Tan-y-Bwlch on Friday evening, 6 September; a few days later the same engine ran up to the Moelwyn Tunnel.

This same year carriage No. 20 was overhauled. The two 1st class compartments were given seats from ex-Mersey Railway electric stock which had been withdrawn at that time; panelling was in hardboard. No. 18 was treated similarly early in 1958, this carriage having but one 1st class compartment. In the winter 1957–8, No. 11 van had its two compartments made into one and the non-van end fitted with large windows, ex-Mersey Railway, and further seats from the same source placed down each side. This became a 1st class observation section divided from the adjacent 3rd class by a door containing a frosted glass panel carrying the crest of the Railway Company. A sliding door into the van enables refreshments to reach the Observation Saloon from the Buffet Car.

When *Prince* was laid off for repair during the winter of 1957, irregularities were found in the assembly of the motion, accounting for its peculiar valve events which had always been noted. It had a curved link with its radius centre forward. Also, its weigh-bar shaft had at some distant date been assembled the wrong way round and in this feature, *Welsh Pony* is also similar. These anomalies were corrected to the improvement of performance. The cause is thought to have been that *Little Giant* was stripped down at the same time as *Prince* early in the War, *Prince* acquiring the other's weigh-bar shaft.

The Boston Lodge engine sheds being considered unsuitable for their original purpose, and inconveniently situated, and having no lighting or water, were now used for storage of rolling stock. After a period of storing engines in the open in the West Yard, the old paint shop was converted into a new loco shed, complete with pit.

By mid-summer 1958 carriage No. 18 was almost ready for service with No. 22 being painted finally. No. 20 was being used but work on it was incomplete. No. 15 was in the erecting shop and reconstruction had begun. One of the Hudson bogie underframes had been fitted out with two tanks to be used for spraying weedkiller.

The 1958 season again began with a short service at Easter, this time reaching the new objective of Tan-y-Bwlch where Mrs. Bessie Jones in her Welsh costume welcomed the arrival of trains. Between Easter and Whitsuntide trains ran on Wednesdays only. Thence trains ran twice in the afternoons throughout the season with a morning train in July, August and early September. A further increase brought the season's passengers to 60,323.

In spring 1959 *Merddin Emrys* was dragged from the shed where it had lain since August 1946 and pushed into the erecting shop. Problems delayed restoration but without a cab the engine worked the peak season of 1961 . . . as *Prince* was by then stripped down, two double engines were in traffic for the first time in almost twenty-five years.

In that same spring, working parties from the Society descended on the Lynton & Barnstaple Railway coach (No. 6993) which had lain isolated on a piece of track at Snapper, N. Devon, since 1935. This was a bogie composite brake vehicle built by The Bristol Wagon & Carriage Works. It had five compartments (one 1st class and four 3rds) and guard's brake and luggage section. There were look-out duckets to the van which would not have passed the Festiniog loading gauge. Seats were nine 1st class and twenty 3rd. Length over body 35 ft. 2 in., body width 6 ft., total height from rail 8 ft. 7 in.

It was necessary, firstly, to arrange purchase of this vehicle, and secondly to organise a series of dismantling and transport parties. As the body was too large in its original form, dismantling was not objectionable. The parts duly arrived at Boston Lodge. It was not intended to rebuild exactly as in L. & B.R. form.

In May, the M.E.T. Staff was restored on the Harbour/Minffordd section and subsequently an intermediate instrument was installed at Boston Lodge.

The winter of 1959–60 was mainly notable for the demolition of the road overbridge near the Cemetery (Rhiw Plas). In connection with the transport of machinery from the Harbour to the new atomic power station at Trawsfynydd, a vast road construction programme was undertaken between the two points. A temporary level crossing, west of the site of the demolished bridge, carried the Festiniog over a temporary road whilst ultimately a new concrete bridge took shape approximately on the site of the old one (*F.R.M.* No. 7, p. 2).

A more worthwhile project for the railway itself was the fitting out of an imposing Booking Hall at Harbour station, undoubtedly then the finest and most up-to-date of any narrow gauge concern.

Passenger traffic, already causing embarrassment to the management by its overwhelming volume in certain seasons, was given a further impetus following a live television broadcast (followed by others at subsequent dates) on 13 July 1960. To help out, the partly finished coach No. 15 was rushed into traffic early in August, and work continued on it after each day's service.

The yards at Minffordd and Glan-y-Mor were now suffering from years of neglect and despite the frightful punishment which the heavy traffic was inflicting on the main line, especially on the upper section, it became more necessary to re-lay portions of these yards completely, in order to obtain access to certain now-inaccessible sidings and prevent derailments during the running season.

During the summer and autumn 1961 the coal stage was built alongside the water tank at the Harbour; a new siding was necessary (*F.R.M.* No. 14, p. 3). At the Works, the machine shop floor was rebuilt and a long-term programme of improvements to make the railway self-reliant, continued. A landmark in the bogie carriage stock took place when No. 11 was taken in for fitting of a steel underframe.

The 1961 season ended with passenger figures at almost 110,000, comparable with those reached in the late 1920s before the slump. Between Portmadoc and Tan-y-Bwlch it appeared that some sort of plateau in statistics might have been reached.

1962–74

(Such was the ever-increasing tempo of restoration, that by the end of 1961 relating the narrative on a year-by-year basis ceases to be convenient. In consequence, the next decade is more happily recorded in departmental form. The headings of earlier chapters make suitable sections to this end.)

The Route: Restoration Portmadoc–Dduallt, and Tan-y-Grisiau–Blaenau Ffestiniog   *Harbour–Boston Lodge*

Towards the mid 1960s it became apparent that the South Snowdon Wharf, lying beyond the end of Festiniog tracks at the Harbour station, was likely to be 'developed' by a property concern. This was the first occasion on which the railway would be affected—right on its doorstep —by building speculation which only rising standards of living and the growth of the holiday industry, could have promoted. By the late 1960s, part of the former end of line had gone, the tracks had been re-arranged, and the three-way point was doing duty at Glan-y-Mor yard.

The station layout saw some considerable alteration too. The point-work for the 70-foot platform's loop line was restored to its older position further along the Cob and a new additional carriage siding along the sea wall and a headshunt made operation less bothersome. The carriage pit was partially covered and a new one put into No. 3 'road'.

In the station itself, a new shop opened in 1968 and from 1975 a two-storied building standing between the present station and the goods shed, provides refreshments at ground level and new administrative accommodation upstairs.

In 1973–4 it was found necessary to alter the terminal end again following conversion of locomotives to oil firing; in 1973 the coal stage was taken down and a new water tank installed; in 1974 the tracks were amended once more.

Further out along the Cob trackwork became urgently necessary in 1968. Bullhead rail materials which had been obtained from the abandoned Penrhyn Quarry Railway were then laid in at the Harbour end. At the Works end the existing bull-head was re-sleepered whilst the length of ex-Welsh Highland flat-bottomed rail from Pitt's Head, Madoc Street and Britannia Bridge survivals, and which comprised the centre section, continued in use; to the latter soleplates, clips and standard screws were added. It was put into the Cob in the winter of 1958–9, replacing pitted rail which had been taken from the tunnel.

Pen-Cob Halt was not re-opened for the 1968 timetable, its effective closing date being 5 November 1967. Boston Lodge Halt was to be used instead.

Proceeding up the line, it is apparent that many former features around and within the Works have disappeared, and new ones have arisen. Among the first buildings to come down was the joiner's shop (1962)—the blacksmith's shop just fell down. It was at this same period that the Locomotive Department was brought into the Bottom Yard and carriages taken out into the former engine shed, the Glan-y-Mor carriage shed (partly ruined by roof falls due to rocks coming down the cliff into it) had been demolished as early as 1956. (Alterations to date were then published in *F.R.M.* No. 20, pp. 10–16). The erecting shop improvements were taken in hand and its area was extended when a second-hand building from Yorkshire was put up partly to this end and partly for carriage storage. The long road of the building now used as an engine shed was extended into it, with sunken facilities for maintenance (1964). Out on Glan-y-Mor a new track layout took shape, embodying the 3-way point from the Harbour (1965).

The sensible decision to use the former engine shed for carriages was restricted by the trackwork giving access to it and it was necessary to re-lay and re-align in 1965. In general, every length of track and especially the old pointwork has had to be renewed over the period, and in 1967 part of the former blacksmith's shop was given over to the Signal & Telegraph Department as a workshop for pointfitters.

There being no more pressing use for the old foundry, it was converted into a second machine shop and additional machine tools were acquired for it. Equipment obtained from slate quarries in the district which were by now closing down very quickly, was purchased as suitable—in this way an air compressor from the Dorothea Quarry, Nantlle, was placed in the new building at Glan-y-Mor.

During 1972 that part of the former engine shed which had been extended years ago in corrugated iron, was taken down and a narrower one built instead; a useful road was brought around it giving access to the Works. The line in the new narrow shed was extended through its end to a loading dock alongside Boston Lodge Halt. This had all been done by spring 1973.

At the period this was taking place, a bigger project for boiler work and steel storage was begun. A site was cleared behind the erecting shop and quarrymen were brought from Ffestiniog to remove loose rock from the cliffs behind. The rock floor level was excavated by three feet and in due course, an 'Atcost' building (prefabricated elsewhere) was erected on the newly-won site.

The 'Atcost' type of building having considerable advantages to the Company, foundations were prepared in spring 1973 for a second one on the Glan-y-Mor site to house four bogie carriages initially, and to be suitable for expansion as stock increased and covered accommodation became difficult to find. The building went up within twelve months, it being intended also to provide facilities for joinery and painting within. The roof was on by the end of the year.

During the same year, a new rail link was built to connect the Bottom Yard and the main line just beside the Toll Gate steps; the points are 'facing' for Down trains and in effect, allow a complete loop off the main line and back on to it again along the fringe of the Bottom Yard, another valuable improvement.

Boston Lodge–Minffordd

On to the environs of Minffordd, where in 1964 an additional siding was laid in alongside the long parallel siding and later, to give accommodation for longer trains, the station loop was extended eastwards— previously it was limited to a double engine, six bogies and six four-wheelers. The same year, the goods shed and an iron shed in the Exchange Yard were vacated by their saw-mill tenants and were taken over by the P.W. Department for sleeper production, etc. A new ballast and coal chute were erected side by side, but signs of a weakening position were evident when the yard's other partner, British Rail, further simplified its layout and demoted its station to an unstaffed Halt from 10 October 1964. Tickets by B.R. were now obtained from the F.R. station when open—a case of 'Last in, first out'. (*F.R.M.* No. 27, pp. 4–5.) By 1966 the Festiniog had taken over maintenance of the standard gauge tracks in the yard; a road was built enabling lorries to unload down the ballast chute. During 1969 the vacant Davies Bros. (slate merchants) premises at the end of the site were prepared for conversion into a carriage shed. This was a considerable undertaking, involving the raising of large slate-roofed timber trusses, supported by slab piers, and infilling between the piers to make a complete wall. Doors were then to be fitted. In October, a 5-ton lifting gantry was erected in the yard.

Welded rails were used below Minffordd and over the crossing at the former weigh house (winter 1968–9).

By winter 1970–1, Davies' sheds had been taken in hand; thus cover would be available for fourteen vehicles. An unusual feature was the provision of a stubpoint giving access to four roads in one of the sheds. The roof of the second shed had been lifted by spring 1972 and then attention was given to the matter of delivery of Company rolling stock by road transport. This was solved by building an end-loading dock in the yard, during summer 1972. Road transport interchange was further improved when British Rail closed their part of the yard altogether and the remaining sidings were lifted in spring 1973. One sunken narrow gauge siding was retained under the ballast chutes (which were improved at this stage) otherwise the site was to be levelled. The year of 1973 saw the goods shed gutted and later converted for the pre-fabrication of track.

Minffordd–Penrhyn

Between Minffordd and Penrhyn, the Pen-y-Bryn Halt was closed on 5 November 1967; it had been open since 20 April 1957.

Electricity pylons, 'giant nude girls that have no secrets', carrying current between Trawsfynydd and Wylfa, Anglesey, dwarfed Minffordd when erected in 1965. Over the Traeth Mawr, the cables were placed underground. Re-laying from Pen-y-Bryn to the upper side of Penrhyn road crossing the same year involved also the extension of Penrhyn station loop. This loop was to be relaid again in the spring of 1969 and the underbridge near Nazareth Chapel was replaced using concrete beams.

In 1966 that part of Penrhyn station which had been used by a local co-operative society became part of a hostel, the P.W. Department store became a Booking Office/Signal Box and the Goods Shed an electrical store. The little-used station building was converted into accommodation (always a problem in the existing circumstances of the undertaking) for volunteer labourers on the line—a feature which would have seemed incredible fifty years ago and may have a quite different impact again, fifty years hence! Part of this was in use during 1971 but was officially opened in spring 1972.

Penrhyn–Tan-y-Bwlch

One hundred and ten years after horse working ceased, the site of the disused passing loop at Rhiw Goch came to life again in early 1973. In order to break up the line with passing loops at approximately the same operating-time intervals, it was considered that this location was a suitable place between Minffordd and Tan-y-Bwlch and more acceptable than Penrhyn station where also the length of loop was limited by road crossings. By the end of 1974 the main trackwork of the loop had been completed using ex-Tilbury Power Station 75 lb. flat-bottomed pointwork and plain rails. It came into use from 14 May 1975.

Continuing up the line, a new Plas Halt, on a new site beyond Tyler's Cutting and before Llechwedd Coed, was opened on 1 June 1963 (*F.R.M.* No. 21, pp. 11–12). Three years later the Economic Forestry Group commenced work on the Tan-y-Bwlch Estate, installing new roads. Considerable re-laying about and below Hafod-y-Llyn during 1966 disclosed that sleepers being taken out were a part of the redundant P.B. & S.S.R. purchase over fifty years before; they were notched to receive the flat-bottomed rails. All old double-head rails on the length out of Penrhyn were exchanged for P.Q.R. bull-head; the Penrhyn loop was lengthened at the Up end and a bull-headed rail turnout from Glan-y-Pwll brought down by road as a replacement top point. On the road crossing a welded length of track made up from eight pairs of P.Q.R. rails was slid in; these had come from the Felin Hen passing loop and were little worn.

Tan-y-Bwlch–Dduallt

Of all places, Tan-y-Bwlch has seen the most complete metamorphosis of all; certain 1954 features remain but almost all functions have changed. Back in 1959 the loop had been shortened and in 1964 all sidings were removed and one new one laid in; this was all part of the clearance plan, starting at Tan-y-Bwlch and extending towards Dduallt (*F.R.M.* No. 25, p. 5). In the spring following not only clearance was in hand but whole sections of track had been relaid including 250 yards between the station and Garnedd Tunnel, which was carried out as part of an Army exercise. To give more stabling room for work trains, petrol trolleys and the like, a new siding was laid at the Up end of Tan-y-Bwlch in 1966 whilst that of 1964 at the bottom end had its point taken out and moved further Down; a concrete-lined inspection pit was provided near the water tower. The new top-end siding required lengthening before the year was out and by Christmas re-laying extended along that exciting location between Tan-y-Bwlch and Coed-y-Bleddiau save for Garnedd Tunnel which was to be the subject of some drastic surgery—beyond Coed-y-Bleddiau the track bed was especially bad almost as far as Dduallt. To avoid mixing rails (old F.R. double-head with anything else) the foregoing section was relaid in P.Q.R. bull-head with the worn running edge laid outwards. Where the original double-head was fit for re-use, it was worked into sections lower down the line where patching was permissible. On curves the double-head proved to be so worn as to be fit only for scrap.

This detail of track replacement is recorded to show the necessity of clearing away original materials completely and as is preferred by track departments, keeping whole sections of similar material together. Later maintenance is thus much eased.

Pressing need elsewhere meant this section had now to be left until Easter 1967 but once more, only a short engagement was possible; during that summer attention was given to the difficulties of improving the bore of the short tunnel but nothing was actually done until the winter following. However, it was possible to follow up the clearance already made and re-lay track as far as Dduallt by October 1967. No ballasting had been done at that date.

This stimulating progress meant that passenger services were billed to reach out to Dduallt from 6 April 1968, but owing to unfinished trackwork, there was as yet no locomotive run-round, so a spare engine was kept at Dduallt to work the train back again. Facilities for passengers were even less forward than for locomotives, and at first they were not allowed to detrain. At the same period the tracks through Tan-y-Bwlch were re-aligned to provide what later became an island platform proper. A highlight of summer 1968 came when *Merddin Emrys* reached Dduallt with nine coaches, the loop being ready from 20 May.

During the summer the floor of the tunnel was dug out, the last assignment in a tricky job which had occupied most of the previous winter when rockmen from Maenofferen Quarry removed the projecting rocks from the roof, these being loaded into wagons stabled on a temporary siding at the tunnel's south end. Welded rails are used through the bore.

Back at Tan-y-Bwlch, a new-old feature came into being again when in July 1971, a footbridge giving access to platform and the footpaths beyond, came into use. By now the station had been given a new look. The former goods shed was now a café; by the time the full service was working through to Dduallt, an island platform was well on the way. Out of sheer necessity, a second water tank was built, only to be removed after a short life and replaced by one ex-road tanker 3,500 gallon tank to replace both existing ones. During the changeover period (May 1969) a hark-back to the occasional use of Dduallt tank was made; this has only a limited storage. In the same month the Coed Llyn Mair Nature Trail was inaugurated, giving both access and added interest to a beauty spot now opened out with planned paths and restrained guidance.

As to operating, to relieve the congestion of passengers which this Up-most road-accessible station provided (Dduallt not being a car-access point) a service along the fine length of line from Tan-y-Bwlch was given by shuttle train between here and the terminus, so enabling those who could not get into ex-Portmadoc trains arriving at Tan-y-Bwlch already full, the chance of a journey to Dduallt and back. For the purpose the tractor *Moelwyn*, two 'Birminghams', Quarrymen's No. 8 and No. 2 van formed the rake.

Another distinction at Tan-y-Bwlch was the building of a 28-lever signal box at the Up end beyond the stone station building, begun in 1971 and since completed. In 1974 a second siding was found to be necessary at the Down end.

On the way Up to Garnedd the wall supporting the 'shelf' which is such a characteristic of this section, has been given a concrete coping wall beside Tafarn Trip. At Garnedd Tunnel itself the state of the bore is still not of a condition to satisfy a fastidious Civil Engineer and thought is being given to means of improving the situation—perhaps by altering the course and using the 1836 formation again? For the moment, a speed restriction of 10 m.p.h. applies through the bore.

Now approaching Dduallt, the most noticeable new item is the short siding and small platform with hut for staff instruments which pro-nounces itself as Campbell's Platform and dates from a start in 1965. It was here that Colonel Campbell of Dduallt Manor below, was able to store his own private stock and bring trains to a stand (under certain conditions). For this a retaining wall and embankment on the south side of the line were built specially, and the 100-foot-long siding is controlled by a two-lever ground frame locked by the staff. His private locos and stock enjoyed conditional running powers over the railway. The siding was connected in 1968 and the Platform appeared in the timetables for 1968.

There is evidence of great changes as soon as Dduallt comes into view. To the south, right *in* the view, stands a prominent feature which the Festiniog of old could never have contemplated, the Trawsfynydd Nuclear Power Generating Station allegedly landscaped to merge into the surrounding National Park. It comes as a reminder that beyond

29L   Livingston Thompson, *as new from Boston Lodge Works, seen from the fireman's side. At Duffws, with Quarrymen's Train stabled behind.*   *(Valentine)*

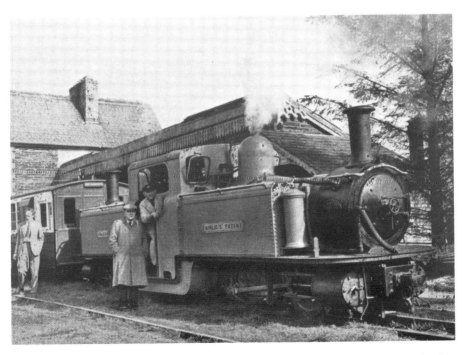

30L   Taliesin *(ex* Livingston Thompson*) restored to service 1956 but as yet in shop grey paint. Minffordd. March 1957.*   *(J. I. C. Boyd)*

31L   *The England engine on typical duty.* Prince *at Tan-y-Bwlch before 1904. The passenger guard stands outside the van and there are two slot machines on hire from*

the North Wales Mutoscope Company. The engine is virtually in the same condition as when taken in hand for working the restored service in the 1950s.

(British Rail; L.M. Region)

32L *Special Working at Tan-y-Bwlch April 1959, with* Prince. *The train was driven by former F.R. employees, brothers Thomas and Evan Davies.* (*J. I. C. Boyd*)

33L Merddin Emrys *returned to traffic in 1961. Seen here in September, running round at Tan-y-Bwlch.* (*J. I. C. Boyd*)

Dduallt a considerable length of this railway has been inundated to provide off-peak electricity, but not by the same resources. The little cutting just on the Down side of Dduallt, has lost its slender footbridge and instead, and adjacently, the main line is spanned by a taller but no less slender concrete bridge which carries the spiral of the new railway, the Deviation, and a second phase of that term in the life of the Company.

It is difficult to imagine the 'old' Dduallt, hardly touched by the clock and largely marked by the change of day into night and the passage of the seasons. At intervals down to 1946 a train would go by, passing between the reedy waters of Rhoslyn and the coppice of pine trees on the other side. The lake survives but encircling the site of the pines the new line swings right and upwards around a hillock on top of which a viewing point complete with picnic site and orientation table, is linked with the station by a new footpath. There is an island platform and on the west side, the recent scars among hill and woodland show evidence of some of the most interesting narrow gauge railway construction of this decade.

At the Up end of the station, the now-disused line directly ahead, plunges into woodland as it has always done, and is used as access temporarily to the accommodation provided at the south mouth of Moelwyn Tunnel, and an occasional works train if, by using this line, access to the Deviation is more convenient than by the incomplete Deviation itself.

Tan-y-Grisiau–Blaenau Festiniog

The Deviation is described separately, but it remains to see what the years 1954–75 have done to the line north of the Long Tunnel. As mentioned before, work to clear the way for the reservoir started in the early 1950s. Brookes' Quarry was cleared of metal by W. O. Williams of Harlech who moved it all to Tan-y-Grisiau station in the period June 1952–January 1953 using a tractor (Ruston & Hornsby Works No. 210955 of 1941, 4-wheel diesel) (*F.R.M.* No. 52, p. 20). The F.R. line was cut by the Electricity Authority access road opposite the L.M.S. Exchange station way back in 1956 but at this time the F.R. line between Duffws and the British Railways (ex-L.M.S.) yard was used by Maenofferen and Votty & Bowydd quarries to bring slate down for trans-shipment. It was by then an isolated length. This traffic ceased in July and November (respectively) 1963. Votty & Bowydd closed. Maenofferen went over to road transport and, except for a short length around Maenofferen which still survives (1975) the Rhiwbach Tramway was ultimately lifted from end to end. A standard gauge link line was built to join former L.M.S. and G.W.R. station sites in Blaenau.* Opportunity was taken to revise the road layout which is taken over the link line on a new bridge. The new railway, begun in summer 1962, received its first (ballast) train in November 1963 and for a short distance, traverses the site of the Festiniog. The G.W.R. station site and all buildings have been cleared for new development. The link line is used in connection with the Nuclear Power Station and involves that part of the former 2-foot-gauge Festiniog & Blaenau Railway (converted to standard gauge) between Blaenau and a point near the Power Station. From here to Bala, and indeed at and beyond Bala itself in either direction, railways have been swept away ruthlessly.

So, within about a century of Samuel and Charles Menzies Holland's dream of robbing the Festiniog of its monopoly of traffic and linking their little F. & B.R. with the Great Western, the Festiniog—now a very different undertaking but today MORE of a monopoly than the Hollands could have ever contemplated!—has lost the last round of keeping the standard gauge to its flanks in Blaenau. For the standard gauge the victory has been hollow enough . . . it too would have collapsed without the Nuclear Power Station traffic, and the thriving Festiniog Railway traffic ridicules a decision to close the Llandudno Junction–Blaenau line. Perhaps Samuel Holland's bitterness for the Festiniog was reconciled when he passed out of the slate business; Charles Menzies can have had little to grumble about though some of his manoeuvres with the F. & B.R. project would be found most distasteful in business today. [He was a wealthy man, and without his financial assistance it is not too much to suggest that I.C.I. in the form it takes today would never have existed, for Brunner and Mond would never have gone into business.]

In 1962 the track was removed from Moelwyn Tunnel (being used elsewhere), and the north end sealed off. The three shafts were filled in later (*F.R.M.* No. 16, p. 2).

In Blaenau the dates of lifting the remaining sections of line have been itemised in Volume 1. Remaining F.R. track east of the former G.W.R. (known then as Central station†) which had survived the major

---

* The link line was built to give rail access to the environs of Trawsfynydd Nuclear Power Station and formed part of an arrangement whereby Liverpool Corporation built a reservoir which flooded the Bala–Trawsfynydd section (part of the ex-G.W.R. Bala–Blaenau Ffestiniog branch). Access from the Bala end of the branch being denied, the new link enabled standard gauge working to be extended from the terminus of the ex-L.N.W.R. branch. To allow the slate quarries east of Duffws continued access to the ex-L.N.W.R. trans-shipment yard, a narrow gauge track was retained but slewed to a new site north of the standard gauge link. The end of rail transport by the quarries (see above) meant the revised narrow gauge link was but hardly used.

† Passenger services suspended 2 January 1960, goods the following year.

lifting of 1963 following quarry closures—see above—was lifted by October 1968, the work occupying a week. Some material could be re-used. Without warning, the commercial successor to its largest customer (the Welsh Slate Company) in the form of the Oakeley Slate Quarry, suddenly ceased operations in autumn 1970, leaving only one large quarry to survive in North Wales, and only a single medium-sized one in the Ffestiniog area. The nails were being driven hard into the coffin of the past. Way back in 1955–6 the Dinas branch had been lifted by scrap merchants, and the last remains went in 1963.

Perhaps this marks the nadir in the story of the Festiniog at Blaenau, for since August 1971 all changes have been of a constructive nature.

At this time clearance began on the Up side of Tan-y-Grisiau, by then a ruin so far as the station building was concerned. Then in the summer of 1973 this was continued in the vicinity of Glan-y-Pwll engine shed, which had formerly been part of the area used by a timber merchant for a saw mill; extending clearance and later the preparation of a new bridge over the Afon Barlwyd near old Dinas Junction site, not only showed the Railway's purpose in a district where the re-incarnation was something that was 'happening elsewhere', but emphasised that the line had a future. Above all, it introduced the Company to a young local generation who had grown up since 1946 in the belief that (latterly) a railway train (B.R. variety) was a mechanical grub which burrowed out of a hole in the hillside, rested awhile and then slunk back again, out of sight, out of mind.

The site of a terminal for the restored line remains uncertain, but must clearly be determined soon. Beyond the London Midland station, the new road and link line contain the narrow gauge and prevent further progress beyond a point almost level with that Region's station. There is more space available in the Glan-y-Pwll area, but this is not con-venient for holiday traffic interchange. But between there and Tan-y-Grisiau, based on the possibility of siting the end of line on the original L.N.W.R. Exchange location (perhaps somewhat enlarged?), work has gone ahead with restoration. Re-laying between Groes-Ffordd and Bod-y-Chain involves re-laying with new rail on jarrah sleepers—materials used elsewhere where complete renewal is demanded. These rails were at first consigned by rail to Blaenau, an early indication that the loss of interchange between the gauges must either be made good at the top of the line whilst reconstruction takes place, or delivery made by road. The availability of a new (alternative) Electricity Board's road to Stwlan Dam will enable the absence of the bridge over the steep road at Dol-Rhedyn to be overcome and reinstatement for road traffic unnecessary. In the vicinity of Tan-y-Grisiau the formation has been widened and the right of way raised by 3 feet.

The Deviation: Dduallt–Tan-y-Grisiau

Earlier in this chapter the compulsory acquisition of part of the route has been described. First notice had reached the Old Company in late 1951. There was sufficient challenge in the actual restoration of the railway—which, to be properly appreciated, was not just making good the depreciation of the last final years of closure but the cumulative results of at least two decades of declining fortune, a much more formidable accumulation. But the loss of a vital part of the through route has proved in retrospect to have been a valuable challenge to those who enjoy humiliating authority. Initially this was probably done for the sheer joy of showing how misguided were the conclusions of the Lords' Select Committee; but, borne on this enthusiasm, a second stronger wave of volunteer constructionalists, many with no great interest in the railway as such, has concentrated sheer physical effort into building a section of railway which, without exaggeration, will have a special place in communication history. In 1974 those responsible for the new railway link, publicised their need for further help under the title '3 more miles to go! Would you like to help?' and stated:

... The restoration of the Railway is, however, far from complete, its access to Blaenau Ffestiniog having been blocked for some years by a reservoir built as part of an electrical pumped-storage scheme. Work on a fresh course to bypass this reservoir was started on a purely voluntary basis in 1965. However, it was not until 1971 that the Company's legal claim for disturbance against the Electricity Board was finally settled. The compensation received does not provide, by a very wide margin, sufficient money to complete the two and a half mile long deviation route, although it will enable some major items to be done professionally. The rest of the effort must come from other resources, and, if reopening to Blaenau Ffestiniog is to be achieved by the target date of 1978, much of the work must be done by voluntary labour. By the end of 1973, one mile of formation was complete, whilst half a mile of track had been laid upon it. The scheduled date for the completion of the whole Deviation is the end of 1976 ... When new formation has been completed, there comes the task of laying track ...

... The new line will join the old one more than a mile from the site of the terminus, which itself has to be built on bare ground. A great deal of effort is needed to rehabilitate this neglected length, ... and to prepare the new station at Blaenau Ffestiniog. In total, three miles or more of track have to be laid or relaid within the next few years, together with bridge rebuilding both under and over the track, drainage, wall repairs, fencing, new telephone wires and cables, signalling, rebuilt and fresh buildings, and all the many other details which go to make up a piece of railway line ...

It is appropriate to examine some of the landmarks which led to this announcement.

It was always the Company's aim, after losing the initial Appeal, to claim for equivalent reinstatement of the railway. A Statement issued ·in 1962 after the dismissal of the Company's case in the Court of Appeal made four points, two of which have been achieved already (*F.R.M.* No. 16, p. 8). The other two were:

3. To negotiate towards completing the link from Dduallt to Tan-y-Grisiau . . .

4. To set about, at an appropriate stage, restoring the section from Tan-y-Grisiau to Blaenau Ffestiniog.

In the matter of adequate compensation *The Times* reported the difficulties of putting a value on a narrow gauge railway (13–14 May 1960) following the three-day hearing of the Lands Tribunal when the Company claimed £180,000–£200,000 from the Central Electricity Generating Board as being the agreed cost of building a replacement line, and it was said that the 'Balance Sheet was neither true nor fair, but in compliance with the law'. Railways as ever proved an emotive subject, and when fact failed, discussion reverted (among those who possibly never permitted themselves such a freedom of comment on other subjects) to such well-loved phrases as 'innocent amusement of running a railway'. The Company failed to convince the Lands Tribunal as to the basis on which compensation should be paid (in respect of notice of entry by the C.E.G.B. on to the railway above Moelwyn Tunnel on 3 February 1956, and on 4 June 1958 for the Tunnel itself) under the Lands Tribunal Act 1949. The Court of Appeal upheld the Tribunal's decision (*F.R.M.* No. 55, p. 17) on 2 February 1962.

The Pumped Storage Scheme was opened by the Queen on 10 August 1963 and in the same month all old F.R. materials from the flooded section were sent back by the C.E.G.B. An official announcement of the proposed route of the Deviation gave a history of ideas involved for avoiding the bottom reservoir; routes along either west or east shores had been considered in turn and both included a new tunnel and spiral works with considerable gradients. At this stage it was intended to use the east route and descend through Brookes' Quarry site, having a tunnel on a curve and a summit at 655 feet (*F.R.M.* No. 24, p. 9).

Between spring 1965 and 1967 all work was in the vicinity of Dduallt, but a large mess hut was placed at the south mouth of the Tunnel. Rolling stock suitable for contract work, plus earthmoving equipment which would never have been suited to the old line, found their way on to the site, ingenuity and appeal both proving fruitful to this end!

A Public Enquiry was held in the Council Chambers, Blaenau Ffestiniog 26–27 January 1967 to enquire into the Company's application for an Amendment to its Light Railway Order of 1923, covering the building of the Deviation between Dduallt and Brookes' Quarry (*F.R.M.* No. 36, p. 9). There were among the objectors, two farmers, and the C.E.G.B. The deliberations may be followed elsewhere, but success was achieved in the form of The Festiniog Railway (Light Railway) (Amendment) order 1968 (1968 No. 178) made on 9 February

1968, which gave powers to build (Section 4(2)) Railway (No. 3) 1 mile
7 furlongs 9 chains commencing by a junction with the principal
railway . . . north of Dduallt station . . . round the hill to the east . . .
crossing the principal railway by a bridge . . . 10 chains . . . from the
point of commencement . . . proceeding westerly, northwesterly,
northerly . . . to Coed Dduallt . . . crossing the Moelwyn Tunnel . . .
southeasterly and easterly to Clogwyn . . . thence . . . terminating near
Brookes' Quarry . . .

It was anticipated it would take five years to complete, but shortly
after an epidemic of Foot and Mouth Disease was to cut down progress
as visitors on the land were discouraged.

The most important advance took place in early 1970, not on the
ground but in negotiation with the C.E.G.B., whose attitude to the
whole matter took on a different hue and almost overnight the Railway
was permitted to use the west shore. None of the existing work was
lost, though now a tunnel of 440 yards would be needed; the line
would be shorter and cheaper and would have to pass through the dam
wall of the abandoned reservoir used for the Incline scheme of 1836.
The following summer, semi-permanent way in second-hand bull-head
track replaced contractor's rails on Dduallt spiral; soon the beams of
the overbridge here were in place and in late 1971 work on the north
side of the ridge had breached the dam wall so draining what was left
of the stored water. Excavation work for the north mouth of the new
tunnel then began and by the end of 1974 the north side work showed
continuous earthworks from the tunnel site, through the old dam and
on to the embankment beyond. Additionally isolated pockets of
progress could be found. Back on the spiral and up towards Gelliwiog,
where new rails had been planned, ex-Tilbury 75 lb. rails were laid
from June 1973, so that by autumn 1974 the track extended almost the
full length of the completed new formation.

Leaving matters on the ground in their existing condition, an answer
was at last to be given to what was becoming a long-outstanding issue.

Commencing on 5 October 1971 and lasting five days, the Company's
claim on the C.E.G.B. before the Lands Tribunal was heard. On 19
November the Tribunal awarded the Company £65,000 plus interest
from 1956, making an ultimate total of £106,710.42p. Perhaps the
man-in-the-street had by then won a hollow victory, but in terms of
purchasing power it would not cover the west shore Deviation completely. A feature of the whole case was that it was the longest (reported)
example in legal history this century with only one exception before
that date. Though threatening so to do, the C.E.G.B. did not in the
event appeal against the decision, and payment was made in the
summer of 1972.

Summarising the period over which work has continued, after a sod-cutting ceremony near Dduallt to mark the commencement of work on 2 January 1965 the work has progressed with remarkable vigour. By autumn 1974 the Dduallt–Gelliwiog length was so advanced that a shuttle service of passenger trains, running independently from the main service, began on 26 May 1975 between these points. If the permanent track on the isolated east end is ready, it is mooted that later another shuttle service might run between Glan-y-Pwll and Tan-y-Grisiau.

Locomotive policy. A historical book is not a place in which to air future locomotive policy, but it may be proper to view it in the light of past events. Two factors stand out most clearly when making comparisons covering thirty years, and the cause is so evident as almost not to require explanation.

Firstly, the parlous state of the existing stud and the age of the boilers on the last two working engines—the others being no younger—underlined the risks involved in spending time and money on equipment whose life-span expectancy might only be short. As traffic grew and forecasts showed it should continue to do so, their unsuitability for re-building except by drastic measures, was clear. To make them completely reliable for future requirements (a Traffic Manager's Elysium), was at that time unthinkable, so additional engines were purchased second-hand from outside sources. Some early acquisitions might have borne an air of desperation, but each was considered on its merits and certainly each had potential. The Penrhyn engines were a fortunate purchase, and it is on the qualities of these that much locomotive experience has been built. For this reason, not all acquired engines have so far been put to use, and it may be expected that they will lose their existing features if new boilers, structural alterations and changed wheel-arrangements are necessary. Their original qualities should remain, however.

In passing, one cannot escape a passing thought for *Moel Tryfan* and wonder if after all, it might not have found a place in the locomotive roster, but at the time it was scrapped this issue seemed beyond all doubt.

Secondly, the work now required of the engines exceeds anything done in the past. Tight timings and heavy loadings have made it essential for them to have modern fittings. The old engines, in the form taken over (even though overhauled) could not have tackled recent timetables and loadings without additional help. This trend in traffic has been self-generating, so making life more difficult for the operating department. So the dice has been thrown and inescapable developments such as standard boilers, superheating, improved bearings, improved suspension and more recently, oil firing with its higher calorific effects, have altered even the acquired stock. Some pleasing former outlines, with pipework hidden away, the smell and problems of coal firing have followed the slate traffic into the limbo of the past.

In recent years certain passenger trains have been worked by diesel power, just fifty years after the Chairman, writing from 'Plas Jack' as the employees dubbed it, sent forth an edict recommending the withdrawal of all steam engines and the beginning of a reign of the internal combustion unit.

Prince. This engine had hardly turned a wheel since 1935. A boiler report of that time, together with its generally poor condition, meant that for two years it was only used in emergency. In 1937 the boiler was condemned. During the War it was arranged that Adamson should build a new boiler, Government approval being essential for such a task. The order was placed in 1943 and delivery made two years later. Closure of the system the following year had the effect of suspending work on re-erecting the engine, and the boiler simply took its place among the more valuable items which might be sold to raise money.

The engine was reconstructed in 1955 using the new boiler as a basis, and for a while gave reasonable satisfaction in traffic. As trains became heavier, lack of adhesion, indifferent steaming, the age of its components and rough riding, all showed themselves. New cylinders were fitted and a 'Kylchap' cowl placed over the exhaust pipe, but when the Penrhyn engines entered traffic and it became possible to select engines for the harder duties, *Prince* was more often seen on lighter passenger workings and works' trains. At the end of 1968 it was taken from traffic and dismantled. No immediate need for its return has occurred since then, but now a project to re-assemble it as a 'non-railway' effort includes putting in a new firebox. It was considered the engine might be a suitable working exhibit for the Rail 150 Exhibition of 1975 to mark the Stockton & Darlington Railway opening, but an opportunity for this did not arise as anticipated.

Taliesin. This double engine had entered Boston Lodge for boiler repairs in 1939; as by this time nothing was done on an engine unless the work was imperative, underlining the fact that conditions had reached the crisis stage. It was intended to undertake tubeplate and other work with urgency, but priorities were changed when war began and the Works was directed to other effort and men left the Company's employ. Dismantled, the engine stood in the Erecting Shop when traffic ceased completely. It should be recalled that the engine carried a boiler supplied in 1905 and that, after 50 years, its life would not be infinite. It had been repaired after a report of 1924, in 1929—an interval of five years when the engine stood idle. When the engine re-entered traffic again in 1959, it was not expected that the boiler would give much further service, but it proved possible to continue its use almost until the end of 1971 when the engine was taken off duty (and it is a matter of opinion as to whether it was withdrawn or simply that it is being rebuilt using some of the existing parts). Certain components have been earmarked for a Phase II version but the remainder, which includes boiler, tanks and the carrier frame, have been put in store—a unique museum piece. Restoration as a historic relic is planned by a select group.

Merddin Emrys. This engine, and *Princess*, having by then the youngest boilers of engines in service, were the last two in use when services stopped in 1946. The engine was run into its shed and remained there, ostensibly ready for its next turn of duty, until 1959. Water left in the side tanks, and atmospheric effects, resulted in tanks and smokeboxes needing renewal, but the boiler served a further nine years; a new one (not identical) replaced it in 1970.

Steam Locomotive Summaries 1954–74 (Original stock)

Princess

1963—Cleaned up for display purposes.
1966—Officially termed as 'Awaiting rebuilding'.
1969—Investiture Year. Placed on display outside Queen's Hotel, Blaenau Ffestiniog.

Prince

1955—New boiler fitted: engine erected using some parts off *Palmerston*. (Note: the boiler fitted was that on hand but not fitted when the line closed in 1946.)
1960–1—New cylinders.
1962—Alterations to framing; 'Kylchap' cowl fitted to improve steaming.*
1963—Replaced in August traffic by *Linda*.
1964—Relegated to less exacting duties.
1966—'Usefulness limited'.
1967—Dismantled but reassembled after boiler inspection.
1968—Working passenger service Tan-y-Bwlch–Dduallt before completion of loop at Dduallt. By November, dismantled again.
1974–5—Reassembly commenced as 'non-railway project'. New firebox.

Palmerston

1966—Officially termed 'Withdrawn'.
1974—July. Remains of engine and an old tender sold for private restoration on condition it would not be operated in North Wales.

* Other engines fitted subsequently.

Welsh Pony

1966—Officially termed as 'Awaiting rebuilding'.

Taliesin (*Earl of Merioneth/Iarll Meirionnydd* from 1961) (Phase I)

(During the period this engine was found to have *Merddin Emrys'* original wheels. A spare set of wheels in the Works' yard were off *Livingston Thompson*; they had cast-iron centres and had clearly proved troublesome.)

1959—Returned to traffic in modified livery.

1963—Overhauled.

1966-7—New bogie cradles and bogie centres fitted. Engine re-erected. To traffic Easter 1967.

1968—Opportunity taken to order new superheated boiler. To be put in store until required.

1969—Under repair, leaving only *Mountaineer* and *Blanche* to work traffic by steam 11 July–6 August. October: new superheated boiler delivered (first of two on order).

1971—Engine withdrawn from revenue-earning service October. Bogies to be placed under *Merddin Emrys*; some other parts to be re-used. 'Superstructure' preserved by restoration group and mounted temporarily on two slate wagon chassis; moved to Minffordd for storage. Ultimate intention to refurbish as *Livingston Thompson* for display (at least), mounted on replica bogies incorporating surviving parts as available.

Earl of Merioneth (Phase II)

(Using new boiler delivered for *Earl of Merioneth I* in 1969, this engine is referred to as the 'Super Fairlie'. Many parts will be new but some existing materials will be embodied. One or both bogies from *Merddin Emrys* are likely to be used, but new side tanks are prepared.)

Merddin Emrys

1959—Dismantled; new smokeboxes, chimneys and side tanks fitted.

1961—Returned to traffic.

1962—Firebox problems; engine out of service.

1963—Returned to traffic, Easter.

1966—Boiler reported as 'going'. Some repair work carried out; back to service September. Found inferior in traffic to *Earl of Merioneth* with weaknesses in flexible joints and foundation rings. Care needed to conserve water during operation. Bottom end cylinders poor.

1967—Partially stripped down.
1968—Top end boiler mid-ring fracture when preparing for season. Loading to Dduallt limited in consequence. Decision taken to rebuild with new superheated boiler; boiler ordered. Bogies to have new cylinders fitted at Hunslet Engine Co., Leeds.
1969—October; new superheated boiler delivered (second of two on order).
1970—Reassembled on modified main frame. New boiler mounted July. Trials November—12-coach loading with satisfactory steaming. New smokeboxes with doors hinged on opposite side to clear vacuum hose pipes.
1971—Bogies overhauled.
1972—Axle broken during summer season; *Earl of Merioneth* bogie used as temporary replacement.
1973—Starting in late 1972, new wheels and axles fitted. Wheels taken out prove to be those off *James Spooner*. Converted to oil burning. On test April; much improved performance with oil firing.

Note on new double-engine boilers: these are virtually two *Blanche/Linda* size barrels with firebox between.

Steam Locomotives (Additional stock)

Blanche: Linda (formerly Penrhyn Quarry Railway, Bangor, North Wales)

Linda, a main line engine on the closed Penrhyn Quarry Railway, was loaned to the Railway in summer 1962 as *Merddin Emrys* had had to be taken out of service. Her performance was most promising and in view of the parlous state of the locomotive position, acquisition of the engine and that of *Blanche*, a sister locomotive, was arranged. Purchase was made in 1963. *Linda* had been fitted with a new boiler in 1936—it had been little used. *Blanche* had received a new boiler in 1946.

Blanche* Named after Blanche Georgiana Fitzroy (1865–1944) who married Edward Sholto Douglas-Pennant, 3rd Baron Penrhyn

1963—Summer; delivered by road; purchased and connected to wooden-framed tender.
1964—Re-gauged slightly to suit F.R.
1965—Given new tender incorporating half-cab.
1966—By this date fully adapted to F.R. standards including sanding

* *Blanche* and *Linda*; pre-Festiniog period history given in NARROW GAUGE RAILWAYS IN NORTH CAERNARVONSHIRE (in preparation).

gear as fitted to *Linda,* vacuum brake, new injectors, etc. Finished in green.

1969—For part of season, along with *Mountaineer* the only steam engines available for traffic.

1970-1—Winter; British Rail, Crewe, to supply prefabricated cylinders with piston valves. April 1971; converted oil burning on same basis as *Linda* (previously converted).

1971-2—Winter; period of work to bring engine to similar standards as *Linda.* New firebox, superheater to be fitted, main frame modified to take leading pony wheels taken from bogie wheels off *Moel Tryfan.* Piston-valve cylinders fitted. By spring 1972 firebox and boiler work at Birmingham (Midland Rolling & Haulage Co.). Boiler returned too late to fit for peak 1972 season. Returned to traffic November 1972. Carries snifting valve behind chimney.

Linda* Named after Linda Blanche Douglas-Pennant (1889–1965) daughter of Blanche (as above)

1962—July; engine on loan.

1963—Wheels re-tyred to F.R. profile and engine purchased. Temporarily attached to George England wooden-framed tender chassis, on which was mounted the body of coal wagon No. 38. Into traffic August, replacing *Prince* in service.

1964—Rpeorted as 'disgustingly reliable in traffic'.

1965—New tender supplied—utilising some parts of old England tender.

1968—Boiler sent to Hunslet Engine Co., Leeds, for fitting new firebox and superheater. Decision to fit leading pony truck.

1969—Boiler returned April but loco not ready. General repair problems at this time with *Merddin Emrys* also in workshops.

1970—Spring; engine ready with superheated boiler and converted to 2-4-0STT. October; converted to burn oil on Laidlaw, Drew system.†

1970-1—Winter; British Rail, Crewe, to supply prefabricated cylinders with piston valves (also for *Blanche*); (cylinders not fitted by 1974).

1971—April; returned to traffic.

Mountaineer‡ Named to perpetuate one of original series of engines supplied to the Railway. Engine carries a bell, a feature—not an original one—of the first engine to bear this name. [The bell still hung

---

* See note on p. 517.

† Details of oil-burning conversion of *Blanche, Linda* and *Mountaineer* given *F.R.M.* No. 60, p. 14.

‡ For early history see *F.R.M.* No. 33, p. 16.

in the derelict Works Yard in 1954, used there to sound the times of work: another bell used to hang in the engine shed, said to be off *Little Wonder*.] *Little Giant* and *James Spooner* also had bells.

Engine acquired privately from Tramway de Pithiviers à Toury in Central France, where it carried No. 3–23 (*F.R.M.* No. 39, p. 10). It was conveyed to London and stored before becoming the property of the Railway. It was taken by road to Portmadoc, unloaded and propelled over the Cob in mid-October 1967; it proved possible to clear Rhiw Plas bridge but not the loco shed entrance, so the cab was removed—the first step in a lengthy series of modifications. On initial test it took eight coaches to Minffordd and it appeared the water capacity of 400 gallons would be adequate. Weight available for adhesion only 10 tons compared with 12 tons of the Penrhyn engines; otherwise, dimensions were similar.

The French tramway on which the engine ran had closed at the end of 1964, the last of their 60 cm. gauge lines and among the first to be built. Latterly, it had relied on sugar beet traffic. The engine had been built originally for the British War Department by the American Locomotive Company in 1916, carrying W.D. No. 1265. In France the engine was dubbed 'une locomotive Cooke', with reference to her origin in the Cooke Works of the A.L.Co. The Tramway ran several similar engines, occasionally on passenger trains; three of them survived at closure.

Comparison of dimensions:	*Blanche* and *Linda* Hunslet	*Mountaineer* A.L.Co.
Cylinders	10½ in. × 12 in.	9 in. × 14 in.
Boiler Pressure	140 lb.	175 lb.
Driving Wheel diameter	2 ft. 1 in.	2 ft. 3 in.
Tractive Effort	6,320 lb.	6,240 lb.
Driving Wheelbase	5 ft. 0 in.	5 ft. 6 in.
Total Wheelbase	5 ft. 0 in.	16 ft. 6 in.
Grate Area	5·2 sq. ft.	5·4 sq. ft.
Total Heating Surface	307 sq. ft.	264 sq. ft.
Weight in working order	12¼ tons	17 tons

1968—Converted to left-hand drive and vacuum brake fitted. Into traffic mid-October with temporary cab. In connection with experiments in chimney proportions, given that off *Linda* whilst that engine dismantled.

1969—Problems in making sufficient steam; in spring double-heading with tractor *Moelwyn* needed. Part of July–August; only steam engine available along with *Blanche*. New steam pipes given. Cavities between smokebox and steam chests filled with concrete. Name allotted at year's end.

1970—Spring; received new smokebox.

1970–1—Considered that the limit of the boiler's steaming rate had been reached due to existing tube arrangement, i.e. too few of too large a diameter.

1971—Autumn; converted to burn oil.

[1975—A new standard boiler is being evolved and this engine will receive one.]

Volunteer (Name not affixed)

This engine was supplied to the Harrogate Gas Works' railway (built in 1908 to 2 ft. gauge and 1¾ miles in length) in 1944 and was of reduced dimensions to allow it to work through a confined tunnel 5 furlongs long, 9 ft. high, 8 ft. wide which included a reverse curve. When the Gas Works line closed in July 1956, W. Grace & Son of Oldham demolished the line and purchased the Peckett; from them the Company purchased it in 1957. It has since been stored and its ultimate form is as yet undecided. The name has been suggested tentatively. In 1966 it was designated as 'Awaiting rebuilding' as its axle loading was too heavy and wheelbase too long for F.R. track conditions when received from Yorkshire (where at first it had run amok with the Gas Works' track whose rails had to be tied to gauge; it also derailed on the sharper curves).

Cylinders	9½ in. × 14 in.	Grate Area	5¼ sq. ft.
Boiler Pressure	200 lb.	Total Heating Surface	300 sq. ft.
Driving Wheel diameter	2 ft. 3½ in.	Total Length	19 ft. 3 in.
Tractive Effort	7,810 lb.	Height from rail level	7 ft. 10¼ in.

Tasmanian Garratt (No number or name allotted)

Built by Beyer Peacock & Co. Ltd., of Manchester for the North-East Dundas Tramway of 2 ft. gauge in Tasmania in 1909 and delivered in 1910, as a compound four-wheeled double-bogie having inboard cylinders. The Tramway closed in 1929 but the engine was retained and brought back to England in 1947 for renovation and display at the maker's works. The firm ceased locomotive building in 1966 and the Gorton, Manchester works was shut down. The engine, stored in the paint shop, was offered to several parties and ultimately bought by the Railway for £1,000, the subject of a special financial appeal. It was delivered to Portmadoc, in three parts, in June 1966.

The North-East Dundas line in the west coast mining area was considered to be the most interesting of the Government lines; it ran from Zeeham on the Emu Bay Company's main line and was essentially an ore-carrying line. There were in effect two branches, one to Dundas and the other to Williamsford (18 miles).

There were two of these engines (which ran as Class K), the first-ever Beyer Garratt type built; the tramway was owned by the Tasmanian Government, and 11 miles long.

Height to chimney top is 10 ft. 9 in. A compound specification was prepared against the wishes of Herbert W. Garratt and never again were cylinders placed in-board—a device in this instance to shorten the steam pipe between high and low pressure cylinders.*

Not surprisingly, the engine is too large in loading gauge for the F.R., approximating more to the former North Wales Narrow Gauge one; its width exceeds the footboards of the latter's coaches by two inches. No steps have yet been taken to modify this unit for Festiniog traffic but the prospect of flexible engines built to two different Patents running on the same system, has considerable historic attractions.

Cylinders (High Pressure under cab)	11 in. × 16 in.
(Low Pressure under smokebox)	17 in. × 16 in. (Width over is 7 ft.)
Boiler Pressure	195 lb.
Driving Wheels diameter	2 ft. 7½ in.
Total Wheelbase	26 ft. 9 in.
Weight in Working Order	34 tons
Tank Capacity	840 gallons
Bunker Capacity	1½ tons
Tractive Effort	17,946 lb.

Rail Tractor Summaries (Original stock)

Mary Ann

1967—Fitted with Gardner 4LK engine. After restoration to service 1955 was, with *Moelwyn*, one of the two original tractors. Put to service, found suitable for restoration purposes, but not as universally suitable for mixed duties as *Moelwyn*. Put to reserve for certain periods up to this date. At this date back on full duties whilst *Moelwyn* in Works.

1968—Given heavy overhaul and engine exchange.

1972—Cab fitted.

Moelwyn

1956—Fitted Gardner 3LW diesel engine; name applied.

1957—Leading pony-truck fitted.

1966-7—Fitted with Gardner 4LK diesel engine and given new cab. (*Mary Ann* deputised in the meanwhile.) Spring 1967, back in service.

* RAILWAY WONDERS OF THE WORLD (Second Series c. 1922) Vol. 1, pp. 27–34 refers.

1969—Working passenger traffic in place of *Upnor Castle* which had to be taken off.

Rail Tractors (Additional stock)

Upnor Castle

1968—Purchased from Welshpool & Llanfair Light Railway Preservation Society and delivered February.* Converted from 2 ft. 6 in. gauge and wheels reprofiled at Hunslet Engine Co. Ltd., Leeds. Already fitted Foden FD6 2-stroke 126 b.h.p. diesel engine. August; into traffic; cab cut down and modified; vacuum brake fitted later.

1969—Put on to passenger train work due to shortage of steam power, but prone to run hot axle boxes; *Moelwyn* substituted whilst *Upnor Castle* under repair.

1970-1—Foden engine replaced by Gardner 6LW. Wheelbase extended and internal ballast moved to improve adhesion and riding qualities. Spring; back in service. Used on certain passenger trains.

Tyke

1964—Delivered from Leeds in March; originally acquired by White Rose Group, F.R.S. October 1962, subsequently overhauled in Leeds. (As built, for War Department, Long Marston. Returned to makers for experimental fitting of three-stage torque converter.)

Alistair

1968—Donated by H. A. Bierrum of Bierrum & Partners (Civil Engineers) for working on Deviation. Standard DL Type 11–13 h.p. Ruston & Hornsby type V.T.O. diesel. Acquired by donors in 1949; delivered summer to Minffordd. Carried name on delivery. Was Tan-y-Bwlch station pilot that season.

Jane

1971—One of two similar tractors owned by Col. A. H. K. Campbell of Dduallt Manor and stored on siding at Campbell's Platform. Formerly St. Alban's Sand & Gravel Co. Ltd., 20–28 h.p. Diesel-mechanical, $2\frac{1}{2}$–$3\frac{1}{2}$ ton type. Built originally for War

* Acquired by W. & L.L.R.P.S. 1962 and name applied, also 'No. 4'.

14Q *Head of Rhiwbach Tramway No. 3 Incline with empties ready to descend. (A small tractor shed is hidden by the right-hand wall.) May 1947.*   (*J. I. C. Boyd*)

1N *Hudson-built steel open wagon No. 87 (acquired) and side-tipping open No. 160, a Company conversion for granite chippings traffic. Minffordd Yard. July 1974.*
          (*J. I. C. Boyd*)

2N *Bogie ballast wagon, Hudson-type, mounted on former Brookes' Quarry bogies. No. 68. Minffordd Yard. July 1974.*   (*J. I. C. Boyd*)

3N Taliesin, *still in grey paint, is reflected in the tidal pools at low water along The Cob.* March 1957. *(J. I. C. Boyd)*

4N Taliesin *taking water at the Harbour headshunt, showing point semaphore signal, tank and three-way point before a Development Scheme swept them all away.* (J. M. Lloyd)

5N Linda, *as first acquired from the Penrhyn Quarry Railway and fitted with improvised tender connections, heads an Up train at the Harbour station. September 1963.*

(J. I. C. Boyd)

6N *A Down train bowls gently round the falling curves below Tan-y-Bwlch, with* Linda. *May 1965.*

(J. I. C. Boyd)

7N Height-of-Season brings saturation to the line's capacity and difficulties in keeping up with the timetable, July 1974. A typical heavy bogie-coach formation leaves Garnedd Tunnel, headed by oil-burning Blanche. (J. I. C. Boyd)

8N Merddin Emrys in 1974 guise threads the woodland below Dduallt water tank on a Portmadoc-bound working. July 1974. (J. I. C. Boyd)

9N   *Tractor* Moelwyn *with empty ballast train, awaits to cross an Up passenger at Penrhyn.*
July 1974.   *(J. I. C. Boyd)*

10N   *The Deviation, 1974. Breach through the old reservoir embankment, with light con-*
struction tractor running round tip wagon. Tan-y-Grisiau is seen beyond the Storage
Scheme Reservoir.   *(J. I. C. Boyd)*

11N Some pictures reveal how little—save for the route—of the old equipment remains. In this case, only the second coach. And above steam power, (locomotive Mountaineer) appears nuclear power. July 1974.
(J. I. C. Boyd)

12N *Reminiscent of mammoth trains a century ago; the pendulum of events brings back such encouraging cavalcades as this spectacular view near Campbell's Platform, of Linda working hard as the train approaches Dduallt. July 1974.* (J. I. C. Boyd)

13N   *'Deviationists'' view of new Dduallt station below, the foot of the new spiral disappearing off centre left, and the old main line going out of sight towards foot of scene. Ultimately, the spiral brings the train in a climbing curve behind the trees (the line is just visible top right) until it passes this point where, at the time, the rails had not been laid. July 1974.*   *(J. I. C. Boyd)*

Department use, September 1940. Donated to F.R. Spring
1971. Delivered cabless to Boston Lodge.
1972—March; left Works with cab and carrying name.

(No Name)

1969—Acquired in dismantled condition; first supplied to New Stubbin
Colliery, Dewsbury (24½ in. gauge, but converted to 24 in. gauge
on transfer to Shaw Cross Colliery, Rawmarsh. Maker's flame-
proof mines type. Diesel-powered. Fitted with Meadow's 70 h.p.
diesel engine.
1974–5—Winter; into Works for overhaul for use on Dduallt–Gelliwiog
shuttle train in summer 1975.

Diana

1974—August; delivered to Glan-y-Pwll for work on restoring isolated
length of main line, ex-Minworth Sewage Works, Birmingham;
acquired through North Staffordshire Group of F.R.S.

Among other self-propelled vehicles, the Railway operates an
inspection-type vehicle Gang-trolley by D. Wickham & Co. Ltd.
(ex-British Rail converted to 2 ft. gauge), carried on four wheels but
driving on one axle only. Fitted J.A.P. 1,000 c.c. V-twin engine.
There is also a Matisa Tamping Machine (delivered September 1968)
which is not yet in use.

Painting

Motive power livery is based on black for boiler tops, tank tops, cab
fronts and surfaces below footplates. Green is used for tank sides, cab
sides and tenders. Green areas may be panelled with 2 in. wide black
border having a ¼ in. wide red or yellow line between black and green.
There may be a red line round the valance; some motions red. Cab
interiors cream or black; some numbers on beams; crests mounted
where appropriate.
For a period oil-burning engine smokeboxes were painted aluminium.

Carriages 1954–74

On 23 October 1954 the derelict carriage shed contained seven
vehicles having the advantage of some protection from the weather:

4-wheeled carriages	2/4/12
Bogie carriages	5/18/20/22

Surviving four-wheelers—in various shades of disrepair—were:
2/3/4/5/6/11/12

STEAM LOCOMOTIVES 1954–74*

No.	Name	Withdrawn from traffic	Returned to traffic	Builder	Works No. and Date	Wheel Arrangement	Origin	Purchased	Notes
1	*Princess*	Stored when line closed 1946	—	*	*	*	—	—	On display from 1969; Blaenau Ffestiniog
2	*Prince*	1937	1955	*	*	*	—	—	Rebuilding: 1975
4	*Palmerston*	1940	—	*	*	*	—	—	Surviving parts sold 1974
5	*Welsh Pony*	1938	—	*	*	*	—	—	Stored 1975
3	*Taliesin* (re-named *Earl of Merioneth*)	1939 (awaiting repair)	1956	*	*	*	—	—	Withdrawn 1971: reboilered, new tanks, etc. 1973–5
10	*Merddin Emrys*	Stored when line closed 1946	1961	*	*	*	—	—	In service
—	*Blanche*	—	—	Hunslet Engine Co. Ltd.	589 of 1893	0–4–0STT rebt. as 2–4–0STT	Penrhyn Qy. Rly.	1963	In service
—	*Linda*	—	—	Hunslet Engine Co. Ltd.	590 of 1893	0–4–0STT rebt. as 2–4–0STT	Penrhyn Qy. Rly.	1963	On loan from summer 1962 by P.Q.R.
—	*Mountaineer*	—	—	American Locomotive Co.	57156 of 1916	2–6–2T	†	1967	In service
(12)	(*Volunteer*)	—	—	Peckett & Sons Ltd.	2050 of 1944	0–6–0ST	Harrogate Gas Works	1957	Not yet used
—	—	—	—	Beyer Peacock & Co. Ltd.	5792 of 1909	0–4–0 + 0–4–0 Garratt type	‡	1966	Not yet used

* Details given in Chapter 14.
† ex Tramway de Pithiviers à Toury (Central France) No. 3–23.
‡ ex Tasmanian Government railways: N. E. Dundas Ty.

RAIL TRACTORS 1954–74*

No.	Name	Withdrawn from traffic	Returned to traffic	Builder	Works No. and Date	Wheel Arrangement	Origin	Acquired	Notes
—	Mary Ann	Stored when line closed 1946	1955	*	*	*	*	*	Name applied
11	Moelwyn	Stored when line closed 1946	1955	*	*	(leading truck fitted 1956)	*	*	Name applied 1956
—	Upnor Castle	—	—	F. C. Hibberd & Co. Ltd.	3687 of 1954	4-wh	ex-Admiralty, for Chattenden & Upnor Rly.	1968	Wt. in W.O. 13 tons delivered, 16 m.p.h. 'Planet' type
—	Tyke	—	—	Hunslet Engine Co. Ltd.	2290 of 1941	4-wh	ex-War Dept., Long Marston	1964 (del'd)	Acquired through members of F.R. Soc. Hudson/Hunslet diesel type
—	Alistair	—	—	Ruston & Hornsby Ltd.	201970 of 1939†	4-wh	ex-Bierrum & Partners (Civil Engineers)	1968 (del'd)	Donated for Deviation work. Wt. in W.O. $2\frac{3}{4}$ tons
—	Jane	—	—	Motor Rail Ltd.	8565 of 1940 (model 12428 36)	4-wh	ex-Col. Campbell	1971 (donated)	Name applied 1972
—	—	—	—	Hunslet Engine Co. Ltd.	4113 of 1955	4-wh	ex-National Coal Board	1969	Acquired in part-dismantled condition. 10 tons
—	—	—	—	D. Wickham & Co. Ltd.	1543 of 1934	4-wh (drive on one axle only)		1962	Converted from standard gauge after delivery
—	Diana	—	—	Motor Rail Ltd.	21579 of 1957	4-wh	ex-Minworth Sewage Works, per S. Grimmar, Shackerstone, Leics.	1974	Acquired through members of F.R. Soc.

* Details given in Chapter 14.
† F.R. publications give variously 1937, 1939 and 1940 as date of manufacture.

FOUR-WHEELED STOCK (NON-PUBLIC PASSENGER)
(Details given in Chapter 15)

Original Series No.	Later Series No.	Returned to traffic	Built as	Returned to traffic as	Notes
5*	2	1958	Quarrymen's Goods Brake Van		Seats 6, open interior
[6*	1	1956	Brake Van		Withdrawn (*F.R.M.* No. 25, p. 15)]
?*	8	1961	Quarrymen's Passenger coach		(*F.R.M.* No. 32, p. 17)

FOUR-WHEELED STOCK (PUBLIC PASSENGER)

Original Series No.	Later Series No.	Returned to traffic	Built at	Returned to traffic as	Notes
—	1	1964	Midland Group F.R.S.	(new vehicle) Multi-purpose pass. coach/ brake van	To replace old 6 (renovated 1) above. 3rd class, open interior. 8 seats (*F.R.M.* No. 26, p. 1)

FOUR-WHEELED STOCK (PUBLIC PASSENGER)
Builders: Brown, Marshalls & Co. (1863–4) Nos. 1–6 originally

Original Series No.	Later Series No.	Returned to traffic	Notes
3	3	1960	Seats 14
4	4	1958	Seats 14
(2) 5	5	1958	Seats 14
(3) 2	6	1958	Seats 14 (1)
12	7	(1970)	(14) Rebuilt as Museum piece in open form: not in traffic

(1)   Given full length doors off original Nos. 11 and 12—used to have drop lights either side central door.

(2/3) Withdrawn winter 1970 for long term rebuild due to deterioration.

From 1961 shock absorbers have been fitted to the outside of bogie frames to reduce body rolling, and some modification has been necessary to springing (*F.R.M.* No. 19, p. 5). This was made more urgent when in 1965 bolster springs breakages needed replacement (*F.R.M.* No. 27, p. 3).

With the centenary of passenger services in 1965 a fresh series of bogie carriages of advanced design commenced with No. 100. Bogies, using the Lynton & Barnstaple coach as example, were built at Boston Lodge with 4 ft. 4 in. wheelbase incorporating primary and secondary suspension. By 1968, bogie component production was on a system basis. At this time it was found desirable to avoid lengths of 24 ft. over bogie centres as it was detrimental to track with existing rail length.

Batch production of the 104–5–6 series marked another step forward; as in older times, bodies (prefabricated in sections) were supplied from outside, the Works providing the rest and assembling the parts.

By 1967 all the original wooden bogie coach bodies had been placed on steel underframes, No. 22 being the last.

During 1972 the Works turned out a number of simple, four-wheeled coaches for Quarry Tours Ltd., Llechwedd, Blaenau Ffestiniog.

The final attainment has seen the inauguration of No. 116, which arrived too late for the peak season of 1972 but went into service just a hundred years after the initial bogie coaches Nos. 15 and 16. This carriage has electrical heating equipment and this has been extended to other corridor vehicles.

Non-smoking compartments have been provided since 1973 and some of the 100 series are having wooden window frames replaced when bodies are overhauled.

Livery

The New Era began by painting stock with ivory upper and green lower panels; ends were red; roofs were light stone or black.

In 1964 No. 24 (later 104) appeared new in varnished mahogany; two thin red lines were added to the waist beading later.

By 1967 the basic main train set was an all-varnish one, a yellow line being painted over the 1st class section. The 'B' train set was still in ivory and green. To denote 1st class where coach construction was appropriate, the adjoining side panels were painted yellow. When No. 22 was returned to traffic in August it was in varnish livery but No. 15, coming out later in the year, appeared in ivory and green. In spring 1969 it was decided the older coaches should be finished in unlined cherry red; the four-wheelers were treated similarly and by the end of 1969, ivory and green had disappeared. Later, the cherry red ends of the foregoing had been changed to black, the carriage numbers being painted on the end so as to be visible from the lineside in a three-quarter view.

In spring 1970 the 100 series too, went over to the cherry red livery.

Goods Stock 1954–74

There is now no goods traffic in the traditional sense. Freight, stores and mineral workings in connection with the Railway's own needs form the bulk of non-passenger traffic. Slate, and more recently, coal traffic has been suspended; some oil traffic for loco purposes has taken the

BOGIE PASSENGER STOCK

(All coaches in existence 1939, stored between end of services that year and date of return to traffic, restored or otherwise)

Original Series No.	Later Series No.	Returned to traffic	Seating	1st	3rd	Notes
2*	10	Period 1955–8	3/3/G	—	12	Used mainly as service vehicle—awaits rebuilding
4*	11	1956	G/1/1/Obs	15	—	1958–9 Rebt. as 1st class observation car; uses Mersey Rly. seats. 1962, fitted steel underframe (first so treated) but old timber side frames retained. Received 12 volt lighting 1957; dynamo fitted
5*	12	1955	3/Saloon-Buffet/G	—	22	1957, side corridor and sales counter fitted; ran with No. 11 with gangway connection, van-to-van. 1963, steel frame and extended by one compartment. 1966, water tank and tea brewing facilities given. 12 volt lighting 1957
—	14†	1963 to service	3/Saloon-Buffet/G	—	26	Ex-Lynton & Barnstaple Rly. (Ex-Southern Rly. No. 6993); body acquired April 1963. Built 1897 by Bristol Wagon & Carriage Works Co. Ltd.; sold 1935 when L. & B.R. closed. Body dismantled; rebuilt Boston Lodge; later guard's section removed. 1964; bogies re-fitted with roller bearings
15*	15	1960	3/3/1/3/3	6	48	1st class now panelled from scrapped Pullman carriage 'Eunice'
16*	16	1969	3/3/3/1/1 coupé/3/3	9	40	Restoration began 1964; last original bogie coach to be rebuilt; 1967, concerted work on body—coupé fitted in lieu 3rd class compartment styled as No. 15.
17*	17	1956	3/3/1/3/3	6	40	12 volt lighting 1957; body overhauled 1966
18*	18	1957	3/3/1/3/3	6	40	Body overhauled as No. 17, 1966–7
19*	19	1963	3/3/1/1/3	12	32	Body reconditioned by outside contractors at Boston Lodge; some components prefabricated outside; 1966
20*	20	1957	3/3/1/1/3	12	32	12 volt lighting 1957. Body reconditioned by local carpenters, in Portmadoc goods shed 1967. Repainting done Boston Lodge

21★	21	—	—	—		1962, body dismantled. (Bogies to No. 26 in summer 1959.) Condition too poor to be worthy of rebuilding
22★	22	1953	3/3/3/3/3/3	—	56	1967, given steel underframe (last wood frame to be so treated)
23‡	23	1955	3/3/3/3/3/3/3	—	56	Ex-Welsh Highland Rly. in store from 1939. Part of reparation received 1936. 1966, given steel underframe, half-doors removed and full doors fitted. Re-roofed
26‡	26	1959	3/3/3/3/3/3/3	—	56	Ex-Welsh Highland Rly. Body sold at auction of W.H.R. assets June 1942; purchased by F.R. from site at Groeslon; placed on bogies ex No. 21. 1965, frame, doors, roof as No. 23
New Series		*Entered traffic*				
—	37§	1971	3/3/3		32	'Tourist Bogie'. Built Boston Lodge on Hudson bogie frame off No. 70. Steel body. Uses half-doors off Nos. 23/6. Slatted seats. Steel floor
—	38§	1972	3/3/3	—	32	'Tourist Bogie'. Built Boston Lodge on Hudson bogie coach frame of 1923 series and some parts off coach No. 38 (derelict by 1939).¶ Steel body. Uses half-doors off Nos. 23/6. Slatted seats. Steel floor

★ Details given in Chapter 15.

† Not an original vehicle of F.R.Co. but listed here for convenience. Strictly it does not conform with rebuilds of original coaches nor new series vehicles, but rebuilding of it gave useful information for future new and re-building.

‡ Supplied to North Wales Narrow Gauge Railways Co. by Ashbury Railway Carriage & Iron Co. Ltd. of Manchester in 1894; given F.R. carriage series numbers in 1923 (ref: NARROW GAUGE RAILWAYS IN SOUTH CAERNARVONSHIRE, pp. 222, 336–40).

§ These are new coaches carrying former numbers, not rebuilds of coaches carrying these numbers.

¶ Frame off original No. 38 coach had meanwhile been used as bogie flat as from 1926; under new regime it had been carrying No. 66.

NEW BOGIE STOCK 1964–75

Series No.	To traffic	Seating	1st	3rd	Notes
100*	1965	G/1 Saloon/1 Obs		18	Numbered to celebrate centenary of passenger service; entered traffic for this event 24 May. Design a development of No. 11, but not including guard's compartment which was incorporated in No. 14. Emulates modern styling of the foregoing. Later modified as No. 101 by being given guard's compartment. This enabled kitchen of No. 14 to be extended.
101	1970	G/1 Saloon/1 Obs		18	Built Boston Lodge; contained guard's compartment from the first, No. 100 being modified similarly later
102	Not used				
103	1968	Buffet/3 Saloon		17	'Super Buffet' coach for inauguration of 3-train service 1968. Built Boston Lodge. Can provide light meals
104*	1964	3 Saloon/1/3 Saloon	4	32	Entered service as No. 24 but series discontinued and renumbered into No. 100 series 1967
105*	1966	3 Saloon/1/3 Saloon/Lav	4	29	Entered service as No. 25 but series discontinued and renumbered into No. 100 series before entering service. First F.R. vehicle to have lavatory accommodation
106*	1968	3 Saloon/1/3 Saloon	4	32	As No. 104
116	1972	3 Saloon/1	4	32	Prototype aluminium panel and frame body supplied as unit by Edmund Crow of Cleator Moor, Cumberland. Bogies and running gear by Boston Lodge. Length 35 ft. 9 in. One 1st class compartment and a large 3rd class Saloon; side corridor at 1st end; inwards-opening doors in end vestibules. Entered service on temporary bogies to assess potential

Bogies of 104, 105 and 106 are a development of No. 14's bogies but with improved bearings and double suspension systems.

Further constructional references, etc. are given in F.R.M. No. 29, p. 4; No. 25, p. 6; Coach No. 100; No. 32, p. 18, Coaches Nos. 104 and 105; No. 56, p. 4, Coach No. 116.

* Numbers marked thus have prefabricated bodies by H. L. Watson Ltd., Birkenhead. Frames and bogies by Boston Lodge.

place of coal. The highest tonnage of non-passenger loading is presently that for ballast, but this is a temporary phase and when the new line and the heaviest renewals have taken place, maintenance will not require the trains and tonnages of today.

Open storage during the closed years decimated much goods stock which was basically of timber construction. Many of the wooden wagons which had been stored at the Harbour station were burned on 21–22 October 1954, the fire lasting several days. Many slate wagons were sold off or simply scrapped to raise finance. Wagons for the conveyance of ballast or track-building or maintenance machinery were scarce in the early years. Out of 1,000, about 100 slate wagons survive.

Some wagons have had their original purpose drastically altered, e.g. a gunpowder van now carries cement; acquired additional stock which once carried potatoes was used for coal and surviving slate or slab wagons may now carry compressors or generators, utilisation unheard-of pre-1954.

Miscellaneous Service Vehicles (*not numbered*)

(Normally restricted to Yard or site use.)

There are a number of miscellaneous service vehicles which carry no numbers and are restricted to Yard or site use at Boston Lodge, in the Permanent Way Department, Minffordd and in connection with the Deviation at Dduallt and beyond.

Miscellaneous Vehicle from Outside Source

F.R. No. 59 rebuilt from cattle van built Swindon 1923 for Vale of Rheidol section. (Latterly carried G.W.R. No. 38089, a similar van carrying the previous number.) Returned to Swindon 1935; regauged and sent to Welshpool & Llanfair section 1937. Body and frame purchased 1959. New body fitted with lower roof and running gear in part from quarrymen's carriages. Vacuum brake pipe; used as stores van.

It should be noted that some wagons were obtained off the Croesor Tramway. In 1963 a quantity of granite and slab wagons came from Maenofferen Quarry. The same year two Hudson bogie opens and the sixteen 4-wheeled steel-sided opens were acquired. (These are listed in the following tables.) The latter were intended for ballast carrying. The same year the last gunpowder van suitable for further use was reconditioned to carry cement bags.

In 1967 a drastic renewal of wagon numbers put the older goods stock

Original Four- and Six-wheeled Stock and Conversions

Original Series No.	Intermediate No.	New Series No.	B = Hand Brake	Body Type	Notes
116	99	99	B	Breakdown van	Previously covered van
8	130	130	B	Open	(Cleminson 6-wh. end door wagon)
Long Load Vehicles					
9	9	131	—	Single bolster close coupled set	Used for telegraph poles etc.
10	10	132	—	Single bolster	Used for telegraph poles etc.
11	11	133	—	Runner	Used for telegraph poles etc.
12	12	134	—	Flat fitted with bolster for carrying boilers	ex-long slab wagon
351	259	135	B	Flat bolster set match wagon	ex-2 ton slate wagon
?	—	136	B	Single bolster close coupled set	
?	—	137	—	Single bolster	
?	—	138	—	Runner	
Miscellaneous Service Vehicles					
985	42	140	—	Flat: tool wagon	ex-3 ton slate wagon
957	152	141	—	Flat: toolbox wagon	ex-3 ton slate wagon
277	122	142	B	M.P.U. E1 mobile generator	ex-3 ton slate wagon
410	106	143	B	M.P.U. E2 mobile alternator	ex-3 ton slate wagon
13	13	144	—	M.P.U. A3 compressor	ex-long slab wagon
?	14	145	—	M.P.U. A4 compressor	ex-long slab wagon
847	167	146	—	M.P.U. A5 mobile generator	(ex-No. 367) ex-3 ton slate wagon
		147	—	M.P.U. E6 mobile generator	
402	105	148	—	M.P.U. W(DC)7 mobile welding generator	(ex-No. 305) ex-3 ton slate wagon
Miscellaneous					
983	15	151	—	Flat with cement mixer	ex-3 ton slate wagon
?	16	152	B	Cement van	ex-gunpowder van
631	267	153	—	Flat with plate roller	ex-2 ton slate wagon
?	—	154	B	Van: end doors. P.W. Dept. welding vehicle	
?	?	155	—	Flat: carries 500 gal. tank	ex-3 ton slate wagon

Tipping Wagons (Iron)

846	17	160	B	Open one-way side tipper	Iron, 2 ton
830	18	161	B	Open one-way side tipper	Iron, 2 ton

Wooden/Iron Open Wagons—Various

19	19	162	B	Single end door, 2 ton	Wooden body
20	20	163	—	Single end door, 2 ton	Wooden body
126	21	164	B	Double end door, 4 ton	Corrugated iron roof fitted. Rebuilt Midland Group, 1966 (F.R.M. No. 32, p. 3) Wooden body
22	22	165	B	Single end door, 3 ton	Wooden body
?	23	166	B	Single end door, 3 ton	Iron body

3 Ton Slate/Granite Wagons

Wood/steel sides, end door.

926	33	150	B

Also New Series Nos. 167–185 inclusive. Only New Series Nos. 177–179 have hand brakes. Some among first to be repaired 1958–9 for loco coal traffic.

2 Ton Slate Wagons

Original Series No.	Inter-mediate No.	New Series No.	B = Hand Brake	Original Series No.	Inter-mediate No.	New Series No.	B = Hand Brake	Original Series No.	Inter-mediate No.	New Series No.	B = Hand Brake
212	205	195	B	1003	248	248	B	367	261	261	B
26	200	200	B	1009	249	249	B	368	262	262	B
57	201	201	B	?	250	250	B	639	268	268	—
154	202	202	B	44	251	251	B	651	269	269	—
206	204	204	B	116	252	252	B	659	270	270	—
411	206	206	B	118	253	253	B	697	271	271	—
567	207	207	B	187	254	254	B	757	273	273	—
602	208	208	B	208	255	255	B	787	274	274	—
618	209	209	B	632	257	257	B	797	275	275	—
634	210	210	B	335	258	258	B	758	276	276	—
642	211	211	B	?	259	259	B	316	277	277	—
22	213	213	B	364	260	260	B	785	278	278	—
		194									

Tool wagon. S. & T. Dept. ex-2 ton slate

Ash Wagons

—	—	196	B	⎫
—	—	197	—	⎬ Iron body, open: ex Croesor Tramway acquired October 1958
—	—	198	—	⎭

Bogie Open or Flat Wagons
(built Robert Hudson Ltd., Leeds)

Original Series No.	Intermediate No.	New Series No.	B = Hand Brake	Body Type	Previous Form	Origin (or other notes)
—	60	60	B	Open	Open	*Smith's Crisps Potato Farm Smith No. 18
—	61	61	B	Flat	Open	*Smith's Crisps Potato Farm (now carries 1,600 gal. tank) Smith No. 35
—	62	62	B	Open	Open (not all same size)	*Smith's Crisps Potato Farm Smith No. 9
—	63	63	B†	Open	Open	*Smith's Crisps Potato Farm (in cherry red and piped 1970) Smith No. 3
4	64	64	B	Oil tank	Open	Carries 2,000 gal. tank
5	65	65	B	Flat	Open (cap. 10 tons)	
6	66	66	B	Flat	Open	Frame used for coach No. 38 winter 1970
7	67	67	B	Open	Open	Carries weedkilling equipment‡
—	68	68	B	Open	Open (fitted 'Feldbahn' type bogies ex-Brookes')	R.A.F. Alrewas, 1963: to traffic 6/1963
—	69	69	B	Open	Open (fitted Hudson 'D' type bogies)	R.A.F. Alrewas, 1963: to traffic 6/1963
§	70	70	B	Open	Open (no doors)	Leighton Buzzard Light Rly. From 1971 carries 1,000 and 3,000 gal. oil tanks
§	71	71	—	Open	Open (no doors)	Leighton Buzzard Light Rly.
§	72	72	B	Open	Open (no doors)	Leighton Buzzard Light Rly.
§	73	73	—	Open	Open (no doors)	Leighton Buzzard Light Rly.

* Smith's Crisps (Nocton, Lincs.) Dropside wagons (not all same size.)
† Vacuum brake piped.
‡ Given 400 gal. tank at each end and pump between (manual)—later mechanised (1963). Withdrawn 1973.
§ ex L.B.Lt.R.: built Gloucester Carriage & Wagon Co. Ltd.: to F.R. winter 1971 (F.R.M. No. 55, p. 38).

Four-wheeled Open Wagons
(built Robert Hudson Ltd., Leeds)

Original Series No.	Intermediate No.	New Series No.	B = Hand Brake	Body Type	Previous Form	Origin (or other notes)
—	97	97	B	Flat	Flat	ex R.A.F. Alrewas. Converted to carry compressor

Intermediate Nos. 83–96 inclusive and No. 98 (New Series Nos. the same) were all acquired in 1963 from R.A.F. Alrewas, Staffordshire. All have steel bodies, drop sides, and are hand-braked: now used for ballast, etc.

3 Ton Slate Wagons and Conversions [Nos. 300 upwards] (see also Nos. 140–43/146–48/151/155 conversions)

(Conversions pre-1955 for granite traffic are listed under Nos. 150/167–185)

[Renumbering from 1xx to 3xx to avoid duplication of Nos. and 100 series coaches]

Original Series No.	Intermediate No.	New Series No.	B = Hand Brake	Notes
7	100	300	B	
256	101	301	B	
330	102	302	B	
396	104	304	B	Carries 500 gal. oil tank
402	105	305	—	(see 148)
469	107	307	—	
947	108	308	B	
969	109	309	B	Converted to Flat
942	110	310	B	
868	117	317	—	Converted as 134
876	119	319	B	
142	120	320	B	One open end
264	121	321	B	One open end
412	123	323	B	One open end
461	124	324	B	One open end
950	125	325	—	One open end
		326	—	Wooden sides: no end door
?	?	327	—	Carries 300 gal. oil tank
955	150	350		
959	151	351		
977	153	353		
980	154	354		
891	156	356		Converted as 134
820	160	360		Converted as 327
819	161	361		
822	162	362		
823	163	363		
824	164	364		
835	165	365	—	One end, one side open
806	166	366	—	(see 146)
847	167	367	—	
828	168	368	—	
829	169	369	—	Converted as 327
841	171	371	—	
852	172	372	—	Converted as 327
854	173	373	—	Converted as 327
	—	378	—	
?	180	380	—	Converted as 320
896	181	381	—	
922	184	384	—	
924	185	385	—	
—	?	387	—	
	188	388	—	Flat: carries 500 gal. oil tank
?	41	400	—	Converted as 320
?	?	401	B	Converted to flat
838	47	402	—	Converted to flat
902	182	403	—	Converted to flat
888	187	404	—	Converted to flat
937	45	405	—	Converted to flat
966	44	406	—	Converted to flat
970	46	407	—	Converted to flat
?	?	411	—	Converted to flat
2 Ton Slate Wagon Conversions				
		412		Flat
		413		Flat: as 134
		414		Flat
		415		2 ton slab wagon

into the 1xx series and the slate wagons into a 3xx series. Numbers now begin at 60 but numbers 100 to 129 inclusive are not used, being reserved for carriage or non-goods stock.

In 1973 some ex-Polish State Railways 60 cm. gauge bogies (plate-framed) salvaged from snowploughs were obtained (others will have diamond side frames), and fitted with F.R. drawgear and bogie centres; these offset the prevailing shortage of bogies and an experimental heavy-duty frame carrying a 2,000 gallon oil tank for a time was mounted on a pair. A new coach for the Gelliwiog shuttle will use them also (*F.R.M.* No. 64, p. 4).

Permanent Way and Signalling

Some description of relaying has already been covered in the section dealing with the Route. Reference has been made to prefabrication of points and plain track parts both at Boston Lodge and in the converted goods shed, Minffordd. From 1963 it became possible to screw chairs into wooden sleepers mechanically, with consequent uplift in output. About the same time compromise-size galvanised screws were introduced but these were too large for most of the existing chair holes. The mammoth task of opening out the cast holes had to be undertaken before the new screws could be used.

Between the start of restoration and the early 1960s a crisis was approaching in terms of rail. Many lengths, some on sharp curves, would need relaying within 4–8 years, and there was no replacement on hand. Fortunately the closing of the Penrhyn Quarry Railway in 1961 led, after negotiation, to the purchase of five miles of bull-head rail (in 24 ft. lengths) and chairs; some of the F.R.'s own double-headed rails, taken from the line in the vicinity of Tan-y-Grisiau, were sold to offset part of the costs of the Quarry rail (*F.R.M.* No. 24, p. 6).

The Penrhyn rail was delivered in weekly 50 ton lots to Minffordd during spring 1965; it was lifted by a contractor (*F.R.M.* No. 24, p. 6).

The Talyllyn and Festiniog Railways combined to purchase a bulk lot of jarrah hardwood sleepers, these coming into Liverpool in January 1970, size 9 in. × 4½ in. × 5 in. A joint purchase was also made of 60 lb. flat-bottomed rails from Bowater's abandoned railway at Sittingbourne. These were laid around Rhiw Plas. Further jarrah deliveries have been made annually.

Whilst jarrah sleepers are expensive and heavy (weighing *c.* 100 lb. each) sources of good second-hand sleepers from British Rail are now scarce. For a time they were bought from contractors lifting B.R. branches, e.g. near Rochdale or ex-Great Central Railway lines.

Bowater rails have been put in above Penrhyn crossing with staggered joints . . . as has Tilbury rail on the Deviation, and all other relaying.

A quantity of ex-Barry Railway flat-bottomed 75 lb. rails was laid on Gwyndy Bank welded into 84 ft. lengths on jarrah sleepers.

In 1972 120 tons of 75 lb. flat-bottomed rail in 36 ft. lengths and six sets of points were purchased from Tilbury Power Station, C.E.G.B.: it was considered too light for modern B.R. motive power there. Much of this has since been laid into the Deviation where new 60 lb. rail will follow when the Tilbury material is exhausted.

Another source of second-hand rails came from A.P.C.M. of Harbury (1972).

The Harbury rails proved to be a 'mixed bag' and confirmed the doubtful value of second-hand purchases. (*F.R.M.* No. 60, p. 8). So early in 1973 100 tons of new 60 lb. flat bottomed rails were ordered for the Deviation—and beyond to Blaenau. These came from the former Workington Iron & Steel Co. premises later in 1973. Ballast presently comes from a local supplier (Minffordd granite quarry) now entirely by road into Minffordd. F.R. bogie Hudson and Alrewas wagons carry it away.

In the long term, flat-bottomed rails are inevitably going to oust the more elderly materials of chaired track.

A new series of mileposts is now in use following re-measuring of the line.

In the winter of 1973–4 new Workington rails were laid on the Sheepfold–Bryn Mawr length; in 1974–5 the Ty Fry–Nazareth length below Penrhyn was similarly relaid, the materials taken out to be used for the approaches on the Down side of the Deviation Tunnel —as yet to be started.

On some sharp curves, ex-main line flange lubricators are in use.

As to signalling, the same problem at first presented itself as was to be found in every other department of the railway, save that neglect was possibly worse on the signal and telegraph side than elsewhere, largely because much of it had become disused before the railway closed. With latter-day working being one engine in steam on three days per week, the only piece of equipment which was vital was the carrying on the train of the appropriate staff, so enabling the remaining ground frames in use to be worked. Semaphore signalling became disused when passenger trains ended in 1939 and by personal observation, it was noted that crossing gates at Glan-y-Pwll and Minffordd, carrying much restricted war-time road traffic, were worked on an 'ad hoc' basis without any formalities, latterly by train crews.

It was at Minffordd crossing that the new operators met some of the three major factors affecting the signalling department. These were that obsolete equipment was unsuited to future use and was unworthy of time spent upon it; secondly there was equipment which the Ministry of Transport might tolerate if restored, but they were likely to insist it be modernised for safety reasons. Lastly, the traffic at the Portmadoc end of the line grew yearly and signalling must be installed to meet anticipated train intervals of some years ahead. In 1957 therefore, Minffordd crossing was given colour light signals whilst Up trains also sounded a warning bell worked on a track treadle. After some problems with the treadle, by 1964 both this and a replacement switch type worked by wheel flanges were replaced by track circuiting (*F.R.M.* No. 27, p. 10) and ultimately, Silic treadles.

By 1965 electric train staff had been given to the Minffordd–Tan-y-Bwlch section and work was in hand for an automatic telephone exchange to cover all internal requirements, at Portmadoc. The cables were placed in a G.P.O. duct along the Cob, allowing F.R. cabling to keep it company; thus the old poles over the Cob disappeared. This work at first began in 1963 when the Gwynedd River Board strengthened the seaward side of the causeway and their crane was used by the F.R. The new telephone system was later extended by means of similar exchanges at Boston Lodge, Minffordd and Tan-y-Bwlch (*F.R.M.* No. 32, p. 2).

A prominent signalling feature of former times was damaged by gales in the winter of 1966–7 and so the three-arm bracket signal from the Cob disappeared at last. A new six-lever frame was installed at the Harbour in spring 1967 and the following winter the ghost of the old bracket signal was placated by a new fitting, involving the marriage of the former Welsh Highland line signal post from the Harbour goods shed side, and an arm from the Liverpool Overhead Railway. By summer 1968 with Dduallt coming into use, No. 1 van was doing duty as an instruments hut there, as by Easter 1968 the automatic phone system was connected right through to Dduallt.

The timetable now demanded that Penrhyn was used for crossing trains, so facilities were made there and at Minffordd enabling both to be used as Block Posts, with opening at Penrhyn optional according to traffic needs. By summer 1969 the 'short section' Electric Train Staff system was available as Minffordd–Penrhyn: Penrhyn–Tan-y-Bwlch. In 1974 even further flexibility of block sections was heralded by work on a new loop at Rhiw Goch and the short section between Minffordd and Penrhyn became a permanent feature.

A fundamental change now took place at Minffordd and Tan-y-Bwlch when colour light signals 'pending the introduction of full mechanical signalling' came into use (*F.R.M.* No. 48, p. 6) by May 1970. Work began on a central signal box at Tan-y-Bwlch. Operating Instructions were issued and the Inspecting Officer of Railways was very satisfied (*F.R.M.* No. 51, p. 24). Again, extremely varied operating requirements according to season will result in a combination of semaphore and colour light signals.

Changes in conditions led to a second semaphore appearing on the Cob for the 1971 season; the existing ex-L.O.R.-armed semaphore (designated the Down Home signal) was joined by a new one, the Up Advance signal. There is an overlap between these two posts, assisted by placing the former some distance from Harbour station along the Cob. The former is locked on the tablet instrument and cannot be pulled to clear unless 'Line Clear' for the section ahead has been received at the Harbour. The second signal prevents a collision between a Down train approaching the Harbour and a shunting movement taking place beyond that station's limits. Ex-Great Northern Railway somersault signals parts were used for both; a reserve stock is on hand for future installation, a number being made available from Holloway. Oddly, they also originally came from the Worcester firm of McKenzie & Holland Ltd.

More recently colour light signalling has appeared at Minffordd, Penrhyn and Tan-y-Bwlch. A policy of fitting every station with Home signals locked with the pointwork and with each other has begun. The former special disc signal above Highgate crossing, Penrhyn, has been replaced by a new signal 250 yards to the west—the old disc is retained as a Caution Board.

For summer 1971 Dduallt's Down end received a new four-lever ground frame; and the following winter saw Tan-y-Bwlch cabin complete but not fitted out. At the same time, the colour lights at Penrhyn, the last intermediate station to be treated, were finished. Back at Dduallt, the Up end of the station was given trapped points to the old main line and a new ground frame put in for spring 1973; a cantilevered post carries shunting disc signals for approaching Up trains.

Further refinements in summer 1974 included an Inner Home signal for use at Minffordd and work on a completely new site, Rhiw Goch. Here a nine-lever frame in a cabin with colour light signals will be used to control the new loop. So the signalling department has worked from reconditioning through to up-grading. Now it moves on to installing sophisticated equipment at a site where since horse-tramway days a 'Station' (for as such it was shown in those times) has re-awakened after slumbering away the century.

AN APPRAISAL OF THE NEW ERA

In two decades of restoration one can expect that the harsh monotony of sweat and toil would be highlighted now and again with peaks of achievement, gloomy setbacks, targets attained—only to be altered shortly afterwards in some other interest; in short, the compression into twenty years of as much activity as had occurred in the life of the

railway in all its years before 1954. The very nature of the re-birth
and the initial restrictions of labour and finance meant that some
features so hardly won back and acclaimed have disappeared. Borne
along by this tide, the Festiniog Railway is today established as one of
the bastions of the Wales Tourist Board. Of international fame in the
1870s, it has risen from the pit to become internationally famous again
—witness the passenger figures—and those who were feebly senti-
mental for the features of the railway's past have been brushed aside
by the sheer weight of business. If Robert Fairlie had been writing
'Railways or No Railways' (a sub-title of his *The Battle of the Gauges*)
today instead of a century beforehand, he too would have grasped a
situation which takes and makes business as it finds it, and makes
mockery of history.

New factors have affected the Railway and these bring new problems
on a scale the old Company never had to face. The loss of a whole
length of line at an early stage has been overcome; if 'profitable' is a
suitable word, the line has shown 'profitability' when its competitors
of a century back have succumbed all round. Inflation makes tourist
business a very speculative affair, with capital tied up in features which
operate for only part of the year. Fairlie's title might now be 'The
Battle of the Wages'.

Three centenaries have been celebrated during the New Era: the
introduction of steam in 1963, of passengers in 1965, and the Fairlie
engine in 1969. With each occasion publicity has made the most of it,
and the forceful intrusion of TV has brought the Railway to every
fireside. Publicity is the strongest feature of the resurgence of the line.
In 1970, the narrow gauge railways of Wales formed a collective
marketing panel and in the same year received the Wales Tourist Board
trophy for 1970 as having given outstanding service to tourism in
Wales. There is isolationism no longer. But the previous year of the
Prince of Wales' Investiture perhaps demonstrated that the Railway
can still be subject to nearby competition, as traffic did not develop
that season until late. The Prince of Wales visited Blaenau Ffestiniog
on 2 July and inspected *Princess* at her outpost outside the Queen's
Hotel.*

Other Very Important Persons actually to travel over the line have
included the Nepal royal family, Dr. Hastings Banda, Lord Snowdon
and the Prime Minister of Senegal. Journeys by prominent people
nearer home, either privately or on special occasion, no longer receive
long write-ups in *The Engineer* even though the mechanical history
of the Company continues to be in the forefront of ingenuity and
improvement.

* This engine was later displayed at the 'Rail 150' Exhibition at Shildon in
August 1975.

Gravity trains continue to run for works trains—a convenient method for instance, of clearing the line of empty wagons when unloading has been completed and saving the stand-by of a locomotive. A gravity-worked slate train was re-enacted on 22 May 1963 for the steam centenary. At the same festival a horse-hauled train ran at the Harbour.

The following year an important issue was reached when a Charitable Trust was formed (*F.R.M.* No. 51, p. 13), and its ambitions are worthy of study.

In autumn 1905, whilst engaged on exercise and a relaying pro-gramme, the Army also operated the train service. The event was not without some hiates! (*F.R.M.* No. 31, p. 2). This was at the end of Passenger Centenary season, somewhat aptly. By 1968 traffic had grown to such proportions that a three-train-set service was inaugurated for the peak season.

During the 1969 Investiture Year festivities, and the centenary of the Double Fairlie Engine, a set of four Railway Letter Stamps was intro-duced on 28 May. Further celebration took place on the Embankment on 8 September 1973 when a cairn was unveiled on the seaward side to mark the 200th anniversary of Madock's birth (17 June 1773)—a date which is customarily accepted as 1774 by some authorities! (*F.R.M.* No. 62, p. 29).

On a different aspect of publicity, and in a feature on which the Railway has never been very strong, a fourth prize was awarded to a poster prepared in 1971 and entered for a competition by *The New Statesman*. The advertisements which formed the basis of the scheme were to demonstrate the advertiser's awareness of his wider social responsibilities (*F.R.M.* No. 53, p. 2).

The Festiniog Railway Trust inaugurated in 1973 a Five Year Plan with several charitable objects in view; one of these is the movement of articles of historic importance in a small relics room at the Harbour station to as-yet temporary display in the former goods shed there. Among other historic items which the Trust has singled out are the restoration of *Prince* and the four-wheeled carriages.

The foregoing are selected at random from a wide choice. To those participating, the highlights of the last twenty years may never appear in print—it is better that some should not! At the beginning of this last section the place of the Railway in the changed national circum-stance has been considered. It is fitting to end with its place on a more parochial level. The Railway is not an undertaking where unlimited opportunities are available for participation by interested supporters—other railway ventures have longer catered for such a democratic out-look. However, the opportunities for laymen to become involved have proved so wide, and the appeal so irresistible, that (professional aid from the Company's staff apart) support from this important quarter has considerably speeded progress—a feature undreamed-of in 1939, and perhaps one aspect of modernisation which our forefathers would find it hard to assimilate. Personal participation, The Tourist Industry, Railway Letter Service, Great Little Trains of Wales, The Gelliwiog Shuttle are among Festiniog phraseology born of the New Era, just as Double Engine, The Birminghams and Crewling were expressions of the past. Perhaps the greatest measure of achievement can be summed up in the thought that no sooner has this new History of the Festiniog Railway appeared in print, than events will have made the book itself a part of history!

Tickets

The greatest part of this account reveals what lies behind the railway and the train which the present-day tourist finds. For him, probably the only tangible evidence of a fleeting acquaintance with a historic institution, is his ticket. Few of the half-million or so tickets in stock were suitable for re-opening in 1955! Having to resolve the problem very hastily, an order was given to Messrs. Harrison who produced a crude card variety in pink, smaller than the Edmundson type. It was cut with nippers to produce singles or half-fares and was basically of only one type; outward and return halves were printed in the reverse of normal custom.

In 1956 a number of original tickets could be used, but Edmondson's advice was sought regarding new printing. (J. B. Edmondson had its archaic plant in premises in Cheetham, Manchester, but closed down in 1960.) The goodwill of Edmondson was taken over by Williamson of Ashton-under-Lyne, and for a time the Railway used their distinctive style with the name 'Williamson' forming part of each ticket.

During the 1960s card tickets gradually gave way to machine-issued paper tickets of various types and with few exceptions, this circumstance continues. It is on the sales of enough of these humble pieces of paper that the future existence of the Festiniog Railway depends.

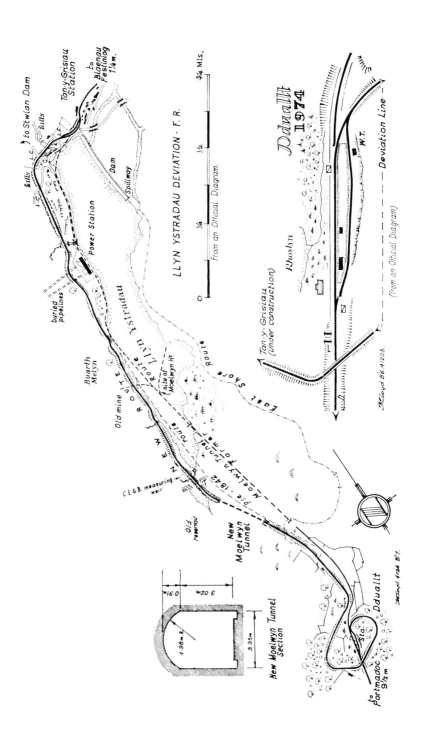

LLYN YSTRADAU DEVIATION · F.R.

from an Official Diagram.

0   ¼   ½   ¾ Mls.

to Stwlan Dam

falls

falls

Tan-y-Grisiau
Station

to
Blaenau
Festiniog 1¼m.

L.C.

L.C.

Dam

Spillway

Power Station

buried
pipelines

Buarth
Melyn

Old mine

ROUTE

Route
LLYN Ystradau

Site of Moelwyn Ht.

East Shore
Route

NEW ROUTE

Moelwyn Tunnel Former

Pre · 1842

C.E.G.B. measuring
weir

Old reservoir

New
Moelwyn
Tunnel

0·91m

3·02m

1·98mR

3·35m

New Moelwyn Tunnel
Section

to
Portmadoc
9½m

Sta.

Dduallt

J.I.C.Lloyd 1984 B 7.

Ddualllt
1974

Tan-y-Grisiau
(under construction)

Rhoslyn

W.T.

Deviation Line

(from an Official Diagram)

J.I.Lloyd B6.4.1205.

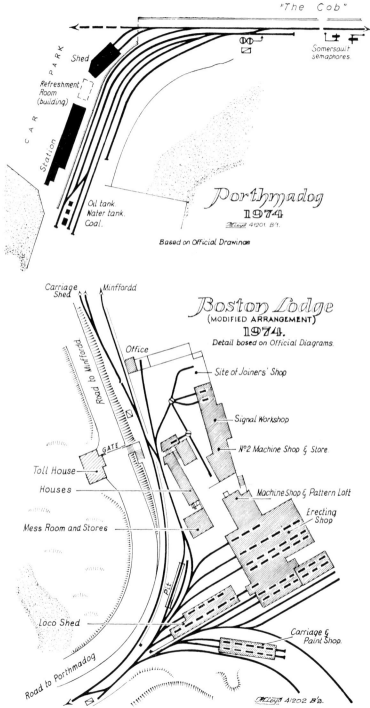

"The Cob"

Somersault
semaphores.

CAR PARK

Shed

Refreshment
Room
(building)

Station

Oil tank.
Water tank.
Coal.

Porthmadog
1974
McLloyd 41201. B'1.

Based on Official Drawings

Carriage
Shed

Minffordd

Boston Lodge
(MODIFIED ARRANGEMENT)
1974.
Detail based on Official Diagrams.

Road to Minffordd

Office

Site of Joiners' Shop

Signal Workshop

Nº2 Machine Shop & Store.

GATE

Toll House

Houses

Mess Room and Stores

Machine Shop & Pattern Loft

Erecting
Shop

Pit

Loco Shed

Carriage &
Paint Shop.

Road to Porthmadog

McLloyd 41202 B'2.

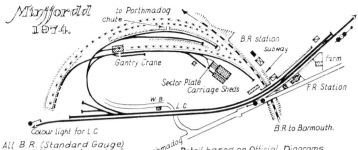

Minffordd
1974.

to Porthmadog

chute

B.R. station

subway

Gantry Crane

farm

Sector Plate
Carriage Sheds

F.R. Station

W.B.   L.C.

Colour light for L.C.

to Porthmadog

B.R. to Barmouth.

All B.R. (Standard Gauge) track lifted and much of the F.R. (Narrow Gauge) track.

Detail based on Official Diagrams.
McLoyd 4220 B/3.

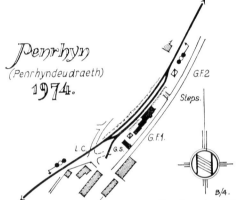

Penrhyn
(Penrhyndeudraeth)
1974.

G.F.2

Steps.

L.C.   G.S.   G.F.1

B/4.

When trains are crossed here a system of hand operated Stop Ground Boards controls movements.

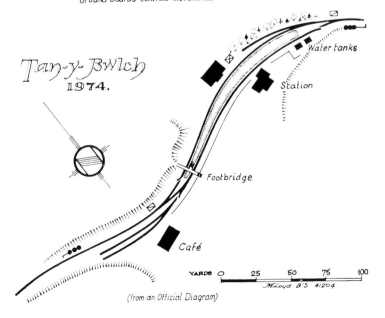

Tan-y-Bwlch
1974.

Water tanks

Station

Footbridge

Café

YARDS 0   25   50   75   100

McLoyd B'5 4/204

(from an Official Diagram)

APPENDICES

APPENDIX 1A

ABSOLUTE GRADIENTS—1869

Distance from Portmadoc Termini				Length of Planes				Ratio of Inclination		Location
M.	Fur.	Chains	Links	Mˢ	Fˢ	Chˢ	Lkˢ			
0	0	7	29	0	0	7	29	Ascending	1 in 246	Commencing at entrance
0	3	3	73	0	2	6	44	,,	1 in 584·69	gate at Northernmost end
1	1	0	73	0	5	7	0	,,	1 in 1343·50	of the W.S.Coˢ Wharf
1	2	2	73	0	1	2	0	,,	1 in 85·65	abutting on Old Quay
1	2	9	83	0	0	7	10	,,	1 in 100·00	at Portmadoc
2	2	8	21	,,	7	8	·38	,,	1 in 90·51	
4	2	6	46	1	7	8	25	,,	1 in 82·71	Rhiwgoch
6	6	4	76	2	3	8	30	,,	1 in 79·82	Tylers Cutting
7	3	5	98	0	5	1	22	,,	1 in 131·68	Hafod Llyn Station
7	5	1	28	0	1	5	30	,,	1 in 87·64	
7	7	8	48	0	2	7	20	,,	1 in 92·50	
10	2	4	02	2	2	5	54	,,	1 in 85·22	Tunnel 60 yards
11	0	2	65	0	5	8	63	,,	1 in 116·59	{ Tunnel 730 yds through Syenite
11	7	9	07	0	7	6	42	,,	1 in 186·00	Tany Gresia Station
12	2	6	45	0	2	7	38	,,	1 in 143·33	
12	6	8	69	0	4	2	24	,,	1 in 94·56	Junction of Branch Line
13	0	4	92	0	1	6	23	,,	1 in 89·75	Rhiwbryfdir Slate Coˢ Incline
13	1	8	29	0	1	3	37	,,	1 in 60·68	
13	2	0	50	0	0	2	21	,,	1 in 104·90	Welsh Slate Coˢ Incline
				13	2	0	50			

(Branch Line to Duffws)

				Mˢ	Fˢ	Chˢ	Lkˢ			
				0	3	3	25	Ascending	1 in 87·89	
				0	2	4	13	,,	1 in 68·69	} Duffws Station
				,,	0	7	24	,,	1 in 92·00	
				,,	6	4	62	Length of Branch Line		

The above is taken from the Company's archives. Another copy, identical to it, is headed differently thus;
Absolute Gradients of Line at present, there having been various alterations of Line since first construction.

APPENDIX 1B

WELSH SLATE COMPANY & HOLLAND'S INCLINE
(5 December 1834 & 16 April 1835)

Chancery Bill: Henry John Temple, Viscount Palmerston and The Honourable William Powlett (the Orators)

Reciting: The Festiniog Railway Act 2 & 3 Wm IV cap xlviii.
Reciting: The limits of deviation referred to in the Act.

Reciting: The powers contained in the Railway Company's Act for others to lay down 'collateral branches' on their own land and that of others 'with the consent of such other persons' but no power to lay branches without such consent.

Reciting: That the Railway Company have since obtaining their Act 'laid down and are proceeding to construct a railway or tramroad from the said quay at Portmadock' and that the Railway Company in concert with Samuel Holland are proposing to build a branch to Samuel Holland's quarries on the common called 'Pen y gesall' part of the farm called Rhiwbryfdir half a mile distant from the railway.

Reciting: That the proposed branch crossed over the Orators land which was leasehold with eight years of the original term or thereabouts remaining unexpired and that consent to such crossing of their land had been refused by the Orators.

Reciting: That the Railway Company threaten and intend to proceed with construction of the branch and that the Festiniog Railway Company's workmen had already entered and commenced work and had been made by the Orators to desist.

Reciting: That upon being made to desist the Railway Company had served a notice on the Orators to acquire a piece of land of a length of 1081 yards and a breadth of 5 yards 'as now staked and marked out from Holland's quarry through Friddgwair to Pantlleidr through Ddolclupia and Ddolfawr to the railway at Ddolman' and that this notice had been dated 8th November 1834.

Reciting: That not all the proposed branch was an inclined plane 200 yards at the railway end and 300 yards at the quarry end being level.

Submitting: That Holland had no power to construct such branch and so went to the Festiniog Railway Company and they 'concerted and arranged' that the Railway Company should build the branch.

Praying: For an injunction against the Railway Company to restrain them from constructing the branch.

Praying: For subpoenas to be directed to Samuel Holland the Festiniog Railway Company 'and their confederates when discovered' to attend and give evidence.
Dated 5th December 1834

Answer by The Festiniog Railway Company:

Reciting: That the railway may be completed in six weeks time.

Reciting: That by a Lease dated 25th March 1821 William Gryfydd Oakley demised to Samuel Holland the land called Rhiwbryfdir and Talywemydd for a term of 21 years and that by an Assignment dated 31st December 1825 Samuel Holland with W. G. Oakley's consent assigned all his interest in the said Lease to Palmerston and Powlett, and that Palmerston and Powlett on 2nd January 1826 granted to Samuel Holland an underlease of part of the land comprised in the original lease of 1821 for the remainder of the term fixed by that lease less 10 days and it was alleged that such assignment contained a grant of a right of way for Samuel Holland. By an assignment dated 5th July 1831 Samuel Holland assigned to Samuel Holland junior his son all his interest in the leasehold property above referred to which had been assigned to him by Palmerston and Powlett.

Reciting: That the quarry owned by Samuel Holland the Defendant was called Rhiwbryfdir or Upper Rhiwbryfdir.

Reciting: That an agreement had been made dated 16th December 1833 between Henry Archer of Tan y bwlch as managing director and on behalf of the Festiniog Railway Company of the one part and Ellis Owen of Harlech and Owen Humphrey Owen of Cefn Milldir near Harlech road contractors of the other part by which the Owens contracted to make and form the bed of two inclined planes and the roads leading to and from them situated near and leading to and from the quarries now worked by Samuel Holland on a farm called Rhiwbryfdir to the Festiniog Railway at the house of Richard Edwards according to marks then laid down and plans made by John Edwards an engineer the work to be done for the sum of £205. The Owens were to cut rocks and form quays and lay the road 'ready for the iron to be laid thereon'. The line was to be double track and for the first 280 yards from the quarry was to be level or on a gentle incline. At the first incline the length of track was to be 260 yards inclined at 12 inches to the yard and at the foot of this incline the track was to be level for 50 yards. The second incline was to be 160 yards inclined at 8 inches to the yard and from the foot of this incline was to be a length of track 80 yards long on a gradient of ½ inch to the yard. The work was to be completed by 15th April next unless prevented by bad weather and the contractors undertook to lay on more men if the Festiniog Railway was completed sooner. The Railway Company was to pay £30 on 31st January next following £30 on 28th February, £30 on 31st March and £115 on completion or 15th April whichever was sooner. The work was to be certified by John Edwards.

Reciting: That the work which the Owens had contracted to do had not been started by 5th April 1834 and the Agreement had been extended to 10th July 1834 the first payment to be made on 7th May and further payments at the same intervals as originally agreed.

Reciting: That an agreement had been made dated 20th December 1833 between Henry Archer of Tan y bwlch as managing director and on behalf of the Festiniog Railway Company of the one part and John Edwards of Penygroes Llanllyfni engineer of the other part under which John Edwards had contracted to make rollers and barrels for the inclines together with walls and masonry work for £250 plus five guineas for superintending Ellis Owen and partners.

Reciting: That John Edwards died in June 1834.

Reciting: The contract to build the inclines contained in the agreement between The Festiniog Railway Company and Samuel Holland dated 27th August 1834.

Reciting: That the only other way of getting rail access to Holland's quarry is by means of a level.

Reciting: That Lord Newborough's quarry lay 799 yards from the end of the railway and that Casson's quarry lay 820 yards from the end of the railway.

Reciting: That work started on Samuel Holland's incline on 20th May 1834 and continued until 12.0 o'clock on 21st May 1834 'when the said complainants sent a number of men to prevent these deponents from proceeding to make the said inclined planes'.

Reciting: That notice to acquire the necessary land had been served on Palmerston and Powlett on 8th November 1834 and that on 11th November 1834 the sum of £7 had been tendered to them in satisfaction.

Reciting: That application had been made to W. G. Oakley for permission to make the said inclined planes over the said land and W. G. Oakley does not object.

Praying: That the injunction granted to Palmerston and Powlett be dissolved.
Dated 16th April 1835.   Common Seal of The Festiniog Railway
                                                    Company
(The Petitioners duly obtained an injunction against both Holland and the Railway Company—see also *The Times*, 12 December 1834.)

[Spelling as in the original]

APPENDIX IC

House of Commons—Festiniog Railway Bill 1831; List of subscribers

'We whose names are hereunto subscribed Do agree to advance and pay the several sums written by us opposite to our names unto   to be laid out and Expended in making and maintaining a Railway or Tramroad from the Quay at Portmadoc in the parish of Ynyscynhaiarn in the County of Carnarvon to and terminating at a certain Slate Quarry or Slate Quarries called Rhiwbryfdir and Diffus Slate Quarries in the Parish of Festiniog in the County of Merioneth Dated this   day of February 1831

	£ s. d.
Henry Archer Gentleman Tanybwlch	8000..0..0
Edw. Keane, Dublin Esq.	3700..0..0
James Smith, Dublin Esq.	5600..0..0
William Read, Dublin Esq.	5000..0..0
Richard Smyth, Dublin Aldn.	100..0..0
Geo. Archer, Dublin Esq.	100..0..0
Geo. Huddart, Dublin Esq.	100..0..0
Stephen Woulfe, Dublin Esq.	100..0..0
Arth. Perrin, Dublin Esq.	100..0..0
John Foster, Dublin Esq.	100..0..0
John Cummins, Dublin Esq.	100..0..0'

Their occupations were given as:

'Alderman Smith

Stephen Woulfe Assistant Barrister

Edwd. Keane 34 N Great Georges Street and Brother in Law to Richd. Farrell Assistant Barrister

George Huddart Police Magistrate

John Foster Receiver to the Attorney General

J. Smith Merchant

Alderman Perrin of the firm of H. George Grigg & Coy. Stock Brokers

William Read   do.   do.

George Archer Town Clerk of Dublin

Henry Archer son to the late Alderman and City Treasurer.'

Official Return of Proprietors 1886

	Average Holding
8 Debenture holders	£1,500
53 Preference shareholders	943
39 Ordinary shareholders	2,210

APPENDIX ID

SLATE WAGON STOCK-TAKING—JUNE 1862

Names of Quarry	No of Waggons on the Bank	No of Waggons on the Road	No of Waggons at the Wharves	Reserve Waggons 'x' on Repairs	Contingent Waggons for Wrysgan Quarry now in small produce 'x' prospect of produce from the Graig ddu Quarry
W Slate Co	55		30		
Rhir. Slate Co	38		25		
Messrs Holland	46		25		
J W Greaves Esq.	30		20		
F S Percival Esq.	30		20		
Maenofferen Slate Co	25	100	15	50	30
The F Slate Co	25		15		Totals
The Cwmorthin Slate Co	25		10		30
The Rhosydd Slate Co					50
by present system of					190
riding	10		10		160
Messrs Casson & Co	45		20		329
on the F. S. Co's Line		60			
Totals	329	160	190	50	759

APPENDIX IE

Extract: Baddeley & Ward's N. Wales Guide *(7th Edition)* [*pre 1865*]

TAN-Y-BWLCH HOTEL.

This delightful and charming place has of late become one of the most fashionable resorts for families and tourists during the summer months. It is situated on a gentle declivity in the centre of the far-famed vale of Ffestiniog, of which the visitor will have a good view from the house; but if he would see it to perfection, he should take a walk through the plantation to the terrace in front of the Mansion of TAN-Y-BWLCH, the residence of Mrs. Oakeley, who kindly permits the visitors from the inn to view the lovely vale from these grounds. This house is embosomed in an extensive and thriving plantation, and commands a splendid and romantic view, embracing the panorama of the entire vale of Ffestiniog, from Blaen-y-Ddôl (the head of the vale) to the ocean in Cardigan Bay. The river Dwyryd, with its serpentine windings through the vale, has a beautiful effect; while the lofty range of the Merionethshire mountains form an admirable back ground to this fine landscape. Mr. Wyndham, who visited this spot in 1774, was quite enchanted with the sight: he says, 'That if a person could live upon a landscape, he would scarcely desire a more eligible spot than this.'

Coins, urns, and inscribed stones, of Roman origin, have been found in the neighbourhood, which are in the possession of Mrs. Oakeley, the owner of this property. The Roman road from Uriconium to Segontium passed through this vicinity, and another from Tommen-y-mur, where England's monarchs oft encamped, also advanced to Caer Gai. Several days might be spent here very agreeably, in viewing the natural beauties of this romantic district. If the weather is fine, it will be a rich treat for the stranger to visit Moel-Gwdion, but one degree lower than that called Moel-Hebog (the hill of the hawk). From hence may be seen a phenomenon common to Wales. 'On the one side,' says Mr. Pugh, 'midnight appeared; on the other, bright day! The whole extent of Snowdon on our left was wrapt in clouds from top to bottom; on the right, the sun shone most gloriously over the sea-coast of Caernarvon. The hill on which we stood was perfectly clear; the way we came up was a tolerably easy ascent; but before us was a precipice of many hundred yards; and below a vale, although not cultivated, has a primitive appearance, and much savage beauty.' The tramroad for conveying slates from the Ffestiniog quarries to Port Madoc passes on a high elevation above the houses. It is one of the most enterprising conceptions of the day, being cut through rocks nearly the whole length of fourteen miles, and forming an inclined plane all the way of 1 inch in 120. The descent from its commencement to its termination is a most delightful ride. Tourists and visitors may enjoy this high treat in perfection without personal fatigue, as a carriage connected with the Oakeley Arms Hotel has been placed on the line.

There are several waterfalls in the neighbourhood, the nearest of which is the one behind the house; each of them is about thirty feet in depth. When looked at from the base of the rock, over which the river descends, it has a sublime appearance. The scenery from the top of the wood above the inn is much admired. Walks either way are exceedingly pleasant and picturesque. About two miles on the Harlech road, up a wooded valley, are two most interesting waterfalls, one called Rhaiadr-Du (the black cataract), and the other Ravenfall.

Extract: Cambrian Mirror (*published 1851: 1883 Edition*)

The Palmerston Slate Quarry.—(*From a correspondent describing a former visit.*)—'While at Blaenau Ffestiniog we made our way to the Palmerston Slate Quarry, which we were told was the largest and most productive in Wales. The landlady of the Baltic Hotel found us a highly respectable guide, who conducted us up the great heaps of shale, and past the 'finishing' sheds to a narrow-gauge line, along which the huge blocks of slate are brought from the pit's mouth on trucks. On one of these we were bidden to take our seats, the guide sitting just behind us and holding us on carefully, whilst two lads pushed us along through a tunnel about 50 yards long, dark and rather moist. On reaching our destination, where we come to more sheds filled with machinery, we alighted and walked down some steps into the first chamber of the black, smoky mine; there are nine beneath it, right into the bowels of the earth. The miners, who number between seven and eight hundred, were then enjoying the open air during their dinner-hour, and were sitting or lying about near the pit's mouth. Considering the fearful atmosphere so many of them have to work in from six in the morning till 5.30 in the evening, they, most of them, looked very robust and healthy, they were all very civil and well-behaved to us as we passed in and out amongst them, and there seemed a great deal of kindly feeling and good fellowship between themselves. The miners earn from 23s. to 25s. a week, and the slate finishers 45s. This mine made £83,000 clear profits last year (1882), but this was unusually good. It yields an average profit of £50,000 or £60,000. The shaft we went down was pitch dark, and the air was most disagreeable to breathe. A miner lad went before us with a lantern; our guide held me by the arm and my sister followed us closely, carrying a bit of lighted candle, set in a lump of clay, in her hand. We came upon bridges across shafts letting air down to the chambers beneath, where we saw, dimly burning, ever so far down, the lights of the poor miners. The quality of the slate in this quarry is very good, and the mine has already been worked 80 years. Our guide showed us the water-works which pump the water out of the mine, and the slate just as it is after it has been blasted—huge blocks worth about £4 each, which are conveyed to the pit's mouth on trucks, part of the way drawn by horses and then by machinery with wire ropes up the steep incline to where the narrow-gauge line takes it on to the finishing sheds, where it is split, cut in squares, and then sent off to the railroad, to be forwarded to all parts of the world. We took a look at the great engine which sets all the different machinery in motion in the finishing shed, where nothing is done by hand now-a-days except the actual splitting of the blocks of slate, which is an easy task when once the two wedges are driven in. The guide has a fixed charge of 5s. for taking people over the mine, and we were glad to give it to him—he was so civil and so careful over us.'

APPENDIX 1F

THE FESTINIOG RAILWAY AND THE NORTH WALES HYDRO-ELECTRIC POWER ACT OF 1955. SUMMARY OF INFORMATION

FIRST notice that the Company was to lose part of their property by compulsory acquisition under the Bill was received during November 1951. Owing to a change of ownership, the old Board was not affected subsequently.

Notice of the impending situation had come to the attention of the new owners shortly after the take-over and consequently the Company was one of two objectors to the project. The following notes are extracted from the Minutes of evidence taken before the Select Committee of the House of Lords, 29–31 March, 1–6 April 1955.

The Petition of the Festiniog Railway against the Bill was supported by Mr. S. Cope Morgan, Q.C.

The Central Electricity Authority (formerly the British Electricity Authority) was first informed that the Festiniog Railway was disused and pointed out that it was shown thus on the Ordnance Survey map. They said the railway company had made an application to abandon their line in 1950 but that the Abandonment of Railways Act of 1850 did not permit an Abandonment Order being issued.

The Festiniog objected to the term 'disused' being used but C.E.A. blamed the Ordnance Survey for inaccuracy if this was the case.

The Festiniog Company had changed hands on 24 June 1954.

There had been an earlier scheme of 1952 for an ordinary hydro-electric scheme which would have submerged part of the railway; the then-owners of the railway had not objected to the scheme at the time.

C.E.A. estimate that it would cost £100,000 to re-align railway to avoid flooding under present scheme, and that it would not be in the public interest to spend money in this manner. After discussions between the F.R. and the C.E.A. Engineer, the C.E.A. found it impracticable to accommodate the F.R. in any way.

(The second objectors to the scheme was a group which included the Council for the Preservation of Rural Wales, The British Mountaineering Council, etc.)

F.R. petition against the compulsory acquisition of their land, saying it is without precedent, further maintaining that the works should be altered in such a way to avoid flooding the line or that a deviation should be built for them at public expense to allow of through running, access to stations, etc.

Counsel for the Authority stated: 'My personal view is that your railway is just a hobby for elderly gentlemen and young men. It is playing trains. I may be wrong in this, but you asked for my personal views.'

It transpires that the edge of the lake formed by the C.E.A. dam would be 20 feet above the north end of the Moelwyn Tunnel.

F.R. propose a deviation to leave the present course along the site of an earlier line (that of 1836) and make a new tunnel 1,900 feet in length to come out above the reservoir on a higher course. The total length would be about one mile and a temporary wooden viaduct round the Generating Station would be replaced by a permanent viaduct in due course. This would permit the through running which the F.R. desired and had always aimed at.

Authority contend that their scheme had been publicised for at least two years before the new owners took any action. This was denied by the Festiniog, who contended that the Authority had not consulted them and that they had tried to 'steam roller' the case. The Authority estimated that a deviation built to *their own plans* would cost £123,000.

(The Clerk to the Festiniog U.D.C. supported the scheme and rejected the opposition put to it by the railway company, saying it would prejudice the Authority's scheme and that the district had been covered by road motor services since about 1923.)

Alan Francis Pegler, Chairman of the Festiniog Railway Company, in evidence, said he had first been interested in the railway in December 1952. A meeting between the B.E.A. and the F.R. took place on 3 November 1954 and the B.E.A. showed they were sceptical of the F.R. Company's *bona fide* intention of reaching Blaenau Festiniog and running a through railway service. They contended that, for instance, three out of five sleepers would require renewal for a start.

The F.R. had asked that they be given a period of time in which to prove their *bona fide* intention and if proved, to obtain their proposed deviation.

Mr. Pegler admitted that he had paid £3,000 for a controlling interest in the Company. (At this juncture the financial structure of the Company was quoted.) B.E.A. assert that this sum was paid for a derelict concern, a fact which the previous owners had acknowledged it to be. At that time the income from rents, etc., was about £600 per annum.

Mr. Pegler quoted from authoritative sources concerning the losses which the Festiniog had sustained, not in running their own line, but in trying to make the Welsh Highland a paying concern.

(Here receipts and traffic figures are given.)

During this, Mr. Cope Morgan interrupted and was told, 'Mr. Cope Morgan, go and play with your trains.'

B.E.A. maintain that in the purchase price of £3,000 Mr. Pegler has obtained about 80% of the share capital. Moreover, they stress that this is only a hobby and that the railway as a through route cannot be of importance. It would not matter if it went nowhere. If the Talyllyn Railway (previously referred to by Mr. Pegler) can run at a profit and yet serve no place of importance, so also can the Festiniog. The new owners cannot prove that the railway will ultimately be a commercial success and B.E.A. contend that public money would be wasted on a deviation if the company failed. In any case, the F.R. would be compensated for the loss of their land and railway. B.E.A. stressed that Mr. Pegler could not bring any figures to prove what costs or profits might be expected and contend that £3,000 has merely been given for an inexpensive way of providing a hobby. There was no evidence that the public wished to use the railway and the people of Blaenau Festiniog have already stated that they 'have a perfectly good bus'.

After consultation, the Chairman of the Committee made the following statement:

'. . . from all I have said it will be appreciated that the Committee are unable to accept Mr. Cope Morgan's amendment. I have been asked to say that they have done that after great searching of heart and with very great regret and on the ground of expense that would be involved in that deviation . . .'

The scheme, known as the Central Electricity Authority's Festiniog Pumped Storage Scheme, was authorised by the North Wales Hydro-Electric Power Act 1955, will be the first of its type in this country and the largest so far contemplated in the world. (1956.) The scheme required the enlargement of Llyn Stwlan as an upper reservoir and the damming of the Afon Ystradau to form a lower reservoir. On the bank of the lower reservoir the generating and pumping station will be constructed. The railway will be either obliterated and/or submerged by the lower reservoir between the north end of the Moelwyn Tunnel and Tan-y-Grisiau station (approx.).

(*Further developments on this subject are covered in Chapter 20*).

Work was commenced in May 1956 and postponed until April 1957 when it began again. The first of the four units were scheduled to be in operation in late 1961 and the whole scheme in early 1963. The Festiniog track was lifted almost to the tunnel mouth by June 1957 and stored nearby. The track through the former L.N.W.R. Exchange station was obliterated by an access road.

The 1962 position found the Festiniog Railway under water almost for the whole of its length between the tunnel north mouth and Tan-y-Grisiau station. The track was *in situ* from thence to Glan-y-Pwll. Track was being reclaimed from the tunnel, the closed north mouth of which is submerged.

In late 1961, the Festiniog Company appealed against the decision given by the Lands Tribunal in March 1961 (a right of appeal is permissible by a party whose land is compulsorily acquired on a point of law). The railway had claimed £180,000 compensation on the basis of Section 2, Rule 5 of the Acquisition of Land (Assessment of Compensation) Act 1919, the case being heard in London on 11–13 May 1960. In March 1961 the Tribunal had ruled that compensation granted to the Company could not be on the basis of reinstatement but was governed by other rules of the above Section 2. The Company appealed against this decision. In their opinion the cost of providing a new link with Blaenau using a new tunnel and extending along the east shore of the dam, equalled the figure above-named. It was proposed to proceed with this scheme even if the claim for full compensation failed.

However, the Lord Justice did not think that, notwithstanding the case was fully merited on many counts, 'the amenity value was such as to justify reinstatement at any cost.' The appeal was dismissed.

(A Summary of the Court of Appeal Festiniog Railway Co. v. Central Electricity Generating Board was given in *The Guardian* 3 February 1962).

(The author is indebted to the Divisional Secretary (North West Merseyside and North Wales Division, Central Electricity Authority) for a copy of the Minutes referred to above, and also assistance in connection with the work in progress.)

APPENDIX IG

UNINTENTIONAL HUMOUR—AND OTHER CORRESPONDENCE

On the Bogie Principle—1885

'The Bogie Principle consists in each pair of wheels moving on a central pivot, so that they can turn while the carriage above remains unbent.' [Murray's *North Wales*, 1885.]

On a Matter of Phonetics—1836

Homfray was quoted at House of Commons Enquiry 1836 regarding rail weights: '... they should be £25 ... and were only £16 ...'

On Access to Tan-y-Bwlch by Rail—c. 1925

'The most amusing way to get to Tan-y-Bwlch is not to walk but to use the Welsh Highland Railway. This narrow gauge railway has champion qualities ...' From a Guide Book of the early 1920s.

On a Matter of Direction—1881

John Parry Jones (driver) describing accident on 14 November 1881—'My engine is an eight-wheeled double bogie Fairlie engine ... I was running chimney first ...'

On a Matter of Disc Signal Aspect—1881

David Davies (driver) reporting on incident at the Harbour and the Down Distant—a Disc Signal: '... as soon as the distant signal was lowered ...'

A Gloomy Prospect—1930

'After working a passenger service for the past sixty-seven years, this once prosperous line closed down on 20 September. It will still be used for goods and slate traffic and one quarrymen's train daily will run from Portmadoc in the morning, returning from Blaenau Festiniog in the evening. All the Fairlie engines have now been scrapped, and the line is worked by the four-wheeled saddle tank tender engines dating back to the early sixties.

The Welsh Highland Railway has been closed for passenger work. During the summer season one train each way on three days a week has been the only service. Goods trains will still be run when required.' [*Locomotive Magazine,* 15 October 1930, p. 353.]

Faults on the G.P.O. Telephone—1913

'As numerous faults on the Department's route on the Portmadoc Embankment have been traced to cotton waste having been thrown by your Company's servants amongst the wires, I am writing to ask if you will kindly issue instructions that will prevent a continuance of the nuisance.' [Letter from Post Office Telegraphs to F.R. Secretary.]

Smoking in Carriages—1906

'I beg to call your attention to the fact that there is only one carriage on the quarrymen's train for smokers and non-smokers, this morning I noticed there were two gangs of platelayers and the brakesmen, besides ordinary passengers in the 3rd class bogie and nearly all of them smoking; it is very awkward especially for ladies to be in a carriage among so many men smoking, you are aware that there are many going up for the L. & N.W. and G.W. Rlys. to have cheap tickets for Liverpool etc. and people that cannot bear smoking and knowing that we have only one carriage for ordinary passengers are obliged to go with the Cambrian via Afonwen. Miss Greaves very often goes up from here and always asks if we have more than one carriage for passengers on the quarrymen's train, as the tobacco smoke is unbearable at times in it she says. Would it not be possible to close one half of the 3rd class bogie for smokers and the other half for non-smokers.' [Letter from R. Evans to Mr. Crick.] 'This is so . . . the tobacco smoked by some of these men is the vilest . . .' [F. G. Crick to J. S. Hughes.]

Smoke in Tunnels—*1901*

'A passenger with a party travelling up to Blaenau yesterday says that he never experienced anything like going through the Tunnel. The smoke with the heat being fearful and he suggested that notices should be put up in the carriages to have the Windows closed before entering the Tunnel. Being strangers he did not know anything about it.' [Letter from D. Owen to J. S. Hughes.]

Loneliness at Dduallt—*1900*

'I beg to inform you that I am feeling very lonely here especially at night and every place here is to [*sic*] far away to go at night would you kindly favour me to go down at night I am quite willing to pay Dd. Davies to come here for me in the morning and I hope you will comply with my request.' [Letter from Dduallt stationmaster to Mr. Hovendon.]

Driver J. Davies's Illness—*1927*

Correspondence between Col. Stephens and R. Evans:

'. . . From enquiries made I understand that Driver J. Davies will not come on duty for some time yet. On the advice of his specialist he is waiting for something like a wart on his nose to get more ripe so that it can be removed. It will take from four to five weeks for this to come out after the first application of a special ointment by the specialist. Personally, I do not think it would be advisable for us to ask Davies to be examined by the Company's doctor as I think he is rather depressed owing to his illness, and one would not know how he would take instructions to be examined, but so far as the complaint is concerned, the doctors here know but very little about the wart referred to, and such warts are treated by a specialist who lives in the country, and no one except himself has the recipe used to remove the warts.'

'. . . I have heard all about these Specialists. There seems to be a certain amount of magic about it, which, I must confess, does not impress me. I suppose you are satisfied that there is no humbug in this matter? I hope I am doing nobody an injustice when I say that, when I hear about people going to a Quack Doctor in the middle of a field, it raises my suspicions that we have not got altogether to the bottom of the case. I do not believe that warts cannot be removed, except by some arrangement with the Evil one, who appears to be invoked in dealing with matters of this description.'

'. . . I am quite satisfied that there is no humbug in the matter as regards Driver J. Davies, being off duty ill. This can be confirmed by Mr. Nevitt. Davies is quite a conscientious man and is not one of these that would lose a day unless he is compelled to do so by illness or some other cause. As regards his complaint, I am afraid that I cannot give a clear definition of this in a letter, but will explain fully to you on your next visit to Portmadoc. The doctor who attends Davies is one of the best known doctors in England and Wales as regards the warts referred to in my letter and not only people from this district visit him to get warts removed, but people from England come to be attended by him.'

'. . . I understood, from Mr. Nevitt, that the wart specialist was a farmer, or some such person. If he is a qualified doctor, my information is incorrect.' [*F.R. Magazine*, No. 6, Autumn 1959.]

APPENDIX 1H (*Calculated from Official Returns*)

MINERAL TRAFFIC

Tons carried per goods train mile: 1864–1912

Year	Tons	Year	Tons	Year	Tons
1864	1·994	1881	1·962	1897	2·629
1865	2·038	1882	1·924	1898	2·564
1866	2·019	1883	1·701	1899	2·474
1867	2·428	1884	1·629	1900	2·367
1868	2·748	1885	1·690	1901	2·380
1869	—	1886	1·560	1902	2·415
1870	—	1887	1·689	1903	2·349
1871	2·408	1888	1·862	1904	2·237
1872	2·767	1889	2·090	1905	2·181
1873	2·664	1890	2·155	1906	2·085
1874	2·648	1891	2·127	1907	2·035
1875	2·860	1892	2·041	1908	2·358
1876	2·265	1893	2·559	1909	2·679
1877	2·313	1894	2·640	1910	3·066
1878	1·759	1895	2·457	1911	3·309
1879	1·768	1896	2·526	1912	3·176
1880	1·877				

Gross Revenue per ton of minerals moved: 1865–1910

Year	£	Year	£	Year	£
1865	0·1579	1881	0·1139	1896	0·0801
1866	0·1446	1882	0·1126	1897	0·0790
1867	0·1471	1883	0·1128	1898	0·0788
1868	0·1457	1884	0·1124	1899	0·0810
1869	—	1885	0·1111	1900	0·0759
1870	—	1886	0·1089	1901	0·0710
1871	0·1480	1887	0·1059	1902	0·0707
1872	0·1318	1888	0·1060	1903	0·0722
1873	0·1295	1889	0·1072	1904	0·0749
1874	0·1250	1890	0·1058	1905	0·0765
1875	0·1202	1891	0·1064	1906	0·0753
1876	0·1111	1892	0·1088	1907	0·0775
1877	0·1144	1893	0·0791★	1908	0·0738
1878	0·1136	1894	0·0775	1909	0·0710
1879	0·1153	1895	0·0736	1910	0·0695
1880	0·1137				

★ Fall in income probably the result of the Rates and Charges Act 1892.

Comparative Tonnages

Tons carried per goods train mile

Year	Festiniog	Croesor (1)	F. & B.R. (2)	G.J.P.R. (3)	T.R. (4)
1866	2·019	—	—	—	—
1867	2·428	—	—	—	0·609
1868	2·748	—	—	—	0·594
1869	—	—	—	—	—
1870	—	—	—	—	—
1871	2·408	3·991	—	—	0·636
1872	2·767	4·141	—	—	0·670
1873	2·664	3·766	—	—	0·623
1874	2·648	3·827	—	—	0·610
1875	2·860	3·378	—	0·343	0·643
1876	2·265	2·767	—	0·502	0·644
1877	2·313	3·007	32·58	0·587	0·744
1878	1·759	4·125	26·62	0·724	0·740
1879	1·768	3·390	15·59	0·455	0·580
1880	1·877	4·476	31·72	0·445	—
1881	1·962	—	51·59	0·380	—
1882	1·924	—	53·05	—	—
1883	1·701	—	—	—	—
1884	1·629	—	—	—	—
1885	1·690	—	—	—	—
1886	1·560	—	—	0·650	—
1887	1·689	—	—	0·104	—
1888	1·862	—	—	0·438	—
1889	2·090	—	—	0·125	—
1890	2·155	—	—	0·262	—

(1) Horse Tramway.
(2) Festiniog & Blaenau Rly. (until part period gauge conversion).
(3) Gorseddau Jc. & Portmadoc Rly.
(4) Talyllyn Railway.

APPENDIX II

Boston Lodge Vernacular—1940

Locomotives

The term 'Fairlie' was not used. On 'Double-engines' the frame in the centre between bogies was 'the cellar'. (The bogies themselves were called 'Top' or 'Bottom').

'Single engine' meant *any* engine not a double-engine.

'Car'board' was a material used, suitably greased, for packing double-engine bogie centres.

Rain strips on cab roofs were 'landers'.

Enginemen were either drivers or stokers. The term fireman was not used.

Wagons

6-wh. No. 8 was 'The Iron Bogie'; and the small iron bolsters were 'Iron Bogies'.

Permanent way trolley was a 'Slave Wagon'.

Bolster runners were 'sledges'.
Slab wagons (vertical) were 'Donkey Trucks'.

Carriages

Any passenger carriage, four-wheeled, 'a Birmingham'.
Quarrymen's carriages or Nos. 21 and 22 'Workmen's'.

Track

A passing loop—'siding'.
Loop Line—the Glan-y-Pwll Deviation.
Dduallt station—Rhos

Quarry Branches

Operating a rake of wagons on an incline was to 'crewl a run'.

Trains in general

A peculiar method of describing the two sides of any vehicle and especially a complete train was related to the positions of the Time Clock and Stationary Engine respectively in the Erecting Shop of the Works. These were to be found on the left, and right, of the building so that the left side of stock became the Clock Side and the right, the Engine Side no matter whether the vehicle itself had ever had occasion to go into the Erecting Shop or not.

Reference to side of stock was often by 'clock side' or 'engine side' in relation to Boston Lodge Erecting Shop (See *F.R. Magazine* No. 39, p. 25).

APPENDIX 1J

Stock on hand   Boston Lodge   30 June 1873

(*extracts*)

Locomotives: *Mountaineer, Princess, Prince, Palmerston, Welsh Pony, Little Giant, Little Wonder, James Spooner;* 5 tenders
Carriages: 1st class 3; 2nd class 4; 3rd class 7; quarrymen's 32; platelayer's 1 (1)
Goods wagons: 40
Iron horse boxes: 11 (2)
Goods wagons, new 4t: 4
Vans: 2
Water truck: 1
Stone trucks: 6
Cattle trucks: 2
Timber trucks pairs 7
Slate wagons: 975 (Details appear in Stock Book)
Break Truck for Minffordd: 1 (3)
Carriages: 2 (4)

New Work:	£	s	d
Work done on new Bogie Vans and cars bogies not included	511.	18.	11
2 Compo carriages from Brown, Marshalls and Co. bogies not included	811.	16.	9
Work done on Bogies—wheels, Axleboxes, Springs etc for 2 Bogie Cars—3 Bogie Vans and 2 composite Carriages	398.	11.	1
Work done Goods Lime and Flour and Timber Trucks including wheels, Axles and Bushes	170.	9.	9

Work done on the Tanybwlch new Station:

    paid to Contractor   £698. 18. 6
      Do by own men   55. 1. 1   753. 19. 7

Stock on hand   Boston Lodge   30 June 1874

(*extracts*)

Locomotive truck £65 and wood packing £6.10.0

10% added to loco stock value (increase in the price of materials)

Carriages: 1st class 3; 2nd class 4; 3rd class 7; Composite carriages 2 (1 1st, 1 2nd, 5 3rd class compartments) (5); Quarrymen's carriages 32; Guards Vans 2 (6); Bogie Guards Vans 2.

Goods Trucks: 40; Iron horse Box wagons 11; Goods trucks bought of W Davies Festiniog 4 (9)

New goods wagons to carry 5 tons 10;

Lime or Flour wagons to carry 5 tons 4;

Water Truck 1; Stone Trucks 6; Cattle Trucks 2; Timber Trucks pairs 7; Timber Trucks new pairs heavier wheels and axles 3;

Break Truck for Minffordd Junction 1 (£14.10.0) (3)

    1 Carriage (Mr Spooner's) £13.10.0 (7)

    1   Do   (Line Foreman's) £9.0.0 (8)

Work on additional rolling stock

    3 Vans

    2 composite carriages

    2 Ballast cars

    (Completed for all excepting one of the Vans)

Notes:

(1) No details.

(2) ex-'Horse Dandies' used for coal traffic.

(3) Possibly for gradient into exchange yard.

(4) and (6) Possibly same item, i.e. 4 wheel Brake Vans.

(5) New bogie stock Nos. 15 and 16.

(7) 'The Boat'.

(8) 4 wheel inspection carriage.

(9) No details.

SUMMARY STOCK RETURNS 1865–1950

End June	Locos	Tenders	4 wheel-coaches			Q'y-men	Bogie Coaches	Bogie Pass. Vans§	Goods Wagons	Cov'd. Wags.	Pairs of Timber Wagons	Cattle Wags.
			1st	2nd	3rd							
1865	—	2	2	2	4	25	—	—	30	—	6	1
1870¶	7	4	3	4	7	32	—	—	51	—	7	2
1875	8	5	3	4	7	44	2	2	65	4	13	2
1880	9	5	5	3	6	43	6	4	85	4	19	2
1885	8	4	4	—	10	44	6	5	100	4	19	—
1890	9	4	5	—	9	33	6	5	108	3	19	4
1895	9	5	5	—	9	35	6	5	114	3	19	4
1900	9	5	4	—	10	37	8	5	119	8	19	4
1905	9	5	4	—	10	37	8	5	117	9	19	4
1910	9	5	4	—	10	36	8	6	114	12	19	—
1915	9	5	4	—	10	33	8	5	—	13	19	—
1920	9	5	4	—	10	33	8	5	B	13	19	—
1925	9	5	4	—	10	36	8†	5	—	13	19	—
1930	9	5	x	—	x	x	8†	5	120	13	19	—
1935	6	4	x	—	x	x	8†	5	110	13	19	—
1938	6	4	x	—	x	x	8†	5	110	13	19	—
1946	6	4	x	—	x	x	9‡	5	110	13	12	—
1950	6	4	x	—	x	x	9‡	5	110	13	12	—

End June	Slate Wags.	Stone Wags.	Water Wags.	P./way Wags.	Bogie Ballast	Coke Wags.	Carriage Truck	4 wh. Pass./ Pass./ Goods Brake Vans	Tool Vans	Trav. Crane	In-spect. Trlly.	Pet. Trctrs.
1865	770	—	—	—	—	—	—	} —	Not separately listed			
1870¶	878	—	—	—	—	—	— Pass	} 3	before 1915			
1875	969	6	I	I	I	I	—	} 3				
1880	988	7	2	I	2	I	—	} 3				
1885	1031	7	I	—	2	I	I	—				
1890	1017	4	I	—	2	I	I	—				
1895	1068	4	I	—	2	I	I	—				
1900	1095	4	I	—	2	I	I	—				
1905	1095	4	I	—	2	I	I	—				
1910	1095	4	I	—	2	I	I	—				
1915	1215*	x	x	—	x	x	I	} 2	I	I		
1920	1215	x	x	—	x	x	I	} 2	I	I		
1925	1219	x	x	—	x	x	I Goods	} 2	I	I	3	2
1930	1095	x	x	—	2	x	—	} 2	I	I	x	2
1935	1043	x	x	—	1C	x	—	} 2	I	I	x	2
1938	1043	x	x	—	1C	x	—	} 2	I	—	x	2
1946	978	x	x	—	1C	x	—	} 2	—	—	x	2
1950	978	x	x	—	1C	x	—	} 2	—	—	x	2

x Not known.
* Includes Open Wagons from 1915 to 1925 inclusive.
† Not including Open 'Hudson' Stock.
‡ Including 1 ex-W.H.R. Carriage No. 23.
§ Including Bogie Vehicles when rebuilt as Compo-Passenger Vans.
C This is the 'Cleminson' six-wheeler.
B See Slate Wagons after 1915 until 1930.
¶ plus 11 'Iron Horseboxes' (1872).
Stock as shown on above Return is not always accurate but is quoted from Annual Reports.

INCREASE AND DECREASE IN NUMBER AND COST OF ROLLING STOCK IN 1907 AS COMPARED WITH 1880

	Increase in Number	Decrease in Number	Increase in Cost £ s d			Decrease in Cost £ s d		
Locomotives		I				987	9	6
Tenders			64	7	6			
Carriages		2ᴬ	1959	13	0			
Vans	Iᴮ		518	16	7			
Goods and Coal wagons	32		1134	3	0			
Slate wagons	103		2220	6	2			
Auto Brakes for Engines, Carriages and Vans from 1892			1884	16	1			
	136	3	7782	2	4	987	9	6
Deduct decrease	3		987	9	6			
Nett Increase	133		6794	12	10			

A *Carriages*
Added 36 Quarr. Carriages of larger size
        to replace worn out smaller size
      2 Compo. Bogie Carriages
      2 Third class   do.
      —
     40
Deducted 42 Worn out Quarr. carriages
        abandoned and replaced by the
        above 36 of larger size
      —
      2 Decrease.
      —

B *Vans*
2 Bogie Vans added
Less 1 Old type abandoned.
  —
  1 Increase.
  —

APPENDIX IK

RETURN OF PERSONS EMPLOYED—1884

Administration
  1 Secretary (also General Manager)
  2 Employed in Secretary's
    Department
  1 Accountant (also Traffic
    Manager)
  1 Assistant Accountant
  1 Clerk
  1 Messenger
  2 Employed in Accountant's
    Department

Traffic Department
  7 Station Masters
  8 Clerks
  2 Passenger Guards
 12 Signalmen
  9 Porters and Messengers*
  3 Inspectors
  6 Goods Guards/Brakesmen
  1 Shunter
  5 Other

Locomotive Department
  1 Locomotive Engineer
  1 Locomotive Foreman
  6 Mechanics
 37 Artisans
  4 Drivers
  4 Firemen
  — Labourers

Civil Engineer's Department
  2 Draughtsmen
  2 Gangers
  2 Artisans
  6 Mechanics
  8 Platelayers
  3 Labourers

Stores Department
  1 Storekeeper
  2 Clerks
  1 Workman

Miscellaneous
  1 Police Inspector

* On the subject of porters generally, they were a race which Spooner apparently did not hold in high esteem for he writes: '... the porters will be able to shunt the trucks and carriages without aid of either horse or engine, which has not only the effect of saving time and expense, but affords fuller employment to the porters, obviating idle habit, under such circumstances so common in that class of officials'.

STATIONS AND STAFF—1920

(From statistics given to Light Railways Investigation c. 1920)

	Station Master	Clerks	Pass. Guards	Goods Guards	Porters or Porter/ Signal-man	Signal-men	Gate Keepers	Oilmen	Shunters	General Waiting Room	Parcels Office	Booking Office	Porters Room	Refreshment Room	Ladies Waiting Room
Portmadoc	1	2	—	—	A	2	—	—	1	x	x	x	x	x	x
Boston Lodge	—	1	—	—	2	—	1	—	—	x	—	x	—	x	—
Minffordd	1	—	—	—	—	—	—	—	—	—	—	—	—	—	—
Minffordd (Weigh Office)	—	3	—	—	—	—	—	—	—	—	—	—	—	—	—
Penrhyn	1	—	—	—	1	—	1	—	—	x	—	x	—	x	x
Tan-y-Bwlch	1	—	—	—	1	—	—	—	—	x	—	x	—	—	x
Dduallt	—	—	—	—	—	—	—	—	—	—	—	x	—	—	—
Tunnel	—	—	—	—	—	1	—	—	—	—	—	—	—	—	—
Tan-y-Grisiau	1	1	—	—	1	—	—	—	—	x	—	x	—	—	x
Exchange L.N.W.	1	1	—	—	—	2	—	1C	1	x	—	x	—	—	x
Duffws	1	1	1	2	1	B	—	1	—	—	—	x	—	—	—
(Unattached)	—	—	—	—	—	—	—	—	—	—	—	—	—	—	—

A Two porters act as guard for 5 and 6 hours respectively, daily. 1 porter acts as pointsman and oilman for part of day. 1 parcel porter—4 porters in all.
B One porter acts as pointsman for part of day—4 porters in all.
C Oilman also acts as porter.

*Extract from Royal Commission on Accidents to Railway Employees Report for
year ended 31 December 1898*

Employees			
Clerks	10 men	3 boys	
Engine Cleaners	5	2	
Engine Drivers	6		
Firemen	7		
Gatekeepers	4		
Greasers	3		
Guards (Goods)	2		
Guards (Passenger)	1		
P.W. Inspectors	1		
Labourers	2		
Lampmen		1	
Mechanics	28	5	
P.W. Men	10		
Pointsmen	1		
Porters	8	1	
Shunters	2		
Signal Fitters	2		
Signalmen	5		
Station Masters	8		
Yardsmen	3		
Miscellaneous	2		
	110	12 = 122	Total

'No employee on duty as driver, fireman, guard or signalman for more than
twelve hours during 1901.'

STAFF DUTY SHEET

DUFFWS STATION

Griffith W. Pugh
(Shunting Guard)
[Minffordd]

July 31st (month) and on—1904

Assist guard check tickets of quarrymen's train on way up in morning. Shunting at Duffws, Dinas, Tan-y-Grisiau, G.W. and L.N.W. sidings.
Weigh slate trains in your charge for L.N.W. and G.W.
To be always quick in clearing main line at Glan-y-Pwll for passenger train.
Hours: 5.40 a.m. to 3.25 p.m.

John L. Jones
(Shunting Guard)
[Penrhyn]

Take charge of special engine and do all shunting at Duffws, Tan-y-Grisiau, G.W. and L.N.W. sidings.
Act as brakesman from Minffordd every Tuesday and Friday and relieve G. W. Pugh at 3.30 p.m. daily and act as guard on Down quarrymen's train.
Hours: 9 a.m. to 6.35 p.m. save Tuesday and Friday when 6 a.m. to 2 p.m. and 3.30 p.m. to 6.35 p.m.

Jonah Jones (Porter) [Genfron Terrace B.F.]	Attend morning and evening trains at Blaenau Junction in turn with R. Pugh. Clean office and waiting rooms. Attend loading and unloading all goods to and from G.W.R. and assist in goods shed and on platform. To relieve oilman when off duty. Hours: Various per different weeks.
David Owen (Foreman Porter) [Tabernacl, B.F.]	Clean offices and waiting room, check goods and wagon unloading and returning, attend passenger trains. To be guard of last Up and Down trains to Tan-y-Bwlch every other week with Robert Pugh. Hours: Various per different week.
Robert Pugh (Oilman) [Diphwys Terrace, B.F.]	Check and oil slate and coal wagons. Sweep out quarrymen's coaches and oil twice weekly. Assist cleaning station. Attend to shunting guard when shunting in station yard and to morning and evening trains at Blaenau Junction in turn with Jonah Jones and to assist generally. To be guard last Up and Down trains to Tan-y-Bwlch every other week with David Owen.

J. P. Roberts, Clerk in charge.
F. G. Crick, Traffic Manager.

UNIFORMS

All employees except cleaners were provided with uniforms.

The two passenger guards had blue frock coats, gold braided, and pill box hats. Gravity slate train workers were provided with oilskins.

All buttons were of brass with coat-of-arms on them, and certain grades had the coat-of-arms on their cap badges. A popular but unofficial form of head gear was a nautical variety of peaked cap.

In the old and spacious days the station staff also had blue uniforms with gold braid, the station masters having a pill box hat.

C. E. Spooner appears to have favoured a top hat but his sons wore bowlers; William Williams preferred the bowler and his successor, Robert Williams, the nautical cap—head gear very popular in the Works.

At Portmadoc and Duffws, town porters with hand carts were employed. The hotels did their own carrying with horse and cart.

WAGES

February 1900

Wm. Williams, Locomotive Superintendent	40/– per week
D. Owen, Station Master, Portmadoc	29/–
S. Crick, Audit Clerk	30/–
R. Evans, Audit Clerk	14/–
G. H. Yoxall, Clerk, Penrhyn	17/–

A. Pritchard, Clerk, Boston Lodge	32/–
A. G. Crick, General Manager's Assistant	34/–
J. P. Roberts, Duffws	27/–
J. D. Jones, Clerk, Duffws	8/–

February 1901

Old hands (i.e. 76 years old) given 5/– week 'for a short time' on retirement.

1906

W. John Evans, Clerk at Blaenau Festiniog station   6/–

1911

W. John Evans, moved to 'Blaenau' station (Duffws)   9/–

1917

Wm. Pugh, Minffordd Crossing keeper (pensioner)   8/– wages + 8/– 'War Bonus'

APPENDIX IL

PERSONNEL

The lesser administration of the Company is complex and tedious; for half its history economic pressures made it necessary to combine duties; these tended to be terminated when the holder retired. In some cases a post was created and held only for the working life of the employee.

There appears to have been no succession in secondary administration, so no attempt is made to list Traffic Superintendents, Traffic Agents, Permanent Way Inspectors, Locomotive Shed Foremen, etc. When a post is in existence, appropriate references are made in the text.

CHAIRMEN OF BOARD—1844–1975

GREAVES John Whitehead	1844–48
DURHAM Andrew	1851–52: 1856–58: 1861: 1864: 1867: 1869–76
GAUSSEN Charles	1862–63
THOMPSON Livingston	1853–54: 1859–60: 1865–66: 1868
HUDDART George Augustus	1855 only
GIBBS George	1849–50
LIVINGSTON John Graves	1877–92
ELLIOTT John W.	1893–1904
HUDDART George A. W.	1907–08
THOMPSON R. Norman	1905–06
GREAVES Richard Methuen	1909–20
JACK Henry Joseph	1921–24
STEPHENS Holman Frederick	1925–30
DAVIES Evan R.	1931–35
DAVIES W. Cradoc	1936–55
PEGLER Alan F.	1956–71 (became President 1972)
ROUTLY E. J.	1972– (in office)

BOARD OF DIRECTORS

1832–1843   As Managing Director (under the Act of Incorporation) Henry ARCHER was a director 1832–37. In 1836 Edward CARREG (see Treasurers), James GANDON and Livingston THOMPSON formed a triumvirate of directors to control ARCHER's decision-making—ARCHER left the Company after dispute in 1837. Some directors must have served additionally 1832–43 but records are incomplete, as there were no Annual Reports prior to 1844. Record for 1859 is incomplete, except where given. Records for 1870–77 do not name all Board.

1844–1955

Name	Years	Note	Description	Location
GREAVES John Whitehead	1844–48: 1850–57	(1)	Quarry Proprietor	Tremadoc
DURHAM Andrew	1844–58: 1860–62: 1864: 1866–76	(2)		
GANDON James	1844–46		Captain	Dublin
GAUSSEN Charles	1844–49: 1851–57: 1860–77		Lawyer	Dublin
THOMPSON Livingston	1844–73*		Attorney	Brynkir
HUDDART George Augustus	1847–58: 1860–64: 1866–73†		—	
GIBBS George	1847–56		—	Donaghadee and
THOMPSON John Graves	1851–58: 1860–63		— changed name from Thompson to Livingston (Lon. Gaz. 12 May 1863)	Clifton
SPOONER Samuel	1850–58			
LIVINGSTON John Graves	1866–69: 1876–95‡	(3)	Major	
KERL Thomas	1874–86		—	
CAINES Thomas Plunkett	1878–88: 1892–93		—	
HALPIN George	1874–87	(4)	Colonel	
HARDY Frederick Norman	1886–90	(5)	Captain	
HUDDART Cuthbert H. Charles	1887–1900	(6)	Doctor	
ELLIOTT John W.	1888–1905	(7)	—	
HUDDART George A. W.	1894–1908	(8)	Reverend Doctor	
THOMPSON R. Norman	1895–1906	(9)	Doctor	
FELKIN H. M.	1899–1903	(10)	—	
COWPER H. A.	1900–06		—	
ELLIOTT John (Jnr)	1904–07	(10a)		
BOWTON Richard	1906–21	(11)	Quarry Proprietor	Ffestiniog
GREAVES Richard Methuen	1907–20	(12)	Quarry Proprietor	Tremadoc
VAUGHAN Frederick	1907–20	(13)	Managing Director F.R.	Portmadoc
ROBGENT (or ROBJENT) Frederick P.	1908–21	(14)	Stockbroker: Company Director	Newport, Mon.
HUDDART George William Otter	1909–13	(15)	—	
MACAULAY John	1914–18	(16)	Surveyor	West Bank, Midlothian
JACK Henry Joseph	1921–25	x (17)	Company Director	Dolgarrog

Name		Role	Dates	Location
DAVIES Evan R.			1921–35	
STEWART Sir John H.	x (18)	Solicitor (b. 1871: Town Clerk, Pwllheli 1894–1920)	1921–23	Pwllheli
WESTALL George	x (19)	Company Director	1924–29	London
STEPHENS Holman Frederick	x (20)	Surveyor	1924–31	Holborn
NICHOLLS Eric H. R.	x (21)	Lt. Colonel R.E. ex Supt. of Line G.W.R. (joined 1884)	1924 only	Tonbridge
WESTALL H. Lander	x (24)	Surveyor	1930–39	London
DAVIES C. Evan	(22)	Solicitor	1932–55	Chadwell Heath
ROBERTS D. H.	(23)	Engineer	1935–43	West Dulwich
DAVIES W. Cradoc		Solicitor	1936–55	Llanberis
WESTALL J.		—	1940–42	Pwllheli

* Also became largest shareholder.

† No precise record but probably served 1874–77 additionally as became one of two paid directors 1875.

‡ No precise record but probably served 1870–75 additionally as became one of two paid directors 1875.

x Also director of Welsh Highland Railway—not necessarily concurrently.

(1) Also Treasurer: 1843–47: 1856–68. Resigned 1869 so as Quarry Proprietor could oppose 1869 Bill.

(2) Died in office 1876: Chairman sixteen non-consecutive years.

(3) Was Chairman sixteen consecutive years: resigned February 1893 'I am getting old'. Died 1895.

(4) Died 1894. Director, Great Northern Railway of Ireland.

(5) Appointed in place of Livingston Thompson, who had resigned due to ill health 1873.

(6) Died 1891.

(7) Died of pneumonia at Royal Sportsman Hotel, Portmadoc, en route for Board Meeting, August 1900.

(8) Died in office 1908.

(9) Died 1907.

(10) Resigned 1900 due to deafness; in favour of Chairman's son (Elliott). Stayed on to 1903 and succeeded by Elliott (Jnr).

(10a) Resigned 1907.

(11) Resigned 1907 but not accepted.

(12) Director of de Winton & Co., Union Ironworks, Caernarvon, as reconstituted 1891.

(13) Appointed first Managing Director: first appointed General Manager. Chosen by Elliott (Snr) to succeed him, 1907. (Vacancy by Thompson's death.)

(14) Solicitor of Newport, Mon., also Chairman, Mold & Denbigh Junc. Rly.: West Somerset Mineral: Director, Didcot, Newbury & Southampton Rly.; Harborne Railway.

(15) Resigned 1914 over Vaughan compromise affair.

(16) Resigned 1918.

(17) Resigned as Chairman, November 1924: as director, November 1925. Director, Snowdon Mountain Railway.

(18) Died in office 1934. Director, Snowdon Mountain Railway.

(19) Resigned 1923.

(20) Died 1930.

(21) Died 1931.

(22) Managing Director, Snowdon Mountain Railway Ltd. from 1930: died 1960.

(23) General Manager, Snowdon Mountain Railway Ltd.

(24) Director, Snowdon Mountain Railway.

COMPANY SECRETARIES—1832–1975

PIM J. Greenwood	during 1833
CARREG Edward	1832: 1834–42
COSGREAVE	–1844
SPOONER James	1844–56 (1)
SPOONER Charles Easton	1856–87
HUGHES John S.	1887–1907
CRICK A. G.	1907–22 (2)
HUSON W. R.	1922–24 (3)
DAVIES C. Evan	1924–55
BELLAMY W. B.	1956
WAYNE F. T.	1957–71
SCOTT R. D. I.	1972– (in office)

(1) 'Clerk' 1844–49.
(2) Started with Company as Assistant Clerk from October 1889: became Traffic Superintendent 1916 when F. G. Crick retired from post: moved to Dolgarrog under F.R./W.H.R. re-organisation. Father was Sydney Crick, Audit Accountant.
(3) Salary £100 per annum: became Secretary to Snowdon Mountain Railway Limited at same date.

TREASURERS—1832–1856

ARCHER Henry	Treasurer to 1831 scheme
CARREG Edward	1832: 1834–42
GREAVES John Whitehead	1843–47: 1856–68
SPOONER Charles Easton	1847–56

LOCOMOTIVE SUPERINTENDENTS—1879–1944 (Post created 1879)

SPOONER George Percival	July 1879–June 1880	(1)
SPOONER Charles Easton	July 1880– 1881	(2)
WILLIAMS William	1881–June 1909	(3)
WILLIAMS Robert	June 1909–May 1924	
STEPHENS H. Frederick	May 1924–October 1931	(4)
AUSTEN W. H.	November 1931–October 1936	
ALEXANDER S.	November 1936	(5)
WILLIAMSON James	1937–1944	(6)

(GENERAL) MANAGERS—MANAGING DIRECTOR—1832–1955

ARCHER Henry	1832 (Managing Director under Act of Incorporation)—1837	
HUGHES John S.	October 1889–December 1908	
VAUGHAN Frederick	January 1909–July 1922 (Managing Director) but July 1921–March 1922 as General Manager only	
TYRWHITT S. C.	April 1922–September 1923*	(7)
NICHOLLS Eric H. R.	May 1924–May 1925	(8)
STEPHENS H. F.	May 1925–October 1931	(9)
DAVIES Evan R.	October 1931–December 1934	
EVANS Robert	January 1933 (acting)	
	January 1935–June 1955	(10)

* John MAY appointed *Superintendent of Line* October 1923–May 1924 whilst there was no General Manager.

(1) Salary £100 per annum.
(2) Assisted by J. S. Hughes at £50 p.a.: C. E. Spooner salary for other posts was £600 p.a.+£50 p.a. as Loco. Superintendent.
(3) Probably began as an 'engineer' employee 1851.
(4) Died whilst in office: held other posts simultaneously.
(5) Also resident engineer of Snowdon Mountain Railway Ltd.
(6) Of Cambrian and Great Western Railway: used as Consultant from 1937 to end of running services—was Assistant Engineer of Cambrian Railways at grouping.
(7) Loaned by G.W.R. as Assistant to General Manager, but due to Vaughan's death became General Manager: was by then General Manager also of North Wales Narrow Gauge Railways Company replacing Aitchison.
(8) Became Managing Director of F.R. and General Manager of W.H.R.: intended to be appointed Engineer but unwilling to act.
(9) Became Chairman and Managing Director at £200 p.a. Later Engineer and Locomotive Superintendent additionally.
(10) Born 1880: joined Company as office boy 1893: retired 1955. Died Prestatyn 1960 (took F. G. Crick's position as Audit Clerk 1916).

ENGINEERS 1847–1944 (Post created 1847)

SPOONER James	1847–August 1856
SPOONER Charles Easton	August 1856– 1889
HUGHES John Sylvester	October 1889–December 1908
JONES Roland	January 1909–September 1921
WILLIAMSON James	October 1921–March 1924
STEPHENS Holman Frederick	April 1924–October 1931
AUSTEN W. H.	November 1931–October 1936
ALEXANDER S.	November 1936–
WILLIAMSON James	1937– 1944

APPENDIX IM

SLATE TONNAGES & PASSENGERS (1913–1946)

Year	Tonnage	Passenger	Year	Tonnage	Passenger
1913	83,000 / Ship 26,926	132,481	1931	50,000	58,165
1914	68,000	Not Pub.	1932	46,000	50,364
1915	45,000	Not Pub.	1933	50,000	65,854
1916	52,000	Not Pub.	1934	54,000	78,001
1917	45,000	Not Pub.	1935	47,000	70,473
1918	43,000	Not Pub.	1936	36,000	65,395
1919	42,000	108,152	1937	36,000	59,300
1920	53,000	117,843	1938	35,000	59,008
1921	53,000	130,612	1939	30,000	46,475
1922	51,000	155,456	1940	14,000	—
1923	52,000	133,592	1941	17,000	—
1924	54,000	111,763	1942	15,000	—
1925	65,000	199,304	1943	12,000	—
1926	66,000	149,234	1944	12,000	—
1927	66,000	145,411	1945	9,000	—
1928	67,000	140,867	1946	4,500	—
1929	67,000	118,159	(to end		
1930	59,000	74,057	of July)		

APPENDIX IN

Miscellaneous Statistics
(as returned by the Company)

CIVIL ENGINEERING (pre-1910 official statistics)

Cutting Width—rock: 8 feet at formation level
     Slope—rock: ¼ to 1
     Depth—maximum: 27 feet
Masonry Embankments Width: 10 feet at formation level vertical walling
                           infilled earth (or)
               slope: 1 to 6
               height—maximum: 60 feet

(17) Stone arch underbridges: 10–15 feet span on masonry abutments
     Culverts on masonry abutments with slab spans: 1–3 feet span
     Culverts ditto but having stone arches: 8–15 feet span
     (Longest span under railway: 19 feet)
     Road overbridges: wrought iron girder spans with cast iron cross girders
     spanned by small brick arches.
     Width between abutments—Single line: 10 feet*. Double line: 17 feet
     vertical clearance rail to overhead structure: 9 feet
(5) Footbridges (and timber or wrought iron cattle)
(2) Tunnels: Garnedd: 60 yds. × 8 ft. wide × 9 ft. vertical (partially lined—
          but no lining when first used)
          Moelwyn: 730 yds. × 8 ft. wide × 9 ft. vertical (three ventilating
          shafts)
     Clearance between adjacent tracks: 4 ft. 6 in.—6 feet (also given as 5 feet)
     Overhang of 4 wh. carriages (6 ft. 3 in. wide): 2 feet each side
     Sidings: 200–400 yards long
     Turntable Sizes (diameter):

		feet	inches
Boston Lodge	(Loco. type)	23	11
Glan-y-Pwll	(Loco. type)	24	4
Portmadoc	(Wagon type)	6	2
Penrhyn, Tan-y-Bwlch, Tan-y-Grisiau	(Wagon type)	6	8

Cranes (1919)	6 hand cranes at stations
	2 do do at Works (½–6T)
	1 travelling crane (¼T)
Sidings (1919)	7 intermediate: all locked from frame
Weigh Bridges	4
Coal Tipplers	1 Minffordd
	1 Blaenau Festiniog (L.N.W.R.) (and used by Brookes'
	for granite)
Cattle Docks	None
Carriage Lights (1919)	Acetylene Gas or Oil
Heating	Footwarmers
Stopping Places	All stations save Dduallt and Moelwyn Halt

* A minimum of 11 ft. 6 in. would have been adopted in 1863, if this had
been practicable.

'*Record*' *Figures quoted from* Railway News, *2 Dec. 1916:*

Heaviest Up train   190 tons
Longest Down Gravity train   440 yards
Largest no. of passengers carried in ordinary train   804
   do   do   do   do   in a year   216,209
   do   annual tonnage: slate   138,958
                  coal etc. (gen. goods)   35,344
Last year of Ordinary Dividend: 1912 $= \frac{1}{2}\%$

APPENDIX 10

ACCIDENT RETURNS 1862–1923

There appear to have been no reportable accidents in the period 1862–71 or in 1873, though immunity from them was far from being the case, as a perusal of the local papers will testify for the above period. The following occasions are quotations from Official Sources only—and occasionally, from *The Mining Journal.*

29 August 1872

On the arrival of an excursion train at Minffordd station a passenger got out of one of the carriages on the wrong side and fell down a slope* on the Cambrian Railways and received such injuries that he died a few days later. [This begs the question as to whether the locking of doors was being carried out?—Author.]

28 October 1872

While a train which was a long one and had over-reached the station and across the high road at Diphwys, Festiniog was standing still a quarryman attempted to cross over the couplings when his leg was caught between the buffers and broken. He had been warned by the Company's servants not to try to cross.

(At this time the Railway bridge at Duffws had not been built.)

11 June 1874

Whilst a passenger train was running near Portmadoc one of the carriages caught a sleeper which was lying too near the rails and consequently left the line as did also another carriage. No one hurt.

19 June 1874

In consequence of some person or persons having placed several stones on the rails of the line in Cae Valley Wood sixteen waggons of a slate train were thrown off the road. No personal injury.

19 November 1874

A loaded slate train came into collision with an engine and three empty trucks which had fouled the Main line. Ten waggons were thrown off the rails in consequence and much damaged. No one hurt.

4 December 1874

An accident occurred to a slate train near the Welsh Slate Company's wharf at Portmadoc in consequence of a stone getting between the points. Three waggons left the road. Slight damage to a wall near.

* Presumably the embankment slope.

17 April 1875

A slate train came into collision at the Dinas Station with some other loaded waggons three of which were thrown off the rails and slightly damaged. No one was injured. The accident was caused by the breaksman of the slate train not being able to stop his train soon enough.

13 May 1875

A truck was being loaded with stone by a contractor and his men at one of the quarries and the break not being properly fastened, when struck by some other trucks it started off and ran down the line to Dinas Station where it came into collision with some loaded coal waggons. No one was hurt but two of the coal trucks were damaged.

4 June 1875

In consequence of a porter failing to open the points at Tan-y-grisiau station the front wheels of an engine when passing over them took a different road to the hind wheels. The engine was travelling at a very slow speed and it came to a stand after running a few yards. No one was injured and very little damage was done.

31 July 1875

Davies, a stoker, was injured when his head came into contact with an over-bridge at Tan-y-grisiau whilst the train was travelling.

14 August 1875

When a passenger train was drawing up at Duffws Station the axle of the driving wheel of the engine broke. The axle was made of a sort of brittle Bowling iron and had been running about three years. The breakage is supposed to be due to bad material and a very sharp corner between the wheel and the bush. There was a previous flaw at the place of fracture.

23 September 1875

A passenger train when approaching Duffws Station came into collision with a waggon which a porter had left standing on the main line during shunting operations. (No one appears to have been injured.)

5 November 1875

As a passenger train was leaving the Duffws Station an iron vice was pitched too near the line by a breaksman and one of the First Class carriages which was empty caught it and was thrown off the rails. The draw-bar of the van was broken and the carriage slightly scratched.

31 December 1875

An axle of a waggon in a slate train broke at Tan-y-grisiau in consequence of which three waggons left the rails damaging the permanent way. The axle was made by Caine & Co. of Liverpool and had been running since 6 July 1867. There was a flaw at the place of fracture.

4 January 1876

The Glanypwll crossing gates near Duffws Station were run through by two slate waggons which had escaped from a siding. No one was hurt.

29 February 1876

In starting a train near Penrhyn Station the draw-bar of a carriage broke dividing the train but the driver and guard succeeded in regulating the speed of the engine and break van so that the carriages came up gently and without doing any damage.

20 March 1876

As a shunting engine was taking a train of empty waggons to Duffws Station it ran over a sheep and some of the waggons left the metals one of them being damaged. The sheep being in a curve the engine driver could not see it until too late to pull up. There was no one hurt.

21 March 1876

Whilst a coal waggon belonging to the Welsh Slate Company was being taken from Duffws Station to a siding at Dinas one of the axles broke and the waggon left the rails. The permanent way was damaged and a portion of a wall was knocked down. The axle was made of Bagnel iron by Messrs. Caine & Co. of Liverpool. It commenced work 12 August 1875 and had run about 1,400 miles. It broke close to the boss of one of the wheels and there was an old flaw at the fracture.

17 May 1876

Whilst a slate train was travelling between Tan-y-grisiau and Tan-y-bwlch an axle of a waggon broke. The axle was made of the best iron by Messrs. Caine & Co. of Liverpool and had been running since September 6th 1870. The fracture occurred close to the boss of the wheel and appeared to have been broken for some time.

24 May 1876

An axle of a waggon in a slate train broke at Tan-y-bwlch Station and seven other waggons left the rails and a quantity of slates were damaged in consequence. The axle was made of Bowling iron by Messrs. Caine & Co. of Liverpool and had been working for about twenty years. The fracture occurred close behind the boss of the wheel and there was a considerable flaw in the middle as though it had not been properly welded.

21 September 1876

When two loaded timber trucks were being moved at Baslon Works [sic] curve about a mile from Portmadoc Station the first pair left the rails and fell over causing the second pair to do the same. The fencing at the side of the line was damaged as were also one or two of the trucks.

26 September 1876

D. Pugh, foreman porter at Duffws had his arm injured during shunting operations.

3 October 1876

The door of an empty waggon opened and came in contact with an iron support in the tunnel near Tan-y-grisiau throwing the waggon off the road and breaking several chairs.

11 October 1876

Seven empty slate waggons and two loaded coal waggons ran away from Duffws Station into the stop-blocks placed on the rails at Glanypwll Junction about a mile from Duffws Station. No one was injured but the slate waggons were a good deal damaged likewise the fencing and walls on the side of the line; the coal waggons kept the line and were not damaged. The accident was caused by the shunting guard not properly securing the waggons by spragging the wheels.

19 October 1876

A goods engine ran into the stop-block at Duffws Station and was thrown from the line and slightly damaged as also was the permanent way.

8 December 1876

As a slate train was travelling near Portmadoc the tyre of one of the wheels of a waggon came off. No one was hurt but the permanent way was damaged. The tyre was made of Bowling iron by Messrs. Caine & Co. of Liverpool and was simply shrunk on to the wheel. The waggon had been running for seven years and there was no flaw or crack in the tyre which had been reduced by wear from $\frac{3}{4}$ inch to $\frac{1}{2}$ inch in the tread.

(After 1876 the Returns contain only bare statistics, though more exactly categorised. The foregoing Inspecting Officers' Reports are the only source of detailed accounts.)

1877 One goods train derailed
One train travelled in the wrong direction through points
One train hit cattle or other obstruction

1878 One collision between goods trains
One passenger train derailed
Two goods trains derailed
Two axle failures
One railway servant injured in accident to train

1879 Two goods trains derailed
One wheel failure
Three axle failures

1880 No accidents reported

1881 One railway servant killed by train travelling in the wrong direction through points
Two passenger trains derailed
One axle failure
Three broken rails

19 February 1881 (*Mining Journal*, p. 226) 'The severity of the recent gale was so great that one of the carriages of the Festiniog Railway was blown off the line near Diphwys. Fortunately no injuries were received and the passengers assisted the officials in replacing the carriage on the rails.'

1882 One passenger train derailed
One goods train derailed
One tyre failure

1883 Two axle failures
One railway servant killed walking on the line to or from home

1884 One railway servant injured during shunting

1885 One goods train derailed

1886 One collision between passenger trains
One passenger train derailment
One axle failure.

1887 One railway servant injured uncoupling vehicles

1888 One train hit cattle or other obstruction

1889 No accidents reported

1890 One passenger train derailed
One railway servant injured through accident to train

1891 No accidents reported

1892 No accidents reported

1893 One train hit cattle or other obstruction
One axle failure

1894 Two axle failures

1895 One collision between a passenger train and a goods train

1896 One trespasser killed
One passenger train derailed
Four axle failures

1897 One railway servant injured getting on or off engines, waggons etc.
One collision between a passenger train and a goods train
One train ran through a level crossing

1898 One axle failure

1899 One passenger train derailed
One axle failure

1900 Three axle failures

1901 Three passenger trains derailed
One railway servant injured coupling or uncoupling vehicles

One trespasser killed
1902 One tyre failure
One passenger train derailed
One goods train derailed
1903 Three axle failures
1904 Two trains ran through level crossings
One 'miscellaneous' train in motion accident
One dangerous slip of cutting or embankment
One axle failure
1905 One trespasser injured
One passenger injured (see next item)
One train ran through level crossing
One tyre failure
1906 One railway servant injured getting on or off engines or waggons
One railway servant injured in 'miscellaneous' accident whilst working on
the line
One railway servant injured in shunting accident
One railway servant injured falling off engine or van at rest
One axle failure
One coupling failure
One axle failure
1907 One trespasser injured
One railway servant injured by stumbling whilst walking on the line
One axle failure
One dangerous slip of cutting or embankment
One railway servant injured whilst attending machinery of engine in motion
One railway servant suffered 'miscellaneous' injury
1908 Two railway servants injured whilst coupling or uncoupling vehicles
One railway servant suffered 'miscellaneous' injury
One railway servant injured whilst attending engine at rest
One railway servant injured by the falling of rails, sleepers, etc.
One railway servant injured by 'miscellaneous' on track!
1909 One railway servant injured whilst coupling or uncoupling vehicles
One railway servant injured working cranes or capstans
One railway servant injured falling from ladder or scaffold
Two railway servants injured 'by miscellany'!
1910 One axle failure
One tyre failure
1911 One railway servant injured whilst coupling or uncoupling vehicles
One railway servant killed getting on or falling off engines, waggons, etc.
One railway servant injured stumbling whilst walking on line
One tyre failure
1912 One railway servant injured whilst attending to the machinery of engines
in motion
One railway servant injured by the falling of waggon doors, lamps, bales,
etc.
One railway servant injured 'miscellaneously'
One passenger train derailment
One train running through gates or other obstacles
One tyre failure
1913 One railway servant injured by falling of rails, sleepers, etc.
One railway servant injured at work on line
One railway servant injured 'miscellaneously'
One passenger train derailment

1914 One passenger train derailment
     One railway servant injured coupling or uncoupling vehicles
     One railway servant injured 'miscellaneously'
1915 One goods train derailed
     Two trains ran through level crossing gates
1916–1919 NO RETURNS PUBLISHED
1920 No accidents reported
1921 One goods train derailed
1922 One goods train derailed
     Two axle failures
1923 No accident statistics published after this date for individual minor railways

('Miscellaneous' would appear to be one of the more dangerous injuries with which the railway employees had to contend!)

Though the aforementioned covers the official list, there were numerous derailments which were never reported. The Letter Books of the Company contain inter-departmental correspondence regarding causes and results of accidents and a few extracts from the 1919–20 period will suffice to show how misleading are the official records.

1919 *Welsh Pony* off the track Duffws station. Signal fitter had repaired points and failed to adjust the blades afterwards.

Bull came through gate of Sandpit Siding at Boston Lodge and was struck by a passenger train. Owing to a long train of wagons on the siding, the gate had been left open.

Both *Palmerston* and *James Spooner* derailed at Harbour station in the same week; the following month the latter burst a cylinder whilst starting the 4.15 p.m. train from Blaenau, a mishap possibly caused by a crack due to the Harbour derailment.

1920 Owing to a broken axle on a gravity train, twenty-two wagons fell into the field at Dduallt.

On the same day two gravity trains collided in Minffordd station (one being stationary) and three vehicles including a brake van were written off for rebuilding completely.

Owing to a rock fall at the Maenofferen Quarry, seven slate wagons were buried; some were only fit for scrap (Nos. 230, 468, 616 and 859). The remainder might be rebuilt. Coal wagons were sent up to the quarry to collect the pieces but Maenofferen filled them with their own scrap and the F.R. discovered them at Glaslyn Foundry.

It was said at this time that every wagon which went out to Rhiwbach came back damaged.

The Mining Journal often reported a tragedy which missed notification elsewhere. Thus (on 29 December 1877): 'The Festiniog Narrow Gauge Railway has enjoyed great freedom from accidents since its construction but on 18th inst. David Evans got jammed between two slate wagons and received injuries which caused his death.'

Nevertheless, the Railway enjoyed a fine record considering its special circumstances. No fare-paying passenger ever received fatal injuries.

APPENDIX 2

SPOONER & CO. (CIVIL ENGINEERS)

The Company of this title (this being the official wording) appears to have occupied the talents and time of the Spooners and others, and to have been openly carried on at least in part from the same building at the Harbour which housed the offices of the Festiniog Railway. Even the Festiniog Manager was known to be on the pay-roll of Spooner & Co. Whilst this may savour of the modern tax racket of being permitted two lots of expenses, the two businesses were so openly worked that there were certainly 'arrangements' between them. It could be the beginnings of the business were a continuation of James Spooner's 'extra-Company' activities after his death in 1856—largely surveying and quarry agency. There would be a natural surplus of energy in terms of steam locomotive design for narrow gauge (1860–63) and on a less parochial basis thereafter. Probably Charles' move from Beddgelert after his wife's death in 1860, to Tremadoc, gave him more opportunity on which he might have been happy to lean at a sad time. However, another ten years at least were to pass before an actual business of this title crystallised!

Many of the drawings which survive at Portmadoc today and which have precious little bearing on the Festiniog itself, may be the early fantasies of those whose minds had expanded far beyond the Festiniog domain, and were concerned with overseas railways' development, of which the Darjeeling system comes readily to mind. In fact, one may ask how many of those early narrow gauge schemes in which the whole Spooner family, each or collectively, were engaged, were born beside the Glaslyn? Possibly more was done here than is fully realised. From evidence, it could be that Spooner & Co. 'just happened'. The Spooner family, from the moment of the successful inauguration of steam power upon the Festiniog, would be the subject of growing enquiry for narrow gauge lines and equipment. It would be natural if they set up a separate business of Consulting Engineers to deal with them on a commercial basis. The Festiniog Company received many questions about gauge, manufacturers, etc., and whilst it could not take advantage of its experience, by setting up under another name, members of its staff *could* do so.

Charles Spooner's son, George Percival, seems to have been the locomotive designer. Charles was then working on passenger stock, probably with Festiniog requirements firstly in mind, with suitable developments for elsewhere. With the whole of the Festiniog line available for experiment and experience and with the lifetime of familiarity, Spooner & Co. enjoyed a unique position. But, the Company does not seem to have flourished as it might. To begin with, Portmadoc was away from industrial centres and it seems that arrangements had to be made with the Vulcan Foundry to build locomotives if required. There were also internal difficulties. There would seem to be an end to Spooner & Co. business shortly after G.P. left.

Suggestions about the designing activities (so far as railway stock is concerned) stem from knowledge of the drawings at Portmadoc, the Spooner & Co. album, drawings in Vignes' remarkable album and in various other places such as books and catalogues—not a very complete background. One may hazard the suggestion that ALL the many schemes for narrow gauge projects of 2 ft. gauge in North Wales, sprang from Spooner & Co. even if they used others as their mouthpieces; they may not have been engaged directly in these schemes but only as engineers to them; the largely-uncompleted North Wales Narrow Gauge Railways enterprise would seem to have been a child of Spooner imagination and one can find the origin of its stock designs in early drawings made at Portmadoc. It would be impossible to say if locomotive and carriage plans for this company were strictly Spooner or Spooner & Co. as there was essentially no difference. The Spooners were in friendly collaboration with the landowners and other gentry who were to form these new companies and the Portmadoc offices would obviously be a centre for local as well as foreign interest.

In this aspect, Spooner & Co. were in direct competition with another local firm, de Winton & Co. of Caernarvon. In the mid-1870s, de Winton put out their first vertical boiler engine for use in the slate quarries where hand or animal traction had held sway. Their first two appeared in 1875 but had only one cylinder each and double-flanged wheels suited to the rough quarry tracks and only to stub-switched pointwork. They also produced the *Rhymney* for Pen-yr-Orsedd (just below Spooner's quarry) in 1875 and within the next two years turned out a number of similar engines.

Three Spooner engines only can be accounted for with certainty, each of them for Spooner's own quarry or a neighbouring one.

Kathleen, *Vulcan Foundry, 805 of 1877. 7 × 12 in. cyls. Class BA*

It is possible that *Kathleen* was the first Spooner engine; it is the earliest yet recorded. It went new from the makers to Alexandra & Moel Tryfan Quarries in May, 1877. Wheels were 1 ft. 9 in. diam. on a 4 ft. wheelbase. The family likeness with engines on the N.W.N.G. and Festiniog is unmistakable. Like the other two to be mentioned later, the boiler had a marine firebox to clear the rear axle and balance the overhangs more nearly. There was a weatherboard reminiscent of the single engine *Taliesin*, and similarity in the boiler mountings, footplate shape, wheel slots and side tanks. The footplate was entered from the left; a coal bunker was on the right. A brass plate on the side tank read 'Specially made for Spooner & Co., Portmadoc'. The name was painted on above this, together with a fleur-de-lis above it and a certain amount of lining out. The overhangs and wheelbase were 3 ft. 4 in. + 4 ft. + 4 ft. 2¾ in. Pressure was 180 lb.; boiler 3 ft. 3 in. × 2 ft. 9 in.; length overall, 11 ft. 6¾ in.; width, 5 ft. 3 in.; height to top chimney, 7 ft. 6 in.

Kathleen appears to have worked in this group of quarries until scrapped. There was one accident which was never forgotten—the original boiler was replaced with a new one by Vulcan in 1896 and this required to be retubed in 1901 (which sounds like indifferent handling), the engine was sent to de Winton for this, probably on a flat truck along the Bryngwyn branch—on 11th February 1907, a tube burst whilst the engine was running footplate first and killed the fireman. The driver managed to stop the engine and was unharmed. Just how the working justified the use of a fireman is not clear, but probably he acted as shunter and pointsman as well. At the Board of Trade enquiry, the fault was laid on the fitter at de Winton's, who 'was illiterate'—the manager of Alexandra, nevertheless, was fined £50, a big sum in those days.

The engine continued to work until March, 1931, when she was abandoned and left to decompose. Some of the usable fittings were put on the mole-like Hunslet saddle tanks which worked through the low tunnel in the same quarry. Finally, the remains were sold as part of the scrap drive in 1940. So *Kathleen* had a fairly long life after all. There was one slight modification which the photo Pl. 2Q (of unknown date) shows; the sister engine *Kelso 2*, working at the same quarries, was cut up in 1916. Her front cab sheet with bent top and different spectacle glasses was put on *Kathleen* when probably the additional 'quarter cab' (a piece of local ironmongery) was added to give more weather protection still. Otherwise, the picture shows the engine little changed, and her driver, Cunnah.

Kelso 1, *Vulcan Foundry, 810 of 1877. 7 × 12 in. cyls. Class B*

This engine was new to Braich Quarry in 1878; the quarry was adjacent to the Alexandra and like it, connected later with the Bryngwyn branch of the N.W.N.G., but had a separate branch line to it from that leading to Alexandra. Though basically similar to *Kathleen*, there were certain differences; there was no footplating forward of the side tanks, the driving wheels were one inch smaller and the footplate was entered over the rear beam. There is no drawing of this engine but the particulars given were supplied by the builders; there survives however, a most interesting photograph which appears to be taken in the precincts of these quarries on Moel Tryfan, though exactly which is not possible to say. The de Winton alongside may be the Cilgwyn Quarry's *Madge*. The maker's plate reads either 1880 or 1889, but it is doubtful if any de Winton's were made in 1889 so an 1880 engine must be chosen.

It is known that a Spooner engine was sold later to the Votty & Bowydd Quarry, Blaenau Ffestiniog, where it was known as *Taffy*. It seems unlikely that the name was actually carried and was probably a nickname. Locomotives of steam origin were rebuilt at certain Ffestiniog quarries, some having overhead double-pole pick-ups to take current from electric cables and having electric motors fitted between the frames. By 1939 *Taffy* was converted into a battery-electric locomotive on the premises, and on closure of the quarry, sold to

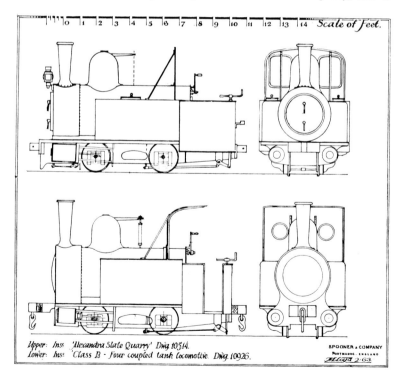

Upper: Inss 'Alexandra Slate Quarry' Dwg 10514.
Lower: Inss 'Class B - four coupled tank locomotive. Dwg. 10926.

SPOONER & COMPANY
PORTMADOC. ENGLAND

Aberllefenni Slate Quarries Ltd. at the head of the former Corris Railway, in August 1963. This conversion worked almost entirely underground and in July 1971 was involved in tipping rubbish from wagons into a disused subterranean part of the workings. Going out of control, it fell over 200 ft. into the chamber where it could not be recovered. In this way the whole unit was lost, the mainframe being the complete assembly of 1877.

The side tanks were jettisoned on to the rubbish tips at Votty where the Author found them in 1943—no marking survived on the sides and only the handrail and curved tank top gave hint of the Spooner 'handwriting'.

Kelso 2, Vulcan Foundry, 832 of 1878. 6 × 10 cyls. Class B

Vulcan Foundry retained dimensions and date for this engine of 1877, but it was only recently that the drawing was discovered (dated 8 February 1878) which agreed with the figures given, even though the date is incorrect. Despite this, there seems no doubt that the drawing is of *Kelso 2*. It may seem odd that two engines with identical names were made for the same quarry in the same period but such a habit is not unknown among industrial concerns. As yet, no picture has been found of this engine, but the curved upper edge of the weather-sheet and the smaller cylinders are confirmed by the drawing. Pen-yr-Orsedd Quarry records show an engine of this name as withdrawn by them in 1916. This quarry was slightly lower down the mountain face and not connected with the N.W.N.G.R. but with the Nantlle Tramway. Transfer could easily be made and perhaps *Kathleen* at that date acquired the weather-sheet of *Kelso 2* which she certainly did not possess if her maker's drawing is to be relied upon for the engine as built.

Almost twenty-five years ago whilst researching in Ffestiniog quarries the Author found a cast oval plate propped up on the weigh-house window ledge at a quarry. In raised letters it reads: SPOONER & CO No. x99 PORT-MADOC. One of the numbers has fallen off, it might be therefore, 199 or more. The remaining figures are pressed into holes by lugs cast on the back of the numbers, a nice touch. The plate probably came off the side of a wagon, in much the same manner as happened to Festiniog stock.

There is another drawing of a developed four-coupled tank, more de-luxe in character, such as might have been used for contracting purposes on the N.W.N.G.R.—no engine to this drawing has been discovered.

The firm's stamp and formal address was 'Spooner & Co., Portmadoc, England', a device possibly employed to facilitate overseas business where 'England' would mean something but 'North Wales' very little!

In correspondence with the late Thomas Spooner Lascelles he referred to an Album of photographs which he said was the property of Spooner & Co. and which had been lost when the family became divided among itself.

Here is a batch of locomotives which had only one common denominator with the three already discussed . . . in that they are attributed to Spooner & Co. Even the Works plates were different.

The evidence of the Album pictures supports the theory that the business seems to have lapsed after G. P. Spooner left. None of the Album pictures is new; the identical illustrations with names (where given) and the Works plates altered, are published in the Brush Bulletin No. 5 dated January 1904. The Brush Electrical Engineering Co. Ltd. was a successor to the Falcon Engine & Carriage Works Ltd. of Loughborough.

There seems to be no connection with the Vulcan batch of the late 1870s and this one; perhaps there had been an interval when little or no business was being done by the Company but fresh impetus had re-opened trade. If all these engines were built by Brush (or more correctly, Falcon) then who designed them, Spooner & Co. or Falcon? There is little doubt that in this second phase of Spooner & Co. they were acting as agents for Falcon products and none of the designs stemmed from Portmadoc.

By and large therefore, the second phase is less Spooner and more Falcon. To widen conception of the firm it is helpful to fill in the blanks with the aid of the Falcon Catalogue (or Brush Bulletin).

(The information on the first line is taken in each instance from the Album.)

Neg. 50 0–4–0T 2 ft. gauge 'Spooner & Co., Engineers, Portmadoc, England'.

The identical illustration appears on p. 7 of the Bulletin except that the buffers and couplings have been removed by photographic process. Painting and lining remain the same; the Works plate is the same shape and in the same position but the plates have been changed (see above). Accepting in all the following cases that the rail gauge usually approximates to the driving wheel diameter we can add dimensions.

Class A No. 9 Code *Moutardier*. Cyls. 7 in. × 12 in. Driving Wheels 2 ft. diam. Wheelbase 3 ft. 6 in. Water 200 galls. Tractive Effort 2,450 lb. Total Heating Surface 138 ft. sq. Grate Area 3½ ft. sq. Weight in Working Order 9½ tons. Suitable for 28 lb. rail. Price £705. Name in catalogue. None.

Neg. 1 0–6–0T 2 ft. gauge *Alosno* 'Spooner & Co., Engineers, Portmadoc'.

Page 9 of the Bulletin shows the identical engine but the side rods are fractionally moved and the handbrake handle has been turned!

Class B No. 1 Code *Mozzicoda*. Cyls. 8 in. × 12 in. Driving Wheels 2 ft. 6 in. Wheelbase 9 ft. 3 in. Water 300 galls. Tractive Effort 2,560 lb. Total Heating Surface 204 ft. sq. Grate Area 4 ft. sq. Weight in Working Order 13½ tons. Suitable for 22 lb. rail. Price £915. Name in catalogue. *Puebla*.

In this instance, no alterations by photographic process.

Neg. 48 0–4–4T 2 ft. gauge 'Spooner & Co., Engineers, Portmadoc, England'.

Probably in primer livery, no name or lining out.

Neg. 52 0–4–4T *Paimoco* 2 ft. gauge. 'Spooner & Co., Engineers, Portmadoc, England'.

(Neg. 48 carries the caption: Minas d'Alosno Railway, Spain, *Alosnito*.)

These two are sister engines and have very slight variations in finish.

The identical picture to *Paimoco* appears in the Bulletin p. 16 and is precise in every detail save that the photographer has clearly used the engine without its name but complete with livery, for the catalogue illustration, and then the signwriter has added the name and the plate has been changed for the Spooner agency print. For this gauge we can obtain the following information:

Class D No. 1 Code *Mulcenda*. Cyls. 8 in. × 14 in. Wheels 2 ft. 3 in. and 1 ft. 4 in. Rigid Wheelbase 3 ft. 6 in. Total Wheelbase 11 ft. 9 in. Water 250 galls. Tractive Effort 3,318 lb. Total Heating Surface 186 ft. sq. Grate Area 4 ft. sq. Weight in Working Order 13½ tons. Suitable for 22 lb. rail. Price £925. Name in catalogue. None. N.B. The later style of Falcon Works' plate with number and date illegible—is used on this illustration.

The engine depicted in Neg. 48 does not appear in the catalogue but apart from slight variations of angle in the pipework, cut-away buffer beams (an odd difference if the engine was to work over the same route as its sister) sloping smokebox door and other detail alterations, there is no vital difference. The sloping smokebox front was a common feature of Falcon products.

Neg. 51 This engine does not appear in the catalogue and may be post-1904 but this is unlikely. Possibly it incorporated features which Falcon did not like, or were found unsatisfactory, or supplied against the builder's recommendations. There is no doubt of its origin; cab, side tanks, boiler and smokebox mountings, cylinders and motion, crosshead pump are all identical with other engines using standard Falcon patterns. From standard sizes quoted, we may deduce leading wheels 1 ft. 4 in. diameter and driving wheels 2 ft. diameter. These would be very small for the metre gauge which the Album gives for this engine. It is the only one of the set with inside frames. Plate reads: 'Spooner & Co., Engineers, Portmadoc'.

Tabulating the Album and catalogue together and adding possible date of origin (having in mind the dates of known products also shown in the catalogue with which the Spooner engines can be compared) shows:

	Built	*Class*	*Date*
Neg. 1 0–6–0T *Alosno* 2 ft. gauge M d'A Rly., Spain	Falcon B	No. 1	*c.* 1884
Neg. 48 0–4–4T *Alosnito* 2 ft. gauge M d'A Rly., Spain	Falcon D	No. 1	*c.* 1887
Neg. 52 0–4–4T *Paimoco* 2 ft. gauge M d'A Rly, Spain	Falcon D	No. 1	*c.* 1887
Neg. 50 0–4–0T — 2 ft. gauge Not known	Falcon A	No. 9	*c.* 1885
Neg. 51 2–4–0T — Metre gauge Not known	Falcon	Not known	*c.* 1893

Among the connections of the Spooner family, conducted through Spooner & Sons or later, through Spooner & Co. (which probably arose as a new title to an established practice when no members of the family were brought in) may be noticed:

A survey for a tramway 6 miles long to Cwm Eigiau from Dolgarrog *c.* 1854

A survey for the Croesor Tramway *c.* 1862

Promotion and engineering work in connection with the North Wales Narrow Gauge Railways project

A plan for a rack railway from South Snowdon to the summit of Snowdon and down to Llanberis on the other side

Evidence that advice (if not actual work done), was given for the Darjeeling-Himalayan Railway

As individuals or in concert the family was linked with the Portmadoc, Croesor & Beddgelert Tram Railway Co.

The Welsh Slate Company (in connection with the working of the mine and survey work)

Surveys for Oakeley Slate Co. (successor to W.S.Co.)

Surveys for Maenofferen Quarry

Surveys for Croesor United Quarry

Surveys in connection with boundaries underground for Diphwys Casson, to which Charles was the first engineer on the formation of the new company in 1863.

Charles had an interest in the Hafod Lâs Slate Quarry west of Bettws-y-Coed. He was also engineer to the Carnarvonshire Railway of 1862, and to the Rhosydd Quarry; there was hardly a quarry in the Ffestiniog area (Llechwedd being a notable exception) to which a Spooner of one generation or another, did not give a service. It will be noted that his son, John Eyrie, died after a fall underground during survey work in a quarry.

The firm's services were called upon for underground boundary surveys, boundary disputes, matters of mechanical or civil engineering and geological investigation. Not all the work they did received acceptance—after being paid £120 for surveying the workings of the W.S.Co. in June 1865, and after C. E. Spooner's recommendation that the walls of the pillars be scaled down, the quarry management ignored the advice, revealing they felt '...a Distinct Danger as a result and that the time was not ripe to do so'. A letter to him followed saying the Company '... do not require his services but they would be happy to consult him professionally, should any occasion arise'. Charles did inspect again the next year to give an opinion on rock falls and of his advice the manager said 'I felt distrust of the operation at the time'.

On another occasion Charles inspected the reservoir of the Welsh Slate Co. in order to advise how to keep water out of the Back Vein (May 1874).

At the time of the North Wales Narrow Gauge Railways project, it was hoped to build a railway from Bettws-y-Coed to Corwen via Cerrig-y-Druidion. At about the same time an independent scheme was promoted to link Cerrig-y-Druidion with Ruthin station on the Denbigh, Ruthin & Corwen Railway. A later reference described this imaginatively as 'part of a line from the coal fields of Minera to the slate districts of Caernarvonshire'. The project was surveyed and prepared by two Ruthin engineers, George Smith and John Anstie, an Act being obtained on 27 June 1876 (39–40 Vic. Cap. 81).

Work began at the Ruthin end but problems too numerous to mention came along and it stopped. There was nothing being done when the *Mining Journal* of July 1889 stated that C. E. Spooner was the engineer but it appears to be none of his doing that powers for a revival, an extension of time and compulsory purchase of land were obtained by a second Act of 3 June 1881. At no time do the few surviving documents make reference to Spooner but they do mention Henry Robertson (of Corwen). Perhaps Spooner may have acted in the meanwhile? The scheme failed anyway, an Abandonment Act being passed on 23 June 1884, and the possibility of Spooner's name being linked with another sixteen miles of Welsh narrow gauge remains to be proven.

Welsh Slate Company Report of September 1883 refers to Mr. John S. Hughes, 'Mr. Spooner's partner' accompanying the elderly John Brunton on a survey following serious rock falls below ground; the next month the quarry records refer to 'Spooner & Co.' by name for the first time and it seems that Spooner himself had probably ceased to do much in mining survey by the late 1880s as the Enquiry into the collapse of the workings at W.S.Co. in December 1886 mentions 'I am not sure if C. E. Spooner is alive ...'. Actually, he was, not dying until 1889. There is no doubt that Spooner's advice on working slate off the pillars which thinned them down and was said to cause the ultimate collapse, lingered on; in February 1866 the manager said it would be imprudent to unroof the walls any further, and it could be fatal to the prospects of the Company. 'All this shows Mr. Spooner's want of practical knowledge.'

By 1869, the Welsh Slate Company's official surveyor was John S. Hughes; he became Charles' partner in 1874, being a Civil Engineer, a Fellow of the Geological Society (he was later to succeed Spooner as Manager and Engineer of the F.R.) and was cited as '... and of other railways in this country and abroad, and in connection with slate quarries throughout the country; also lead and copper mines'. By 1886 he had become Consulting Engineer to Lord Penrhyn's Quarries. In another reference to Hughes it says 'In 1876 the Welsh Slate Co. workings were surveyed by him and partly by Mr. Edmund Spooner who is now in Ceylon' and again 'In 1876 (Mr. Edmund Spooner) was about 21 or 22; he is now on public works in Ceylon, and had not done any underground quarry work before 1876'. (This reference to 'Edmund' should be Edwin, b. 1853, third son of Charles Easton.)

Reverting to Charles Easton Spooner once more; he was associated with several Patents:

No. 3605
(provisional) 26 November 1868   For Rail Joints   (with G. A. Huddart)
No. 1487   14 May 1869   ditto   ditto

No. 2854	1 October 1869	For Rail Joints	(with G. A. Huddart)
No. 2896	5 October 1869	For Rail Bending Machine	
No. 1315	1 May 1872	Locomotion from turbine and water pressure pipes	(with J. S. Hughes)
No. 2874	29 August 1873	Point Locking Apparatus	

Among other sundry papers in the Portmadoc records are drawings Nos. 2205 and 2206 (reproduced here) of 2 ft. 3 in. gauge cattle and sheep trucks, probably the products of the Spooner office but stamped 'Festiniog Railway'; these are only about 6 ft. in height. Among correspondence is a letter from C. C. Kleberg of St. Petersburg regarding the possibility of supplying narrow gauge rolling stock to Russia (6 November 1875).

G. Percival Spooner took out Patent No. 2512 of 22 July 1873 for centre buffer couplers, already mentioned in reference to coaches Nos. 15 and 16.

Hughes' contribution was that he already acted for several Ffestiniog quarries and brought with him established connections. He conceived an imaginative plan to build rack railways to the summits of some of the highest mountains in England, Scotland, Wales and the Isle of Man; these were to climb Skiddaw, Ben Lomond and Snaefell (his plan for a line up Snowdon has been mentioned earlier). The original conception was possibly a joint dream with Charles Spooner but Hughes continued with it after Spooner's death. Landowners defeated these projects. They were not big enough to call for statutory backing, and only two succeeded, but not because of Hughes.

The Patent he and Spooner took out for a water-powered locomotive operated by water pressure on a turbine. The tube laid between the rails savoured of early atmospheric railways.

Hughes was made Engineer as well as Secretary to the F.R. during Spooner's lifetime, a Minute of 21 August 1889 reads that he was to become Engineer and General Manager at £300 per annum from 1 October 1889. A condition was that he should retire from his partnership with Spooner and give his entire time to the service of the Company, but might undertake consulting work at the sanction of the directors. Alfred Crick was to be Assistant Clerk to help him.

The last actual survey for a railway which can be attributed to Spooner & Co. to come to notice so far, was for a railway to connect the F.R. with the Deudraeth Sett Co. Ltd.'s quarry; this would have branched off to the left about half way up Gwyndy Bank and by two reverse curves would then have travelled westwards to the quarry—today the large Minffordd granite quarry. Documents are dated 16 September 1874.

Hughes supplied 'memorandum and plans' concerning the Darjeeling-Himalayan Railway to the Cape Government Railways on 16 March 1901, suggesting but not confirming that the plans were carried out at Portmadoc. T. S. Lascelles maintained that all the Darjeeling-Himalayan Railway plans were carried out under C. E. Spooner's supervision.

The last member of the family to be associated with the firm was Thomas James Spooner, youngest son of James Swinton Spooner.

Nº 2206

SHEEP TRUCK

Scale one inch to the foot

SIDE ELEVATION

Plan of Cab with 2' Wheels

HALF SIDE ELEVATION

HALF TRANSVERSE SECTION

5' 0"

Brown Marshalls & Cº's mark here ?

Reconstructed from fragments of the original. *M.Lloyd* 70213.

FFESTINIOG RAILWAY ENGINEER'S OFFICE PORTMADOC

No. 2205

CATTLE TRUCK

Scale ⅛ inch to the foot

Brown Marshall & Co.
BRITANNIA WORKS
BIRMINGHAM

Drawn by H.W. Ross

Weight 1 ton 8 cwt with 2 wheels
C.C.3

Bibliography

PERIODICALS—NEWSPAPERS—ANNUALS

The Festiniog Railway Magazine
Skinner's Register of Defunct
  Companies
The Stock Exchange Year Book
Journal of Transport History
Bradshaw's Railway Manual
Bradshaw's Timetables
The Locomotive, Railway Carriage
  & Wagon Review
Engineering
The Engineer
Railways (Railway World)
The Railway Magazine
Journal of County Record Office,
  Caernarvon
Quarry Manager's Journal
The Railway Register
The Railway Engineer
Proceedings: Institution of
  Mechanical Engineers
Proceedings: Institution of Civil
  Engineers
The Quarry

The Mining Journal
The Railway News (British N/G
  Rlys.) Series II No. IV
Herpath's Railway & Commercial
  Journal
The Railway News
Transactions of the Caernarvonshire
  Historical Society
Transactions of the Merionethshire
  Historical Society
Postal History Society Bulletins
  (76 and 78, 1954–5)
The Slate Trades Gazette
The Railway Gazette
The Engineering & Mining Journal
The Weekly Reporter
The Law Times
The Carnarvon & Denbigh Herald
The North Wales Chronicle
The North Wales Gazette
The Times
Mines and Minerals

RAILWAYS
(*Reference Number from 'A Bibliography of British Railway History'—Ottley*)

2256	Narrow Gauge Railways	C. E. Spooner	1871
3668	The Battle of the Gauges	R. F. Fairlie	1872
5699	Etude Technique sur le Chemin de Fer Festiniog et quelques autres Chemin de Fer a Voie Etroite de l'Angleterre	M. E. Vignes	1878
—	Mittheilungen uber Localbahnen insbesondere Schmalspurbahnen	W. Hostmann and Richard Koch	1882
6927	The Hay Railway	C. R. Clinker	1960
—	The Chester Division of the G.W.R.	G.W.R.	1924
—	Running Powers of the G.W.R.	G.W.R.	1924
—	Industrial & Independent Locos. & Railways of North Wales	Bradley and Hindley	1968
6348	Railway Reminiscences	G. P. Neele	1904
—	How Ffestiniog got its Railway	M. J. T. Lewis	1965
2182	Light Railways	Mackay	1896
—	Report of Investigating Committee on Light Railways 1920–1	M.O.T.	1921
—	R.C.H. Handbook of Railway Stations	R.C.H.	Various
—	Reports of Proceedings under Lt. Rlys. Acts		1896–1939

2251 Locomotive Engines (What they are etc . . .)	R. F. Fairlie	1864
— Light Railway Construction	R. M. Parkinson	1902
6393 Conway Valley Railway	R. G. Harman	1963
— Chester & Holyhead Railway	C. E. Stretton	1898
6369 The Chester & Holyhead Railway	J. M. Dunn	1968
— The Festiniog Railway for Passengers	H. W. Tyler	1865
— Government & Railways in 19th Century Britain	H. W. Parris	1965
5698 A Descriptive Account of the Construction and Working of the Festiniog Railway . . .	C. E. Spooner	1870
— Brookes Industrial Railways	S. A. Leleux	1972

STATUTORY AND LEGAL

Index to Local & Personal Acts 1801–1947	H.M.S.O.	
Halsbury's Statutes of England (2nd Edit.)	Burrows	
The Law List		
Proceedings of Courts of Chancery		
The English & Empire Digest of Cases (56 volumes and 4 supplements)	Butterworth & Co. (Supplemented to 1974)	
Railway Passengers & Railway Companies	L. A. Goodeve	1876
The Law specially relating to Tramways & Light Railways	S. Brice	1898
A Treatise on the Law of Railways (7th Edit.)	W. Hodges	1888
Acts of Parliament relating to Wales 1714–1901	T. I. J. Jones	1966
Registers & Records	T. M. Aldridge	1964

MINING—TOPOGRAPHY—COMMERCIAL—LOCAL HISTORY

Treasures of the Mawddach	H. J. Owen	1950
The Slates of Wales	F. J. North	1946
Slate Quarrying in Wales	Morgan Richards	1876
British Mining	R. Hunt	1887
Views in North Wales	W. J. Loftie	1875
Enquiry into Slate Mining in Merioneth		1894
Atlas Sir Caernarfon	E. H. Owen	1954
Index to Parliamentary Papers on Mines & Quarries 1800–1949 (privately circulated)	J. S. Wilkinson	1972
Index to Parliamentary Papers on Railways 1800–1949 (privately circulated)	J. S. Wilkinson	1971
Slate Quarries in Wales (reprint from 'Mining Journal')	T. C. Smith	1860
Slate Quarries as an Investment (ditto)	J. Bower	1865
The Slate Trade of North Wales (ditto)	J. Kellow	1868
Slate Quarries of North Wales (rep. Carns. & Denb. Herald)	anon.	1873
Merionethshire—History of Slate Industry (pp. 70–4)	A. Morris	1913
A Treatise on Slate & Slate Quarrying (4th Edit.)	D. C. Davies	1899

Llechwedd Caverns	I. W. Jones	1973
Reports of Inspectors of Metalliferous Mines	P.R.O.	
North Wales (3rd Edit.) (Inst. of Geol. Science)	H.M.S.O.	1961
Hanes Porthmadog	E. Davies	1913
List of Plans of Abandoned Mines Vol. 4	Mines Dept.	
Welsh Slate Quarry Industry. Committee Report	H.M.S.O.	1947
Guide to the Geology of Portmadoc Area	P. J. Kiteley	1972
A Bibliography & Index of Geology & Allied Sciences for Wales & Welsh Borders 1536–1896	D. A. Bassett	
Mineral Wealth of Wales	Trevor M. Thomas	
Hanes Plwyf Ffestiniog*	G. J. Williams	1882
Echoes of Old Merioneth	H. J. Owen	1944
Royal Commission on Land in Wales & Monmouth		1893
Historian's Guide to Ordnance Survey Maps	Harley & Phillips	1964
Classified List of Historic Events, Mechanical & Electrical Engineering	Science Museum	1955
The Light of Other Days	Alison Hamson	(Recent)
A Description of Caernarvonshire 1809–11	E. E. Hall	1952 repr.
Prince Madoc, Discover of America		1909
Miscellaneous Pen & Ink Sketches (of N. Wales)	Richard Richards	1868
Some Aspects of the Industrial Revolution in South East Caernarvonshire: Traeth Mawr	W. M. Richards	1944
History of Traeth Mawr—a dissertation in connection with University Degree—Aberystwyth	W. M. Richards	1925
Rhosydd Slate Quarry	Lewis & Denton	1974
Immortal Sails	Henry Hughes	1946
Brief Glory	D. W. Morgan	1948
The Industrial Revolution in North Wales	A. H. Dodd	1950
The Memoirs of Samuel Holland	Samuel Holland	1952 repub.
Canals of South Wales & the Border	C. Hadfield	1960
A History of Caernarvonshire 1284–1900	A. H. Dodd	1968
Topographical Dictionary of Wales (4th Edit.)	S. Lewis	1850
Tours in Wales	Pennant	1883
Anglesey & North Wales Pilot	H. Glazebrook	1961
Royal Commission on Ancient Monuments—Caernarvonshire		1924
The Book of North Wales	Cliffe	1850

BIOGRAPHY

Madocks and the Wonder of Wales	E. Beezley	1957
George and Robert Stephenson	L. T. C. Rolt	1960

* There is an earlier edition of 1871 by 'Ffestinfab' (a Llechwedd Quarry Manager) on which the 1882 edition is entirely based.

Thomas Telford	L. T. C. Rolt	1958
The Life of Lord Palmerston	H. L. Bulwer	1870
Historical Portraits 1800–50	C. F. Bell	1919
County Families of the United Kingdom	E. Walford	1883
Annals and Antiquities of the Counties		
& County Familes of Wales		
The Memoirs of Sir Ll. Turner	J. E. Vincent (Ed.)	1903
A History of the Family Holland	W. F. Irvine	
I.C.I.—A History 1870–1926	W. J. Reader	1970
Life of Ludwig Mond	J. M. Cohen	1956

BIOGRAPHICAL REFERENCE SOURCES

Burke's Peerage — Who's Who?
Burke's Commoners of Great Britain — Who was Who?
Burke's Landed Gentry — The Directory of Directors
Who's Who in Wales? — The Universal Directory of
Dictionary of National Biography — Railway Officials
The Complete Peerage

SOURCES

Primary

County Record Offices: Deposited Plans & Sections, Book of Reference
Legal Material
Newspapers
Slate Trade Documents
especially: Quarry Proprietors, Solicitors' Documents, Estate
Papers, Quarry Records, L.N.W.R. District
Engineer's Records
National Library of Wales: Collections—Festiniog Railway: Glynliffon:
Stokes: Longueville: Henry
Robertson: Madocks: Holland:
Davies Bros.: Piercy: Morris:
Bronwylfa
University College, Bangor: Collections—Porth-yr-Aur: Carter Vincent:
Searell: Bangor: Cynhaiarn
Public Record Office: Statutory Records material
Board of Trade (and subseq.)
Official Returns
House of Commons/Lords: Statutory Records
Sessional Papers
British Transport Historical Records: Documents concerning neighbouring
standard gauge railways
Festiniog Railway Company: Company's Collection of Records & Manuscripts

Secondary

The John M. Lloyd Collection
The J. I. C. Boyd Collection (incorporating the work of Donald Mackereth and
Frank Hewitt)
The A. M. Davies Collection
Records of the Spooner Family—per T. S. Lascelles
Wagon Records per L.M.S.R. Earlestown and G.W.R. Swindon
Kenneth Brown Collection—John Rylands Library
Plans & Sections of Light Railway—per Freeman Fox & Partners
Vulcan Foundry Records—City of Liverpool
Quarry and Mining Records—J. S. Wilkinson

TABLE—LOCOMOTIVE TRIALS, FESTINIOG RAILWAY 1869-70

No.	Date	Locomotive(s)	Train Weight	Tons Cwts.	Length	Av. Speed	Remarks
1.	18 Sept. 1869 (Inspection by B.O.T.)	Little Wonder 0440 (Loco new)	111 Slate Wagons 6 Coaches 60 Passengers 12 Goods Wagons Loco	74 0 9 0 4 10 26 6 20 0 133 16	1348 Ft.	—	Test run to Dinas. Train divided at Hafod Llyn owing to danger of stalling in tunnel. Time in tunnel 1 min. 5 sec., speed 23 mph. Division proved unnecessary. On return journey with coaches and a few wagons, speed 35 mph. on relaid track.
2.	20 Sept. 1869 (Ins. by B.O.T.)	Little Giant 040	49 Wagons and Passengers	51 0	—	—	Coal consumption 22 lbs. per mile. Loco found to "shoulder" load.
3.	11 Feb. 1870	Little Wonder 0440	90 Slate Wagons 7 Coaches & Vans 57 Passengers Loco	57 10 13 10 4 0 19 10 94 10	854 Ft.	14.5 mph	Test run to Blaenau Festiniog with train.
4.	12 Feb. 1870	Little Wonder 0440 Welsh Pony 040 Mountaineer 040	Nil Nil Nil		— —	Confined 12-15 mph	Test of steadiness of running on Traeth Mawr Embankment. 040s had strong vertical oscillation and less lateral. On 0440 no noticeable oscillation at all. NB. Track was original 30 lbs. cast iron rail with no fish plates.
5.		Welsh Pony 040	50 Wagons Passengers Loco	123 10 3 10 10 0 137 0		—	Stalled on 1 in 85 near Boston Lodge loco shed: pressure 160 lbs.

No.	Loco	Load	Weight	Distance	Speed	Remarks
6.	Welsh Pony 040	25 Wagons Passengers Loco	59 7 3 10 10 0 72 17	—	—	(Not known.)
7.	Welsh Pony 040	30 Wagons	—	—	—	Attempted to start on 1 in 85, but wheels did not revolve. No lack of adhesion, therefore.
8.	Welsh Pony 040	26 Wagons Passengers Loco	62 6 1 10 10 0 73 16	—	5 mph	Up 1 in 85 successfully until purposefully stopped with pressure at 150 lbs.
9.	Little Wonder 0440	72 Slate Wagons Empties Passengers Loco	138 17 43 13 4 0 19 10 206 0	648 Ft.	—	Started with 165 lbs. pressure, ran up 1 in 85 and stopped with 125 lbs. and low fire (purposely); backed down to point where trial 8 started and pressure rose 170 lbs. Restarted, attained 5 mph and speed increased as ran up 1 in 100. Purposely stopped with pressure at 170 lbs.
10. 16 Feb. 1870	Little Wonder 0440	22 Wagons Coal 21 Wagons Slate 2 Bogie Timber Passengers 2 Flat Wagons 1 Coach Loco	64 18 49 3 4 18 1 1 1 4 12 19 10 141 6	407 Ft.	11¼ mph (15 max.)	Test run to Blaenau Festiniog. Portmadoc dep. 5.41p.m. Penrhyn (pass) 5.58 Hafod Llyn arr. 6.18 Hafod Llyn dep. 6.26¾ Dduallt (water) 6.40 Tunnel 7.2 (2 min. 10 sec. pass) Tanygrisiau (pass) 7.9 Dinas arr. 7.15 Total time 1 hr. 34 min. excluding stops 1 hr. 10½ min. Average pressure 175 lbs. Slipping at start from watering, in tunnel and at Glanypwll Junc. (where slate trains stand for Down train to pass, and drop oil on rails).

Weather fine; strong head wind against train.

Trials to show limitations of four coupled engines

Very strong head wind against train.

	Loco	Load	Tons cwt	1323 Ft.	mph	Remarks
11. 17 Feb. 1870	Little Wonder 0440	140 Slate Wagons 7 Coal Wagons	100 16 Total	—	12½ mph (16½ max.)	Test run to Dinas. Speed on return journey averaged 25 mph and 30 mph maximum.
12. 18 Feb. 1870	Little Wonder 0440	Train Loco	81 11 19 10 101 1	—	13–22 mph	Test run. Pressure 145–60 lbs.
13. 8 July 1870	Little Giant 040 Welsh Pony 040 (Coupled)	75 Slate Loaded 8 Slate empty Passengers Locos & Tenders	183 13 5 0 1 0 22 8 212 1	—	8¼ mph	Pressure 150 lbs. Slipping at start, sand used. Pressure fell to 155 and 140 lbs. and finished 165 and 150 lbs. Both locos slipping from foot 1 in 85 at Embankment end, up 1 in 100 and 1 in 90; pulled up by load 50 yds. short Minffordd Level Crossing (1m 5f 3ch) Dep. 4.52 p.m. stop 5.4 p.m.
14.	Little Wonder 0440	Train as No. 13 above		—	13 mph	Slipping at start and couplings broken, Sand used. Speed increased over Embankment, slackened up 1 in 85/100/90, maintained for ½ mile beyond Minffordd. Train then purposely stopped, pressure 155 lbs. Dep. 5.45 p.m., stop 5.55 p.m. (2m 1f 3ch). Restarted with sanded rails and 160 lbs., speed increased for ¼ mile, then purposely stopped. Pressure then 170 lbs. and speed was over 6 mph and gaining.

Weather warm and dry.

Comparative Locomotive Figures
1926—1931

	September 1926		May 1927		August 1927		January 1928		January 1930	August 1930	June 1931
	Miles	Coal: lb. per train mile	Miles	Coal: lb. per train mile	Miles	Coal: lb. per train mile	Miles	Coal: lb. per train mile	Mileages only		
Princess	1096	22.86	413 F.R. / 257 W.H.R.	25.14 / 34.97	673 F.R. / 993 W.H.R.	31.26	859	28.35	—	1407	1178
Prince	1043	28.81	1153 F.R. / 18 W.H.R.	26.95 / 46.66	1947 F.R. / 181 W.H.R.	26.90	—	—	1220	1383	900
Palmerston	617	31.31	1215 F.R. / 126 W.H.R.	23.16 / 43.33	1082 F.R. / 1229 W.H.R.	27.68	1557	19.87	946	—	—
Welsh Pony	847	31.40	43 F.R. / 36 W.H.R.	45.58 / 38.88	168 F.R. / 183 W.H.R.	35.49	—	—	—	2696	1910
Little Giant	—	—	—	—	—	—	—	—	—	—	—
James Spooner	—	—	—	—	—	—	—	—	—	—	—
Taliesin	—	—	2927	52.22	3054	52.31	—	—	—	—	—
Merddin Emrys	3043	59.07	—	—	—	—	2509	41.23	2508	—	203
Livingston Thompson	—	—	—	—	—	—	—	—	—	—	—
Russell	1700 W.H.R.	26.02	1627 W.H.R.	23.42	932 W.H.R.	27.87	—	—	—	—	—
Baldwin	—	—	50 W.H.R.	44.80	703 W.H.R.	27.00	—	—	—	—	—
Moel Tryfan	—	—	—	—	135 W.H.R.	31.31	—	—	—	—	—
	No separate figures given for W.H.R. mileages.		Note higher coal consumption of first three when on W.H.R. _Welsh Pony_ obviously not in good working order.		A typical August with F.R. 0-4-0 working over W.H. Section.		Only 3 engines in service.		Simplex 380 / Baldwin 208	Simplex — / Baldwin	Simplex 640 / Baldwin —
										Apparently no double engines in use	

Essex Chambers,
104 King Street, Manchester.
Sept. 29th 1869

Capt. Tyler, R.E.
London.

Dear Sir,

Observing a long article upon the Festiniog Ry. in last weeks Engineering Journal, and containing a quotation from your Report upon the line and Engines (date 1865), I have written to ask for a correction of that part of your report wherein you say "Mr. England was employed under Mr. C. E. Spooner, the Secretary and Engineer of the Company, to design an Engine, etc" — — — —

As the original party who proposed in 1860 that locomotives should be applied to the Ry. and afterwards at Mr. Spooner's request prepared drawings for same and secured an order from the Director to obtain Tenders for the Engines and get them built, I am naturally, as a young Engineer, anxious to have my share of whatever credit may apertain to this; and Mr. Spooner has written to my Father on the subject some time since and says in his letter: "As the latter part of this statement bestows a credit which is due to another I think it right that you should know that Captain Tyler in that paper must have formed some erroneous impression and fallen into error as the party under whose control and direction the Locos were made is Mr. C. M. Holland." — I should therefore be much obliged if you would kindly correct this on any future occasion when any mention is made about the first Engines.

Mr. England has I think unfairly to me appropriated the credit for building and **designing** the Engines for as the Engineer who brought him the original design and accepted his Tender for that design and afterwards supervised the construction of the Engines and was solely responsible to the Company for so doing—I naturally regard them as my own design. The main proportions were arranged afterwards between Mr. England and myself and he certainly deserved every credit for his work— but I cannot allow him to pass over my claim as the designer of the Engines and had indeed some trouble to perswade him to tender for them—.

That the original design was partly abandoned I admit but under any circumstances I should have the credit due to the designer—I hope you will excuse this longer letter than I purposed writing but I wished you to understand my position in the matter.

and remain

Dear Sir,

Yours truly,

C. M. Holland

FESTINIOG RAILWAY

Locomotive Power Costs per train mile

Year	£	Year	£
1865	.0103	1888	.0211
1866	.0171	1889	.0264
1867	.0196	1890	.0240
1868	.0223	1891	.0259
1869	.0254	1892	.0263
1870	.0580	1893	.0224
1871	.0306	1894	.0261
1872	.0337	1895	.0255
1873	.0295	1896	.0297
1874	.0303	1897	.0241
1875	.0303	1898	.0273
1876	.0375	1899	.0267
1877	.0292	1900	.0302
1878	.0338	1901	.0294
1879	.0285	1902	.0291
1880	.0270	1903	.0284
1881	.0246	1904	.0306
1882	.0247	1905	.0325
1883	.0263	1906	.0270
1884	.0254	1907	.0329
1885	.0294	1908	.0369
1886	.0249	1909	.0371
1887	.0201	1910	.0314

MILEAGES BETWEEN EACH STATION AND TRAIN TIMES
FEBRUARY 1921

Mileage m. ch.	Station	Time Running minutes	Time at Station minutes
2 23	Portmadoc to Minffordd	8	2
1 14	Minffordd to Penrhyndeudraeth	5	1
4 4	Penrhyndeudraeth to Tan-y-Bwlch	16	2
2 20	Tan-y-Bwlch to Dduallt	8	1
1 19	Dduallt to Moelwyn Halt	4	1
54	Moelwyn Halt to Tan-y-Grisiau	3	1
1 2	Tan-y-Grisiau to Glan-y-Pwll Box	4	–
12	Glan-y-Pwll Box to Blaenau	1	1
30	Blaenau to Duffws	2	–
13 18		51	9

APPENDIX 5 Timetables

During the existence of the Festiniog&Blaenau Railway, and to clarify timetables in connection with through-working to it, Festiniog timetables reversed Up and Down terms, Down trains being shown as Portmadoc–Duffws with connection Duffws (F&BR station)–Llan Ffestiniog, this also being a 'Down' working where the F&BR was concerned. It is strange that the larger and long-established railway thus fell into line with the smaller, younger one. Bradshaw's Guide appears to have continued to show the two Company Tables separately and the change was possibly made to simplify local timetable bills.

FESTINIOG RAILWAY

TIME TABLE

From NOVEMBER 1st, 1875, until further Notice.

No Sunday Trains.   1st, 2nd and 3rd Class Carriages.

Down Trains	Mondays only 1	2	3	4	5	6
	a.m.	a.m.	a.m.	p.m.	p.m.	p.m.
PORTMADOC... ...	6.00	8.00	10.35	1.00	3.20	5.00
‡ MINFFORD JUNC.	6.10	8.10	10.45	1.10	3.30	5.10
PENRHYN...	6.21	8.21	10.56	1.20	3.40	5.19
TAN-Y-BWLCH ...	6.42	8.42	11.19	1.44	4.05	5.47
TAN-Y-GRISIAU ...	7.09	9.09	11.44	2.09	4.30	6.14
DUFFWS	7.17	9.17	11.52	2.15	4.38	6.20

Up Trains	1	2	3	4	5	6
	a.m.	a.m.	a.m.	p.m.	p.m.	p.m.
DUFFWS	6.12	8.12	10.50	*1.15	3.35	5.15
TAN-Y-GRISIAU ...	6.19	8.19	10.56	1.22	3.42	5.22
TAN-Y-BWLCH ...	6.42	8.42	11.19	1.44	4.05	5.47
PENRHYN...	7.00	9.06	11.41	2.06	4.23	6.07
‡ MINFFORD JUNC.	7.05	9.13	11.46	2.15	4.30	6.12
PORTMADOC... ...	7.15	9.23	11.56	2.25	4.40	6.22

‡ Change for Cambrian Railway   * This Train will have low-fare Carriages on Saturdays only.

Day Tickets issued on Saturdays are available for return on the Day they are issued or on the Monday following, but Tickets issued on other Days of the week are only available on the day they are issued.

The Company cannot guarantee these times being kept under any circumstances, nor will they be responsible for delay.

Omnibuses run between the Portmadoc Stations of the Cambrian and Festiniog Railways, meeting every train.

The Village of Festiniog is 3½ miles by Rail from Duffws.

FESTINIOG RAILWAY.

TIME TABLE
for
UP AND DOWN SLATE TRAINS,

For July, August and September, 1890.

Up Empty Trains.	1.	2.	3.	4.	5.	6.	7.
	A.M.	A.M.	A.M.	A.M.	P.M	P.M.	P.M.
Portmadoc leave	5 35	6 45	8 30	10 40	12 50	3 20	4 50
Minfford Junction „	5 45	6 55	8 40	10 50	1 0	3 30	5 0
Dinas Junction arrive	6 30	7 42	9 25	11 37	1 45	4 18	5 48

Down Loaded Trains.				Except Saturdays	On Saturdays only. 4 5		
	7 48	9 30	11 45				
	A.M	A M	A M	P.M.	P.M.	P.M.	P.M.
Dinas Junction leave	6 55	8 30	10 50	12 50	1 30	3 25	5 0
Tan-y-grisiau „	6 58	8 40	10 56	1 0	1 36	3 31	5 6
Tan-y-bwlch „	x7 18	x9 3	x11 13	x1 23	1 53	x3 53	x5 23
Penrhyn ... „	7 35	9 20	11 30	1 40	2 10	4 10	5 40
Minfford Junction ar.	7 38	9 23	11 33	1 43	2 13	4 13	5 43
Portmadoc ar. ° 7·30	9 30	10 15	12 30	3 0	*0 0	5 15	*0 0

PORTMADOC,
July 1st, 1890.

J. S. HUGHES,
General Manager.

E. Jones, Printer, &c., Portmadoc.

TIME TABLE
UP and DOWN SLATE TRAINS
For July, August and September, 1897.

UP EMPTY TRAINS	1	2	3	4	5	6	7
	a.m.	a.m.	a.m.	a.m.	p.m.	p.m.	p.m.
Portmadoc depart	7.00	8.15	11.00	..	1.00	3.15	4.25
Minffordd „	7.10	8.25	11.10	..	1.10	3.25	4.35
Tan-y-bwlch „	7.35	8.50	11.35	..	1.35	3.50	5.00
Dinas Junc. arrive	7.55	9.10	11.55	..	1.55	4.15	5.20

DOWN LOADED TRAINS						Except Sats.	
	a.m.	a.m.	a.m.	p.m.	p.m.	p.m.	p.m.
Dinas Junc. depart	6.55	..	9.20	..	2.00	4.30	..
Tan-y-grisiau „	7.05	..	9.23	..	2.03	4.33	..
Tan-y-bwlch arrive	x7.25	..	..	..	..	x4.50	..
„ depart	7.55	..	9.40	..	2.20	5.20	..
Penrhyn „	8.12	..	9.57	..	2.37	5.37	..
Minffordd arrive	8.15	..	x10.00	..	x*2.40	5.40	..
Portmadoc „	9.15	..	11.30	..	4.00	6.00	..

x Cross Passenger Train   * Stops at Minffordd on Saturdays, arrives at Portmadoc 7.30 Monday morning.

PORTMADOC,
July 1st, 1897.

J. S. HUGHES
GENERAL MANAGER

FESTINIOG ' RAILWAY.

TIME TABLE

For NOVEMBER 1890, and until further Notice.

Up Trains	Ply. 1.	2.	3.	4.	5.	6.	7.
	A.M.	A.M.	A.M.		P.M.	P.M.	P.M.
PORTMADOC ... dep.	BC5 35	8 30	11 18	..	2 10	5 10	
†MINFFORDD JUNCTION	5 45	8 40	11 28	..	2 20	5 20	
PENRHYN....	5 49	8 45	11 33	..	2 25	5 25	
TAN-Y-BWLCH	6 7	9 5	11 53	..	2 45	5 45	
DDUALLT	A	A	..	..	A	Sat.	
TAN-Y-GRISIAU	6 25	9 23	12 11	..	3 3	6 3	
§BLAENAU FESTINIOG L & N.W.R.	6 33	9 28	12 16	..	3 8	6 8	
,, ,, G.W.Ry.	6 34	9 29	12 17	..	3 9	6 9	
DUFFWS .... arrive	6 35	9 30	12 18	..	3 10	6 10	
L.&N.W.R. { Blaenau Festiniog depart	7 0	9 55	12 20	..	..	6 30	
Llandudno Junction ar.	8 16	11 9	1 32	..	..	7 46	
Chester ... ,,	9 58	1 6	3 35	..	..	10 0	
G.W.R. { Blaenau Festiniog depart	8 5	11 55	12 42	2 10	..	7 5	
Bala ... ... arrive	9 13	Festiniog Saturdays excepted.	fynydd Sat. only	3 19	..	8 13	
Chester .... ,,	11 26			5 35	..	10 33	

Down Trains.	A.M.	A.M.	A.M.	A.M.	A.M.	A.M.	P.M.
L&N.W.R { Chester .... depart	..	6 30	..	10 0	11 43	..	2 30
Llandudno Junction ,,	..	8 40	..	11 43	1 55	..	4 15
Blaenau Festiniog arrive	..	9 51	..	1 0	3 17	..	5 32
G.W.R { Chester .... depart	..	..	7 10	9 0	..	..	From Festiniog Sats.
Bala .... ,,	..	..	9 36	11 21	..	..	
Blaenau Festiniog arrive	..	..	10 45	12 30	..	..	5 25
DUFFWS .... depart	..	9 50	E12 28	1 0	3 40	G5 15	6 20
•BLAENAU FESTINIOG G.W.Ry.	..	9 51	12 29	1 1	3 41	5 16	6 21
§ ,, ,, L.&N.W.R.	..	9 52	12 30	1 2	3 42	5 17	6 22
TAN-Y-GRISIAU	..	9 57	12 38	1 7	3 47	5 25	6 27
DDUALLT	..	A	A	A	..	A	A
TAN-Y-BWLCH	..	10 15	12 58	1 25	4 5	5 45	6 47
PENRHYN....	..	10 35	1 23	1 45	4 25	6 5	7 5
†MINFFORDD JUNCTION	..	10 40	1 28	1 50	4 30	6 10	7 10
PORTMADOC .... arrive	..	10 50	1 38	2 0	4 40	6 20	7 20

†Change for Cambrian Railway.
§Change for L.&N.W.Ry.
•Change for G. W. Ry.

(A) Stop by Signal to take Up and set Down when required. Notice to be given to the Guard at the preceding Station.
(B) On Mondays will leave Portmadoc at 5-45 a.m.
(C) After the 10th inst. will leave at 5-50 a.m. except Mondays.
(E) On Saturdays only. (G) Does not run on Saturdays.

Return Tickets are available for return on the following day.
The Company cannot guarantee these times being kept under any circumstances, nor will they be responsible for delay.
☞ Omnibuses run between the Portmadoc Stations of the Cambrian and Festiniog Railways, meeting every train.
The Village of Festiniog is 3½ miles by G.W. Railway from Duffws.

PORTMADOC, November 1st, 1890. J. S. HUGHES, General Manager.

E. Jones, Printer, Portmadoc

FESTINIOG RAILWAY

TIME TABLE

RECEIVED 15 JUL 1902 No. 163 R
BOARD OF TRADE

For JULY, AUGUST and SEPTEMBER, 1902.

CAM. RYS.		A.M.	A.M.	A.M.						
Aberystwyth .. .. depart	..	..	7 15	..	10 5	12 15	1 10	3 0	3
Barmouth .. .. ,,	..	..	9 16	..	12 29	2 0	4 0	4 45	6 15
Minffordd .. .. arrive	..	..	9 58	..	1 6	3 23	4 33	5 26	6 55
Pwllheli .. .. depart	..	7 25	..	9 50	11 15	1 40	4 0	..	4 45
Criccieth .. .. ,,	..	7 50	..	10 23	11 32	2 5	4 30	..	5 15
Minffordd .. .. arrive	..	8 9	..	10 44	E	2 25	4 50		E

UP TRAINS.

		Ply. 1	2	3	4	5	6	7	8	9
		A.M.	A.M.	A.M.	A.M.	A.M.	P.M.	P.M.	P.M.	P.M.
Portmadoc .. .. depart		5 35	6 30	8 20	9 50	10 50	1 0	3 30	4 45	6 50
Minffordd (Cam. R.) ,,		5 45	6 40	8 30	10 0	11 0	1 15	3 40	4 55	6 58
Penrhyn .. .. ,,		5 50	6 45	8 35	..	11 5	1 18	3 45	5 0	7 3
Tan-y-bwlch .. .. ,,		6 10	7 5	8 55	10 18	11 25	1 35	4 5	5 20	7 21
Dduallt .. .. ,,		6 20	A	A	10 28	A	A	A	A	A
Tan-y-grisiau .. ,,		6 28	7 23	9 13	10 38	11 43	1 53	4 23	5 38	7 41
§ Bl. Festiniog (L.N.W.R.) ,,		6 33	7 28	9 18	10 43	11 48	1 58	4 28	5 43	7 46
• Bl. Festiniog (G.W.R.) ,,		..	..	9 19	10 44	11 49	1 59	..	5 44	..
Duffws .. .. arrive		6 35	7 30	9 20	10 45	11 50	2 0	4 30	5 45	7 48

L. & N.W.R.						P.M.				
Blaenau Festiniog .. depart		..	8 5	9 55	..	12 15	2 15	4 45	..	7 55
Bettwsycoed .. .. arrive		..	8 40	10 30	..	12 51	2 50	5 20	..	8 30
Llandudno Junction .. ,,		..	9 19	11 11	..	1 32	3 35	5 57	..	9 10
Chester .. .. ,,		..	11 32	1 5	..	3 30	5 24	7 25	..	10 52

G.W.R.										
Blaenau Festiniog .. depart		..	..	9 35	..	12 10	2 45	..	7 5	..
Festiniog .. .. arrive		..	..	9 39	..	12 25	2 58	..	7 19	..
Bala .. .. ,,		..	..	10 44	..	1 10	3 50	..	8 12	..
Llangollen .. .. ,,		..	..	11 58	..	..	4 44	..	9 23	..
Chester .. .. ,,		..	..	1 2	..	3 35	5 53	..	10 30	..

DOWN TRAINS.

L.&N.W.R.		A.M.		A.M.	A.M.		A.M.	P.M.			P.M.
Chester .. .. depart		2 46	..	6 0	9 0	..	10 5	12 10	..	..	3 52
Llandudno Junction .. ,,		4 25	..	8 20	10 20	..	11 30	2 5	..	..	5 20
Bettwsycoed .. .. ,,		5 25	..	8 59	10 54	..	12 2	2 46	..	..	6 5
Blaenau Festiniog .. arrive		6 12	..	9 41	11 37	..	12 52	3 27	..	..	6 47

G.W.R.					A.M.	A.M.		A.M.			P.M.
Chester .. .. depart		..	..	..	6 48	..	8 55	..	..	..	3 5
Llangollen .. .. ,,		..	..	..	8 15	..	9 58	..	..	..	3 34
Bala .. .. ,,		..	..	7 45	9 30	..	11 34	..	..	..	5 15
Festiniog .. .. ,,		..	..	8 41	10 23	..	12 25	..	3 40	..	6 5
Blaenau Festiniog .. arrive		..	..	8 57	10 40	..	12 40	..	4 0	..	6 20

		Ply. 1	2	3	4	5	6	7	8	9	10
		A.M.	A.M.	A.M.	A.M.	P.M.	P.M.	P.M.	P.M.	P.M.	P.M.
Duffws .. .. depart		6 40	8 30	9 50	11 55	C12 25	1 10	3 40	4 55	D 5 50	6 55
Bl. Festiniog (G.W.R.) ,,		..	..	9 51	11 56	..	1 11	..	4 56	..	6 56
Bl. Festiniog (L.N.W.R.) ,,		6 42	8 32	9 53	11 57	12 29	1 12	3 42	4 58	5 52	6 57
Tan-y-Grisiau .. ,,		6 47	8 37	9 58	12 2	12 38	1 17	3 47	5 2	5 57	7 2
Dduallt .. .. ,,		A	A	A	12 10	12 45	1 25	3 55	5 10	6 5	7 9
Tan-y-bwlch .. .. ,,		7 5	8 55	10 18	12 20	12 58	1 35	4 5	5 20	6 15	7 21
Penrhyn .. .. ,,		7 25	9 15	10 36	12 40	1 18	1 55	4 23	5 38	6 35	7 38
† Minffordd (Cam. Rys.) ,,		7 30	9 20	10 40	12 45	1 23	2 0	4 27	5 45	6 40	7 42
Portmadoc .. .. arrive		7 40	9 30	10 50	12 55	1 33	2 10	4 35	5 55	6 50	7 52

CAM. RYS.						P.M.					
Minffordd .. .. depart		..	10 0	..	1 8	..	3 25	4 35	6 58	..	8 22
Criccieth .. .. arrive		..	10 18	..	1 27	..	3 45	4 55	7 15	..	8 45
Pwllheli .. .. ,,		..	10 50	..	2 0	..	4 20	5 20	7 40	..	9 10
Minffordd .. .. depart		8 9	..	10 44	..	1 30	2 25	4 50	..	..	7 44
Barmouth .. .. arrive		8 47	..	11 30	..		3 15	5 40	..	..	8 32
Aberystwyth .. .. ,,		10 55	..	1 30	..	Harlech Sat only	7 55	..	..	..	

§ Change for L. & N. W. Railway.
• Change for G. W. Railway.
† Change for Cambrian Railway.

A Stops by Signal to take **Up** and set **Down** when required. Notice to be given to the Guard at the preceding Station.
B (Quarrymen's Train) on Mondays will leave Portmadoc at 5·45 a.m.
C (Quarrymen's Train) Saturdays only.
D (Quarrymen's Train) Saturdays excepted. **E** Change at Portmadoc.

Return Tickets are available to return on the following day. The Company cannot guarantee the times being kept under any circumstances, nor will they be responsible for delay.

Portmadoc July 1st, 1902.   **J. S. HUGHES, General Manager.**

W. O. Jones, Printer, 27, High Street, Portmadoc.

Combined Companies Working Timetable 14th July 1924

Distance from Dinas	Station		Passenger and Workmen's Carrs.	Minerals (Brooks) (R)	Tractor, Goods, etc. (R)	Passenger and Goods	Minerals (Brooks) (R)	Passenger and Goods	Goods and Minerals (R)	Passenger and Goods	Tractor,
M. C.			a.m.	a.m.	a.m.	a.m.	a.m.	a.m.	a.m.	a.m.	p.
	Dinas Junction	dep.						8 10			
2 0	Tryfan Junction	arr.						8 18			
	" "	dep.						8 21			
	Bryngwyn	arr.									
3 60	Waenfawr	"						8 28			
	"	dep.						8 31			
4 40	Bettws Garmon	"						8 35			
	Salem	"						A			
	Plas-y-Nant	"						A			
7 20	Quellyn Lake	arr.									
	" "	dep.						8 50			
9 20	South Snowdon	arr.						8 58			
	" "	dep.						9 1			
10 24	Pitts Head	"						A			
11 20	Hafod Ruffydd	"						A			
13 25	Beddgelert	arr.						9 26			
	"	dep.						9 30'			
15 43	Nantmor	"						9A 38			
16 25	Hafod-y-Llyn	"						A			
17 25	Hafod Garregog	"						A			
17 77	Croesor Junction	arr.						9 52 / X			
	" "	dep.						9 56	10 45		
18 27	Ynysfor	"						9A59			
19 27	Pont Croesor	"						10A 3			
	Gelert's Siding	arr.							10 58		
	" "	dep.							11 13		
21 22	Portmadoc (New Station)	arr.						10 12 / X	11 14		
	" " "	dep.						10 28		11 5	
21 57	Portmadoc (Old Station)	arr						10 32		11 9	
	" " "	dep.	5 15		7 49	8 15		10 33		11 12	12
22 57	Boston Lodge	arr.									
	" "	dep.									
	Minffordd Wharf	arr.				8 22				11 21	
	" "	dep.				8 26				11 23	
24 0	Minffordd	arr	5 24		7 59	8 27		10 42		11 24	1
	"	dep.	5 25			8 29		10 43		11 26	
25 14	Penrhyndeudraeth	arr.	5 30			8 33		10 47		11 30	
	"	dep.	5 31			8 34		10 48		11 31	
29 18	Tanybwlch	arr.	5 49			8 52 / X		11 2		11 53 / X	
	"	dep.	5 53			8 55		11 6		11 57	
31 38	Dduallt	"	A			A				A	
31 57	Moelwyn Halt	"	A		7 40		10 27				
33 31	Tanygrisiau	arr.	6 11			9 12				12 13	
	"	dep.	6 12			9 14				12 15	
34 33	Glanypwll	arr.			8 0		10 47			X	
34 45	Blaenau Festiniog (L.M.S.)	arr.	6 17			9 19		11 27		12 20	
	" "	dep.	6 18			9 20		11 28		12 21	
34 66	" " (G.W.R.)	arr.	6 20			9 21		11 29		12 22	

only.   R Conditional Trains and are run to meet traffic requirements.   X Trains cr

Workmen's Carrs.	Passenger	Slates (R)	Minerals (Brooks) (R)	Passenger and Goods	Tractor, Goods, etc. (R)	Goods and Minerals (R)	Passenger and Workmen's Carrs.	Passenger	Passenger	Passenger (Thursdays and Saturdays only until 13th September.)	Passenger
.m.	p.m.	p.m.	p.m.	p.m.	p.m.	p.m.	p.m.	p.m.	p.m.	p.m.	p.m.
O		SX	SX		SX	SX					
15	12 36			3 0			4 25		7 20		9 35
16	12 37			3 1			4 26		7 21		9 36
18	12 38			3 3			4 28	5 18	7 23		9 38
X		1 10	2 17	X							
22	12 42			3 7			4 32		7 27		9 42
23	12 43			3 8			4 33		7 28		9 43
			2 29								
A							A				
A	A			A			A		A		A
41	1 2	1 53		3 28			4 52	5 39	7 48		10 0
		X		X			X	B			
42	1 3	1 54		3 31			4 54	5 40	7 49		10 1
55	1 16			3 43			5 7		8 1		
56	1 17			3 44			5 8		8A 2		A
2	1 21	2 34		3 50			5 13	6 0	8 8		10 19
4	1X35			3 52	3 30		5 15	6 2	8 10		10 21
14	1 44			4 2	3 45		5 25	6X11	8 20		10 30
15	1 45			4 3			5 27				
19	1 49			4 7			5 31				
X	X			X			X				
25	2 25			4 13			5 40			7 35	
A33	2A33			4A21			5A48			7A43	
A38	2A38			4A26			5A53			7A48	
41	2 41			4 29			5 56			7 52	
X										X	
44	2 44			4 31			5 58			7 55	
A	A			A			A			A	
A	A			A			A			A	
A55	2A56			4A42			6A 9			8A 6	
6	3 7			4 53			6 20			8 17	
	X			X			X				
	3 25			4 56			6 24				
	A			A			A				
	A			A			A				
	3 55			5 26			6 54				
	X						X				
	3 57			5 32			6 57				
	4 5			5 40			7 5				
	4 8			5 43			7 8				
	A			A			A				
	A			A			A				
	4 19			5 54			7 19				
	4 24			5 59			7 24				
	4 27			6X 1			7 27				
						3 55					
	4 34			6 8		4 20	7 34				
	4 37			6 10		4 24	7 37				
	4 45			6 18		4 35	7 45				

via Minffordd. SX Saturdays excepted. SO Saturdays

Combined Companies Working Timetable 14th July 1924

Distance from Blaenau Festiniog			Passenger and Goods	Minerals (Brooks) (R)	Slates (R)	Passenger and Goods	Goods and Mineral (R)	Passenger and Goods	Minerals (Brooks) (R)	Tractor, Goods, etc. (R)	Passenger
			a.m.	a.m.	a.m.	a.m.	a.m. SX	a.m.	a.m.	a.m.	a.m. SX
M. C.											
	Blaenau Festiniog (G W.R.)	dep.	6 50					9 30			11 35
0 21	" (L.M.S.)	arr.	6 51					9 31			11 36
	"	dep.	6 52					9 32			11 37
0 33	Glanypwll	"		7 15	8 10				10 0		
1 35	Tanygrisiau	arr.	6 56					9 36			
	"	dep.	6 57					9 37			
2 9	Moelwyn Halt	arr.	6 59	7 27					10 12		
	"	dep.	7 0								
3 28	Dduallt	"	A								
5 48	Tanybwllch	arr.	7 14		8 50 X			9 53			11 56 X
	"	dep.	7 15		8 53			9 54			12 2
9 52	Penrhyndeudraeth	arr.	7 28					10 7			
	"	dep.	7 29					10 8			A
10 69	Minffordd	arr.	7 34		9 33			10 12			12 24
	"	dep.	7 35					10 13		11 30	12 30
	" (Wharf)	arr.									
	" "	dep.									
12 9	Boston Lodge	arr.	7 40								
	"	dep.	7 44								
13 9	Portmadoc (Old Station)	arr.	7 48					10 22		11 45	
	" "	dep.				9 20	10 10	10 23			
13 44	Portmadoc (New Station)	arr.				9 25	10 14	10 27 X			12 45 X
	" "	dep.				9 38	10 15	11 25			1 25 X
	Gelert's Siding	arr.					10 16				
	"	dep.					10 25				
15 39	Pont Croesor	"				9A46		11A33			1A33
16 39	Ynysfor	"				9A51		11A38			1A38
16 69	Croesor Junction	arr				9 54 X	10 35	11 41			1 41 X
	" "	dep.				9 57		11 44			1 44
17 41	Hafod Garregog	"				A		A			A
18 41	Hafod-y-Llyn	"				A		A			A
19 23	Nantmor	"				10A 8		11A55			1A55
21 41	Beddgelert	arr.				10 20 X		12 7 X			2 6
	"	dep.				10 24		12 11			
23 46	Hafod Ryfydd	"				A		A			
24 42	Pitts Head	"				A		A			
25 46	South Snowdon	arr.				10 54 X		12 41 X			
	"	dep.				10 56		1 0			
27 46	Quellyn Lake	arr.				11 4		1 8			
	"	dep.				11 8		1 11			
—	Plas-y-Nant	"				A		A			
—	Salem	"				A		A			
30 26	Bettws Garmon	"				11 19		1 22			
31 6	Waenfawr	arr.				11 25		1 27			
	"	dep.				11 27		1 30			
—	Bryngwyn	"									
32 66	Tryfan Junction	arr.				11 34		1 37			
	"	dep.				11 36		1X40			
34 66	Dinas Junction	arr.				11 44		1 48			

NOTES. A Stops if required.   B Stops if required to pick up passengers for G.W.R. only.

Passenger and Goods	Minerals (Brooks) (R)	Passenger and Goods	Goods and Minerals (R)	Passenger	Passenger	Passenger	Passenger
a.m.	p.m.	noon	p.m.	p.m.	p.m.	p.m.	p.m.
9 50		12 0	1 20		3 5	5 40	
9 58		12 8	1 35		3 13	5 48	
10 1		12 11	1X45		3 16	5 51	
			2 11				
10 8		12 18			3 23	5 58	
10 11		12 21			3 26	6X 0	
10 15		12 25			3 30	6 4	
A		A			A	A	
A		A			A	A	Thursdays and Saturdays only until 13th September.
10 30		12 40			3 45	6 19	
10 40		12 49			3 54	6 28	
X		X			X	X	
10 57		12 52			3 59	7 0	
A		A			A	A	
A		A			A	A	
11 22		1 17			4 24	7 25	
X				X	X		
12 15		1 20		3 15	4 58	7 29	8 30
12A23		1A28		3A23	5A 6	7A37	8A38
A		A		A	A	A	A
A		A		A	A	A	A
12 37		1 42		3 37	5 20	7 51	8 52
		X				X	
12 40		1 45		3 39	5 22	7 54	8 53
12A44		1A52		3A44	5A26	7A59	9A 0
12A48		1A57		3A49	5A30	8A 3	9A 5
12 58		2 5		3 57	5 38	8 12	9 13
X		X		X	X		
1 20		2 40		4 10	6 5	8 20	9 15
1 24		2 44		4 14	6 9	8 24	9 19
1 25		2 50		4 15	6X12	8 28	
		2 59					
		3 3					
1 33		3 4		4 24	6 20	8 37	
X							
1 34		3 10		4 26	6 21	8 38	
1 38		3 14		4 30	6 25	8 42	
1 39		3 15		4 31	6 26	8 43	
1 53		3 30		4 46	6 41	8 58	
X		X		X			
1 57		3 34		4 53	6 44	9 1	
A		A		A	A	A	
	2 45	A					
2 12		3 49		5 8	7 0	9 16	
2 14		3 51		5 10	7 1	9 18	
	3X 4						
2 19		3 58		5 15	7 6	9 23	
2 20		3 59			7 7	9 24	
2 21		4 0			7 8	9 25	

at these stations.

FESTINIOG AND WELSH HIGHLAND RAILWAYS

Down Trains (Weekdays)

Stations		a.m.	a.m.	p.m.	p.m.	p.m.	p.m.
Bl. Festiniog (G.W.R.)	dep.	....	11.50	1.49	4.22	5.27	8C00
„ (L.M.S.)	„	....	11.55	1.50	4.25	5.30	8C03
			p.m.				
Tan-y-Bwlch	„	....	12.20	2.15	4.50	5.55	8C25
Penrhyndeudraeth	„	....	12A40	2.35	5.10	6.15	8C45
Minffordd	„	....	12.50	2.43	5.17	6.21	8C52
Portmadoc	arr.	....	12.59	2.52	5.26	6.30	9C01
„	dep.	10B45	2.00	3B55	....	....	....
Aberglaslyn	„	11B09	2.24	4B19	....	....	....
Beddgelert	arr.	11B20	2.35	4B30	....	....	....
„	dep.	11B30	3.15	4B50	....	....	....
South Snowdon	„	12B25	3.50	5B35	....	....	....
Dinas Junction For L.M.S. Rly. }	arr.	1B15	4.35	6B15	....	....	....

Up Trains (Weekdays)

		a.m.	p.m.	a.m.	p.m.	p.m.
Dinas Junction	dep.	....	....	11.25	1B30	4B50
South Snowdon	„	....	....	12.15	2B15	5B35
Beddgelert	arr.	....	....	12.45	2B45	6B03
„	dep.	....	....	12.55	2B55	6B05
Aberglaslyn	„	....	....	1.06	3B06	6B16
Portmadoc	arr.	....	....	1.30	3B30	6B40
„	dep.	10.20	12.30	3.10	4.15	6C50
Minffordd	„	10.35	12.38	3.20	4.25	7C00
Penrhyndeudraeth	„	10A40	12A53	....	4A30	7A05
Tan-y-Bwlch	„	11.00	1.13	3.45	4.55	7C25
Bl. Festiniog (L.M.S.)	arr.	11.23	1.35	4.07	5.17	7C47
„ (G.W.R.)	„	11.25	1.38	4.10	5.20	7C50

A—Stops if required.   B—Runs to 12 September only.
C—Runs 3 to 29 August inclusive.

The above Services form suitable connections with the L.M. and S. and G.W. Coys. in both directions at Blaenau Festiniog, also at Dinas Junction with the L.M. and S. Railway. Time is allowed at Portmadoc for break of journey in each direction.

The Company give notice that they do not undertake that the trains will start or arrive at the time specified on the time tables, nor will they be accountable for any loss, inconvenience, or injury which may arise from delays or detentions, but every endeavour will be made to ensure punctuality as far as practicable. Passengers booking at intermediate stations can only do so conditionally upon there being room in the train.
July 1936.

By Order.

Bradshaw's Timetables show the final years:

Issues	Service
October 1930 to May 1931	Workmen's only
June 1931 to September 1931	Tourist
October 1931 to May 1932	None
June 1932 to September 1932	Tourist
October 1932 to May 1933	Workmen's only
June 1933 to September 1933	Tourist
October 1933 to April 1934	Workmen's only
May 1934 to September 1934	Tourist
October 1934 to May 1935	None
June 1935 to September 1935	Tourist
October 1935 to April 1936	None
May 1936 to September 1936	Tourist
October 1936 to April 1937	None
May 1937 to September 1937	Tourist
October 1937 to May 1938	None
June 1938 to September 25th 1938	Tourist
September 26th 1938 to May 1939	None
June 1939 to September 24th 1939	Tourist

The final service shown in the issue for September 1939:

10.20 a.m.　)
12.30 p.m.　) from Portmadoc to Blaenau Festiniog (L.M.S.) calling at Minffordd,
3.10 p.m.*　) Penrhyndeudraeth* and Tan-y-Bwlch (the 3.10 p.m. not calling at
4.15 p.m.　) Penrhyndeudraeth).

11.48 a.m.*　)
1.53 p.m.　) from Blaenau Festiniog (L.M.S.) to Portmadoc calling at same
4.23 p.m.　) stations as above (the 11.48 a.m. not calling at Penrhyndeudraeth).
5.30 p.m.　)

Illustrations published in *"Etude Technique sur les Chemins de Fer a Voie Etroite de l'Angleterre"* by M.E.Vignes (1878)

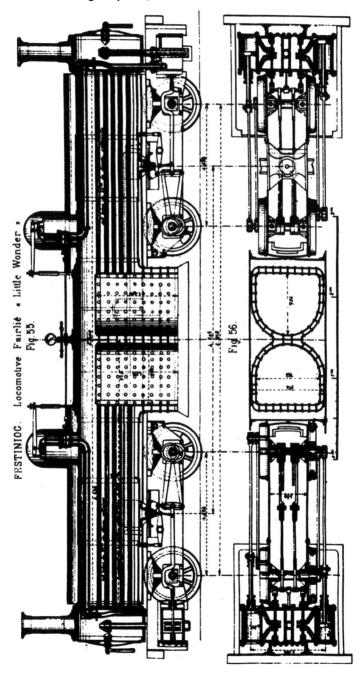

FESTINIOG. Locomotive Fairlié « Little Wonder »
Fig. 55.
Fig. 56.

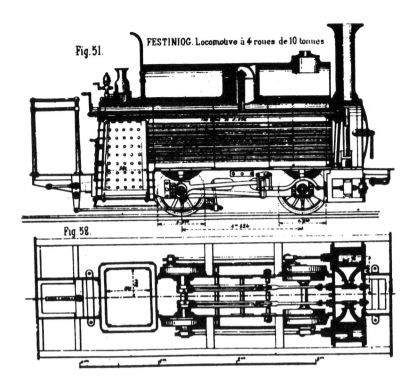

Fig. 51.

FESTINIOG. Locomotive à 4 roues de 10 tonnes

Fig. 52.

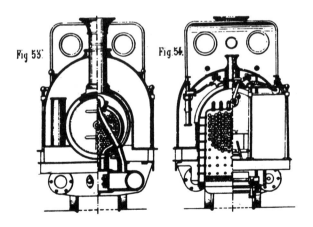

Fig. 53.

Fig. 54.

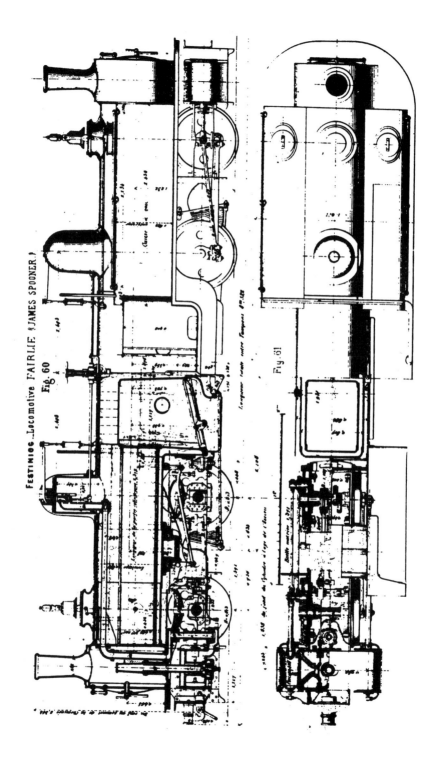

Festiniog._Locomotive FAIRLIE. (JAMES SPOONER.)

Fig. 60

Fig. 61

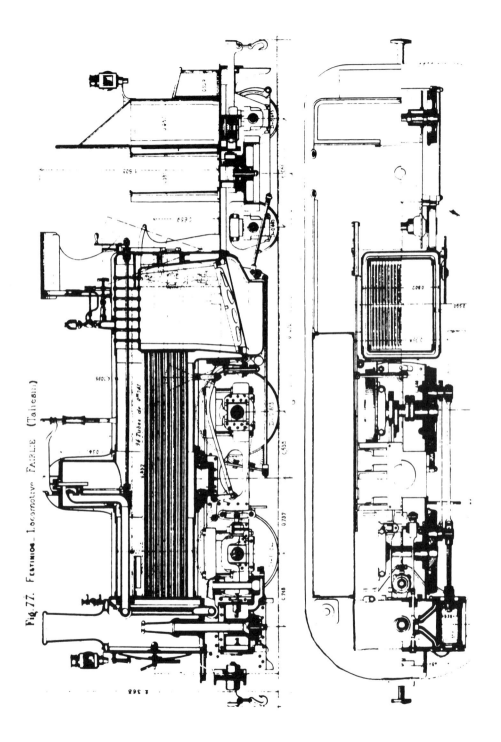

Fig.77. Festiniog. Locomotive FAIRLIE (Taliesin.)

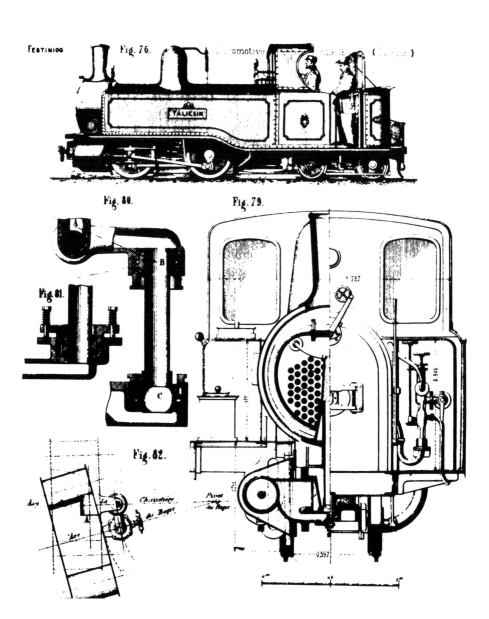

Festiniog   Fig. 76.   omotive   ( )

Fig. 80.   Fig. 79.

Fig. 81.

Fig. 82.

FESTINIOG Voiture a banquettes longitudinales

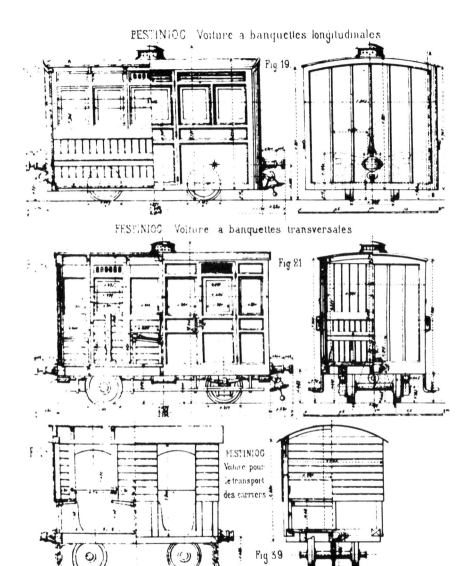

Fig 19.

FESTINIOG Voiture a banquettes transversales

Fig 21

FESTINIOG
Voiture pour
le transport
des carriers

Fig 39

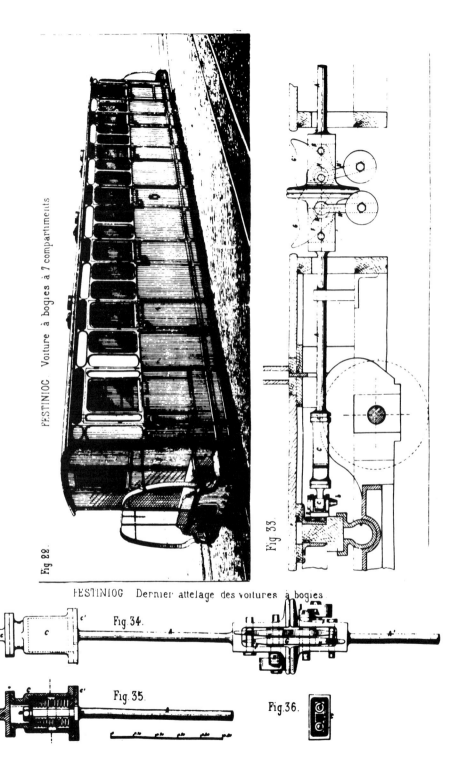

FESTINIOG Voiture à bogies à 7 compartiments

Fig 28.

Fig 33.

FESTINIOG Dernier attelage des voitures à bogies

Fig. 34.

Fig. 35.

Fig. 36.

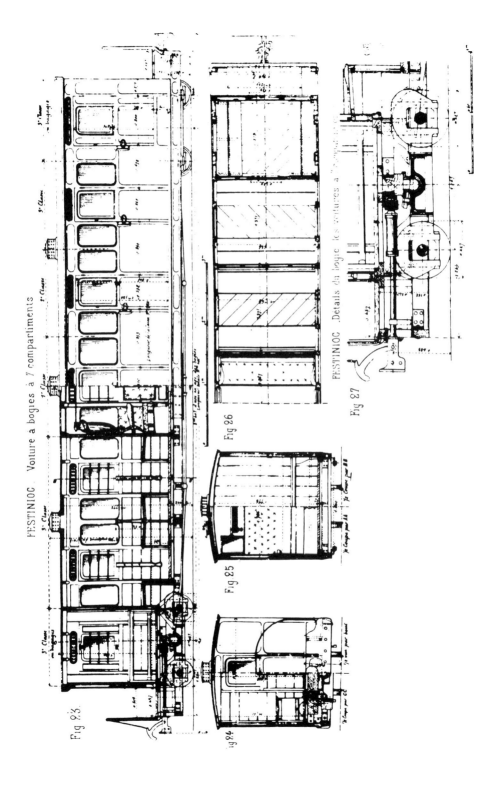

FESTINIOG . Voiture à bogies à 7 compartiments

Fig. 23.

Fig 24

Fig 25

Fig 26

FESTINIOG . Détails du bogie les voitures à ...

Fig 27

	1864	1865	1866	1867	1868	1869	1870	1871	1872	1873	1874	1875	1876	1877	1878
Maintenance Works and Way	4,219	2,965	1,757	1,499	1,841	1,692	5,855	1,156	1,571	2,317	2,760	2,788	1,845	3,336	3,603
Locomotive Power	1,950	638	1,506	1,729	2,008	1,792	2,932	2,895	3,427	3,139	3,251	2,977	4,161	3,961	4,537
C. and W. maint. and repair	799	814	938	993	1,351	2,006	1,406	1,486	1,496	1,270	1,799	2,098	2,957	3,344	1,890
Traffic Expenses	-	1,932	2,129	2,152	3,897	3,205	3,376	3,277	4,412	3,697	3,974	3,607	3,739	4,002	4,174
Net Receipts	2,761	6,517	6,994	10,494	11,003	26,125	5,349	8,335	8,494	9,893	9,487	9,532	7,822	8,996	10,351
Goods and Minerals Total	39,877	61,586	87,640	88,103	89,941	70,529	50,536	94,458	101,412	106,134	107,178	98,135	110,692	135,202	134,028
Passenger Traffic Total	-	23,105	67,835	82,821	92,920	-	99,385	91,982	113,568	128,634	150,774	157,844	175,851	195,205	215,455
Ordinary Dividend %	Nil	Nil	2	2	6	5½	9	10	5	4	4	5	5	5½	6½

	1879	1880	1881	1882	1883	1884	1885	1886	1887	1888	1889	1890	1891	1892	1893
Maintenance Works and Way	3,603	2,358	2,846	2,377	2,270	1,862	1,543	1,671	1,859	1,726	1,918	2,006	1,968	1,389	1,214
Locomotive Power	3,565	3,470	3,166	3,356	3,390	3,114	3,534	2,921	2,417	2,416	2,648	2,228	2,580	2,624	2,246
C. and W. maint. and repair	1,926	3,080	2,907	2,815	2,170	1,727	1,818	1,487	1,260	1,475	1,642	1,473	1,338	1,186	1,423
Traffic Expenses	4,142	4,191	3,968	4,161	3,986	3,656	3,527	3,379	3,143	3,076	2,844	2,884	2,860	2,932	2,974
Net Receipts	7,776	8,517	8,848	9,017	6,670	7,825	7,278	6,700	7,321	7,462	6,723	7,667	7,324	7,700	8,034
Goods and Minerals Total	124,753	128,195	128,671	135,673	128,707	122,268	119,921	116,902	119,677	114,003	100,041	92,818	99,583	99,456	99,984
Passenger Traffic Total	188,418	192,561	179,286	181,576	176,563	168,366	161,765	149,987	143,533	142,183	139,810	144,327	139,727	137,726	150,660
Ordinary Dividend %	4¾	4	5	5	2¼	3	3½	2¼	3½	3½	3	3½	3½	3½	4

* An exceptional total under 'Holders of Season and Periodical Tickets' of 6,582 for this year was brought about by adding in '6,578 workmen's Weekly Tickets' total value returned as £658. There were four other season ticket holders in 1882; up to now the average had been ten from 1872 when this Return began. It read 141 for 1883, 144 for 1884 and grew until this century. workmen's Tickets were added in for 1882 only and are not returned again for any year.

Maintenance works and way	1894	1895	1896	1897	1898	1899	1900	1901	1902	1903	1904	1905	1906	1907	1908
Maintenance works and way	1,219	1,526	1,315	1,734	1,586	1,274	1,796	1,675	1,571	1,345	1,542	1,374	1,267	1,352	1,663
Locomotive Power	2,750	2,591	3,177	2,591	2,891	2,839	3,211	3,097	3,047	2,980	3,241	3,383	2,822	3,399	2,746
C. and W. maint. and repair	1,239	1,182	1,510	1,579	1,757	1,610	1,323	1,372	1,216	1,334	1,362	1,315	1,239	1,128	1,258
Traffic Expenses	3,000	3,017	3,231	3,232	3,311	3,248	3,250	3,076	3,133	3,139	3,105	3,167	3,061	2,987	2,699
Net Receipts	9,075	7,090	7,841	8,747	8,116	8,556	5,970	4,663	5,129	5,827	5,340	4,165	3,939	2,328	1,788
Goods and Minerals Total	105,149	101,378	106,690	107,485	105,624	106,226	106,210	104,996	104,449	104,714	105,781	103,808	104,469	103,125	74,397
Passenger Traffic Total	155,581	167,262	171,464	179,253	198,048	187,781	175,419	155,239	157,610	168,243	162,925	149,718	157,602	125,342	117,706
Ordinary Dividend %	4½	3½	4	4	4	4	3½	1½	¾	1¼	1¼	½	Nil	Nil	Nil

	1909	1910	1911	1912
Maintenance works and way	1,372	1,266	1,088	1,078
Locomotive Power	2,553	2,186	2,302	2,348
C. and W. maint. and repair	1,080	888	1,106	1,028
Traffic Expenses	2,561	2,510	2,477	2,461
Net Receipts	2,395	3,660	4,330	3,815
Goods and Minerals Total	68,308	69,544	66,452	62,944
Passenger Traffic Total	115,129	120,856	131,726	124,763
Ordinary Dividend %	Nil	¼	½	½ *

Form of Returns altered 1913

	1913	1922	1923	1924	1925	1926	1927	1928
Maintenance of Works and Way	1,353	2,883	2,754	2,498	1,892	1,574	1,718	1,767
Locomotive Power	397	1,076	1,359	1,308	910	1,024	1,009	)
Carr. maint. and repair	274	571	659	900	490	343	397	1,946)
wagon maint. and repair	462	365	665	800	783	894	428	)
Traffic Expenses	2,264	5,906	4,887	4,104	3,810	3,363	3,793	3,420
Carried forward to next year	77	377	Dr. 2,587	Dr. 6,988	Dr. 6,985	Dr. 6,598	Dr. 6,596	

No Returns made for the years 1914 – 1921, but the following amounts were carried forward:

	1919	1920	1921
	115	136	DR. 763

* Last Dividend on Ordinary Shares

INDEX TO DRAWINGS

INDEX

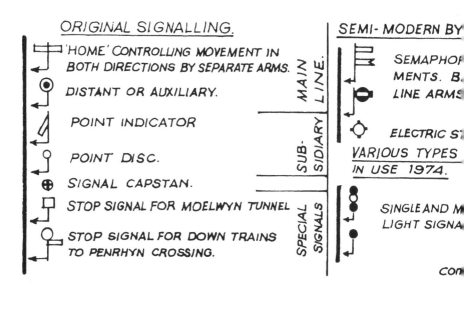

ORIGINAL SIGNALLING.

'HOME' CONTROLLING MOVEMENT IN BOTH DIRECTIONS BY SEPARATE ARMS.

DISTANT OR AUXILIARY.

POINT INDICATOR

POINT DISC.

SIGNAL CAPSTAN.

STOP SIGNAL FOR MOELWYN TUNNEL

STOP SIGNAL FOR DOWN TRAINS TO PENRHYN CROSSING.

MAIN LINE.

SUB-SIDIARY

SPECIAL SIGNALS

SEMI- MODERN BY

SEMAPHOR
MENTS. B.
LINE ARMS

ELECTRIC S
VARIOUS TYPES
IN USE 1974.

SINGLE AND M
LIGHT SIGNA

con

Standard Symbols and Abbrevi

RAILWAYS:

NARROW GAUGE   STANDARD GAUGE

BUILT.
PROJECTED.
ABANDONED

MIXED GAUGE :
ON SOME DIAGRAMS, F.R. PASSENGER LINES
ARE DISTINCTIVELY MARKED:
QUARRY LINES UNDERGROUND:

xxxxxxxxxxx

•THE ABOVE SYMBOLS AND ABBREVIATIONS, WITH THE EXCEPTION OF THRE
WHICH WERE USED IN THE EARLIER WORK, ARE STANDARD THROUGHOUT T
EXAGGERATION IS INTRODUCED WHERE NECESSARY TO CLARIFY DETAI
THE PERIOD BUT MAY NOT CONFORM TO PRESENT DAY USAGE.